IMAGINING
PEACE

BEN LOWE

IMAGINING PEACE

A History of
Early English
Pacifist Ideas,
1340–1560

The Pennsylvania State University Press
University Park, Pennsylvania

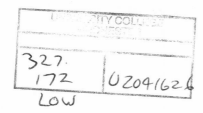

Library of Congress Cataloging-in-Publication Data

Lowe, Ben
    Imagining peace : a history of early English pacifist ideas / Ben
Lowe.

        p.   cm.
    Includes bibliographical references and index.
    ISBN 0-271-01688-4 (cloth : alk. paper)
    ISBN 0-271-01689-2 (paper : alk. paper)
    1. Peace—History.   2. Peace movements—Great Britain—History.
I. Title.
JX1942.L69   1997
327.1'72'09420902—dc21   96-50136
                                                             CIP

It is the policy of The Pennsylvania State University Press to use acid-free paper
for the first printing of all clothbound books. Publications on uncoated stock
satisfy the minimum requirements of American National Standard for
Information Sciences—Permanence of Paper for Printed Library Materials,
ANSI Z39.48-1992.

For Lisa

CONTENTS

PREFACE

Very little research has been attempted on the growing interest in peace in late medieval and early modern England. Robert P. Adams's works, culminating in his *Better Part of Valor: More, Erasmus, Colet, and Vives on Humanism, War, and Peace, 1496–1535* (1962), were groundbreaking in their explorations of humanist thought on the subject; but Adams did not extend the parameters of inquiry to consider conceptual and discursive developments. Other historians, such as John Hale, Philippe Contamine, C.S.L. Davies, Christopher Allmand, and Malcolm Vale, have recently drawn a more expanded context for the military histories of the period, so that the roles of literature and ideology are given a place in the overall treatment of warfare. In fact, it is Hale's pronouncement (in his *War and Society in Renaissance Europe* [1985]) that a great change in the connotations of peace had accompanied the early modern military revolution, which first led me to question the value and place of peace in Tudor England. These historians have produced a wealth of understanding concerning the political and social forces that led to and operated in times of war, but they have neglected almost entirely the ideational character of war itself. The more systematic nature of the following study of war and peace is an effort to demonstrate that ideas, and the values attached to them, can play an integral part in how a nation views itself and how its leaders determine policy.

Throughout this book I have modernized spellings, especially those in Middle English, since the older forms are more difficult to read and might engender some confusion or misunderstanding among those unfamiliar with early writing. The letters "u" and "v" are rendered according to modern usages. Short titles for works are used unless the longer title is particularly significant.

It is with pleasure that I acknowledge the assistance I have received in completing this research. I have benefited from the work of literary critics, political scientists, philosophers, and sociologists as well as historians. The pioneering efforts of James Turner Johnson, Arthur Ferguson, Janet Coleman, and Christopher Allmand stand out especially. I thank JoAnn Moran for encouraging my initial interest in the project after I presented a preliminary paper on ideas of peace among English Protestants during a seminar at Georgetown University. She kept me focused and made me see the value of clear writing. Other debts go to A. G. Dickens, who directed me to many early printed works that had been sorely neglected; Thomas Mayer, whose comments on a draft article helped me be more consistent methodologically; and Joe Slavin, for introducing me to the greater pleasures of Tudor intellectual history while directing a wonderful seminar, "Property, Power, and Politics," at the Folger Shakespeare Library in the fall of 1987.

Many of the conclusions put forth in this study are the result of countless discussions among colleagues and friends who offered an abundance of fresh perspectives and tolerated my obsession with peace discourse and intellectual history with great patience. These include Paul Fideler, Dale Hoak, Joe Martin, Linda Levy Peck, and Melinda Zook. I am deeply indebted to James Turner Johnson, who read this work closely and contributed many excellent suggestions, especially on how peace discourse interacted with the European just-war tradition. I would also like to thank John Roth for carefully reading large portions of the manuscript and offering valuable advice. Of course, I am totally responsible for what has finally come out on paper. My time in England was enhanced by the helpfulness of librarians at the British, Bodleian, and Cambridge University libraries and made affordable by a research grant from Georgetown University. The debt of gratitude I owe to the staff at the Folger Shakespeare Library, including some long-distance assistance by Georgianna Ziegler, can never be repaid. This wonderful facility became a second home for three years, and it is only through the collections and seminars available there that I could have completed this research. The Folger Institute's Center for the History of British Political Thought offered numerous forums for pursuing the nascent ideas from which this research originated, and I am indebted to its director, Lena Cowen Orlin, and seminar participants, including John Pocock, David Harris Sacks, Lois Schwoerer, James Muldoon, and Ralph Pollack, for their insights and direction. A 1992 grant from the National Endowment for the Humanities enabled me to complete a significant portion of this research and to discuss it with fellow participants of a seminar conducted by Hans Hillerbrand at Duke University. I also would like to extend my appreciation to Peter Potter, Cherene Holland, and Andrew Lewis at Pennsylvania State University Press for guiding me through the editing process efficiently and painlessly.

Finally, I thank my family for their sustaining love and patience, and most of all, Lisa Robeson, whose inspiration, encouragement, and belief in the research and in me, got me through many ponderous moments.

ABBREVIATIONS

BL	British Library
BN	Bibliothèque Nationale
Bod. Lib.	Bodleian Library, Oxford
C4S	Camden Fourth Series (London: Royal Historical Society, 1964–)
CW	*The Complete Works of St. Thomas More.* New Haven, Conn.: Yale University Press, 1963– .
CWE	*Collected Works of Erasmus.* Toronto: University of Toronto Press, 1974– .
DN	*Dictionary of National Biography*
EETS ES	Early English Text Society, Extra Series
EETS OS	Early English Text Society, Original Series
LP	*Letters and Papers, Foreign and Domestic, of the Reign of Henry VIII, 1509–47.* Edited by J. S. Brewer, J. Gairdner, and R. H. Brodie. 21 vols. and addenda. London: HMSO, 1862–1932.
PMLA	*Publications of the Modern Language Association of America*
PRO	Public Record Office
PS	Parker Society
RS	Rolls Series
SCH	Studies in Church History
Span. Cal.	*Calendar of Letters, Dispatches and State Papers Relating to the Negotiations between England and Spain, Preserved in the Archives at Vienna, Simacas, and Elsewhere.* Edited by M.A.S. Hume, Royall Tyler et al. 13 vols. London: HMSO, 1862–1954.
SP Dom., Edw. VI	*Calendar of State Papers Domestic Series of the Reign of Edward VI, 1547–1553, Preserved in*

	the Public Record Office. Revised ed. Edited by C. S. Knighton. London: HMSO, 1992.
STC	*A Short-Title Catalogue of Books Printed in England, Scotland, and Ireland and of English Books Printed Abroad.* Edited by A. W. Pollard and G. R. Redgrave. Revised by W. A. Jackson, F. S. Ferguson, and Katharine F. Pantzer. 2d. ed. 3 vols. Oxford: Oxford University Press, 1976–1992.
TRHS	*Transactions of the Royal Historical Society*
TRP	*Tudor Royal Proclamations.* Edited by Paul L. Hughes and James F. Larkin. 3 vols. New Haven, Conn.: Yale University Press, 1964–69.
Ven. Cal.	*Calendar of State Papers and Manuscripts Relating to English Affairs Existing in the Archives and Collections of Venice, and in Other Libraries of Northern Italy.* Edited by Rawdon Brown. Vols. 2–8. London: Longman, 1862–81.

INTRODUCTION

Few debates in human history have engendered such intense scrutiny or evoked the amount of ideological fervor as those over whether or not to go to war. Violent struggle, inherent in the human condition, according to Thomas Hobbes, has characterized social behavior as far back as written and archaeological records exist. A major function of civil society, however, is to legitimate, regulate, and organize certain types of violence in order to mitigate their harmful excesses and channel public violence, or war, into productive purposes, as necessary.[1] In the West, war was rarely condemned out of hand until more recent times, largely because it often served particular desirable ends, not the least of which was the resumption of some form of peace. Thus the value accorded life and concord in the Judeo-Christian tradition has been at times overridden by moral imperatives that seemed achievable through war. This uneasy and constant tension is mirrored in the ethical literature that overwhelmed intellectual circles during the European Middle Ages and early modern period, as writers attempted to define clearly those instances when violent conflict was justi-

---

1. Thomas Hobbes, *Leviathan, or The Matter, Forme, & Power of a Common-wealth Ecclesiasticall and Civill* (London: Andrew Crooke, 1651), 2:17–18, pp. 85–94.

fied. The concept of just war thus became the lightning rod for a rich and variegated literature whose many lines and hues of argument have persisted in debates over warfare to this day.[2]

In describing the main characteristics of the just war we need to realize that they did not really cohere until the later Middle Ages. Using the categories described in detail by J. T. Johnson, we can divide just-war theory into the *jus ad bellum* and *jus in bello* traditions.[3] The former refers to the law or right to go to war; the latter, with ethical behavior *in* war. Ancient Roman law held that wars should be fought only if proclaimed by the emperor and for redress of wrongs, thus contributing two major components to the *jus ad bellum:* proper authority and just cause. With Augustine, right intent (love or charity toward the enemy) and the goal of peace were added. The concepts of proportionality (whether the effects of war are comparable to the wrong being avenged) and last resort are implicit in Augustine but were not made explicit until the medieval canonists, beginning with Gratian's *Decretum* (ca. 1140).

The *jus in bello* only entered the mainstream of just-war ideology in the late eleventh century when the *jus armorum* (law of arms) was beginning to form and become regularized in the chivalric code. In the previous century church councils had initiated moves to restrain violence in warfare with the Peace of God and Truce of God movements. After Urban II launched the first crusade in 1095, however, this side of the just war supplanted the *jus ad bellum* as the main focus of educated opinion. The growing list of concerns contained within the *jus armorum* cannot be recounted here, but interested writers all dealt with certain general issues, including treatment of noncombatants and prisoners, rights to plunder, tactics and subterfuge, weapons used, and the overall behavior of soldiers on and off the battlefield. The apogee of *jus in bello* formulation was probably reached in Honoré Bonet's *L'Arbre des batailles,* Christine de Pisan's *Les Faits d'armes et de chivalrie,* and Nicholas Upton's *De studio militari,* which appeared during the long and exhausting Hundred Years War (1337–1453) between France and England.[4]

2. Michael Howard, "Constraints on Warfare," in *The Laws of War: Constraints on Warfare in the Western World,* ed. Michael Howard, George J. Andreopoulos, and Mark R. Shulman (New Haven, Conn.: Yale University Press, 1994), 1–2.
3. Most of the following discussion of the just war is taken from James Turner Johnson's *Ideology, Reason, and the Limitation of War: Religious and Secular Concepts, 1200–1740* (Princeton, N.J.: Princeton University Press, 1975), and *The Quest for Peace: Three Moral Traditions in Western Cultural History* (Princeton, N.J.: Princeton University Press, 1987).
4. Johnson, *Quest for Peace,* 50–66, 75–91, and *Ideology,* 5–11.

During this time the *jus ad bellum* and *jus in bello* came together to form the "classic just-war doctrine," and it remained in this form, with some slight variation, until religious wars between Protestants and Catholics gave rise to both holy-war justifications and naturalist explanations that devalued the *jus ad bellum* (admitting that both sides could be right) and emphasized more a *jus in bello* that was basically secular and founded on early principles of international law. Since this development moves us into the seventeenth century and beyond, I do not treat it in this book. It is my belief, however, that with the corresponding maturation of peace discourse in the late medieval and early modern periods, a much more complex just-war ideology developed that took into account the expanding repertoire of pacifist ideas and made even holy war between Protestants and Catholics problematic. Not a few of the confessionally rigid simply wanted the right to practice their beliefs according to conscience, hoping that prayer and good example would be enough to move their oppressors toward greater charity.[5]

By the sixteenth century, war had become so cruelly violent and debilitating for large sections of the population in England that the fruits of peace gradually came to cover a multitude of slights to honor and differences over points of dogma. But both the complexity of the just war and its overall flexibility have enabled critics to question certain of its tenets while at the same time making their own contributions to what constitutes proper authority, right intent, and just cause. For this reason, although no absolute consensus on what comprises a just war has ever emerged, there has been agreement on occasion about the categories of analysis; and by the later Middle Ages, those who believed the entire framework of debate needed to be redirected away from the rights and benefits of war to the rights and benefits of peace were taking issue with all versions of the just-war argument.[6]

Most of those who engaged in this moral debate believed that they were engaging in matters of life, death, and eternity. To be sure, self-interest and contests for power marshaled moral, legal, and philosophical opinion in brazen support of questionable wars, but these actions served to add nuance to theories and concepts that were in permanent states of flux. And as the nature of wars shifted within changing historical contexts, the argumentative forms legitimizing them were also modified, and new considera-

---

5. Johnson, *Ideology,* 18–48.

6. See Chapter 5 for more on Protestant peace discourse and its connection to holy-war ideas.

tions were introduced. The extent to which the concept of peace entered
into this dialogue provides one of the most significant developments in late
medieval and early modern formulations of the just war. In England especially, the confluence of centralizing political and religious institutions,
broadened theaters of war, a burgeoning educated elite, overall laicization,
and the rebirth of legal studies impelled a growing and interested number
of writers to offer pacifist alternatives to war.[7] For much of the period
between 1337 and 1559 England was fighting France to maintain a territorial (and sometimes jurisdictional) foothold in that country, the origins
of which dated back to the Norman Conquest. With the outbreak of the
Hundred Years War and the devastation it produced, questions arose over
the king's right to the French crown and to territory across the Channel.
Some wondered if perhaps the cost of the war did not outweigh the justice
of it, or whether more might be achieved in working toward a lasting
peace with France. Within this context the concept of peace expanded to
include a number of new meanings reflective of cultural changes taking
place in England. Just-war advocates were more attentive to pacifist ideas
and sometimes unhesitatingly argued from a pacifist stance. Perhaps for
the first time in England's history, between 1340 and 1560, English writers
and officials could imagine the establishment of real and lasting peace. The
conceptual forms varied and evolved during this period, moving from calls
to end hostilities so that order could be reestablished, to ethical and ped-
agogical efforts, and finally, to realistic proposals for workable, pragmatic
peace policies. This book is largely devoted to uncovering the origins of
and mutations in peace discourse as it emerged among the English people
in debates over specific wars, from the outbreak of the Hundred Years War
to England's complete expulsion from the Continent with the final loss of
Calais. It describes the various ways that emerging peace ideas intersected
with both just-war theories and policy decisions made during this time.
While a few areas here have been treated in other studies, especially the
"pacifism" of late-fourteenth-century writers and early-sixteenth-century
humanists,[8] this book attempts to provide some thematic coherence over
time — to demonstrate that there were important textual and contextual
traditions that connect these two peace discourses (among others). I hope

7. John Guy, *Tudor England* (Oxford: Oxford University Press, 1988), 1–52.
8. See, for example, R. F. Yeager, *"Pax Poetica:* On the Pacifism of Chaucer and Gower,"
Studies in the Age of Chaucer 9 (1987): 97–121, and Robert P. Adams, *The Better Part of
Valor: More, Erasmus, Colet, and Vives on Humanism, War, and Peace, 1496–1535* (Seattle:
University of Washington Press, 1962).

to build on and extend Robert Adams's groundbreaking work on the early English humanists, *The Better Part of Valor*, by fitting his subjects and their successors into a larger cultural milieu that had extensive roots, not just in antiquity, but in the Middle Ages as well. Rather than simply analyze the specific ideas of peace advocates and how they corresponded, we will investigate the language of peace, including its labored construction, various ideological components and practical emphases, and connections to larger developments in English political culture.

In this effort I intend to examine peace discourse and how it was modified and given new emphases according to changes in the historical contexts from which it arose. To do this I begin by introducing the basic components of the just-war tradition to demonstrate the impact on it of the emerging peace discourse.[9] In Chapter 1, therefore, I argue that as Europeans became less tolerant of perpetual violence, early literature stressing spiritual peace and the endemic nature of warfare was supplemented by calls for civic order and legal rationalization of war. In a time when petty jurisdictional disputes could erupt easily into war, the canonists stressed aspects of proper authority, and a debate ensued over who had the right to wage war. English clerics studying in Paris under the tutelage of Peter the Chanter made some allowance for individual judgment and thus opened up the question of just wars to wider deliberation, if not solely to individual conscience. This development enabled a wider range of opinion to emerge in England which repudiated conventional calls to arms by popes, kings, and emperors to reclaim lost territory or honor. A desire for peace as a temporal condition could then become an important factor in deciding when to fight a war and perhaps delay the taking of such a momentous step.

Not only was there a transforming dialogue on the right to engage in wars (*jus ad bellum*) during the later Middle Ages, there was also one devoted to how they should be fought once initiated (*jus in bello*). Chapter 2 traces the development of the law of arms, especially within an English context, and describes the various proposals for restraint in war offered to calm a very volatile European landscape. Once again, the changes that occurred in this arena influenced how peace would come to be understood. As the martial codes multiplied and were altered to accommodate the

---

9. It is not my aim to treat exhaustively the juridical and institutional efforts to ensure peace in the Middle Ages; this has been done more than adequately elsewhere. See Johnson, *Quest for Peace*, 67–132, and Frederick H. Russell, *The Just War in the Middle Ages* (Cambridge: Cambridge University Press, 1975).

many exigencies of contemporary warfare, more exacting standards of conduct were applied to knights, their retainers, and even commoners who fought. At the same time, however, egregious violations came under harsh attack from a growing number of moralists who believed that the *jus armorum* was either ineffective or unenforceable. At this juncture I consider the effect of medieval wars on social and political developments in England, where a greater tradition of consent existed mainly through the institution of Parliament. Opposition to war levies forced successive royal governments to resort to propaganda to secure popular support for wars. Such heightened participation in the process of warmaking within a context of an emerging law of arms spurred greater criticism of specific wars by the fourteenth century, along with calls for real reform. The specter of war and its train of higher taxes, destruction of property and crops, and general fears of injury or death engendered resentment among people who could neither afford nor morally tolerate perpetual conflict.

With this foundation laid, therefore, Chapters 3 and 4 catalog the actual tide of English antiwar rhetoric and peace discourse that the Hundred Years War unleashed. This literature suggests great dissatisfaction with much of the reasoning employed in *jus ad bellum* arguments and also castigates contemporary behavior in war and the insufficiencies of *jus in bello* restraints. The extensive and rich variety of polemic is staggering. They include moralists such as John Gower and Thomas Hoccleve, clerics both heterodox and orthodox such as Thomas Brinton and John Wyclif, "popular" poems, economic treatises, and works of fiction by noted writers such as Geoffrey Chaucer, William Langland, and John Lydgate. They all expressed a common aversion to the Hundred Years War and a predilection for peace that sometimes bordered on outright pacifism, although the extent of the latter varied. These writers argued a much broader definition of peace, and I construct a typology that delineates their configurations of peace as spiritual, godly, orderly, and pragmatic. (By the end of the war, the impoverishment of the realm guaranteed the appeal to pragmatism.) As a result, the just-war concept could continue to develop and expand, taking into greater account the many fruits of peace these writers had spotlighted.

The pacifist beliefs associated with Erasmian humanism entered England by the late fifteenth century, and the courts of Henry VII and Henry VIII both encouraged their incorporation into new curricula and educational programs. Chapter 5 argues that the first half of the sixteenth century witnessed the emergence of an uncontested peace ethic developed by hu-

manists who stressed particular interpretations of Christ-like behavior and
the value of educating people into higher moral and humane activities.
Their tendency to idealize the concept of peace could not help but meet
with disappointment, as it did by the 1520s; nevertheless, its worth was so
taken for granted that even Henry VIII and his chief minister, Cardinal
Thomas Wolsey, found the motif serviceable in their attempts to fashion
themselves as the arbiters of Europe. The reiteration of classical ideas of
peace and good government—including the new emphasis on nonmartial
service to the king by more refined noblemen—added an even greater dimension to peace discourse during these years which disillusionment could
not completely void.

English Protestants, feeling besieged by Catholic threats from overseas,
held to a more pessimistic view of human nature and remained instinc-
tively skeptical about plans for true and lasting peace. In England, however, many of those sympathetic to reform were also humanists who
greatly admired the Erasmian concept of *philosophia Christi*, that is, mod-
eling one's life on what Christ did or would do. Chapter 6 describes the
early stages of the English Reformation when many Protestants and royal
supremacists who wrote on war portrayed it as terribly problematic—a
sinful activity that Christ had condemned when he declared, "Blessed are
the peacemakers." Unlike Augustine, they often portrayed war itself as an
evil—more a culmination of sin rather than a corrective for it. Here, the
Christian's responsibility to create a better, more godly world is presented
as an injunction to promote peace and as manifest in the profitable, noble,
and altogether good qualities it brings societies. They contrasted the evils
of war with the fruits of peace, thereby constructing a bold dichotomy to
encourage repentance, reform, and obedience. Protestants also valued
highly the pragmatic and orderly aspects current in the peace discourse of
their day. In tying this broader configuration to the just war, it is significant that now for a war to be legitimate, it must not only have a just cause
but also not endanger the commonwealth. The latter criterion became a
major addition to the concept of the just war for a growing number of
English people in the sixteenth century and inhibited England's involvement in foreign conflicts.

In Chapter 7, I place the ideas of peace traced earlier into the mid-Tudor
context of war and peace policymaking. The 1540s and 1550s witnessed
the most sustained period of war in England since the Hundred Years War,
and once again we find victims of war weariness challenging certain aspects of just-war theory and proposing peaceful alternatives. But this time,

with the introduction of humanist and Protestant elements, the practical argument emerges boldly—especially as it relates to a healthy economy and prosperous commonwealth—and finds its way into the highest reaches of government. Those most involved in carrying out the war effort (Stephen Gardiner, William Paget, and Edward Seymour), openly questioned whether breaches of honor or ancient feudal claims were sufficient justification for the impoverishment of the nation when the returns seemed so uncertain and inconsequential. Their letters, proposals, and treatises are full of allusions to classical and Erasmian maxims regarding the sensible and preferable state of peace for human society, and to what best promotes the commonwealth. Of course, many of those who wrote about war and peace during these crisis years had numerous and diverse motivations and expectations for their positions, but one common theme can be found in most of them—the necessity of peace to the economic vitality of the nation. Clearly, by mid-century, the practical value of peace was recognized and would henceforth be placed alongside just-war arguments in the national debate, however limited, over whether or not to go to war.

A fitting, if incomplete, coda to these developments is offered in the final chapter. By the time of Elizabeth, Europe was encountering a "price revolution," and religious wars had broken out all over the Continent. A large part of the queen's public policy was devoted to protecting England's security, which usually meant either staying out of wars or supporting others to carry out the unpleasant task. The fact that she did not drain precious English resources in foreign campaigns made her a hero at home, and she encouraged the colossal outpouring of iconography, pastoral literature, poetry, pageantry, and other cultural products that eulogized her for her pacifism. The ease with which she tapped into a substratum of popular desires for prosperity-inducing peace demonstrates the place ideas and images of peace could have in practical governance in the later sixteenth century.

Since this is a study of peace discourse I should perhaps define these terms as is appropriate at this juncture. Timothy Reiss denotes discourse as a "coherent set of linguistic facts . . . caught within a network of contextual relations, within a definable if exceedingly complex environment."[10] Keeping this in mind, we might better notice the interaction between historical context and conceptual development, and how this relationship is best

10. Timothy J. Reiss, *The Discourse of Modernism* (Ithaca, N.Y.: Cornell University Press, 1982), 9–10, 27–28.

identified in written or oral representations. Or in other words, attitudinal changes based on wider historical developments affect the meanings that ideas come to convey. At the same time I accept Quentin Skinner's premise that "there *is* no history of the idea to be written, but only a history necessarily focused on the various agents who used the idea, and on their varying situations and intentions in using it."[11] For this reason, it is impossible to say much here about what we mean by "peace," because the term is far from static during our period. The Latin word *pax* is often associated with *tranquillitas* and *concordia,* and in either case can refer to civic order as well as to the absence of war. In the Middle Ages, the initial emphasis was on public peace and the end of widespread lawlessness, but as political and religious consolidations resulted in more effective concentrations of power, this became less of a pursuit. Simultaneously, wars became more devastating and disruptive, even to peoples not directly involved in them.

Obviously, a topic such as the development of peace discourse and its place in English political culture is a broad one. Any one of the trends, thinkers, or policies discussed here can be given more specialized treatment. My purpose, however, is to present the larger picture and still offer enough specificity to support an overall thesis, while concurrently trying to make the material accessible to the general reader who may not be familiar with the personalities and events described. To strengthen my argument I have taken care to present in some detail the historical contexts for developing peace ideas—such as the introduction of Protestantism into England—even when the connections are not immediately clear. I have also attempted to show the relationship between English peace ideas and developments on the Continent. For this reason, I cite writers as far afield as Philippe de Mézières, Erasmus, and John Calvin. While there are many unique elements that come out of English experiences, they cannot be analyzed in a vacuum.[12] As is probably obvious at this point, many different forms of literature will be used to provide a wide range of evidence. Writers could serve a variety of purposes through what they penned, and

11. Quentin Skinner, "Meaning and Understanding in the History of Ideas," in *Meaning and Context: Quentin Skinner and His Critics,* ed. James Tully (Princeton, N.J.: Princeton University Press, 1988), 56. I would also agree with some of Skinner's critics who question his unilateral focus on authorial intent, as if such a pursuit were epistemologically possible, much less, beneficial. In the same collection also see Joseph V. Femia's "An Historicist Critique of 'Revisionist' Methods for Studying the History of Ideas," 156–75.

12. For more on the Continental pacifist traditions, see Johnson's *Quest for Peace,* which mirrors my interest in cultural change, yet emphasizes more the philosophical and religious trends rather than conceptual and linguistic developments.

their place in the contemporary political culture was usually either as advocate (even propagandist) or critic. Works by the latter, on which this study is largely focused, most often reflected on events by pointing out what was wrong, then usually pushed thought into new realms by suggesting alternatives. Tudor historian Alistair Fox has shown the value of viewing literature in this way: "Early Tudor literature indicates more clearly than any other sort of evidence the aspects of Tudor policy and political circumstances that caused anxiety. Examination of the ways in which writers tried to allay such anxieties allows one to infer the source of them." He goes on to say that literature is also a "means of saying things that otherwise could not be said within the constraints of existing social codes."[13] If this is true, then antiwar rhetoric and suggestions for peace may have been more important than heretofore realized and probably had an indirect effect on larger cultural attitudes as they developed and changed.

Finally, there has been a historiographic tendency of late to downplay the importance of ideas, especially humanist and Protestant ones, in Tudor government and policy. Given the perhaps exaggerated claims of an earlier generation,[14] the recent debates over historical evidence,[15] and the more cynical age in which we live, this trend is not surprising. It is encouraging that a reaction is currently in the making,[16] for as this study will show, there is tremendous utility in placing ideas within historical contexts and observing their dissemination into wider culture through various linguistic adaptations. What may be even more disturbing, however, is the all-too-frequent dismissal of earlier ideas that seem to deviate markedly from current understanding. The assumption in this instance is that twentieth-century pacifism has little or nothing in common with sixteenth-century peace discourse and to believe that it does is whiggish and presentist. Annabel Patterson alerts us to the potential dangers of such reasoning when she

13. Alistair Fox, *Politics and Literature in the Reigns of Henry VII and Henry VIII* (Oxford: Basil Blackwell, 1989), 5–6.

14. W. Gordon Zeeveld, *Foundation of Tudor Policy* (Cambridge: Harvard University Press, 1948; reprint, Westport, Conn.: Greenwood Press, 1981); James K. McConica, *English Humanists and Reformation Politics under Henry VIII and Edward VI* (Oxford: Clarendon Press, 1965); Arthur B. Ferguson, *The Articulate Citizen and the English Renaissance* (Durham, N.C.: Duke University Press, 1965).

15. For a good summary, see David Harlan, "Intellectual History and the Return of Literature," *American Historical Review* 94 (1989): 581–609.

16. See, for example, John Stephens, *The Italian Renaissance: The Origins of Intellectual and Artistic Change before the Reformation* (London: Longman, 1990), and Annabel Patterson, *Reading Holinshed's Chronicles* (Chicago: University of Chicago Press, 1994).

asserts that "the notion of anachronism in *language* seems to me a shib-boleth that permits modernity to shore up its own reputation for advanced thinking against earlier primitivisms."[17] Others view peace ideas as having been too marginal to the values of early modern society to have had any real impact. Obviously, peace advocates did not win the day in Tudor England any more than they have in contemporary Britain, but to varying degrees each have affected the policies of their governments and the lives of their fellow countrymen and countrywomen. To minimize or ignore the contributions of any "minority voice" unfortunately imposes artificial restrictions on what we can learn from the past by assuming any impact to be negligible from the outset. In the words of Miriam Eliav-Feldon: "Historians cannot ignore the corpus of peace literature for it provides a valuable collection of documents reflecting their own times—reflections on changing political realities, opinions on particular acts of belligerency, certain strains of political thought, views of human nature, contemporary hopes and aspirations, and what at the time were considered to be feasible solutions."[18] A number of years ago the well-respected historian of war and technology, John U. Nef, made an important and still useful connection between the early modern English penchant for peace and the foundations of industrialization in that country. To him, by the early seventeenth century, England was unique in Europe for its reluctance to engage in foreign wars and for its hostility toward standing armies. The Thirty Years' War (1618–48), which embroiled most of the Continent, gave rise to a popular saying among contemporary Europeans, "Peace with England and war with all beside."[19] While this might have been an exaggeration, since the English did not completely stay out of that conflict, it still captures well the political culture in England at the time. A year after the war erupted, in 1619, Thomas Middleton perhaps put the sentiments of his countrymen and countrywomen best when he wrote

> Peace is the passage from life to life, come then to the factory of peace, thou that desirest to have life. . . . The Nobility, who were wont to be strangers in their native country, leading the ranks of blood and death against their enemies, have now no enemy. . . . For

17. Patterson, *Reading Holinshed's Chronicles*, xii.

18. Miriam Eliav-Feldon, "Grand Designs: The Peace Plans of the Late Renaissance," *Vivarium* 27 (1989): 53.

19. John U. Nef, *War and Human Progress: An Essay on the Rise of Industrial Civilization* (Cambridge: Harvard University Press, 1950), 22.

Honour is the Rumour of a beautiful and virtuous Action . . . which
turns to a great peace; . . . blessings which were never yet found in a
Blood-shedding. . . . Let our Souls be bound for our Bodies, our
Bodies for our Souls. . . . As we have kept the Peace, we shall be
rewarded with Peace, and kept in Eternal Peace. Amen.[20]

New ideological configurations of war and peace were being fashioned
in late medieval and early modern England, and as this study will demonstrate, coherence or clarity was often the price paid for hammering them
out. The sources are, for the most part, those of a literate elite who left
written traces; but its members were contributing to more general beliefs
about war and peace, as evidenced in the attention given to many of their
writings by those in power at all levels. And the flow of ideas was hardly
in one direction. A variety of sources, including popular ballads, court
testimony, and civic responses to increased taxation for war, suggest
clearly that the *vox populi* made itself heard as well. The social dimension
in determining prevalent attitudes toward war and peace, therefore, cannot
be underestimated. Middleton assessed quite well the direction English
government and society was moving as contemporaries imagined and then
worked for a real peace that benefited the commonwealth. He echoed
many of his contemporaries who shared an abiding belief in peace's enduring value by simply stating without qualification that it "is the passage
from life to life."

20. Thomas Middleton, *The Peace-Maker, or Great Brittaines Blessing. Fram'd for the
Continuance of That Mightie Happinesse Wherein This Kingdome Excells Manie Empires.
Shewing the Idlenesse of a Quarrelling Reputation, Wherein Consists Neyther Manhood nor
Wisdome. Necessarie for All Magistrates, Officers, Masters of Families, for the Conformation
of Youth, and for His Maiesties Most True and Faithfull Subiects: To the Generall Avoyding
of All Contention, and Bloud-shedding* (London: Thomas Purfoot, 1619), sigs. A4v–B4v,
D4r–E4r.

1

EARLY JUST-WAR IDEOLOGY
AND ITS CRITICS

In order to trace the development of a peace discourse and ethic in England during the late medieval and early modern periods it is necessary first to consider the just-war positions that developed and how they were affected by cultural changes occurring in the Middle Ages. Legitimations of war took their cue from Roman and early Christian formulations, but by the twelfth century the tensions created by political exigencies that had led to war and contributed to its ethical underpinnings had caused these formulations to mutate into a wide range of opinion. With the outbreak of the Hundred Years War more writers reflected on the various arguments used by the crown and its supporters to justify Edward III's claim to the French throne. By then, a conceptual foundation had been laid for more individualistic assessments of cause, intent, and authority, the prime considerations before entering into battle.[1] The rhetoric underwent no dramatic change, and just-war advocates employed their arguments with the same assurance as always. The difference lies in the development of a literature that extolled the virtues of peace and disparaged some contemporary

---

1. Robert P. Adams, "Pre-Renaissance Courtly Propaganda for Peace in English Literature," *Papers of the Michigan Academy* 32 ([1946]–48): 437.

motives behind warmaking. The debate that ensued reinterpreted and
added to Continental positions pioneered by canonists and theologians
who represented a more internationalist approach to the subject by associating just wars with religion or with dynastic territorial claims. In England at least, a few voices spoke to the heightened sense of incongruity
between theory and reality, and they ultimately came to enlarge the construct to include concerns for real and lasting temporal peace, hoping to
prevent just-war positions from turning into casuistries for selfish religious
and lay powers.

This chapter will explore the changing nature of the concept of the just
war — the patristic, canonical, and scholastic permutations that developed
as it came to emphasize particular themes and trends in medieval Europe.
Its great flexibility, however, in adapting to political, social, and religious
changes while solidifying its philosophical base, nevertheless, could open it
up also to greater criticism, especially during the time of the Crusades. By
the fifteenth century the new fiscal and technological realities of sustained
war set the stage for a spirited dialogue between certain just-war theorists
and peace advocates, both of whom felt the changes necessitated greater
adherence to their positions if the all-important goal of order and stability
were to be achieved.

The Just War Before the Crusades

It is necessary to look carefully at the just war as a developing theory
during the Middle Ages in order to fathom the philosophical vulnerabili-
ties in usage it faced once it appeared to have lost all relevance to the real
world of warfare. Ancient Roman constructions of the *bellum justum* provide the initial building blocks of the medieval just-war tradition. During
the empire, proper imperial authority was required before any war could
be undertaken, and then it should be fought to redress wrongs, to reclaim
lost goods, or to punish evil. Any war conducted outside these parameters
was immoral and strictly forbidden. Such limits characterized the just-war
tradition in the West for centuries to come, but during the earliest years of
the Christian era certain Fathers — Tertullian and Origen, among others —
tended toward outright pacifism in their rejection of all that was Roman
and pagan.[2] Even though traditional treatments of early-church beliefs on

2. Tertullian, *On Idolatry,* chap. 19, and *De Corona,* chap. 11, in *The Ante-Nicene Fa-*

war have emphasized this aspect, the devotion to absolute peace may not have been as unilateral as it first appears.[3] Beginning with Clement of Alexandria and further explored by Ambrose of Milan and Augustine, a less separatist attitude developed that stressed the Christian moral obligation to be *in* the world and to make it a better place. That world included sin and violence, the products of human nature. In such a context, Christians still valued peace, but they could also hold to a just-war position that regulated violence and promoted peaceful resolution of differences. Ambrose went beyond Roman (Ciceronian) tenets that wars be defensive in nature when he suggested that violent subjugation of heretics was valid and moral. Continuing this line of thought and insisting that only when the intention was right could a just war be fought, Augustine added to the Roman concepts of proper authority and just cause the last major component of the medieval *jus ad bellum*.[4]

Although a number of Augustine's works refer to war and when it may be fought legitimately, he offered no systematic treatment of the problem. He did, however, contribute particular insights and an overall framework that were useful to canonists who organized the various aspects of just-war theory into more coherent form in the twelfth and thirteenth centuries. For this reason, and because he maintained that peace be the consequence and goal of all wars, his thought needs to be examined in more detail if we are to trace the development of peace ideas in Western history.

In *Contra faustum Manichæum*, Augustine contended that war was instituted by God as a means for inflicting punishment, but in such a way that it performed a necessary cleansing function by eradicating great sin in

---

thers, ed. Alexander Roberts and James Donaldson, vol. 3 (Grand Rapids, Mich.: William B. Eerdmans, 1956); in the same collection, also see Origen, *Origen Against Celsus*, bk. 2, chap. 30, and Pseudo-Clement, *Recognitions of Clement*, bk. 2, chap. 29.

3. Johnson, *Quest for Peace*, 30–50. For ancient and early patristic attitudes, see Aristotle *Politics* 1.2.16–19, 3.7–8; 7.13.7–8, 13–17, and *Nicomachean Ethics* 10.6–7; Russell, *Just War*, 3–6, 10–12; Arthur Nussbaum, "Just War—A Legal Concept?" *Michigan Law Review* 42 (1943): 453–54; Wallace E. Caldwell, *Hellenic Conception of Peace* (reprint, New York: AMS Press, 1976), 108–39; Peter Brock, *Pacifism in Europe to 1914* (Princeton, N.J.: Princeton University Press, 1972), 7–11; and Peter Calvocoressi, *A Time for Peace: Pacifism, Internationalism and Protest Forces in the Reduction of War* (London: Hutchinson, 1987), 10–12. The model of pure early-church pacifism is distilled most thoroughly in Cecil John Cadoux, *The Early Christian Attitude to War* (London: Headley Bros., 1919; reprint, New York: Seabury Press, 1982).

4. Ambrose of Milan, *Of the Duties of the Clergy*, in *A Select Library of Nicene and Post-Nicene Fathers*, ed. Philip Schaff and Henry Wace, 2d ser., 10:1–89 (New York: Christian Literature, 1896), 1.40.195–98; Louis J. Swift, "St. Ambrose on Violence and War," *Transactions and Proceedings of the American Philological Association* 101 (1970): 533–43; Johnson, *Quest for Peace*, 53–61.

society. "The real evils in war are love of violence, revengeful cruelty, fierce and implacable enmity, wild resistance, and the lust for power, and such like."[5] Wars were not always fought, therefore, with moral intentions, and those that contributed to chaos, disorder, and uncontrollable abandon were particularly abhorrent. It was every Christian's duty to love his fellow man and woman, and to obey divinely instituted authorities with moral acknowledgment. If war was fought in the "interests" of the enemy, however, it could become a positive exercise. If love was the motive or intention, then one could argue that a particular war was even *required* at times. Any means, claimed Augustine, could be used to achieve this greater good; and injury to noncombatants was an unfortunate side effect that could not be avoided in this world. Because the earthly city would always remain fallen, war would be a perpetual condition among men, who would fight the battles of good against evil as part of an eternal struggle. Since no soldier was able to offer a proper verdict on a war's justice, he who fought or killed in an unjust war was freed from guilt if he acted under the command of a legitimate authority.

Despite his seemingly passionate embrace of legitimate wars, Augustine believed that the true end of all warfare, however, should be peace, even though that peace was largely spiritual and could never be lasting or complete. While his argumentation lacks careful precision this early Father's interest in peace is remarkable in that it suggests that violence organized strictly and properly could serve as an appropriate expedient for bringing society to a state where godly conduct is ensured. Thus, peace, while virtually unattainable, can still be valued in the abstract and perhaps even approximated in reality — but only if the spiritual condition precedes the temporal one.[6]

Since these precepts proved a touchstone for much subsequent discussion of the just war, they may be important for determining how medieval

---

5. Augustine, *Contra faustum Manichæum*, in *Opera omnia*, vol. 8 (Paris: Gaume Fratres, 1837), 22.70–79. See also his *De civitate Dei*, in *Opera omnia*, vol. 7 (Paris: Gaume Fratres, 1838), 1.21, 26; 3.10; 19.7, 12 (1), 13 (1–2), 15, 21; Russell, *Just War*, 16–26; Albert Marrin, ed., *War and the Christian Conscience: From Augustine to Martin Luther King, Jr.* (Chicago: Henry Regnery, 1971), 52–60; Nussbaum, "Just War," 455; and R. A. Markus, "Saint Augustine's Views on the 'Just War,'" in *The Church and War*, ed. W. J. Sheils, SCH, vol. 20 (Oxford: Basil Blackwell, 1983), 1–13.

6. Augustine, *Contra faustum Manichæum*, 12.70, 74, 78, *De civitate Dei*, 19.7, 21; Russell, *Just War*, 17–20; Richard Shelly Hartigan, "Saint Augustine on War and Killing," *Journal of the History of Ideas* 27 (1966): 195–204; Michael Walzer, "Exodus 32 and the Theory of the Holy War: The History of a Citation," *Harvard Theological Review* 61 (1968): 5–8.

people perceived the institution of war and why they engaged in it. If war were a natural condition and used by God, then it could be held properly to the bosom of Christian Europe and exalted.[7] But for Augustine's ideal — that war could be a means for good to triumph over evil — to be operative required adherence to strict moral guidelines, the construction of which preoccupied medieval writers who witnessed the most grievous sins emanating from their own cause or countrymen's behavior on the battlefield. By the end of the Middle Ages, with the cumbersome, languishing campaigns, full of plunder, and dependent on technological innovations that wrought tremendous destruction in battle, it was hard to believe that soldiers had altruistic or charitable motives in going to war or that peace was their ultimate goal. Because of unique political, social, and intellectual contexts that heightened literate awareness of the international scene, the evils that Augustine found in war seemed so inexorably bound up in practice that it became more difficult to separate the act from its effects. The canonists dealt with this problem by rationalizing further the process for determining just cause, right intent, and proper authority in warfare. Others, however, began to consider the institution of war itself evil, thus initiating alternative outlooks promoting peace.

These intellectual currents would not blossom, however, until the twelfth century. Before then, little attention was given to Roman and Augustinian views on war. The Christian church realized the evil excesses of war and dealt with them more-or-less in a sacramental manner. Before the first millennium A.D. warfare was endemic and mostly local. The political instability that resulted led many lay and ecclesiastical authorities to derogate wars connected with the desultory cruelties perpetrated on populations by roving bands of soldiers or by renewed invasions of Norsemen, Magyars, and others. They hoped to inculcate a "hegemonic peace," either universally or territorially, but the random violence and ubiquitous factionalism made this an almost impossible task. Just as Augustine — and before him, the Stoics — believed that concord must eventually replace the disruptions of war, the concept of *tranqillitas ordinis* (tranquillity of order) was a major pursuit of medieval authorities, especially the clerical hierarchy, which possessed the most centralized political structure in medieval Europe. Order and stability were prerequisites to good government, which no matter how effective, could not flourish if powerful warriors might resort to hos-

7. Josef L. Kunz, "*Bellum Justum* and *Bellum Legale*," *American Journal of International Law* 45 (1951): 528–34.

tilities whenever the slightest jurisdictional disputes broke out. Until the High Middle Ages and the incorporation of the law of arms into the classic just-war theory, the Church provided some mitigation by requiring penance from anyone who participated in the shedding of blood. Such a step called attention to how easy it was to kill for the wrong reasons when battling the enemy. A penitential of Bede required a soldier who killed in a war to fast for forty days. After Hastings, penance was imposed on William's army even though it fought "under a papal banner and against a perjurer." Other expiations for the sin of killing without charity in battle were promulgated in Charlemagne's first general capitulary (ca. 769).[8] Despite clerical efforts, however, the pervasiveness and unpredictable nature of violence made it difficult for people of the earlier Middle Ages to distinguish between times of war and peace, which they simply envisioned as "two poles of a single concept." Peace, for example, was often depicted as the goddess of victory. According to J. M. Wallace-Hadrill, Germanic notions implied the "absence of hostility within a specified context . . . but it is nonetheless negative, resting as it does on the knowledge that the world at large . . . is naturally hostile."[9] Peace was little more than an interruption between bouts of violent conflict, often the result of uncontrollable factors such as the weather, casualties, or inadequate supply.[10] By the end of the tenth century, with the cessation of the Norse invasions and the growing control being exerted by the Church Universal after the Cluniac reforms, the papacy looked for more effective ways to curb excessive violence, especially among the lay nobility, but also among a now less-acceptable warrior clergy.

The twin Continental movements, the Peace of God (*pax Dei*) and the Truce of God (*treuga Dei*), were sincere efforts by the Church to contain those groups of soldiers, including certain noble retainers, landless brigands, and mercenaries, who threatened the safety and property of ecclesiastics and other noncombatants. Organized between 975 and 1139, these movements were the product of a number of councils restricting who

8. Russell, *Just War*, 32; Philippe Contamine, *War in the Middle Ages*, trans. Michael Jones (Oxford: Basil Blackwell, 1984), 267–69; Thomas Renna, "The Idea of Peace in the West, 500–1150," *Journal of Medieval History* 6 (1980): 146–56.

9. J. M. Wallace-Hadrill, "War and Peace in the Earlier Middle Ages," *TRHS*, 5th ser., 25 (1975): 157–61. Wallace-Hadrill does find, however, among the Anglo-Saxons a less militaristic temperament than prevailed among the Franks and notes that King Alfred and Bede were particularly intrigued by the possibilities of a prolonged peace.

10. Georges Duby, *The Legend of Bouvines: War, Religion and Culture in the Middle Ages*, trans. Catherine Tihanyi (Berkeley and Los Angeles: University of California Press, 1990), 58.

might fight, when soldiers could engage in battle, and what weapons could be employed. Coming in three separate phases, beginning with the most important Peace of God, the regulations promulgated were backed up with papal sanctions of excommunication and interdict, and as such were successful in compelling some obedience to ecclesiastical authority in protecting Church property and in laying the groundwork for later *jus in bello* retrains in war that became part of the chivalric code. The Truce attempted to curtail daily violence and warmaking by outlawing battle on certain holy days and at certain times of the year. The weapons outlawed at the Second Lateran Council (1139) were those usually employed by mercenaries, who were more likely to engage in acts of unrestrained, disruptive violence outside the emerging code of chivalry, which was a major problem at the time. It was still licit, however, to use any weapon against heretics and infidels, all of which points out a major consequence of these movements on the political powers and claims of Rome. By curtailing localized, private violence, the Church hoped to harness martial energies and channel them into just causes. The Peace, for example, would not allow anyone to fight against the Church but permitted the pope to command that Europeans take up causes he termed legitimate, which meant sanctioning crusades. As J. T. Johnson puts it, "Not only is such a position hardly pacific, it is self-centered in the extreme."[11]

Certain aspects of the Peace were more successful than others, such as keeping clerics immune from and barring them from participating in authorized violence; but since the institution of warfare itself did not come under any careful scrutiny, it is easy to see in both movements other motives than just a desire for peace. For one, it helped separate war among Christians from war between Christians and non-Christians, thereby diverting more extreme martial activity toward fighting heathens. As a result, one scholar has maintained, there was actually an "intensification of warfare in the eleventh century."[12] Also, it has been argued ably that both the *pax Dei* and *treuga Dei* were attempts by the Church to tame the warrior instinct of the knightly class without undermining the practice of war as a

11. Johnson, *Quest for Peace,* 82, and *Just War Tradition and the Restraint of War* (Princeton, N.J.: Princeton University Press, 1981), 128–30; Contamine, *War in the Middle Ages,* 270–72. See also Roger Bonnaud-Delamare's "Fondements des institutions de paix au XIe siècle," in *Mélanges d'histoire du moyen âge dédiés à la mémoire de Louis Halphen* (Paris: Presses Universitaires de France, 1951), 21–26, which finds a more spiritual foundation for both the *pax Dei* and *treuga Dei.*
12. Robert C. Stacey, "The Age of Chivalry," in Howard, Andreopoulos, and Shulman, *Laws of War,* 29.

whole (and perhaps further to separate the clergy from the worldliness of battle and from the command of lay rulers).[13] Yet the Peace was most effective in melding the interests of the Church with the emerging chivalric code, which viewed knights as protectors of the weak and innocent. It accomplished this objective most impressively by enjoining a particular social class, charged by the pope to do his bidding, with the immediate need of going on crusade. By removing any taint of sin from papally sanctioned fighting, and by directing martial activity into "legitimate" outlets, eventually the privileges and immunities given to these warriors would transform Europe into the most elaborately bellicose society of its day.[14]

England, strangely, was little affected by these ecclesiastical developments. For the most part the "peace movement" remained a Continental phenomenon, perhaps because there was less need in England to control warring noble families or private armies, which were terrorizing the countryside and contributing to general lawlessness elsewhere at this time.[15] The nation's ever peculiar relationship to the papacy (as plainly seen in the Thomas Becket affair) allowed many of these experiments to become only superficial exercises of little urgency perhaps by virtue of the greater distance from Rome. With the coming of the Crusades, however, England entered into the mainstream and maelstrom of international warfare — clearly not so much out of a national interest but as a collection of individual advance guards seeking fame, fortune, and the defense of Christendom.[16]

The Just War During the Crusades

Before considering the advent of this new manifestation of holy war, we must examine further developments in the theoretical basis for just war — which coincided with the Crusades. Although England had little affinity

13. Richard Barber, *The Knight and Chivalry* (New York: Charles Scribner's Sons, 1970), 213.

14. Contamine, *War in the Middle Ages*, 273–76; Johnson, *Just War Tradition*, 132–42; C. J. Holdsworth, "Ideas and Reality: Some Attempts to Control and Defuse War in the Twelfth Century," in Sheils, *Church and War*, 63, 68–69.

15. Roland H. Bainton, *Christian Attitudes Toward War and Peace: A Historical Survey and Critical Re-evaluation* (New York: Abingdon Press, 1960), 104–11; Wallace-Hadrill, "War and Peace in the Earlier Middle Ages," 173–74.

16. For a discussion of the relationship between the *pax Dei / treuga Dei* and the crusade as well as their utility in curbing domestic disorder in France, see Duby, *Legend of Bouvines*, 57–75.

for much of Roman law, the decretal position on just war was to have a great impact on later scholastic arguments. Gratian's *Decretum* appeared around 1140, and during the second half of the twelfth century, a flood of commentaries on the work followed.[17] In *causa* 23 Gratian delineated what was to become the basis for later debate on the just war through his incorporation of the Roman legal stipulation that both just cause (redress of injuries) and proper authority be present. He added particulars, such as when righting wrongs left unattended by the enemy, a formal pronouncement first must be issued enumerating the reasons for going to war; and although wars for religion are acceptable, anticipating imminent or future actions that would justify war or engaging in preemptive strikes is not. In other areas, Gratian's strong moral tone can be traced to Augustine's influence, especially when he insists that since right intent and the *jus gentium* regulate warfare, loving the enemy and desiring peace legitimizes war. He went on to insist that to fight with these motives meant that uncontrollable violence and personal vindictiveness would never be part of just wars. With Gratian, therefore, the *jus in bello* (the law of war) began to take a position beside the *jus ad bellum* (the right to make war) and to become a part of the chivalric ideal.[18] The difficulties inherent in trying to conform to what would become a very precise and rigid "law of arms" will be considered later, but for the legitimacy of war itself, the decretists established a legal definition that could be challenged only when restraints appeared brittle and war raged with unparalleled ferocity.

The *Decretum* attempted further to deal with the problems of what to do with heretics, noncombatants, and clergy who fight. Much of the pressure was taken off the individual soldier, for he was to obey even "evil commands" if enjoined to fight by a proper authority. Gratian declared at one point that "wars should only be undertaken on the command of God or some legitimate *imperium*."[19] In *quaestio* 8 he allowed clerics certain rights in declaring war, with the pope exercising the greatest authority. But

17. Contamine, *War in the Middle Ages,* 282–84; Nussbaum, "Just War — A Legal Concept?" 456. For a thorough discussion of Gratian's impact within the Roman law tradition (mainly on the Continent) see Russell, *Just War,* 41–85. The author provides nearly complete summaries and analyses of the important commentators Stephen of Tournai, Sicard of Cremona, and Huguccio (pp. 86–126).

18. Russell, *Just War,* 83–85; Johnson, *Just War Tradition,* 152–62, and *Ideology,* 53–64; Calvocoressi, *Time for Peace,* 24–32.

19. Gratian, *Hoc presens Graciani decretum una cum apparatu Bartho. Brixen in suis distinctionibus et causis bene visum et emendatum* (Basil: Michael Wenssler, 1481), *causa* 23, *questio* 8, fols. dd1v–dd4v; Russell, *Just War,* 69.

following the strictures of the peace movement, the jurist forbade those in orders to take part in combat directly. Only bishops in regalia, acting on their temporal authority, could actively participate (*"ecclesia imperatoribus non sunt obnoxie"*), as long as they refrained from committing violent acts themselves. The Church also maintained coercive powers over heretics and could force true religion on them against their will. According to the *jus gentium* care should be taken to protect noncombatants whenever possible.[20] Yet the *jus ad bellum* still took precedence in Gratian's arguments, and like Augustine, he believed that the innocent would be hurt sometimes in the achievement of an overall good. A tension arises in the *Decretum* between proper political authority and individual conscience, although it is not immediately apparent. Since the argument presented is essentially a moral one set forth in a legal manner, any absence of an agreed-upon spiritual authority — such as the pope — could potentially sow seeds of doubt about certain wars.

Three English canonists and theologians who studied and taught in Paris (ca. 1190–1220) under the tutelage of Peter the Chanter offered a unique gloss on the *Decretum* when it came to defining the just war and the limits of obedience it might impose on combatants.[21] Because they invoked an authority more personal and complex than the temporal or sacerdotal *imperium* of Gratian, they paved the way for the scholastic theologians who would emphasize the right-intent aspect of the just war as the means for transcending the otherwise un-Christian tolerance for unmitigated violence that often accompanied the command of a recognized authority. But even with these English decretists there was a reluctance to engage fully with the leading implications of their thought. They found in their own day that purely legal interpretations of just warfare were too limiting and did not sufficiently address the greater moral issues that both a revival of Aristotelian logic and the quagmire of holy war made urgent.

Robert of Courson, Stephen Langton, and Thomas of Chobham provided major commentary on the standard canonist definitions of just war. Their ideas were not unique to English theologians in their day, but the chord they struck over ethical issues in armed conflicts resonated within a

---

20. Gratian, *Decretum, causa* 23, *questio* 8, fols. dd1v–dd4v; Russell, *Just War*, 70–81, 83–85.

21. Most of the following discussion is taken from John W. Baldwin's excellent compendium and analysis of twelfth-century Parisian social and political thought. John W. Baldwin, *Masters, Princes and Merchants. The Social Views of Peter the Chanter and His Circle*, 2 vols. (Princeton: Princeton University Press, 1970).

nation that exhibited a particular antipathy toward war among some of its leading figures. Perhaps this is what led such men to consider these problems so deeply and respectfully. All three were interested mainly in a most difficult aspect of the just war — obedience to a proper authority. Gratian had declared that soldiers were to obey established authorities completely unless to do so would contravene "divine precepts" — even if the one in command was himself acting sinfully by going to war. Responsibility rested completely on the latter's shoulders, shielding the dutiful knight from all blame. This early canonical position may have been so simply put because the complex moral dilemmas of later crusades and dynastic conflicts were not yet evident in the first half of the twelfth century.[22]

As the century progressed, however, the decretists were confronted with a growing number of *in bello* contingencies that led them to create a more specific, legal interpretation of proper authority, yet one flexible enough to expand the relevant categories as new situations arose. Focusing on the feudal and contractual nature of warfare, canonists such as Huguccio and Simon of Bisignano accepted fully the just cause, right motive, and proper authority formula for the just war, but added a broader emphasis, however, on good intentions. These men permitted disobedience to schismatics, heretics, and excommunicates, regardless of particular feudal obligations owed by a vassal to his lord. The effort to limit brigandage disguised as just war and legitimized through legalisms is clearly demonstrated here and was an extension of the earlier Peace of God movement. The Church would determine who was in the right and thus promote greater political and religious unity and stability.[23]

By Peter the Chanter's day early theologians, still mostly canonists in practice, were considering proper authority along moral lines. They were much more suspicious than their medieval predecessors of the motives behind wars, thereby demonstrating the change in climate that followed recent campaigns. Since they believed few armed conflicts were justified, it became increasingly important for the individual combatant to examine and properly evaluate his own behavior. Simply following the orders of supposedly more knowledgeable, sometimes competing authorities meant soldiers could no longer count on the assured refuge of an automatic pardon. The greater attention on individual choice carried over into other issues as well, including treatment of civilians and prisoners, plunder, and

22. Russell, *Just War*, 69–70.
23. Ibid., 103–4.

so on. In the end, the problems of conflicting jurisdictions that plagued
earlier canonists were simply transcended by grounding the justice of a
war in an ethical determination of proper obedience, meaning that some
evaluation of intent might be required as well.[24] Only one side in a conflict
behaved correctly, and so *this* became the basis for choosing one's allegiance, regardless of responsibilities and duties bound up in feudal obligations. Obedience was still a bedrock of the just war even as it became an
increasingly divisive issue, since more powerful princes were demanding it
from their subjects without question. But what constituted proper behavior, and once again, when could a soldier disobey his superior? These were
the burning questions for the early theologians in Paris at the turn of the
thirteenth century.

In his *Summa,* Robert of Courson concentrated his discussion of war on
Old Testament *exempla,* much like Augustine, acknowledging the justice
of conquests that were under God's direct leadership. In those times, it was
clear which offensive actions were legitimate and which were not. In the
present day, however, he argued that these types of wars could be justified
only when there was a proper authority, such as that provided by the
Church against its enemies. But even that authority did not automatically
designate a war as just.[25] For Robert, only holy wars were unequivocally
lawful. Like the Hebrew conquest of the Amorites (Numbers 20:17–21),
so the Crusades are sanctioned for their attempt to recapture Christendom's rightful inheritance. More than Gratian, Robert made just cause the
preeminent determinant of legitimate warfare. The clearly secular exploits
of other Old Testament and ancient warriors, such as Nebuchadnezzar,
Sennacherib, and Alexander were forthrightly and unapologetically condemned.[26]

A just cause still needed a proper determination, and so as inquiries
were made into which authorities could sufficiently deem a conflict just or
holy, an ancillary question also arose over whether the "subject" (*sub-
ditus*) should be permitted any role.[27] Thomas of Chobham, by arguing
that all wars fought without the "judgment and counsel of the realm"
were unjust, thereby determined just wars to be essentially judicial matters.

24. Ibid., 215, 218, 222.

25. Robert of Courson, *Summa,* MS Paris BN 14524, xv, 2, 3: fols. 63vb–64ra, quoted in
Baldwin, *Masters, Princes and Merchants,* 1:208, 2:147.

26. Robert of Courson, Summa, MS Paris BN 14524, xxvi, 10: fol. 92rb–va; xv, 2, 3: fols.
63vb–64ra; fol. 64va–vb; Baldwin, *Masters, Princes and Merchants,* 1:206–9, 2:146–7.

27. Baldwin, *Masters, Princes and Merchants,* 1:209.

This "implied right of discussion," however, omitted any mention of which part of the kingdom should be included.[28] Robert of Courson proved nearly as vague in his claim that traditional human law, which denied a subject the right to inquire into the justice of his prince's war, contradicted divine authority. Still, he also refused to explicate who would be permitted to offer opinions and judgments concerning war.[29]

In his *Questiones,* Stephan Langton came closest to solving this particular quandary. First, he declared that if a war was found to be just in the royal court, which was most knowledgeable, then there was no right of discussion by the people. This reasoning, however, served to create another problem simply one step removed, even as it attempted to set limits. Now one needs ask, Who at court should be involved in decisions of war and can there be a clear, unassailable right to fight when more than one opinion is expressed? A somewhat tentative answer may be found in the individualism detectable in Stephen's answer to the question of whether a knight is obligated to fight in an unjust war. Having in mind the example of Philip Augustus's campaign against Plantagenet holdings in France (and England's eventual loss of Normandy), Stephen supposed an unjust war was being waged by the French king against the English king.[30] The French soldier must choose either to disobey God or to commit treason against his lord. To save his honor and his faith, he should remain loyal in supporting the conflict but personally withdraw from battle once it begins.[31] Any time the king himself, however, is attacked, the knight must come to his defense even if the enemy is in the right. Stephen thus made a clear distinction between offensive and defensive wars, whereas Augustine and Gratian found no demarcation or reason for introducing such categories.

Arguing in a similar vein, Thomas of Chobham laid it upon the bishops to persuade soldiers to withdraw from unjust wars, but only "if the people were unanimous and if this could be accomplished without schism or sedition." Individual knights are required to remain loyal to the prince, even in an unlawful conflict, but they are not to shed blood. And if there was

---

28. Ibid.; Thomas of Chobham, *Summa confessorum,* ed. F. Broomfield, *Analecta Mediævalia Namurcensia* 25 (1968): 430.

29. Robert of Courson, *Summa,* MS Paris BN 14524, xxvi, 10: fol. 92rb, quoted in Baldwin, *Masters, Princes, and Merchants,* 1:209, 2:147.

30. Stephen Langton, *Questiones,* MS Avranches 230, fol. 261v; MS Paris BN 16385, fol. 69va–vb; MS Vatican Lat. 4297, fol. 62va; Baldwin, *Masters, Princes, and Merchants,* 1:209–10; 2:147–48; F. M. Powicke, *Stephen Langton* (London: Merlin Press, 1965), 49–74.

31. Langton, *Questiones,* MS Avranches, quoted in Baldwin, *Masters, Princes, and Merchants,* 1:209–10, 2:148.

pressure to kill Christians or to plunder, they were duty-bound to resist even with force if necessary.[32] Using the analogy of the Eucharist, Stephen contended that as the priest must offer publicly the sacrament to all, even mortal sinners, it is necessary that he refuse to do so privately. In the same way, the knight must ultimately resist direct combat in an unjust conflict when he himself is called upon to kill in a private act of violence against the "enemy."[33] Harkening back to needed assurances of just cause, Robert of Courson considered the possibility of being faced with having to fight either a partly just war or a completely unjust one. He believed the dilemma could be overcome by simply going on crusade. Since this was the only war justified without a doubt, it was the most lawful war, and thereby excused the knight from following his prince in a less than fully just war and from endangering his own salvation.[34]

In sum, these three English canonists stretched the intent of the *Decretum* to near the breaking point. They were most consistent with Gratian in their support and justification for crusades, but even here, they were less than wholehearted in their enthusiasm. Their judicial approach to the just war added a critical element to the overall discussion of the theory, especially when one considers the early, medieval roots of political consent as part of the English constitution. The extent of their influence, however, even within their own circle, was probably minute. But they do provide a window into what may be a peculiarly "English" understanding of just and holy wars, built upon a uniquely "English" experience in Continental affairs, which as we have seen, made them, if not indifferent, at least aloof in their attitude toward papal and imperial politics (William of Ockham notwithstanding). And domestic cultural and institutional developments offer a whole other set of possible influences. In terms of philosophical consistency or even rudimentary logic, these three writers did leave much to be desired. Their attempt to be theoretically orthodox and yet empirically penetrating on the subject of war exposed what would be a common

32. Thomas of Chobham, *Summa confessorum,* 430; Baldwin, *Masters, Princes, and Merchants,* 1:210.

33. Langton, *Questiones,* MS Cambridge, St. John's College. 57, fol. 204vb, and MS Paris BN 14556 fol. 220va, quoted in Baldwin, *Masters, Princes, and Merchants,* 1:210–11, 2:148.

34. Robert of Courson, *Summa,* x, 15: fol. 50va, vb; xxx, 9: fol. 107ra; quoted in Baldwin, *Masters, Princes, and Merchants,* 2:148–49; see also 1:209–11. The penalty for refusing a military summons included forfeiture of property (as payment), which befell the bishops of Lincoln and Salisbury and the abbot of St. Edmunds. Baldwin, *Masters, Princes, and Merchants,* 1:207–8, 2:148 n. 36.

characteristic of later theologians who offered "contradictory and confusing" advice that often proved unworkable in practice.

By the early thirteenth century canonists throughout Europe began commenting more on papal legislation than on the *Decretum*. These decretalists, including William of Rennes, Innocent IV, and most important, Hostiensis, specified further the legal categories that incorporated the just war. Going into more detail about what constituted a just cause, proper authority, and right intent in waging war, they expanded previous theories by permitting a loose interpretation of the original Augustinian position.[35] Most of their emphasis, however, went to defining proper authority, which unlike the earlier decretists, they relegated to a supreme authority only. The decretalists, however, consciously went beyond Gratian's interpretation and tried to reinvigorate the feudal contract as a means for curbing unjust wars. Peter of Salins determined that a soldier could fight a war in which the cause was just and the intention (such as cupidity) was not. Only if the lord violated divine law or broke faith with his vassal could he be disobeyed. Hostiensis and Innocent IV both upheld the rights of a vassal to maintain his inheritance if he refused to fight in an unjust war. There should be no legal recourse for wicked lesser lords. In some ways these later decretalists complicated the issue of proper authority by making, for the first time, the cause of national defense (embodied in the will of a legitimate lay power) superior to personal rights and claims.[36] By allowing wars to be initiated exclusively by those kings and emperors who had no temporal superiors they completed the adaptation, begun by the decretists, of just-war theory to feudal law. Since the feudal relationship lent itself to clear lines of military obligation — which were "legalized" by the decretalists — it could also be absorbed by the Church for its own purposes, which were often, during the initial years of the Crusades, in accordance with the personal interests of the knight. According to Frederick Russell: "Authority compelled obedience, and the lure of property made such obedience attractive. The prospect of confiscation on a grand scale when coupled with spiritual and legal benefits granted by the papacy made the Crusades possible."[37]

---

35. Russell, *Just War*, 127–55; Jonathan Barnes, "The Just War," in *The Cambridge History of Later Medieval Philosophy*, ed. Norman Kretzmann, Anthony Kenny, and Jon Pinborg (Cambridge: Cambridge University Press, 1982), 772–77.

36. Russell, *Just War*, 127–211, 215, 218.

37. Ibid., 211.

The crusade or holy war, as a movement of the High Middle Ages, is beyond the scope of this study. Yet in terms of its impact on perceptions about the institution of war itself, it should be given at least a glance. Without a doubt the Crusades created a greater tolerance for violence directed against a universal enemy. Moral apprehensions over killing or the legitimacy of a war were muted, and papal directives made the need to evaluate just causes unnecessary for many.[38] The effect this development had on a prince's proclivities for battle spurred Etienne de Fougères and Guillaume le Clerc to write some exceptional antiwar poetry in the early thirteenth century, praising kings who eschew war and dissension for peace and concord (*tranquillitas ordinis*).[39] Monastic pacifism went by the way as well, as military orders such as the Templars and Hospitalers (also known as the Knights of St. John) were founded.[40] More than anyone, Gregory VII gave form to the Christian warrior by transforming the meaning of *militia Christi* from involvement in spiritual struggles into armed combat against God's enemies. He began offering absolution for sins in return for military service in the "army of God."[41] To die while taking up the Cross became a path to salvation and by the early thirteenth century, a huge number of spiritual benefits were conveyed to those who fought.[42]

This "sanctification of warfare" took just-war arguments to such heights — especially the inherent premise that any controls limiting violence were unnecessary when fighting heretics — that the crusade came under increasing attack as time went on and military successes were fewer. By the thirteenth century, the plenary indulgence was devalued and weakened "by setting up inner tensions between the spiritual purpose of the instrument

38. See E. O. Blake, "The Formation of the 'Crusade Idea,'" *Journal of Ecclesiastical History* 21 (1970): 12.

39. Mary Morton Wood, *The Spirit of Protest in Old French Literature* (New York: Columbia University Press, 1917; reprint, New York: AMS Press, 1966), 18–22.

40. Bainton, *Christian Attitudes,* 114; B. H. Rosenwein, "Feudal War and Monastic Peace: Clunaic Liturgy as Ritual Aggression," *Viator* 2 (1971): 129–57.

41. I. S. Robinson, "Gregory VII and the Soldiers of Christ," *History* 58 (1973): 178–80; Russell, *Just War,* 35; Keith Haines, "Attitudes and Impediments to Pacifism in Medieval Europe," *Journal of Medieval History* 7 (1981): 379–81.

42. Besides the infamous crusade indulgences, release from excommunication and interdict was available, and confessors could grant pardons for "homicide, matrimonial consanguinity, bastardy, irregular ordination, perjury and pluralism" — all powers normally reserved for papal jurisdiction. A crusader's vow could substitute as well for other vows made previously, such as those made to enter a monastery or to live chastely. See James A Brundage, *Medieval Canon Law and the Crusader* (Madison: University of Wisconsin Press, 1969), 22, 145–57.

and its practical application in the context of the crusade."[43] The edge was being taken off the Church's spiritual and moral authority. Theorists, including canonists, were influenced more by the actions of crusading armies; wars were less often conducted according to original just-war principles.[44]

Recent scholarship has demonstrated clearly that those who supported crusades, or holy wars in general, from the eleventh to the seventeenth century, usually employed just-war reasoning to justify their positions. Thomas Aquinas exemplified this correlation in a quodlibetal question written near the time he wrote his position on the just war in the *Summa theologica*. According to Aquinas, the three criteria for obtaining a valid crusade indulgence mirrors those proposed for just wars, each necessitating legitimate cause, intention, and authority. The holy war, for example, is fought to defend the Holy Land and includes the redress of wrongs done to Christians living there. It is initiated by the pope and should be conducted with charity toward the enemy. There was no wholesale permission given to kill innocent noncombatants, even if they were heathens. Theoretically then, Thomas and other like-minded theologians posited that crusades ought to be conducted with the same care and concern for moral and legal principles as other just wars. In practice, however, this was often not the case because religious arguments are easily disposed to extremes of praxis. As LeRoy Walters states, "The classic just-war theorists can perhaps be faulted for insufficient sensitivity to the absolutizing tendencies of religiously sanctioned warfare." Gradually, all semblance of concern for enemies disappeared, and their treatment belied charitable intentions. Raymond Schmandt contends that by the Fourth Crusade the excesses had so tainted the movement and corrupted the just war that many came to have serious reservations about certain prevalent assumptions that *any* action was permitted against an enemy. Overall, the Crusades caused consternation and widespread rethinking about war itself for the first time perhaps since the pacifist literature of the early church fathers.[45]

England was not at this time a central theater for the debate that ensued. In some cases English kings and nobles were denied altogether the right to

43. Maureen Purcell, "Changing Views of Crusade in the Thirteenth Century," *Journal of Religious History* 7 (1972): 17; Brundage, *Medieval Canon Law*, 24.
44. Raymond H. Schmandt, "The Fourth Crusade and the Just-War Theory," *Catholic Historical Review* 61 (1975): 191–221.
45. LeRoy Walters, "The Just War and the Crusade: Antithesis or Analogies?" *The Monist* 57 (1973): 587–94; Schmandt, "Fourth Crusade and the Just-War Theory," 191–221; Johnson, *Ideology*, 134–46.

take up the Cross, as is evidenced in the confrontation between Henry II
and Abbot Samson of Bury St. Edmunds. Others made their own choice
not to participate in the Crusades because they interfered with and took
away from particular personal interests. A recent study has characterized
English contributions to the Crusades as "modest." Neither Henry III nor
Edward I exhibited much enthusiasm "and the workings of social structure
ensured that this would have a profound bearing upon the level of crusading activity of their subjects." In the end, the Crusades did not exert a
"profound or decisive impact upon English historical development in other
ways."[46] Edward purposely planned his coronation for the same time the
Council of Lyons was to make preparations for a new crusade. In the
process he kept other high-ranking men of the realm home and demonstrated clearly that he "had had his fill of crusading."[47] There seems to
have been, however, little overt, theoretical condemnation of the Crusades
in England at that time. Since any expressed dissatisfaction with them
could be construed as heresy (recalling the pacifism of the Waldensians),
orthodox critics of war had to be careful not to come under censure by the
papacy.[48]

On another level a few English Franciscans did criticize the intentions
and actions of crusaders when they took up their founder's argument that
missionary activity should replace all holy war.[49] In 1250 Adam Marsh
could commend Henry III for his perfunctory crusading endeavors, all the
while insisting that peaceful conversion was the superior course, even if it
led to martyrdom.[50] Roger Bacon was more outspoken in his abhorrence
for holy wars; indeed, around 1268 he wrote that crusades hindered rather
than assisted the conversion of pagans. He concluded that unbelievers
were not "converted in this way, but they are slain and sent to hell," while
"survivors of the wars and their sons are angered more and more against

46. Simon D. Lloyd, *English Society and the Crusade, 1216–1307* (Oxford: Oxford University Press, 1988), 87, 244, 247. Real skepticism about the efficacy and practice of crusading came especially after the disastrous failure of the Third Crusade. See William of Newburgh, *Historia rerum Anglicarum,* in *Chronicles of the Reigns of Stephen, Henry II, and
Richard I,* ed. R. Howlett (London: Royal Society, 1884), 1:374–75, 379–80.
    47. Palmer A. Throop, *Criticism of the Crusade: A Study of Public Opinion and Crusade
Propaganda* (Amsterdam: N.V. Swets & Zeitlinger, 1940; reprint, Philadelphia: Porcupine
Press, 1975), 220–21.
    48. Bainton, *Christian Attitudes,* 118–21.
    49. Ibid.
    50. Adam Marsh, *Epistolae,* in *Monumenta franciscana,* ed. J. S. Brewer, RS, no. 4 (Lon-
don: Longman, Brown, Green, Longmans & Roberts, 1858), 1:416, 435; Throop, *Criticism
of the Crusade,* 132.

the Christian faith because of those wars."[51] Unlike some of the early four-teenth-century Old French and Provençal poetry that denounced the Cru-sades as part of a larger attack on the papacy, the English Franciscans condemned current practice later in the century out of a simple, even naïve personal ethic of showing love to all people, without seriously engaging with the right-intent facet of the just war. Still, their sentiments, especially those of the eminent Bacon, are noteworthy and illustrative of profound discontent with the types of wars being sanctioned by the pope in the thirteenth century, and of the rising conflict between temporal and eccle-siastical interests.[52]

If we return to theory, it is the schoolmen who seemed most affected by holy-war proclivities toward greater violence and their possible negative influence on the just war or the practice of legitimate warfare itself. For this reason, the Thomist just-war position emphasizes right intention rather than the proper authority stressed by the decretalists.[53] In the wake of these alternative and expanded means for evaluating war (including the crusade) the *jus in bello* received greater attention, and at the same time, an underlying practical skepticism slowly materialized.

The Just War Among the Theologians

In their own day the theologians who commented on warfare were not as influential as the canonists whose work became part of an extensive and widespread legal tradition. Popes, who often contributed to decretalist opinion, preferred to justify crusades in this way because it seemed more concrete and manageable. The theologians, however, found such legalism part of the problem with contemporary just-war reasoning. Returning to abstract arguments based on Aristotelian logic, scholastic theologians tried to rationalize and humanize the just war by basing it on achievement of the common good. They still made Augustine their touchstone, even if he was filtered through the canonists, and accepted, by and large, the tradi-tional categories of analysis.

51. Roger Bacon, *Opus majus,* ed. and trans. Robert Belle Burke (Philadelphia: University of Pennsylvania Press, 1928), 2:111. See also Bacon's *Compendium studii,* in *Opera hactenus inedita,* ed. J. S. Brewer, RS, no. 15 (London: Longman, Brown, Green, Longmans & Rob-erts, 1859), 395, and Throop, *Criticism of the Crusade,* 133.
52. Throop, *Criticism of the Crusade,* 26–30, 285–86.
53. Walters, "Just War and the Crusade," 585–94.

The most influential theologian, Thomas Aquinas, streamlined the criteria for just wars by basically reducing them to just cause, proper authority,
and right intent. He provided, however, a different basis for determining
the conditions when all three would be valid. His views on the first two
are consistent with the Christian *jus ad bellum* doctrine of his day, which
held that wars are just which right grievous wrongs and are carried out by
a godly authority wielding the sword against evil. The "right side" then,
according to Thomas, has been offended and has a right to some form of
retribution. Such reasoning may legitimate only defensive wars but first
strikes are permitted, especially when the evil perpetrated — such as heresy — is not of a military nature.[54] Thomas's particular interest in the third
criteria, right intention, can be attributed in part to the Crusades, which
had made the schoolmen increasingly suspicious of military service, even
though they would not condemn war out of hand, as already seen in Peter
the Chanter's circle. By incorporating with even greater force the Aristotelian position that just wars promote the common good, they laid much
of the moral determination about any particular war, again, on those who
fought it rather than on the authority that had declared it.[55]

In the *Summa theologica* Aquinas divides the question of the just war
into four parts: (1) Are some wars permissible? (2) May clerics engage in
warfare? (3) May belligerents use subterfuge? and (4) May war be waged
on feast days? He gave much attention naturally to the first section where
most of the *jus ad bellum* aspects are addressed. Taking for granted Aristotle's belief that humans are naturally social and political beings, for
Aquinas, government was a positive good whose chief end is to promote
the public welfare. For this reason, "since the care of the commonweal is
committed to those in authority they are the ones to watch over the public
affairs" and "on whose command war is waged."[56] If just cause and
proper authority are so construed, then, like many of his contemporaries,
it is understandable that Thomas would return to Augustine for guidance
on the third component. Right intention, which Aquinas took to be the
motive "to promote good and to avoid evil," means that a man must take

54. Johnson, *Ideology*, 38–40.
55. Russell, *Just War*, 214–18, 297; Contamine, *War in the Middle Ages*, 286. J. Leclercq,
"St. Bernard's Attitude Toward War," in *Studies in Medieval Cistercian History*, vol. 2, Cistercian Studies Series, no. 24 (Kalamazoo, Mich.: Cistercian Publications, 1976), 1–39.
56. Thomas Aquinas, *Summa Theologica* (New York: McGraw-Hill, 1972), 2-2, q. 40, pp.
81, 83.

up arms on occasion "for the common good or even for the good of his opponents."[57]

The experience of the Crusades caused the schoolmen to comment not only on the reasons for war but to reexamine the conduct associated with it, including the role of clerics. In the second question Aquinas argued that "fighting in war is quite inconsistent with the duties of a bishop or a cleric" because he is prevented from contemplating divine things and profanes the sacrament by shedding blood. Still those in orders may do everything short of fighting to promote wars that are just.[58] Thomas found the just war, however, to be meritorious when fought with proper intent and so does allow for subterfuge and fighting on feast days when such is necessary for the protection of the commonweal. "To act otherwise in the face of such peril would be to tempt God."[59] Such a rationale betrayed a concern over injury to noncombatants and a condemnation of plunder even if these were not expressed points of the argument. At the same time, both actions were permissible if circumstances warranted them. For Thomas there was a justice to the just war that aided those who had been wronged, had property seized, or in any other way been deprived of the protection of their *patria*. The Church could wage war against the infidel but only if these same conditions of just cause, proper authority, and right intent determined the recourse to crusade.[60] "Mere infidelity no longer served as sufficient justification for a Christian crusade of conquest."[61] Here the most confusing aspect of Thomas's position on the just war comes into view. Supporting almost every tactic promoted by the Church as justifiable in holy war, he enjoined the soldier and sovereign to determine whether the war itself is just, but denied that crusades for conversion fit this category.[62]

The attempts by theologians like Aquinas to combine legal and moral theories of just war drove them to offer some early *jus in bello* limits to the prosecution of wars. Blended with analogous contributions by Gratian, Hostiensis, and other canonists, they were supplementing a newly emerging institution that had its own, more secular, rationale. The *jus armorum*

---

57. Ibid., 83–85.
58. Ibid., 85–87.
59. Ibid., 91–93.
60. Walters, "Just War and the Crusade," 587.
61. Russell, *Just War*, 286; Bainton, *Christian Attitudes*, 106–9.
62. That is, outside the holy land, to which Christendom had a historic and spiritual right.

had developed into an international code of knightly behavior by the thirteenth century, providing yet another ethic for fighting. The English (and indeed most of Europe) soon realized that the *jus ad bellum* alone could not regulate martial activity sufficiently. The Crusades looked more and more like colossal failures, and the Church's motives, often perceived as full of self-aggrandizement, did not always correspond with those of lay authorities. It had become increasingly urgent for temporal powers to contain the behavior of free companies and force them to acknowledge rules and principles that secured the public peace (*tranquillitas ordinis*) under a more centralized governmental structure. While canonists did introduce *jus in bello* limits on behavior in warfare, it was the law of arms that had the true advantage of becoming a means for curtailing the excesses, even if it never measured up to the standard over which its admirers rhapsodized.

In many ways the new reliance on the *jus in bello* underscores a reorganization wherein militaries no longer protect feudal rights and duties but serve as organs of consolidating princely prerogatives, a transition already occurring in some areas during the High Middle Ages. Even before the end of the Crusades the moral authority held by the Church over the issue of war had been greatly shaken by these ventures. Territorial and national interests began to eclipse religious enterprises, and discipline within ranks began to be valued more highly. If then the "just war is really an ethical and religious doctrine surfaced with an often thick veneer of legality,"[63] it would have to be fully resolved and complemented by regulating more carefully its practice. While still embracing the *jus ad bellum* as it had been defined by the Church over many centuries,[64] with its important role in intellectualizing a destructive activity, excesses could be mitigated through a code of strict behavior in the actual arena of combat. Thus by creating a new moral ground for war—one predicated on personal conduct—warfare could be more thoroughly institutionalized in medieval Europe even if its theoretical base remained open to manipulation. At the end of the Middle Ages these two components of "classic just-war theory" came together and remained a unified, complementary doctrine at least until the Refor-

63. Russell, *Just War,* 306.
64. The only known case wherein a Christian ruler actually asked the pope to decide on the legitimacy of a war came with the Portuguese dilemma over whether to continue its conquest of the Canary Islands in 1436. See James Muldoon, "A Fifteenth-Century Application of the Canonistic Theory of Just War," in *Proceedings of the Fourth International Congress of Medieval Canon Law, Toronto, 21–25 August 1972,* ed. Stephen Kuttner (The Vatican: Biblioteca Apostolica Vaticana, 1976), 467–80.

mation.[65] While in England the just-war positions were never given the attention they received on the Continent, nevertheless they infiltrated educated opinion on the subject of war. Still, such ideas seemed to have remained rather tenuous and fragile until given new life during the Hundred Years War — a conflict which by its end had sapped the nation of much of its fighting spirit and fostered alternatives to just-war reasoning.

The Just War in Medieval England

Except for the expatriate canonists in late twelfth-century Paris — and their arguments were often weak and logically suspect — English opinion on the just war does not really make itself felt until the fourteenth century. By that time the Crusades had wound down into complete disaster and a renewed conflict with France took their place as the primary martial activity for the knights. Growing nationalist sentiment led many of the first skeptics of contemporary just-war assumptions to appear at this time, brandishing in one hand a disaffection with causes unrelated to dynastic concerns, and in the other, a sword poised to strike fiercely against the French usurper. As the war progressed, however, and its unprecedented destruction was felt, the critiques began to focus on the larger dynastic issues as well.

It would be absurd to deny that in England, as well as in the rest of Europe, a devotion to the "just war" existed throughout the Middle Ages. The countenance of this devotion, however, possessed a number of peculiarities once Englishmen examined the actual motives behind conflicts such as the Hundred Years War. Due to the education of knights' sons into the law of arms and prowess from the age of twelve, "warfare and battle became the *sine qua non* of knighthood."[66] But this compliance with the rites of chivalry extended only to a small if influential number of Englishmen. A much wider social and intellectual range of people, who were familiar with aspects of just-war theory, saw problems with what it was exhorting Christians to advocate. Contemporary observers like John Gower and John Wyclif, who were in the thick of the international events of their day, could find only so much valuable in Thomist justifications for war and thus helped initiate a dialogue that challenged existing rationales.

65. Johnson, *Ideology,* 33–48.
66. Haines, "Attitudes and Impediments," 381.

When corrupt leaders are able to manipulate soldiers into thinking that their behavior in battle is meritorious and even blessed by God, how could the scholastic notion of proper intent be gauged properly? What if an individual moral decision appeared to conflict with the common good that Thomas said war was to protect? These questions and others like them emerged during the late fourteenth century and forced those who once accepted and promoted "just wars" to rethink their positions. In times when theory appeared to conflict with reality some made serious attempts to revise the theory while others simply refused to admit that any correlation existed between the two. In England a number of factors, ranging from earlier national unity, technological backwardness, and royal incompetence to economic hardships and their impact on parliamentary oversight, made the latter course increasingly less acceptable by the fifteenth century. These historical developments and how they impinged on attitudes toward war are discussed in Chapter 2, since they parallel neatly those changes occurring in the *jus armorum*. Here we will concentrate on ideological critiques that were based largely on specific activities that took place during the Hundred Years War, and which called into question how the *jus ad bellum* was being invoked at the time. While it is true that more criticism of war in medieval England came from those who had grown cynical about the role of knights, a few argued that the justice of contemporary warfare itself should be called into question, although this must not be taken to mean that there was anything approaching a systematic or coherent body of thought emerging.[67]

Of these men of peace (as opposed to the anachronistic term "pacifist"), the poet John Gower and Oxford theologian-heretic John Wyclif developed the most substantive appraisals of the just war. When Gower wrote *Mirour de l'omme* around 1376–78, he appears to have supported Edward III's claim to the French throne. By the end of the next decade, however, he had retreated fully from that position. As will be shown later, much of his disgust for the war came from what he saw to be the corruption of the nobility who fought, which in turn further delegitimized the justice of the conflict.[68] How could Edward's claim be just when all of the subsequent destruction brought inordinate hardship on the English and French people? In his address to Henry IV soon after the latter's accession

---

67. Scott L. Waugh, *England in the Reign of Edward III* (Cambridge: Cambridge University Press, 1991), 129–30.

68. John Barnie, *War in Medieval English Society: Social Values and the Hundred Years War, 1337–99* (London: Weidenfeld & Nicolson, 1974), 122–23.

in 1399, Gower acknowledged that "a king may make war upon his right," yet all the while he admonishes his king to "keep charity, and draw pity to hand, maintain law, and so the peace shall stand."[69] The author's hope that Henry would forsake greed and stake out the higher moral ground with France by working for peace proved somewhat naïve. Gower had earlier spelled out what he thought of kings and nobles who abused the right to go to war, in book 3 of *Confessio amantis:*

> You might a great example take,
> How they their tyranny excuse
> Of that they stand of one accord,
> The soldier forth with the lord,
> The poor man forth with the rich;
> As for courage, they are likely
> To make wars and to pillage
> For lucre and for no other skill.[70]

Here the writer complained that the just war was being used to justify the pursuit of plunder, a criticism that would become standard over the next century.

Yet Gower did not put all of the blame on the corrupt knights; he also charged the Church with fostering a bellicosity among men that was contrary to Christ's teachings. In book 7 of *Vox clamantis* he made a pointed reference to Jesus' warning to Peter that those who live by the sword shall die by the sword. Peter seemed to have listened, but his successor, the pope, continued to disobey: "Peter preached, of course, but today's Pope fights. The one seeks souls, the other greedily seeks riches. The first was killed for God's law, the second kills, and yet God maintains no such law as that. The one arouses faith through his innocence, not by force; the other rouses armies on parade."[71] Most likely Gower had in mind here the scandalous *pugil ecclesiae,* the Norwich Crusade of 1383, which pitted Christian against Christian under the pretense of a holy war.[72] In *Confessio*

69. John Gower, "Address to Henry IV," in *Political Poems and Songs,* ed. Thomas Wright, vol. 2, RS, no. 14 (London: Longman, Green, Longman & Roberts, 1859–61), 6, 15.

70. John Gower, *Confessio amantis,* lines 2352–60, in *Complete Works,* ed. G. C. Macaulay, vol. 2, bk. 3 (Oxford: Clarendon Press, 1900), 289–90. See also Barnie, *War in Medieval English Society,* 130.

71. John Gower, *Vox clamantis,* in *The Major Latin Works,* trans. and ed. E. W. Stockton, bk. 7 (Seattle: University of Washington Press, 1962), 125–26.

72. Led by Henry Despenser, bishop of Norwich, this campaign was an unfortunate at-

amantis, after the Lover asks if it is right to go on crusade, the Confessor replies that it is lawful to suffer and die for the faith, "but as for killing, about that I hear nothing." By this he points to the example of the Apostles who were martyrs and never forced conversion by the sword. If they had, Christianity would "yet stand in the balance." The present crusade proved that since the Holy Church "has abandoned preaching, and has the sword received," many areas have been lost to the Gospel.[73] In the hands of Gower and others like him, the holy war became the launching pad for a more devastating attack on the just-war concept as it was being argued in their day. For them the papacy had turned its back on its pastoral calling and rent Christendom into a society of sinful, warring fragments. Gower's overall position on the just war is unclear, and since he did not condemn its component parts (just cause, right intent, proper authority) out of hand, he most likely had no problem with it in theory. His dissatisfaction with it rested more in its corruption and in his growing realization that it was being manipulated brazenly for personal gain. In Chapter 3 we will see how this disillusionment drove him to champion alternative bases for international relations built around peace.

For Wyclif, Rome had cultivated this deplorable state of affairs, and even now as an international power it has continued to lose much of its moral and political hold over the people of Europe. Given refuge by the duke of Lancaster and others who believed the papacy (residing in Avignon before the Great Schism of 1378) was partial to France, Wyclif held that the Holy See looked to remain politically strong by letting (or even encouraging) potential national powers to languish in their dynastic bloodletting. His criticisms were based almost exclusively on assessments of current jurisdictional disputes and how they were being exploited by those in power with little concern for their effects on women's and men's souls. As other English clerics would do during the Reformation, Wyclif returned to an early, unadulterated, often pre-Augustinian, Christian view of war and peace as he launched his unrelenting attacks against the Church militant. For one, he contended that the apostolic understanding of the *militia Christi* is the proper one, since "Christ taught not His Apostles to fight with a sword of iron but with the sword of God's word, which standeth in

---

tempt to assist the Flemish towns that had risen against their French overlords and to protect English trade interests there. Justified as a crusade to free Flanders from the yoke of an Avignon pope, the whole experience showcased the corruption and inefficiency of the English civil and ecclesiastical administrations at that time.

73. Barnie, *War in Medieval English Society,* 123–25. See Chapter 3 herein.

meekness of heart, and in the prudence of man's tongue."[74] In addition, he was reluctant to permit wars that claim charitable intent as part of their justification: "For Saint Paul bids that all our deeds be done in charity; and by God's law we should love our enemies, and so make them friends by the strength of charity." Since we no longer fight to avenge God's injuries at his leading (as in the Old Testament), or with charity as the motivation, "it is a known thing that men should not now fight."[75] The problem of determining what proper authority can call for a just war is dispatched here with ease. Unlike the tortuous and meticulous deliberations of Peter the Chanter's group, Wyclif simply regarded all war as improperly instituted, since only when God directly leads one is it legitimate; and God seemed to have relinquished that role a couple of millennia ago.

Wyclif leveled his greatest vituperation, however, against the papacy. Not only had it twisted and shamed the peaceful Gospel of Christ by justifying illicit wars, but it had godlessly led people to hell by teaching that fighting for the Church can bring salvation. In the highly critical *Of Prelates* he censured the compliant clergy who endorse the pope's false teaching: "Also they preach not Christ's gospel in word and deed, by which Christian men should live holy lives in charity, but blabber forth the antichrist's bulls which make Christian men war with each other in the hope of winning heaven by such wars."[76] In other sermons and tracts the early reformer vented his spleen repeatedly against both the spiritual and physical harm brought by the clergy upon the people. Because its ranks (including monks and friars) desire to "maintain their possessions and worldly lives," they incite wars, encourage senseless bloodshed, help perpetuate the "robbery of their poor tenants, . . . maintain many men of arms to kill

---

74. Josiah Leeds, *Wiclif's Anti-War Views,* 2d ed. (London: Friends Tract Association, 1902), 9–10.

75. John Wyclif, *On the Seven Deadly Sins,* in *Select English Works of John Wyclif,* ed. Thomas Arnold, vol. 3, chap. 13 (Oxford: Clarendon Press, 1871), 137. In chapter 14, Wyclif betrays a philosophical departure from the traditional just-war position when he challenges the validity of both the "just cause" and the "proper intent" requirements of Augustine. Even if there is the danger that one might lose all of his earthly possessions, it is still not lawful to fight: "And if we if we fight thus for love, it is not love of charity; for charity seeks not proper good in this life, but common good in heaven by virtous patience." And any excuses of fighting for charity will be uncovered on Judgment Day (Domesday) when the guilty will be punished (chap. 14, pp. 137–38). See also Leeds, *Wiclif's Anti-War Views,* 8; L. J. Daly, *The Political Theory of John Wyclif* (Chicago: Loyola University Press, 1962), 141.

76. John Wyclif, *Of Prelates,* in *The English Works,* ed. F. D. Matthew, , chap. 9, EETS OS, no. 74 (London: K. Paul, Trench, Trübner, 1902), 73; Daly, *Political Theory,* 138.

Christian men in body, and they themselves kill many thousands in soul and body."[77] In a manner similar to Gower's, Wyclif bemoaned the applications of the just war, as they had evolved from the experience of the Crusades, to excuse heinous crimes against humanity, both now and for all eternity. In England, the Hundred Years War seemed to give even greater substance to these views and to the perception that the papacy was covertly supporting the French.

Despite the writings of men such as Wyclif and Gower, the just-war tradition was still vibrant in late medieval England, but Wyclif and Gower believed that much of its moral base had eroded. England's enemies, namely the French king and the "French pope," had permitted senseless violence that clearly contradicted the spirit of Augustine, the canonists, and the theologians, who insisted that conditions be scrupulously met before engaging in war, and then that charity govern how it is prosecuted. And both would chastise their own countrymen in other related criticisms. Neither writer could conceive that wrongs avenged in these cruel ways might rest on very sure foundations. Their attacks were restricted to the geopolitical concerns of the day and how they corrupted governments and religion.

Political and religious arguments, however, were not the only tack taken by opponents of just-war usages in Wyclif's or Gower's day. Another diatribe against sin exhibited the more fundamental social differences that may have divided the English people on the ethics of extended warfare. In the moralistic dialogue, *Dives and Pauper,* written around the turn of the fifteenth century, a poor man educates a rich man into his simple yet wise understanding of righteous living. The effects of the Black Death in Europe (after 1348) had raised the status of peasants, and works such as *Piers Plowman,* presented them as upholding a more just manner of living, especially when contrasted to the warring, havoc-wreaking actions of the upper classes. The poor man (Pauper) in *Dives and Pauper* proffers his moral instruction to the dissolute rich through an exposition of the Decalogue. On the fifth commandment: "Thou shalt not kill," Dives asks that if killing is wrong "why does God suffer so much war on earth and so many battles"? Pauper answers that God ordains "the law of the sword and of chivalry" to bring men to peace who will not subscribe to the "law of charity and reason." He then goes on to argue that war is justified if there

77. Wyclif, *Of Prelates, Of Clerks Possessioners,* in *English Works,* chap. 23, p. 90; chap. 26, p. 132.

is proper cause, right intent, and the "authority of a lawful prince," thus giving full acknowledgment to the conditions of the *jus ad bellum,* even quoting Augustine at one point. Proper authority, however, in this instance is that of the sovereign king, with no mention being given to the power of the pope to declare just wars. Pauper makes an even more noticeable departure when he proclaims that if one is "in doubt whether the cause that they fight for is true they are excused by the precept of their prince for virtue of obedience."[78] And if a soldier is absolutely sure that the cause is false, there is no alternative but that he refuse to fight, for "if the prince is a man out of good governance, frantic or brainless, or he is living in open rebellion against God, then the people ought not obey the prince of heaven who bids him fight unless they know for sure his cause is true." Therefore, despite the allegiance to current just-war theory, this treatise presents a major qualification, not totally unlike Gower or Wyclif in its implications. In his final bit of wisdom on the problem of war, Pauper offers some interesting insights when he warns Dives about the terrible abuse which has accompanied "just" wars: "All day you men see what vengeance falls for shedding men's blood, every year more and more. Other nations kill us on every side and rob us, and we have little or nothing to show but the death of our own nation. Therefore, beware of God's sword and of man's sword also, and do not justify what God damns."[79]

Once again, a cynicism about the possibility of legitimate wars accompanies the original doctrinal statement permitting them and warns those who fight without a truly just cause that their punishment is coming. But there is also here a detectable concern with the effects of war and how they steal from the people. As will be shown more specifically in Chapter 2, the writer may have been tapping into a deep-seated resentment against those who would fight wars and leave the land vulnerable to great devastation for slight reason. The separate roles taxpaying commons and plundering nobles played in the making of war could not help but generate serious social tensions.

All of the English writers examined so far who wrote on just-war applications in the later Middle Ages were very concerned with the behavior of soldiers engaged in campaigns, and how that could reflect on the cause itself. The situations to which they referred in their rebuffs of current practice helped produce additional works that attempted to combine the right

78. *Dives and Pauper,* ed. Priscilla Heath Barnum, vol. 1, pt. 2, chap. 14, EETS OS, no. 275 (Oxford: Oxford University Press, 1976), 54–56.
79. Ibid., 56–57.

to make war with an exacting code of military conduct, that is, the *jus ad bellum* with the law-of-arms aspect of the *jus in bello*. Perhaps the most popular treatise of this type is the *Book of Feats of Arms and of Chivalry* by Christine de Pisan, which Caxton published in 1490, in translation, but which was originally written in French around 1408–9. From the very start Christine hit hard on the need for certain wars as long as they were properly initiated and conducted according to a strict law of arms: "It appears manifestly that wars undertaken in a just cause are permitted and suffered by God, as we have found in Holy Scripture many places where our Lord himself commanded captains of armies against their enemies." She went on to acknowledge that it "may seem to some that wars and battles should be accursed things and not proper," but contended that this is so only because they were not being fought properly and according to law. Again, as with English writers on this theme at the time, proper authority rests solely with the temporal sovereign, that is, the king, who is concerned only with the welfare of the nation and "like the good shepherd exposes his life for his sheep." She then delineated five reasons for war: for justice, against oppression, against usurpation, for revenge, and for aggression. The first three she considered lawful, the last two, "wilful" and illicit. Yet to further circumscribe just causes and to eliminate abuse, even under this seemingly self-contained rubric of legitimate authority, Christine restricted the king from making war without consulting an impartial councillor and attempting arbitration (for which the Church would provide its good offices).[80]

While the intent of her treatise was not to justify war, Christine clearly wanted to demonstrate how traditional *jus ad bellum* criteria complemented chivalric principles if they were used in tandem whenever questions of going to war arose. The rules associated with this second aspect of classic just-war theory, the *jus in bello,* helped revitalize the just war and compensate, to some extent, for the growing moral confusion over just cause, right intent, and proper authority which its more theoretical counterpart, the *jus ad bellum,* found itself facing in the midst of a cruel and violent age.

80. Christine de Pisan, *The Book of Fayttes of Armes and of Chyvalrye,* trans. William Caxton, ed. A.T.P. Byles, EETS OS, no. 189 (London: Oxford University Press, 1932), 9, 11–13.

2

CULTURAL CHANGE AND THE LAW OF ARMS IN THE LATER MIDDLE AGES

As military campaigns and capabilities for widespread destruction multiplied in the thirteenth and fourteenth centuries, a feeling grew among Europeans that it was incumbent upon Christians to curb and restrain the worse aspects of warfare. The *jus armorum* was developed for just this reason, and over time it became a disciplined code of behavior. Besides "humanizing" warfare these "moral imperatives governing the behaviour of soldiers" helped "reinforce the effectiveness of armies," thereby serving the dual purposes of limiting war while at the same time enhancing the chances for victory.[1]

The Law of Arms as a Justification for War

An important step in creating a "law of arms" was to eradicate the associations made by the early medieval church between warfare and the possibility of performing a grievous wrong by killing with wrong intention. The plenary indulgence promulgated during the Crusades remitted the tempo-

1. Contamine, *War in the Middle Ages,* 290; Barnes, "Just War," 783.

ral sins of soldiers who died in battle before making confession. Pious
intention was requisite but this usually meant simply having the desire to
reclaim Christian lands wrongfully seized by heathens. Beyond that, pure
motives were hard to come by as soldiers got caught up in the rhythm of
violence, so this measure actually served to break down certain moral bar-
riers that might have inhibited extreme behavior. As has been shown already, Gregory VII's actions, including the use of the indulgence, may have
encouraged this tendency. To spotlight the differences from just a short
time earlier, as late as 1076 — only twenty years before the First Crusade —
it was determined at the Council of Winchester that one year of penance
be required of anyone who killed in war. Those soldiers who were unsure
of how many of the enemy they had killed in battle were obligated to
perform penance one day each week throughout their lives; and all archers
were to do the same three times during a forty-day period.[2] In early
twelfth-century England, there was still the fear that one could commit
mortal sin in warfare; clause 68-12 of the *Leges Henrici Primi,* for example, states that "anyone who kills a man in a national war or in defence of
his lord shall do . . . penance . . . on bread and water for forty days; and
for three periods of Lent together with lawful feast days, he shall abstain
from flesh and drink."[3] The rigorous application of penitential correctives
for martial activities that may have been performed with sinful intent
became less common in practice during the course of the Crusades. In
England, however, ethical quandaries lingered into Stephen's reign (1135–
57), when those who should have been exacting penance from their war-
like brethren were themselves caught with blood on their hands. According
to the king's moralistic chronicler, the bishops of Lincoln and Ely "disregarded the holy and simple manner of life that befits a Christian priest and
devoted themselves utterly to warfare and the vanities of this world," and
so astounded those in court when they appeared shamelessly with their
large retinue of knights. Do such actions indicate an eroding belief in the
defiling nature of warfare by the Church? It is hard to say, but here at
least, English commentators echoed canonist and theological opinion critical of clerics directly involved in fighting.[4]

Martial exploits came under greater scrutiny as the period progressed,

2. Bainton, *Christian Attitudes,* 109.
3. *Leges Henrici Primi,* trans. and ed. L. J. Downer (Oxford: Clarendon Press, 1972),
clauses 68-7, 68-12, pp. 217, 219.
4. *Gesta Stephani,* trans. and ed. K. R. Potter (London: Thomas Nelson & Sons, 1955),
48–49, 104.

and lay military captains often made deathbed confessions asking forgiveness for excessive bloodlust during their lifetimes. Whether William Marshal feared he had done wrong by going to war or for what he had accomplished while at war, he nevertheless exhibited much guilt when, during his final moments in 1219, he confessed that "the clerks are too hard on us [knights]" and "if for this reason [warring] the kingdom of God is closed to us, I can do nothing about it." He contended that only now was he able to repent of all his sins, and that "unless the clergy desire my damnation, they must ask no more. But their teaching is false — else no one could be saved."[5] There is some evidence, therefore, that in England, even after the Crusades were well under way, a strong sentiment remained which took the corruptive nature of warfare seriously and questioned whether these holy wars could be fought morally. As seen in Chapter 1, the theologians, influenced by Aristotelian ethical principles, kept the spirit of penitential correctives in warfare alive by emphasizing the importance of right intent. This concern was Europe-wide; Frederick Russell maintains that the "moral suspicions attached to warfare or at least killing in the early medieval penitential literature went underground but did not cease to exist in the high Middle Ages, where it re-emerged as the scholastic hesitation to assimilate the crusades wholly into the just war theories."[6]

Despite some apparent uneasiness with the practice of war, especially during the Crusades, "peace was not regarded in the Middle Ages as the natural condition of states," and it was hard to differentiate between times of war and times of peace. Endemic to the period, war had by the twelfth century become a muddled exercise with private vendettas being fought alongside deep-seated international conflicts. The feudal levy had become outdated, and contracts for pay took the place of formal service. After the Statute of Winchester in 1285, English armies were raised through commissions of array, which chose men (aged sixteen to sixty) from local areas to serve at the king's wages. Pardons, good wages, and chances for plunder attracted many, but this system also created additional problems. Local communities complained about the expenses of arrays, and pay for hobelers, mounted archers, and men-at-arms was often in arrears.[7]

---

5. Sidney Painter, *William Marshal* (Baltimore: Johns Hopkins University Press, 1933), 285–87.

6. Russell, *Just War*, 294.

7. M. H. Keen, *The Laws of War in the Late Middle Ages* (London: Routledge & Kegan Paul, 1965), 23–24, 64; May McKisack, *The Fourteenth Century, 1307–1399* (Oxford: Clarendon Press, 1959), 234–47.

As English campaigns on the Continent became extended in the late thirteenth and early fourteenth centuries, there existed a concomitant need for a more reliable source of soldiers. The arrays proved one way to get at this problem, but in taking a page out of papal directives, after 1294, much of the army was recruited by pardoning criminals, which helped contribute to greater domestic chaos and to a consequent "breakdown in law and order."[8] In France, the Peace of God movement was revived and transformed "into something like a royal peace" to serve the security interests of the crown, while in England, this initiative by the Church never entered into attempts to maintain public order. The king's peace there became a separate model of control, unique to itself and caught up in extending the parameters of royal jurisdiction into broader legal and political spheres, thereby giving rise to both common law courts and Parliament.[9]

For much of these "early" campaigns against France the expectation for victory and the rewards that accompanied it probably meant that most English people supported the king's motives for and manner of fighting, even if they did not really understand either. The upper classes were definitely caught up in the reigning ethos of heroic warfare. William Fitz-Stephen wrote that the nobles in twelfth-century London, when not in actual combat, "made pretence at war, carrying out field exercises, and indulging in mimic combat. . . . Each is inflamed with the hope of victory. . . . Theirs is an age greedy of glory; youth yearns for victory, and exercises in mock battles in order to carry itself more bravely in real battles."[10] Among the nobility there did exist in fact a great love for war, and it was difficult still at this time for monarchs to exercise thorough control over their newly raised "national chivalries." Much of the independent spirit for personal gain and autonomous companies remained, and thus in an international context the law of arms developed to create a uniform code that would circumscribe wayward and extremely violent behavior. As campaigns became large enterprises, the need for order became even more evident.[11] Chivalry as a social institution among the knights provided a means to enhance their position as an estate, to order their behavior, and to reinvigorate the legitimacy of war by giving it a *jus in bello* rationale

8. Michael Prestwich, *War, Politics and Finance under Edward I* (Totowa, N.J.: Rowman & Littlefield, 1972), 282–90.

9. Richard W. Kaeuper, *War, Justice, and Public Order: England and France in the Later Middle Ages* (Oxford: Oxford University Press, 1988), 6–12, 145–53.

10. Haines, "Attitudes and Impediments," 381–82; Kaeuper, *War, Justice, and Public Order,* 338.

11. Johnson, *Just War Tradition,* 45–49.

alongside some of the *jus ad bellum* rationales that were coming under greater attack for their incongruity with warfare as it was practiced at the time. It is here that the laws of arms intersected with the right-intent strain of the *jus ad bellum*. A war honorably waged was often considered just for that reason alone. The excessive behavior associated with crusade indulgences could be mitigated, some forms of moral guilt assuaged, and musters streamlined, as the work of canonists, scholastic theologians, and codifiers of the *jus armorum* coincided more harmoniously than ever.

The classic exposition of the law of arms[12] comes from the compilation made by the Frenchman Honoré Bonet at the end of the fourteenth century. His *Tree of Battles* extolled "a very ancient system of war theory and soldierly custom" and provided a set of rules that contributed to the developing "law of nations."[13] The *jus armorum* was only gradually recognized as universally applicable, and Bonet's precepts were mainly an anthology taken from various legal, customary, and classical sources.[14] Even though the exemplary knight functioned according to the author's design — as an ideal type embodying an absolute standard — Bonet and others (including his famous disciple, Christine de Pisan) hoped the soldier would practice his craft according to Christian principles and so approximate the archetype as much as was possible. Like the Augustinian and decretal formulations that allowed proper intent to make war a glorious enterprise, these apologists for chivalry made their case by calling the nobility to a higher standard of behavior. They were most responsible for uniting the two components of the medieval just war in order to ensure that the practice of war matched the philosophical justifications for it.

Like his more theoretical just-war predecessors, Bonet proclaimed at the outset of his treatise that "war comes from God, and not merely that He permits war, but that He has ordained it."[15] But then he went on to say

12. It is well beyond the scope of this study to try to elucidate in any more than a cursory manner just what constituted the law of arms. For a more detailed picture one should begin with G. W. Coopland's edition of Bonet's *Tree of Battles* (Cambridge, Mass.: Harvard University Press, 1949) and then move on to Keen's *Laws of War in the Late Middle Ages.*

13. N.A.R. Wright, "The *Tree of Battles* of Honoré Bouvet and the Laws of War," in *War, Literature and Politics in the Late Middle Ages,* ed. C. T. Allmand (Liverpool: Liverpool University Press, 1976), 13–14. See also Coopland's introduction in Bonet, *Tree of Battles.*

14. There were in addition to the treatises like the *Tree of Battles,* laws of war promulgated in England which tried to control soldiers' behavior according to specific standards of conduct. Heralds were often given the task of enforcing laws of war and of keeping soldiers in line. See C. T. Allmand, *The Hundred Years War: England and France at War, c.1300–c.1450* (Cambridge: Cambridge University Press, 1988), 50.

15. Bonet, *Tree of Battles,* 125.

that war is derived from divine law which is the "law of nature because everything is inclined by its nature to contradict its evil form."[16] War is that means of combating wrongs and perversions of good. The traditional *jus ad bellum* concept crucial to Bonet's argument is that of proper authority, which he related to the rights and actions of kings, who as God's captains on earth, desire to maintain order as is divinely ordained but often corrupted by sinful human nature. A wise prince can best determine the justice of a cause and the motivations behind any recourse to fighting. From this premise, Bonet understood war's purpose as setting wrongs right and replacing dissension with peace, as is testified to by Scripture (mainly the Old Testament). Echoing Augustine's warning about wrong intention: "And if in war many evil things are done, they never come from the nature of war, but from false usage,"[17] Bonet also drew a connection between the legitimate authority's role in proclaiming just wars and his responsibility to regulate how they are fought. Behavior, then, becomes the ultimate determinant of whether a war is "just," and here the role of the prince is limited, if important, thereby setting up the need for an enforceable code of conduct. If a knight behaves contrary to the "laws" of his vocation, then he is acting against both natural and divine law and so encourages evil rather than good. To maintain proper decorum and chivalric honor, therefore, specific codes of conduct should be stipulated and universally applied. This objective provides the focus for the rest of his book.

The advantage of Bonet's catalog of knightly virtues is to raise issues that would be of some concern later to those who would condemn wars because of glaring contradictions between law and practice. This is the case especially with Bonet's own contention that "in all wars poor labourers should be left secure and in peace," acknowledging that "in these days all wars are directed against the poor labouring people and against their goods and chattels. I do not call that war, but it seems to me to be pillage and robbery." In addition, he called the knights back to a time when "noble warriors . . . upheld justice, the widow, the orphan and the poor," while

> nowadays it is the opposite that they do everywhere, and the man who does not know how to set places on fire, to rob churches and usurp their rights and to imprison the priests, is not fit to carry on war. And for these reasons the knights of to-day have not the glory

16. Ibid., 126.
17. Ibid., 125.

and the praise of the old champions of former times, and their deeds can never come to great perfection of virtue.[18]

Because recent wars had been so unruly and destructive Bonet set down other rules against unjust reprisals, coercing certain people to fight (old people, women, children, and the infirm), excessive plunder, injury to non-combatants, and wars of conquest or conversion (except in certain threatening circumstances).[19]

As stated, Bonet's exposition of the laws of war drew from many traditions, including canon law, civil law, and the imprecise customs that princes had kept throughout time. He also incorporated ideas from Vegetius and other classical authors. Augustine's belief that the temporal ruler has an obligation to bear the sword in order to secure peace resounds throughout, for war is only evil when practiced immorally, never in the abstract. These formulations catered to a widespread European sentiment of the later Middle Ages that war be conducted honorably, justly, and with less cruelty. The *Tree of Battles* was a genuinely respected and authoritative work, widely read in England, and as already stated, the basis for Christine de Pisan's *Book of Fayttes of Armes*. But did it have any impact on the nature of war or its justification in the later Middle Ages? One influential historian argues that the law of arms may have invigorated the just war by giving it a set of rules, which were "something more than a vague set of principles of loyalty and honour," and which could have heightened the distinction between the real and the ideal.[20] For some this dichotomy would prove to be a serious problem of the age, but for most, especially lay authorities, chivalric principles could be incorporated into "national" codes of military discipline and thus provide a more secure and legitimate foundation for wars they deemed appropriate to fight. By the fifteenth century, because the law of arms and its international standards for knightly behavior had proved inadequate to the task of regulating warring armies, military discipline now required the firmer grounding of a sovereign's sanction.[21]

By declaring war to be a natural and morally sound rite of human association, Bonet helped institutionalize war and relegate much discussion

18. Ibid., 189.
19. Ibid., 127–30, 153–54, 154–58; Johnson, *Just War Tradition*, 142, 150; Wright, "*Tree of Battles*," 16–17.
20. Keen, *Laws of War*, 137–85; 241–45.
21. Stacey, "Age of Chivalry," 39.

concerning its morality to *jus in bello* arguments.[22] He was also instrumental in taking the burden of judgment as to the justice of a particular war off the individual knight and placing him more within a context of duty to his lord and to his people. Bonet wanted a more civilized warfare in Europe, and with this in mind, it is most likely that his work was more a "programme of reform" than a statement of how things were.[23] His ideas for a better class of knights were later incorporated into the training of princely armies; but he could not foresee the places in his justification for war where the *jus armorum* might be compromised or criticized seriously. His refusal to contend with the possibility that war undertaken by a proper authority could be wrong indicates just how mighty and secure the code of chivalry had become even as the feudal relationship on which it rested was breaking down. Setting themselves up for a big fall, many English nobles throughout the fourteenth and much of the fifteenth centuries continued to place hope in a revived knighthood to bring the nation to glorious honor, prosperity, and peace. In truth, however, this predilection for war with its cursory and sometimes disingenuous regard for intentions did nothing but engender the opposite of what was hoped for; another Agincourt would have only prolonged the ill effects of war, not remedied them. The consensus on the just war that had begun to cohere in the later Middle Ages was powerful but not monolithic. As warfare and society experienced major changes in the fourteenth century, with more aimless violence between battles being directed toward noncombatants, a few would begin to write boldly about the need for peace to supersede all other determinations of public policy.

The Law of Arms and Nationalism

Ostensibly, the chivalric ideal, despite its elusiveness in reality, did attempt in some form to mitigate against bloodshed or violence, with the knight "posing before all the world as the champion of justice who does not hesitate to sacrifice himself for his people."[24] The law of arms, and the code of honor that surrounded it, helped also create a spirit of duty to

22. Johnson, *Ideology,* 68.
23. Wright, *"Tree of Battles,"* 30–31.
24. Johan Huizinga, "The Political and Military Significance of Chivalric Ideas in the Late Middle Ages," in *Men and Ideas,* trans. and ed. James S. Holmes and Hans van Merle (London: Eyre & Spottiswoode, 1960), 200.

one's country (king or lord primarily), and with a subsequent concern for the protection of the people as a whole, transformed it eventually into an early type of patriotism.[25] By the end of the fifteenth century the principle that primary allegiance was due the prince had been acknowledged in Western Europe. Jean de Bueil in his fifteenth-century "allegorical military romance," *Le Jouvencel,* concluded that it is no honor to "seize another's possession" and put one's self in danger to hurt someone else, especially since it impedes a greater duty to the nation, as the knight "neglects war, his king's service, and the public weal."[26] This movement toward nationalist sentiment had the effect of giving new life to the chivalric code by placing it (with different emphases) under the discipline of monarchs, thus prolonging its hold on popular imagination well into the later Middle Ages and beyond.[27] At the same time, warfare in the name of the people gave knights another, loftier justification for going to war.

Nationalist sentiment was very strong in England, where by the thirteenth century a great deal of autonomy had been achieved already in church affairs. There existed as well a more centralized administrative structure and a growing tide of xenophobia, which by Edward I's reign (1272–1307) had helped encourage foreign wars. These wars, in turn, assisted in accentuating national differences.[28] Yet in the Middle Ages, early forms of nationalism coexisted with strong local attachments because of limited contacts between areas and differing parochial interests. The person of the king, however, unified people across regions as he came to personify the nation. In 1312, for example, the Proclamation of Peace read: "The king has received the government of the realm by provision of God, by whom he is held to the defense of the realm itself and of all his subjects, clerk and lay."[29] As defense was the crown's primary obligation (along with justice), support for the king's right to make war became a test of loyalty. Within a nationalist framework warfare received yet another important sanction at this time, reconfiguring proper authority so that it held an even more prominent place in the just war.

---

25. Ibid., 203–6.
26. Jean de Bueil, *Le Jouvencel,* ed. Léon Lecestre (Paris: Librairie Renouard, 1887), 2:100–104; M.G.A. Vale, *War and Chivalry: Warfare and Aristocratic Culture in England, France, and Burgundy at the End of the Middle Ages* (Athens: University of Georgia Press, 1981), 170.
27. Vale, *War and Chivalry,* 168–74.
28. Barnaby C. Keeney, "Military Service and the Development of Nationalism in England, 1272–1327," *Speculum* 22 (1947): 534–36; Johan Huizinga, "Patriotism and Nationalism in European History," in *Men and Ideas,* 116–18.
29. Keeney, "Military Service," 537.

The bulwark of just war could be supported as well through a nationalist explanation for why men fight and how order could be restored once military duty was fulfilled. The return to Vegetius's *De re militari* in the fourteenth century, and its popularity into the early modern period, coincided neatly with a renewed emphasis on the notion that wars that seek peace can be justified.[30] A model for Bonet, as already mentioned, Vegetius's work influenced jurists, theologians, and commentators on war. According to this early Christian writer, because wars can bring about peace, there is the implication that they do not create social disharmony, but rather become "the chief means of attaining the restoration of an order which had been broken by other causes."[31] Therefore, war serves as another way in which kings can deliver justice to their people. Since kings have complete power to defend and execute justice, all other considerations about the legitimacy of a conflict are subservient to their private determination. Even in defeat the monarch claims that justice is on his side and that God is simply chastising the people temporarily for some particular sin for which they must atone.[32] The king and nation, therefore, were becoming inextricably bound in an idealistic purpose that often found itself being played out in international wars. The question must then arise: As this unity of purpose involved a greater number and variety of English people, and as wars in the late Middle Ages were being fought on a much grander and thus costlier scale, at what point did such harmony become discord? While nationalist feeling could provide a wider base of support for foreign enterprises, it also left open the door to "public opinion" and the possible swift erosion of that support, both philosophically and practically.

---

30. Stacey, "Age of Chivalry," 27.

31. Allmand, *Hundred Years War,* 37–38. A fifteenth-century verse paraphrase of Vegetius's work, *Knyghtehode and Bataile,* underscores this point in making specific reference to England's fratricidal wars between York and Lancaster. The writer invokes the need for knights to follow ancient precepts of warfare with the intention of bringing about peace. *Knyghthode and Bataile, A 15th Century Verse Paraphrase of Flavius Vegitus Renatus' Treatise "De Re Militari,"* ed. R. Dyboski and Z. M. Arend, EETS OS, no. 201 (London: Humphrey Milford, Oxford University Press, 1935), bk. 3: lines 1108–10, 1685–98, pp. 41, 62.

Vegetius was first translated into English in 1408 for Thomas, Lord Berkeley, who was fighting Welsh rebels. The English editions were notable for their additions, which critique "Christian knights that war for no other skill but for the cruelty of wrecking or else out of covetousness." Diane Borstein, "Military Manuals in Fifteenth-Century England," *Medieval Studies* 37 (1975): 469–71.

32. Allmand, *Hundred Years War,* 39–40.

Support for War in Late Medieval England

During the Hundred Years War the English people became acutely aware of the deprivations and hardships occasioned by long and continued states of emergency preparedness. They were drawn into the war personally by the "commissions of array, requests for subsidies, seizures of goods and services, alerts and alarms against invasion, and barrages of propaganda and counter-propaganda."[33] The clergy were most instrumental in serving as channels of royal persuasion in efforts to garner support for various wars. Writs sent to clerical officials announced royal decisions and demanded compliance with them. Edward I revived the system of prayers *pro rege,* which became "a kind of royal news service" or "propaganda agency for influencing public opinion." King and Council also directed Chancery to issue writs instructing the clerics to conduct special services (including prayers, sermons, vigils, and processions) to obtain divine favor, protection, and guidance — most often just before the nation embarked on major military engagements. They were permitted to offer indulgences on occasion as well.[34] Throughout these efforts the French and Scots were portrayed unfavorably while the English cause was represented as completely just, all of which was "evidently designed to elevate the popular view of the wars from mere squabbles over feudal rights to a grand defense in England's security and honor."[35]

Aside from propaganda, the clergy's next most important contribution came in its role of enhancing the revenues needed to prosecute wars. Taxes were approved in both ecclesiastical convocations and then collected by their members. Also, poll taxes were tried briefly with well-known disastrous results in 1380–81. Attempts at tapping the wealth of chantry and stipendiary chaplains were abandoned as well in the mid-1400s. There was much opposition and difficulty in collecting these taxes and often clerics paid more than their fair share. The prohibitions against direct clerical

33. W. R. Jones, "The English Church and Royal Propaganda During the Hundred Years War," *Journal of British Studies* 19 (1979): 18.

34. Ibid., 19–21; Herbert James Hewitt, *The Organization of War under Edward III: 1338–62* (New York: Barnes & Noble, 1966), 28–29; G. R. Owst, *Preaching in Medieval England* (Cambridge: The University Press, 1926), 200–202.

35. Jones, "English Church," 30; C. T. Allmand, ed., *Society at War* (Edinburgh: Oliver & Boyd, 1973), 190. For a good summary of the growing attention to public opinion in these matters, see Charles Ross, "Rumour, Propaganda and Popular Opinion during the Wars of the Roses," in *Patronage, the Crown and the Provinces,* ed. Ralph A. Griffiths (Gloucester, Eng.: Alan Sutton, 1981), 26.

participation in war had been successfully incorporated into the laws of war by the fourteenth century; nevertheless, prelates were involved in all activities just short of actual combat. They provided much of the organization for foreign campaigns, such as in financing expeditions, keeping disbursement records and even ordering equipment.[36] At the same time, however, the English clergy was hardly unified in its support of the Anglo-French conflict. Criticism became fiercest during periods of military setback or economic hardship, and those conditions became practically endemic in the fifteenth century.

As already noted, a certain amount of consensus among the subnational localities was necessary for national wars to be carried out effectively. The social context is explored more fully in the next section, so at this point, we will examine the policy changes that were intended to help create greater support for royal wars. Edward I was probably the first to make consultation of Parliament a central part of his war policies. In the next reign discussions over the Scottish campaign (1322) and French war (1324) were still controlled by the king, but with contracts beginning to replace feudal obligations, he had to ensure local cooperation in order to raise an adequate military. Ironically, those communities which had longer traditions of political participation were looking at the same time for ways to reduce their military obligations. The indentured contract was one attempt to circumvent parliamentary consultations but Edward III's war in France created a financial need that required exceptional measures.[37] By the fifteenth century Parliament had expanded greatly its role in advising the king on his war and peace policies. Contracts, viability of campaigns, and supply had all come under parliamentary oversight, and the result was the opening of a new arena for public complaint about war.[38] Some of the

36. A. K. McHardy, "The English Clergy and the Hundred Years War," in Sheils, *Church and War*, 171–75, and "Liturgy and Propaganda in the Diocese of Lincoln during the Hundred Years War," in *Religion and National Identity*, ed. Stuart Mews, SCH, vol. 18 (Oxford: Basil Blackwell, 1982), 215–27.

37. Michael Rhys Powicke, *Military Obligation in Medieval England: A Study in Liberty and Duty* (Oxford: Clarendon Press, 1962), xi, 227–37. See E. B. Fryde, "Parliament and the French War," in *Essays in Medieval History Presented to Bertie Wilkinson*, ed. T. A. Sandquist and M. R. Powicke (Toronto: University of Toronto Press, 1969), 251–69, on the delicate negotiations between crown and Parliament over financing the initial stage of the Hundred Years War. Even at that early juncture outcries over purveyance and "the hurts done to commune people" were being heard.

38. Powicke, *Military Obligation*, 242–50; Allmand, *Society at War*, 189; J. R. Lander, *The Limitations of the English Monarchy in the Later Middle Ages* (Toronto: University of Toronto Press, 1989), 14–17.

first topics turned to concerned the status of knights, the burden of unsuccessful war, and the need to compromise on "just war" claims to the French throne.

The decline of chivalry in the late Middle Ages can be attributed not only to nonchivalric practices in the conduct of war but also a great deal to technological and organizational changes. Obviously artillery and the firearm were the most notable inventions of the time and their easy adoption only created a greater disparity between the chivalric ideal and the reality of war.[39] This development was accompanied by an expanded employment of mercenaries. After 1343, those who were opposed to serving might pay to be exempted. The money collected then could be used to hire foreign soldiers.[40] Often these mercenaries were drawn from the most reckless and irresponsible ranks of society. The mercenary companies of the Hundred Years War were notorious for their savagery and destructiveness. To recruit these men, especially from Swiss and German lands, was to acknowledge a "crueller and more brutal" kind of warfare, which also eroded the "chivalric ethic and increased the horror of war."[41] Military organization underwent significant change by the fifteenth century as well. A recent study of Lancastrian Normandy between 1420 and 1450 details the switch from expeditionary to occupation forces since the previous century, along with a more bureaucratic contractual army that attempted to set up a system to control division of spoils, procedures regarding prisoners, and in some fashion, decisions affecting pay, weaponry, and discipline. There was also a simultaneous division made between garrison and the more mobile field forces. Constant reinforcements and replacements helped relax personal loyalties (as contracts expired), and retinues lost their hold as personal plunder seemed more lucrative and available.[42]

Add to these developments innovations in strategy, siege warfare, and tactics, and it becomes obvious that within only the hundred years of this war, the art of war had been altered vastly. Despite all these changes, the

39. M.G.A. Vale, "New Techniques and Old Ideals: The Impact of Artillery on War and Chivalry at the End of the Hundred Years War," in *War, Literature and Politics in the Late Middle Ages*, ed. C. T. Allmand (Liverpool: Liverpool University Press, 1976), 72.
40. Hewitt, *Organization of War*, 37.
41. Vale, *War and Chivalry*, 155–57.
42. Anne Curry, "The First English Standing Army? Military Organization in Lancastrian Normandy, 1420–1450," in *Patronage, Pedigree and Power in Later Medieval England*, ed. Charles Ross (Totowa, N.J.: Rowman & Littlefield, 1979), 193–201. See also M. R. Powicke, "Lancastrian Captains," in Sandquist and Powicke, *Essays in Medieval History*, 371–82.

individual soldier had not moved away at all from his own selfish motivations for going to war; after all, what we conceived of as strong, effective
military discipline did not exist, and in fact, seems to be one of the last
acquired stages of modern warfare.[43] With the technological and organizational breakthroughs, fourteenth- and fifteenth-century knights were
loosed from a code of honor that constrained individual behavior, while
finding little divine providence in a war that seemed unending. In France
they pursued a regimen of "looting, destruction and burning" and exercised extreme cruelty toward noncombatants. Captains, who were supposed to be responsible for imposing discipline, often behaved in like manner, and only exceptional commanders could control the excesses. At other
times, maintaining order and restraint entailed extreme and bloody measures, especially when conquest or victory seemed to hinge upon it. Since
part of the *jus armorum* permitted the killing of captured soldiers who
were not knights, the French at Crécy and Henry V at Agincourt massa-
cred countless prisoners.[44] The chivalric code may have assisted in restrain-
ing excessively violent behavior among the knights, but as more men-at-
arms came from the other ranks of society, limitations of this kind became
less and less applicable. There was much inherent in late medieval warfare,
then, keeping it from becoming more humanized.[45]

   The Wars of the Roses were not marked by the near total abandon that
occurred in France, largely because of the more immediate local and personal dangers intrinsic to civil war. These "wars" were essentially a "series
of short, sharp engagements," usually unplanned and interrupted by long
periods of peace. Armies were raised quickly and disbanded soon after
battle. There was such order throughout the land during most of this time
that the traveler, political observer, and councillor to Louis XI, Philippe de
Commynes, remarked during a visit that "England enjoyed a peculiar
mercy above all other kingdoms, that neither the country nor the people,
nor the houses were wasted, destroyed or demolished," and that the "ca-
lamities and misfortunes of the war fell only upon the soldiers."[46] Soldiers
did resort to plunder and destruction but at nowhere near the scale as

   43. Allmand, *Hundred Years War,* 53.
   44. Hewitt, *Organization of War,* 94–96, 111; Vale, *War and Chivalry,* 157; Stacey, "Age
of Chivalry," 33. See also André Corvisier, "Le Mort de soldat, depuis la fin du Moyen Age,"
Révue Historique 254 (1975): 3–30.
   45. See also Contamine, *War in the Middle Ages,* 290–91.
   46. Philippe de Commynes, *Mémoires,* ed. H. G. Bohn (London: H. G. Bohn, 1855), 1:
394; J. R. Lander, *The Wars of the Roses* (London: White Lion Publishers, 1965), 20–23.

outside England, meaning there was little disruption of everyday life overall. Pay, however, was often in arrears, and with inferior equipment, it did
become difficult sometimes for commanders to force troops to leave noncombatants undisturbed.[47] A more recent study of these years goes even
further and suggests that there was a conscious design by commanders on
both sides to limit bloodshed in order to win popular support.[48] In effect,
these wars were not very violent when compared to other contemporary
examples of civil strife, and the worst savageries charged to either side
were largely the creations of later propagandists. The gentry often hesi-
tated to commit itself to one side or the other because it did not want to
take a gamble on who would emerge victorious.[49]

Yet battles were fought and they punctuated the English countryside
for well over thirty years. For some, they were further evidence of a
disastrous situation in which failure in one war (Hundred Years War) had
brought on another one, which had in turn, led to a complete breakdown
in national government. There were complaints about the "lack of governance" in the realm and the rise in violent crime during these years, but
since no one favors civil war there is really no antiwar literature directed
specifically to the Wars of the Roses by a disgruntled English people.
Rather, diatribes concerned with the restoration of good government took
prominence, and while it lasted, attacks against the French war remained
numerous.[50] The latter were often leveled at those who still maintained
the legitimacy of that conflict and the claim that sustained it, although
the sufferings it produced had escalated beyond anything supportable in
good Christian conscience. But by the late fifteenth century the internecine wars were perceived also as both "shocking and memorable,"[51]
providing the growing opposition to warfare with greater legitimacy.[52]
With two types of war now difficult to justify, it became easier to condemn the entire institution.

47. K. B. McFarlane, "The Wars of the Roses," in *England in the Fifteenth Century: Collected Essays* (London: Hambledon Press, 1981), 237, 242; Anthony Goodman, *The Wars of
the Roses: Military Activity and English Society, 1452–97* (London: Routledge & Kegan
Paul, 1981), 197–217.

48. John Gillingham, *The Wars of the Roses: Peace and Conflict in Fifteenth-Century England* (Baton Rouge: Louisiana State University Press, 1981), 1–32, 49–50, 254–57.

49. McFarlane, "Wars of the Roses," 246; Gillingham, *Wars of the Roses,* 27.

50. Lander, *Wars of the Roses,* 25–27.

51. Gillingham, *Wars of the Roses,* 255.

52. McFarlane, "Wars of the Roses," 260.

Social and Political Alignments

The groundswell for peace that was building as the Hundred Years War progressed stemmed not only from economic and political hardships but also from the social realignments they produced. Just-war theory, as far back as Augustine, had argued that the restoration of tranquillity of order (*tranquillitas ordinis*) must be the end result of all war. The nobility received the bulk of invective from peace advocates for hindering the attainment of this lofty objective in the prosecution of the war with France. When clergy or king appeared responsible, they came under attack also, although for obvious reasons, perhaps, not so overtly. The injustices that resulted, such as unfair tax assessments and the general lawlessness of returning soldiers, provided a further indictment of the war. In the ebb and flow of its long course, as any semblance of *tranquillitas ordinis* seemed a distant memory, the near universal cry for peace denoted a cultural shift, extending across social class, demanding an end to war and asserting a predilection for ideas that supported such. But it would take years of political, social, and economic change and concomitant debate, before this point was reached.

The conflicts between Church and nobility extended well back to the early Middle Ages and the attempt by the former to prescribe and regularize fighting through the Peace of God movement. Some accommodation of interests was achieved in the initial stages of the Crusades but this quickly dissipated as powerful nobles and warriors made the papacy's agenda secondary to their own. In England, the positions were not so neatly delineated during the great war with France. We can no longer speak of the Church's position per se since the English pope was not the French pope from 1378 to 1417, and before this, there was great mistrust of the Holy Father in Avignon. This may help explain how an orthodox bishop like Thomas Brinton and the heterodox John Wyclif could both criticize the martial spirit of the pope with only a qualitative variance in tone separating them. While the outcry against the Church remained constant until the return to Rome in 1417, the real domestic problem associated with continuing the war centered on the deterioration of the relationship between king and nobility and between nobility and commons throughout the course of the war.

By the end of Edward III's reign a number of important interests in England came to resent the doddering king's lack of concern for the deteriorating state of good government and peace. International trade was disrupted and domestic costs for fortifications and scarce goods skyrocketed. Some towns like Newcastle-upon-Tyne and Southampton had to keep ships at the ready to meet a possible invasion. The added tax burden only exacerbated the misery of the peasants, who were already suffering from the ravages of pestilence and insecure harvests. The demands of purveyance were particularly onerous and reviled. The fiction that commoners wanted war because they could obtain employment in the army becomes obvious when measured against the greater fear of leaving tenements for dangerous and unknown situations abroad. Pay was usually in arrears, and there was an overriding, and perceptive, suspicion among the people that wars were corrupt enterprises that benefited only the knights and merchants. Social advancement during the war was extremely rare. Instead, most of the English suffered, as the French had, the base strategies of early campaigns and *chevauchées* (raids for plunder) at the hands of returning knights who had found their terroristic ways difficult to abandon. From what evidence there is of popular opinion on the war it was not at all supportive of aristocratic, or even royal, aspirations.[53]

It was at this juncture that the interests of nobility and king often parted company, which made it possible for the former to become the target of a growing tide of antiwar literature that found support among both clerics and commoners. Edward III had "negotiated consent" for his war only by making concessions to nobles, clergy, and commons alike. He used the anticlerical mood of the day to gain control over provisions (appointments to benefices) and "bombarded parliament with speeches, newsletters, and propaganda on behalf of his policies."[54] He never took this support for granted and always seemed able to find common cause with his people—at least until his final years. With Richard II (1377–99), however, the situation changed drastically. His novel means for constructing a government created many enemies among the established nobility and members of Parliament. By preferring household officials to traditional aristocratic counsel in making government decisions he challenged accepted practice and made it difficult to gain support for his policies. A truce was announced in July 1389 and renewed in 1392, 1393, 1394, and 1396, but all hope for a permanent peace faded when the chief nobles, most of whom were related to the royal family, fell out over who would get the lion's share of the spoils in Gascony. John of Gaunt, duke

53. Waugh, *England in the Reign of Edward III*, 93–96.
54. Ibid., 208–9.

of Lancaster and the king's major rival, had support from the Gascons to transfer this territory over to the duchy of Lancaster. Arundel and Gloucester were not happy at being passed over. But in the end the truce was acceptable, since it enabled domestic agendas to dominate once again, and some hoped to reap further benefits at royal expense. Only now it led to the usurpation of 1399 by Lancaster's son, Henry Bolingbroke (Henry IV), when Richard committed his final miscalculation and attempted to confiscate his property.[55]

Throughout the war another clear alignment was being formed between the commons and the educated elites, many of whom were involved in some aspect of government service. Writers such as Gower, Geoffrey Chaucer, and Thomas Hoccleve, among others, adopted a highly moralistic style that suggests they considered it their role to act as arbiters of social policy. These *literati* identified with the rebels' grievances during the Peasants' Revolt of 1381 and certainly found allies among the common people in their attacks on unscrupulous landlords, government ministers, and clergy. Most of the blame for existing social ills was laid at the feet of the nobility, whose insatiable greed was responsible for all misery, including the continuation of a costly and agonizing war in France.[56] Class divisions were thus accentuated, and eventually the outcry began to affect concessions that Parliament demanded before granting further subsidies to continue the war. As early as 1354 the Commons responded enthusiastically to Edward's proposal for a permanent peace with France.

While some found personal reasons for complaining publicly, there was nevertheless a serious concern among many with the plight of the poor which obviously had the potential to affect government policy in a way that was unique to Europe. A stream of protest resulted and found expression in a variety of literary genres, from poems and prophecies to sermons and satires. Important national figures, including the bishop of Rochester, Thomas Brinton, "made wealth and taxation moral issues . . . lashing out at lords and ministers, lay and ecclesiastical alike, for seeking their own profit at the expense of the poor and failing to work for the common good."[57] By the fifteenth century fewer clerics and moralists supported the war, and many were pleading with the government to find a way out of it.

55. J. Anthony Tuck, *Richard II and the Nobility* (London: Edward Arnold, 1973), 90–92, 104–5, 156–63.
56. G. G. Coulton, *Chaucer and His England* (London: Methuen, 1908), 231.
57. J. R. Maddicott, "Poems of Social Protest in Early Fourteenth-Century England," in *England in the Fourteenth Century: Proceedings of the 1985 Harlaxton Symposium,* ed. W. M. Ormrod (Woodbridge, Eng.: Boydell Press, 1986), 140–44; Waugh, *England in the Reign of Edward III,* 223, 235.

Except for a few particular moments (such as immediately after the victory at Agincourt), it is no exaggeration to say that by the turn of that century only the upper nobility and on occasion, the king, pushed the English claim to the French throne as a legitimate cause for continuing the war overseas.

With the removal of Richard in 1399, Henry IV (1399–1413) was immediately faced with renewed French activity in Gascony. The royal dukes of Burgundy, Berry, Bourbon, and Orléans had wrested control of French war policy from an increasingly unstable and unpredictable Charles VI. Between 1403 and 1405 they assisted the rebellion of Owen Glyn Dwr in Wales and thereby turned the English government away from their territorial gambits in southwest France. Burgundy's disputes with the other dukes gave both Henry IV and Henry V added incentive to renew the war and send another invasion force into France.[58]

J. R. Lander has concluded that war could only be successful in the later Middle Ages if there were "a king who was an able military leader, an enthusiastic ruling class (both aristocracy and gentry) prepared to fight and command the armies, and a people willing to bear the cost through taxation."[59] After Agincourt (1415) only the first criterion remained operative. But even that celebrated campaign met with great resistance initially and did not get under way until 1415. Opposition to new taxes had reached an all-time high. Until the last moment Parliament insisted that Henry V (1413–22) first expend all possible diplomatic energy to achieve peace. The king agreed but the negotiations of 1414–15 broke down without a settlement. Within two years after the battle the king was greatly distressed that "the clergy, resenting his heavy taxation, *tepide causante*, were ceasing to pray for the success of the war."[60] By 1418 "Henry was finding it increasingly difficult to finance the war." After another campaign that finally produced the English triumph secured in the Treaty of Troyes (1420), Parliament refused further grants, and soon thereafter, Henry unexpectedly died, leaving his kingdom to a six-month-old infant, Henry VI (1422–61).[61]

58. G. P. Cuttino, *English Medieval Diplomacy* (Bloomington: Indiana University Press, 1985), 105; Robin Neillands, *The Hundred Years War* (London: Routledge, 1990), 193, 204.

59. J. R. Lander, "The Hundred Years War and Edward IV's 1475 Campaign in France," in *Tudor Men and Institutions: Studies in English Law and Government,* ed. Arthur J. Slavin (Baton Rouge: Louisiana State University Press, 1972), 70.

60. *The Register of Henry Chichele, Archbishop of Canterbury, 1414–1443,* ed. E. F. Jacob (Oxford: Clarendon Press, 1947), 4:176; Lander, "Edward IV's 1475 Campaign," 73.

61. Christopher Allmand, *Henry V* (Berkeley and Los Angeles: University of California Press, 1992), 130, 284–85; Lander, "Edward IV's 1475 Campaign," 73.

The post-Agincourt campaigns (1417–21), therefore, indicate an eroding respect for the king's claim to the French throne. Most crucial is the
loss of support for the war among the ruling class. The number of aristocratic participants fell from more than one-half before 1415 to barely one-
third afterward. No "parliamentary barons" led contingents either, and
virtually the entire leadership of Henry VI's forces had changed. The ratio
of archers to men-at-arms decreased to about one in sixteen in some of the
greater non-noble companies, reflecting "the growing disenchantment of
the English middle-class with the war in France."[62] Only a very few of the
"court aristocracy" insisted that the war effort be maintained, and after
1422, they had lost either the support or the involvement of the king. By
1426, while Henry VI was still a child, this party released a flurry of propaganda to convince a skeptical populace that their king did have a just
claim to the French throne.[63] This final stage of the war was most inglorious and did the greatest damage to royal and national prestige. The
luster of Agincourt was completely gone, and division over a whole range
of policies (including the war) led to a preoccupation with domestic disputes that finally erupted in the Wars of the Roses. By 1453 it was all over.
No treaty was signed, and the English seemed resigned to retaining only
the coastal city of Calais.

When Edward IV (1461–83) attempted to garner support for another
invasion of France in 1475, the interest in such a course had reached an
all-time low. Lander's final assessment is noteworthy:

> It is perhaps, no exaggeration to claim that the majority of the aris-
> tocracy and gentry were no longer enthusiastic for continental war,
> nor particularly fitted for it, and that Edward IV's claim to be wag-
> ing defensive war was true. The old enthusiasm (such as it had
> been) for the king's claim to the French throne had long since de-
> parted and the campaign of 1475 was not so much a fervid renewal
> of ancient glories as a defensive reaction of the government to the
> complications and dangers of the international situation in north-
> western Europe as it had developed since 1453.[64]

62. Powicke, "Lancastrian Captains," 371–82.
63. J. W. McKenna, "Henry VI of England and the Dual Monarchy: Aspects of Royal
Political Propaganda, 1422–32," *Journal of the Warburg and Courtauld Institutes* 28 (1965):
145–62; Lander, "Edward IV's 1475 Campaign," 75–77.
64. Lander, "Edward IV's 1475 Campaign," 118.

The point is an important one in the context of emerging peace positions in that century and the next. Kings could no longer count on support from any one of the three estates for "just wars." The aristocracy had turned its interest away from purely martial matters, and English society as a whole was coming to agree with much of the complaint against the war that had been made over the previous century. While those attacks were directed specifically at the war with France, as Chapter 3 will show, sometimes the critiques turned into an indictment of the institution of war itself. If there was even the possibility of another war of such magnitude and hardship based on a similarly unachievable claim of just cause, then perhaps the whole basis for war was questionable, or at least, problematic. Peace positions, argued with the same philosophical rigor as the just war, were being heard clearly for the first time. The contest for the hearts and minds of the English people would lead to a lively debate that reached deep into the national consciousness. The unique opportunities for participation across a wide social spectrum in England permitted creative approaches and new positions on the side of peace to develop.

The Decline of the Law of Arms

A final assessment of the law of arms is in order. As public sympathies for the war with France shifted over the course of nearly a century, and since during most of that time the warrior nobility was held responsible for the ill effects of continued fighting, it is no surprise that there was a great deal of skepticism expressed in antiwar polemic about the efficacy of the *jus armorum*. Neither did the devaluation of the *jus in bello* and chivalric honor go unnoticed by the rest of English society, which found knightly behavior responsible for a great number of society's ills and became less concerned about whether they acted according to the strictures of their code. These warriors were no longer engaging in localized campaigns restricted to a defined set of combatants. One of the most astonishing and important legacies of the Hundred Years War is the great outcry it produced against both soldiery and war. Especially by the reign of Richard II, many began to write about the deplorable state of the realm and the corruption that caused it. The enemy no longer received the bulk of hatred and invective, which was now transferred to domestic failures. Sermons likened the nation's propensity for war and corruption to a similar state of affairs during the late Roman Empire. Gower and John Erghome linked politics with morality and insisted that failures in both realms went right to the top.[65] By the time of Henry VI's disasters in France a full-scale attack had been launched against the king's councillors and family. The royal estate was being squandered and the public welfare disregarded. Peace, for the first time in English history that we know of, had become an over-whelming cry of the day. The role of the nobility and its warring arm, the knights, in creating this atmosphere by obstructing peace is crucial. Jean Froissart, the great chronicler of the Anglo-French conflict, claimed that the peace negotiations of 1390 failed because of "the less well-off knights, esquires and archers of England, who appreciated its [the war's] comforts and, indeed, maintained their status through war. You should understand that by no manner of means whatever could love, peace or concord exist or be brought about by these parties."[66] French observer Diez de Games believed that Richard II was killed by those who feared he would bring about "peace perpetual" with France, even though many English people praised Henry IV initially for his bringing peace to the realm.[67]

The unchristian brigandage perpetuated by the companies in France was prolifically chronicled. Such commentaries of the time provoked two forms of complaint literature. One responded to the decline of chivalry with he-roic calls for its reform and rejuvenation. This approach was most vividly adopted by romantics such as William Caxton and — to a less obvious ex-tent — Thomas Malory, and by chivalric commentators like Christine de Pisan, Bonet, and William Worcester. Henry V's first venture into France in 1415 had a great deal of support from the nobility but by the time of the next one, in just two years, this had dwindled tremendously.

The only truly native medieval handbook on the law of arms, Nicholas Upton's *De studio militari*, was written some time before 1446, when Humphrey, duke of Gloucester, to whom it is dedicated, died.[68] In it, Up-ton, a veteran of the successful French siege of Orléans, admitted to a prevailing lack of concern for the chivalric code or any rules governing soldierly behavior among what was fast becoming a new, mixed, even

65. Barnie, *War in Medieval English Society,* 117–18.
66. Allmand, *Society at War,* 31.
67. Barnie, *War in Medieval English Society,* 125–28.
68. John of Salisbury's *Policraticus* (1159) does include in book 6 a substantial discussion on the necessity of a well-trained militia that would take special care in recruiting moral and God-fearing soldiers, as well as enforcing a rigorous code of ethics. John of Salisbury, *Poli-craticus, the Statesman's Book,* ed. Murray F. Markland, bk. 5, chap. 8 (New York: Frederick Ungar, 1979), 82.

motley group of combatants. Thus he devoted most of his discussion to categorizing punishments for soldiers who fail to follow strict military discipline. These included procedures for ridding camps of prostitutes, stopping assaults, protecting safe conducts, and behaving properly in battle.[69] Violence by soldiers toward particular noncombatants, such as spiritual men and women, received severe condemnation from Upton, who was at the time of writing pursuing a career in the Church. Since they did not carry weapons, he commanded that they should not be taken as prisoners and "moreover that no person be so bold as to lay violent hands upon any religious people, either men or women, or in unlawful manner to touch them wearing the habit of their order without fraud or guile."[70] The composition of armies (including more commoners) and attitudes toward war were changing, and the law of arms had difficulty adapting to them. It had become impossible to socialize current soldiers into the class-based code of chivalry. Furthermore, the effects of contemporary warfare had enlarged the panorama of government policy and no longer would major decisions concerning peace and war be made exclusively by the elites. C. T. Allmand describes how this development went right to the heart of whether the king's reasons for war were really worth it:

> The public rights of subjects were of greater importance than the private rights of kings: so that those who negotiated peace terms between France and England in 1439 were reminded. It brings home to us the increasing awareness that dawned during the period that a monarch's legal rights were not worth fighting for if the material interests of his people were to suffer as a direct consequence of a war fought in his name.[71]

The personal, even if nationalized, ethic of the knight devoted to the prince was too far removed from a consideration of the public welfare. It is to those who would obscure this "higher" mission that much of the early antiwar literature is addressed. Yet there was also a concern that the nobility assume more fully other responsibilities aside from fighting.[72] Many

69. Nicholas Upton, *The Essential Portions of Nicholas Upton's De Studio Militari, Before 1446*, trans. John Blount, ed. Frances P. Barnard (Oxford: Clarendon Press, 1931). Upton eventually became the precenter of Salisbury Cathedral in 1446.

70. Ibid., 35.

71. Allmand, *Society at War*, 192.

72. See Edmund Dudley, *The Tree of Commonwealth*, ed. D. M. Brodie (Cambridge: The

nobles raised troops during the 1400s only with the greatest reluctance.
Even if the idea of a military career may not have been exactly passé before 1450, as one historian has recently contended, it was quickly losing
ground in the minds and hearts of many. Both Lancastrians and Yorkists
threatened any knight who tarried in his military obligations, sometimes
with death. Even when the French imperiled the East Anglian coast in
1457 it was difficult to muster and sustain an adequate force to defend the
area around Norwich. Lander's assessment of the situation is noteworthy:
"The taste of the nobility and gentry for continental campaigns to support
the dynastic claims of their rulers to foreign territory was distinctly limited. . . . The English political nation, therefore, became withdrawn and
insular — in their safety from attack and aggression less military, more ci-
vilian in character, and able, unlike continental subjects, to deny the monarchy an adequate taxation base."[73] Indicative of the calls for more aristocratic attention to good government, Sir John Fortescue, while in exile
with the royal family between 1468 and 1471, advised Prince Edward (son
of Henry VI) in *De laudibus legum Angliae* to focus on upholding the law:
"I wish that I observed you to be devoted to the study of the laws with the
same zeal as you are to that of arms, since, as battles are determined by
arms, so judgments are by laws."[74] The chief justice's words were unusual
for a noble society that still held to the belief that excellence in prowess
was the highest aspiration for one of that class. William Worcester may
have had Fortescue in mind when in *The Boke of Noblesse* (1475) he
expressed the more traditional view and encouraged Edward IV to win
back the aristocracy to the arts of war. He chastises the nobles of his day
who have neglected prowess to "learn the practice of law" or estate management and thereby choose civil careers so that they "waste greatly their
time in such needless business."[75]

University Press, 1948), for a late medieval understanding of what is expected of the "chivalry" as an integral component of the commonwealth.
   73. Lander, *Limitations of English Monarchy,* 15–17; Powicke, "Lancastrian Captains,"
371–82.
   74. John Fortescue, *De laudibus legum Angliae,* trans. and ed. S. B. Chrimes (Cambridge:
The University Press, 1949), 3, 5.
   75. William of Worcester, *The Boke of Noblesse: Addressed to King Edward IV on His
Invasion of France in 1475,* ed. John G. Nichols (London: J. B. Nichols & Son, 1860), 76–
78. This advice manual was first prepared for Henry VI, enjoining him to be like his father in
France (1450s), before being reworked in order to obtain Yorkist patronage between 1461
and 1472. Its final incarnation in 1475 was directed toward Edward IV. See K. B. McFarlane,
"William Worcester: A Preliminary Survey," in *Studies Presented to Sir Hilary Jenkinson,* ed.
J. Conway Davies (London: Oxford University Press, 1937), 198–214.

It is, however, William Caxton who best embodied the nostalgia and romanticism that had grown up around the knight in the late fifteenth century. The monumental attempt of England's first printer to recapture an idealistic vision of a past that had never existed is well known. His own personal feelings are perhaps best expressed in his famous eulogy to the knights of yore that appears at the end of his translation of Ramon Llull's work on chivalry, published between 1483 and 1485. This famous passage mourns the passing of the "exercises of chivalry not used, honored, nor exercised as it had been in ancient times." Caxton calls on the knights to forsake their warm baths, sleep, and other comforts that have made them soft. He suggests "that every knight should have horse and harness and also the use and craft of a knight," and that the king, Richard III, decree jousts at least once a year and command that Llull's book be read to young lords so "that the noble order of chivalry be hereafter better used and honored than it hath been in late days passed."[76] The trouble with this and other similar remedies for a decrepit and unworkable code of chivalry — simply to force a revival — is their failure to deal with the changing nature of warfare and the composition of armies. Chivalry's legacy would be found in how some of its principles came to be used by early modern monarchs who were creating manuals of military discipline and laws of war to govern the behavior of all types of soldiers; and, of course, some chivalric precepts could be adapted to this more expansive type of military.

A different kind of rejoinder to Caxton's historically suspect view of an idyllic past, however, came from moralists like Gower, Thomas Hoccleve, Thomas Brinton, and John Bromyard, who believed that even if armies were still composed only of knights, the *jus armorum* would still be unable to stem adequately the greed and love for violence typical of that class. These men called also for a reformation but of a much more sweeping kind. Instead of a simple return to a nonexistent past they required a more rigorous philosophical and pragmatic consideration of war and the difficulties it generated. While they were not so much seeking new ways to deal with the severe problems now encountered by an ineffective administration and corrupt knighthood, they found much about war that was objectionable and so wanted the issues debated with the focus put on workable solutions. In this way they paved the way for the more thorough evaluation and policy overhaul that characterized the sixteenth century.

76. William Caxton, trans. *The Book of the Ordre of Chyvalry*, ed. A.T.P. Byles, EETS OS, no. 168 (London: Oxford University Press, 1926), 121–25.

3

ANTIWAR DISCOURSE DURING THE HUNDRED YEARS WAR

Comparative and Early Literary Responses

Having pinpointed some shifts and developments in the just war and the law of arms, and the problems encountered in satisfactorily legitimizing warfare by the fifteenth century, we should now turn to those writers who no longer felt encumbered by these constructs or inhibited from offering alternative ideas on the issue of war. It is difficult to find in any of these works a sweeping indictment of warfare as a whole, and it is certainly asking too much that we even look for such a pattern. Just the same, the full-scale debate that erupted during the last quarter of the fourteenth century, while concentrated mostly on a specific war, was carried on with enough vehemence to suggest that in some cases more far-ranging attitudes existed. For this reason it is imperative that the alternative of peace be studied in all of the ways it is used by those polemicists who opposed the Hundred Years War. Is peace merely a pause in hostilities as presumed within the chivalric temperament? Is it a personal, spiritual quality that maintains only a tenuous or coincidental relationship with the society at large? Or as Augustine and his successors contended, is peace an ideal end (impossible to realize on earth) such that even war can be justified when predicated on efforts toward its ultimate achievement? It is my contention

that all of these connotations of peace existed in the literature of late medieval England, but also that they become less prevalent as the nature of war
continued to degenerate into a morass of violence that, at times, could not
be justified adequately according to just-war and chivalric explanations.
Peace discourse throughout this period continues to expand as it becomes
associated with acts of state and the economic prosperity of the kingdom.
It will be shown in the ensuing discussion that this "pre-pacifist" literature
is a major, predominant strain of later medieval English political and social
discourse that has not been treated systematically by scholars.

The value of using literature in describing political and social trends (as
opposed to relying solely on chronicles, official documents, and other such
primary sources) is best summed up by Christopher Allmand in his recent
study of the Hundred Years War:

> If we regard literature as a mirror, we see reflected in it something
> of a growing awareness of what war was, what it was doing to
> society, and how change was coming about. It was through litera-
> ture that society thought aloud, commented on changing moral and
> political values, and reacted to developments of which it disap-
> proved. No one writer could be the common voice on all matters
> which concerned the public, his importance might lie in him being a
> voice in the wilderness. But some notice of what people wrote, how,
> and when they did so, can give the historian an idea of reaction to
> events and developments.[1]

It is with this exhortation and rationale in mind that the problem of war
will be considered. Even though there was a large body of work that
treated the motivations and practices of war, it is crucial that we examine
the other side of the coin also, that is, the literature that expressed dissatisfaction with late medieval assumptions about war's necessity or utility.
Because such a study has not been attempted yet, there is some need to
inventory the evidence that exists. The following discussion, therefore,
takes a more-or-less chronological approach followed by an analysis of
themes that stretch over the entire period between 1345 and 1470, en-
abling us to construct a late-medieval typology of peace that broadly expanded earlier definitions.

1. Allmand, *Hundred Years War*, 151.

Understandings of Peace since Augustine

As we have seen, the abstract nature of peace and the consequent possibilities for its being perceived as a good in itself were not really considerations of early medieval thinkers. Considered as nothing more than the absence of war or conflict, peace does not even exist as a "distant political
ideal." Not until the Hundred Years War does a tide of dissatisfaction with
just-war theories and military codes draw writers to contemplate the good
of peace in isolation from the necessity for wars; and only with the Erasmian humanists positing peace as an attainable ideal, can the abstract idea
be given the concrete value needed in constructing practical means for
achieving it. Before then, always contrasted with war, which was still perceived as a refiner's fire where good and evil could be sorted out, peace
remained a vaguely construed term devoid of sustained interest as an issue
or condition in itself.

Peace as an idea profitable to Christian kingdoms, however, has a legacy
extending far back into antiquity. Augustine incorporates much of the Hel-
lenistic, Roman, Judaic, and Christian definitions when he describes peace
as merely the other side of war and an unnatural condition in a sinful
world. As we have seen, in both *Contra faustum Manichæum* and *De
civitate Dei* he declares that war is a constant condition among men, with
the forces of good pitted against the forces of evil in an eternal struggle,
because the earthly city is and will always remain mired in sin. Since even
Heaven knows no perpetual peace, how can the earthly city expect to attain such a true and lasting order? Throughout the early Middle Ages this
supernatural and dialectical understanding of peace was accepted ortho-
doxy, especially within the Church, with Germanic martial mores giving it
an even greater basis in culture.[2]

Augustine and his successors, therefore, emphasized the spiritual rather
than temporal nature of peace, for it was here, through the empowering of
the Holy Spirit in the individual, that progress could be made toward its
true achievement. The regenerate Christian, by living a godly life and treating his fellow man and woman well, could find the joy of salvation and
most effectively bring about God's kingdom on earth. Peace was viewed as
a right relationship with God which would produce a people who showed
love toward one another. In fact, for Augustine, individuals could only be
responsible for themselves and their own actions. Thus, we see why this

2. Wallace-Hadrill, "War and Peace," 159, 161.

early church father and the schoolmen who followed him, found wars completely worthy if they were entered into with the proper attitude of charity toward the enemy. War was not a societal blight just as perpetual peace was not an objective that even Christian realms could ever attain.[3] By the time of the Crusades, the notion of a holy war could very easily exist alongside the Church's earlier promotion of the *treuga Dei* and *pax Dei*. All of this points out the idealistic way in which peace was discussed. Again, going back to Augustine, peace on earth may have been what Christ was sent to bring but it would never exist as long as there was sin, which, in turn, could only be eradicated in the final judgment. By keeping temporal peace outside the realm of attainment, this argument invoked peace in a limited manner, and then largely in millennial or unrealizable forms.

While this Augustinian formulation of "spiritual peace" carried great weight throughout the medieval period, especially in the works of the canonists and scholastic theologians, it ceased to be the primary locus of peace discourse by the end of the fourteenth century. Augustine upheld the goal of peace in his discussions of just wars but its realization would depend on more than the good intentions of authorities. In the later Middle Ages the objective itself seemed to have been forgotten, and the peace concept took on nuances that were more practical and conceivably attainable. A typology of peace developed in England that came to embrace at least four distinct notions.[4] The changing political, economic, and social structure that arose out of the unprecedented destruction of the Hundred Years War (and other concurrent crises) helped create an intellectual environment wherein we find the first sustained discourse of peace. Alongside the spiritual ideal already mentioned, peace became associated more concretely with the need to restore order and stability, with rigorous Christ-like behavior, and finally, with pragmatic policy. All of these constructions were appositional to the evil of war as it was being experienced, but only the first and earliest definition linked understandings of peace to a justification of war. In other words, by the late fourteenth century war and peace were no longer simply two poles of the same concept.

Those who wrote about peace in the fourteenth century, whatever their particular literary genre, were enamored of the expanding possibilities for words and the consequent conceptual broadening which a formative lan-

---

3. Markus, "Saint Augustine's Views," 1–13; Hartigan, "Saint Augustine on War and Killing," 195–204.

4. For the sake of simplicity these types of peace will be referred to as spiritual peace, orderly peace, Christ-like peace, and practical (profitable) peace.

guage like English offered. As will be seen, there were many points of contact among them as they read each other's works and fashioned for themselves similar roles as moral reformers and spokesmen for the lower orders. They appear to have been consciously attempting to push the frontiers of meaning beyond traditional conventions, especially for recognizable values like peace. Each new notion of peace created, in turn, a set of interpretants which then gave rise to a greater acceptance of future appropriations of related, if novel, understandings. A growing number of explanatory traditions were born and legitimized, thereby becoming the bases for the constant reintroduction of new ideas into a more open-ended conceptual framework.[5] The authors needed to fasten new information onto the old schema with which the reader (and sometimes hearer) was already familiar, with the result being that these semantic building blocks eventually constructed multiple layers of meaning, all in an unprecedented manner when compared to the information comprehended when discourse occurs within a more restricted semantic environment.[6]

Because of the many meanings that peace had come to harbor by this time, it is important that they be discussed with the various distinctions in mind, with a view to comprehending the intended illocutionary forces that gave them particular communicative values. There was a great deal of interconnection, nevertheless, among writers on when and how they would invoke the idea of peace. For some, like John Gower, the need for social harmony was predicated on personal ethics, while others, such as John Wyclif, determined that the Christian life could not be maintained as long as people were in violent conflict with their neighbors. Above all, however, peace was a restorative idea, and in all four usages, the terms "rest" and "tranquillity" (usually tied to aspirations for social and political unity) often accompany it. Depending on the particular context, the emphasis did change, even if within these categories the definitions remained largely constant.

Continental Peace Discourse

Before surveying the various strains of English antiwar literature it would assist our appraisal of their originality by surveying the corresponding Continental literature. Aside from the international theological and canon-

5. Paul Ricoeur, *Hermeneutics and the Human Sciences* (Cambridge: Cambridge University Press, 1981), 163–64.
6. Wallace L. Chafe, *Meaning and the Structure of Language* (Chicago: University of Chicago Press, 1970), 210–33.

ical positions on war and peace, already discussed, the Hundred Years War proved a catalyst for a more national-based critique of war that stressed moral and practical concerns rather than legal and logical considerations. England's enemy, the French king, was particularly sensitive to any criticism of his handling of the war. Given the endemic factionalism among his vassals, and the persistent shifts in loyalty for which they became famous, it was even more important that a patriotic spirit develop which could unite the various portions of the realm in a concentrated effort to expel the English. This goal was not realized until after the siege at Orléans was raised through the efforts of Joan of Arc in 1429. Until that time the French cause counted on the propaganda of enthusiasts like Jean Froissart to rally the people.

Froissart himself typified a unique development in the law of arms as practiced by French knights in the course of the war. Recent scholarship has noted his expansion of what constituted proper behavior in war by gradually including acts of greater cruelty and violence into the chivalric code. Adapting the *jus in bello* to his particular cultural milieu, through fancy, exaggeration, and irony, Froissart blurred the distinction between pillage and rapine committed by companies "and the legitimate profit that accrued in time of declared war to the soldiers of a royal army fighting under the aegis of the law of arms and the code of chivalry," by his and his contemporaries' "grudging or secret admiration for the resourcefulness of the former."[7] The *jus armorum* had always allowed brutal treatment of the enemy within certain military contexts, but with the French chroniclers of the Hundred Years War, the apparent sanctioning of increasingly violent acts demonstrated just how much the code was being determined according to the "custom and practice of senior knights, marshals, and heralds, rather than books."[8]

A few French writers wrote in obvious contrast to Froissart, such as Jean de Venette and the writer of *Les Voeux du Héron* (The Vows of Heron), both of whom were quite critical of French knighthood. In his chronicle, which covers the years 1341 to 1368, Venette, offering a different perspective from Froissart, gave less attention to feats of arms and more to peace efforts, especially those of the English, whom he felt were particularly active in trying to end the war. The imaginative poem, *Les Voeux du Héron*, which was written soon after the English victory at Crécy in 1346, lashes out against those of high position who make rash

---

7. Peter F. Ainsworth, *John Froissart and the Fabric of History: Truth, Myth, and Fiction in the Chroniques* (Oxford: Clarendon Press, 1990), 82.

8. Ibid., 82–83; Wright, *"Tree of Battles,"* 19, 21.

vows that lead to warmongering. Both works reflect a distaste for the fri-
volity that sometimes surrounds the decision to fight. Yet there is no
sweeping condemnation of the institution of war or even of this particular
conflict. Venette's clear war-weariness never extended to analysis, and the
poet championed love and prowess when combined in a chivalric ideal
tempering the pride that leads to unjust wars.[9]

The most celebrated critic of French conduct in the war, Philippe de
Mézières, in his *Oratio tragedica,* or *Epistre lamentable et consolatoire,*
admonished the knights defeated at Poitiers to leave off the self-promotion
found in chivalric behavior and submit to the greater discipline of coordi-
nated strategy that is more likely to win battles. Mézières's fullest plea for
peace between France and England, however, is found in his *Epistre au roi
Richart,* a "jumble of allegory, parable, and figurative writing," composed
in 1395. While the writer cautioned that a cause found just according to
human understanding may not be so by God's wisdom, the work is striking for the degree to which peace is subsumed by just-war posturing. Like
his English contemporaries Mézières detailed the impoverishments of constant battle but, in his case, made no appeals to social or economic needs
that peace would help satisfy. Simply put, his overriding desire to repair
the Schism and launch a crusade against the Ottoman Turks (who had just
won a major victory at Nicopolis) was predicated on obtaining peace with
England. Crusades were the most just of wars and should be the martial
priority of nations. This tendency to champion peace as an expedient was
less pronounced in English peace discourse, or at least there was less reliance on traditional, scholastic formulations of the just-war and a greater
variety of alternative approaches.[10] Both Mézières and Venette accepted
some wars as legitimate but focused on the *jus in bello* as a way to restrain
and confine their worst elements. They were also signaling the movement
toward a French national army that had made chivalry nearly obsolete by
the end of the war.[11]

Chivalric attitudes ran deep in France and were much more difficult to

9. Jean de Venette, *The Chronicle of Jean de Venette,* trans. Jean Birdsall, ed. Richard A.
Newhall (New York: Columbia University Press, 1963), 98–107 (negotiations surrounding
the Peace of Brétigny, 1360); *The Vows of the Heron (Les Voeux du Héron): A Middle
French Vowing Poem,* ed. John L. Grigsby and Norris J. Lacy (New York: Garland Publishing, 1992), 15–18, 32–57, 59.

10. Philippe de Mézières. *Letter to King Richard II: A Plea Made in 1395 for Peace
between England and France,* trans. G. W. Coopland (Liverpool: Liverpool University Press,
1975), xxv–xxxii, 3–11, 21–24, 53, 63–72, 126; Contamine, *War in the Middle Ages,* 288.

11. Ainsworth, *Jean Froissart,* 84–85.

uproot. Aside from Mézières, Bonet and the renowned cleric Jean Gerson criticized knightly behavior with an eye more toward reform than extending critiques to the code itself or to the war as a whole. This persistent and fervently embraced culture may best be understood by looking at Bueil's *Le Jouvencel,* which was dedicated to portraying the ideal knight but within the realistic setting of contemporary warfare. The hero regards war as his profession, not tilts and other games. Nobles unfit for war face sneers and derision. For Bueil, glorious feats of arms equaled honor and true nobility. Just after returning from an expedition the Jouvencel rejoices in the exploits just accomplished and of war in general when he proclaims,

> What a joyous thing is war. . . . When war is fought in a good cause, it is fought for justice and the defence of right. War . . . is a proper and useful career for young men, for which they are respected by both God and the world. You love your comrade so much in war. . . . When you see that your cause is good and your blood is hot, tears come to your eyes.[12]

In this paean to just wars, Thomist notions of wars for the common good are thoroughly engulfed with the spirit of vengeance, once again demonstrating the late medieval penchant for diluting just-war exhortations to right intent.

Aside from Mézières, Georges Chastellain was probably the least impressed observer of French chivalry at this time; yet even he was profoundly gratified by the gift of the spurs of knighthood two years before his death.[13] These deeply ingrained values point out that an obvious difference between English and French military culture at this time would be England's ability to withdraw from France with little threat to its security. The French, however, were far from unified and considered war necessary to achieve that goal. Opposition to war and peace ideas, then, could develop among the English with much less at stake than they might be among the French.[14] And the former criticized the conspicuous loss of

12. Bueil, *Le Jouvencel,* 2:20–21; Raymond Lincoln Kilgour, *The Decline of Chivalry as Shown in the French Literature of the Late Middle Ages* (Cambridge, Mass.: Harvard University Press, 1937; reprint, Gloucester, Mass.: Peter Smith, 1966), 148–49; 318–32; Vale, *War and Chivalry,* 30.

13. Kilgour, *Decline of Chivalry,* 392–93.

14. G. R. Elton, "English National Self-Consciousness and the Parliament in the Sixteenth

honor and Christian charity in the *jus armorum* with an urgency that seemed quite alien to the latter (thanks to the efforts of Froissart among others). Maurice Keen has recently contended that what held the writers of these chivalric handbooks together was their desire for internal, even national peace. As a consequence Mézières, Bonet, Llull, and Christine de Pisan tended to uphold worldly honor over the "crown of salvation" that ecclesiastics offered crusaders. An ensuing breakdown in a unified concept of honor in the midst of widespread devastation by the companies caused the French writers to divert their attention naturally away from warmaking to the value of peace, but only within the context of restoring law and order within the kingdom. Christine, therefore, revived Vegetius's description of Roman military discipline in order to apply it to her own nation's soldiers.[15] But perhaps the most noticeable difference between the peace discourses of these two nations by the end of the war is the continued utopian and scholastic influences on Continental ideas and the clearly emerging economic, social, and overall practical concerns of the English.

Reflecting a more developed millenarian tradition, many Italian, German, and French writers throughout the Middle Ages hoped for a *renovatio mundi* that would include a most Christian world leader to usher in a prolonged if not eternal period of peace. Prophets, like Joachim of Fiore, spoke of a third and final age of the Holy Spirit and of a new Charlemagne, or Emperor Frederick, who would usher in this new world order.[16] The influence of the early fourteenth-century works, Dante's *Monarchia* and Marsilius of Padua's *Defensor pacis,* are hard to measure. Both envisioned peace as a secular concept, a condition brought about by this world leader or emperor. The authors believed that it was not in Augustine's city of God where peace would most likely appear, since the Church itself had caused most of the disorder that had led to wars. Law and justice are the prerogatives of lay rulers who are under a mandate from God to bring perpetual peace and order.[17] Such ideas resonated in both England and

---

Century," in *Studies in Tudor and Stuart Politics and Government,* vol. 4, *Papers and Reviews, 1983–1990* (Cambridge: Cambridge University Press, 1992), 131–33.

15. Maurice Keen, "War, Peace and Chivalry," in *War and Peace in the Middle Ages,* ed. Brian Patrick McGuire (Copenhagen: C. A. Reitzels, 1987), 97–110; Philippe de Mézières, *Le Songe du vieil pèlerin,* ed. G. W. Coopland (Cambridge: Cambridge University Press, 1969), 1:531–52.

16. Marjorie Reeves, *The Influence of Prophecy in the Later Middle Ages: A Study of Joachimism* (Oxford: Clarendon Press, 1969), 306–58.

17. Christian L. Lange, *Histoire de la doctrine pacifique et de son influence sur le développement du droit international,* Academy of International Law, Recueil des cours, no. 3,

France during a time when many looked for strong kings to reestablish tranquillity and stability within their own realms. As will be seen, Marsilius especially was held in high regard in England in the 1530s when Henry VIII was challenging papal authority. But overall the English found these theories to be of limited utility in the fourteenth and fifteenth centuries. Even when the Continental humanists borrowed some of Dante's and Marsilius's "utopian" language, many English writers felt compelled to temper their hopeful, humanist sensibilities with a strong dose of pragmatism. The complaint literature of the Hundred Years War offers the first clues to this aspect of English peace discourse, reaching its clearest statement in the *Libelle of Englyshe Polycye* (1436–37) and in the works of John Lydgate. By contrast, the French peace advocates, including Pierre Dubois and Mézières, continued to perpetuate Dantean idealism. Mézières's *Le Songe du vieil pèlerin* visualized a future free of crime, violence, heresy, war, and all malevolence.[18] While William Langland and Thomas More harbored utopian visions as well, both used their pens to lash out candidly against existing corruption and injustice; and neither truly believed that a future reign of peace could be found this side of heaven.

Another major component of Continental peace discourse was founded on the continued legacy of canonist and scholastic interpretations of just wars. As already recounted to some degree in Chapter 1 and to be considered again in this chapter, many English moralists were seriously questioning the hegemony of clerical opinion in this area. The works of Christine de Pisan, Chastellain, and Gerson, however, suggest this cynicism may not have been as widespread in France. Christine's *Le Livre de la paix* promotes eloquently the benefits of peace and the need for its achievement, but it argues that peace must come honorably. Gerson also desired peace deeply but claimed it should not be at any cost, reiterating the assumption that a just war is preferable to an unjust peace.[19] During the English Renaissance, a number of politicians, religious leaders, and humanists pointedly eschewed this notion and revived the Ciceronian dictum that held the most unjust peace is better than any just war. As exemplified by these

---

vol. 13, pp. 171–426 (The Hague: Academy of International Law, 1926; reprint, New York: Garland, 1973), 203–4; Johnson, *Quest for Peace*, 113–32.

18. Contamine, *War in the Middle Ages*, 292–93; Mézières, *Songe du vieil pèlerin*, 1:224, 231, 2:421; Allmand, *Society at War*, 159–61.

19. Jean Gerson, *Oeuvres complètes*, ed. Palemon Glorieux (Paris: Desclée, 1966), 7:219; Christine de Pisan, *Le Livre de la paix*, ed. C. C. Willard (The Hague: Mouton, 1958); Contamine, *War in the Middle Ages*, 293.

French writers, however, it appears that much thought regarding peace was still bound within the strictures of older just-war theory which included employing *jus in bello* means for bringing about a legitimate end to conflict and a period of true peace.

Late-medieval classicists interested in applying ancient virtues to justifications for war were a minority but illustrative of trends prevalent later among Renaissance humanists. The utilization of Virgilian/Ciceronian views of friendship (*amicitia*) in idealist ambitions for peace and harmony between the empire and the papacy can be found as early as the tenth century in the letters of Gerbert, archbishop of Ravenna. One historian has argued that this strain of peace thought ran contrary to Augustine's pessimism and came to influence Dante, Bernard, and even Thomas and their dreams of a Christian commonwealth.[20] Aquinas's *On Kingship* draws from Cicero in its advocacy of the public good over private interest, which promotes "friendship among inhabitants." The Florentine Remigio de' Girolami wrote in 1304 that such amity could be equated with peace when peace promotes the common good more than the restitution found in a just cause.[21] By placing these classical concepts into a timeless vacuum and not integrating them sufficiently into a rapidly changing political and military context, these well-intentioned and still largely scholastic works did little to make temporal peace the moral imperative it would become in the sixteenth century when Erasmians believed it could actually be realized.

Finally, we can detect with greater frequency in the fourteenth century a sectarian response to war that promoted peace as a worthy alternative. Not all heterodox movements, however, preached an end to war. The Hussites found armed battle quite serviceable to their own desires for an independent church in the early fifteenth century. But after the establishment of the mendicant orders in the thirteenth century and the subsequent growth in lay piety, a series of religious and social factors combined to produce a number of sects that wished to live according to monastic ideals without becoming members of established orders. Clerics aspiring to perfection were nonviolent and viewed battle as full of sin, even if it was justified on occasion. Waldensians and the Cathars who rejected armed conflict based

20. Brian P. McGuire, "The Church and the Control of Violence in the Early Middle Ages: Friendship and Peace in the Letters of Gerbert, 982–97," in McGuire, *War and Peace in the Middle Ages*, 30–55.

21. Antony Black, *Political Thought in Europe, 1250–1450* (Cambridge: Cambridge University Press, 1992), 24–25.

their beliefs on a need to imitate Christ to the devaluation of worldly, and therefore futile, attempts to improve society. Tendencies of this kind, which in effect laid claim to a separate law and determination of proper public and private morality, were unacceptable to political powers in late medieval Europe. Most adherents to such ideas were hunted down and brutally punished, usually with death.[22]

Being in the world but not of it did not have to lead to social disintegration, but the refusal to deal with the realities of human social and political intercourse pushed many sectarian ideas of peace so out of the mainstream that they lost all practical value. As will be seen, while the Lollards in England offered the most radical critique of war in the later Middle Ages, they had virtually no lasting influence or impact on developing peace discourses — except for perhaps some Protestants in the sixteenth century who read the Bible as they did and adopted a similar form of the *imago Christi*. One may again find here some evidence of a social division in the unilateral attachment to temporal peace. In Bonet's words, "Everyone knows well that when it is a question of deciding on war or ordering it, the poor do not intervene because as far as they are concerned they only wish to live in peace."[23] Those least consulted and most affected in times of war were also the most likely to participate in outbreaks directed against war taxes, or as in this case, to join sects opposed to war. As concerns for the commonwealth grew in England during the fifteenth century, and as attacks were launched against the devastation caused by war and misgovernment, the protests of the commons found support in the moralists who wrote forcefully on their behalf then and well into the next century.

In summary then, European peace ideas in the later Middle Ages were still largely circumscribed by the just-war tradition, as well as by movements of laicization and secularization that promoted peace in the overall cause of reform, encouraging the idealism that was often a by-product, and by sectarian visions of a world released from dissension and differing spiritual vocations, given over instead to a universalized ethic of Christ-like behavior. These threads, once plunged into the dye of incessant war and unique religious and social and political conditions, were taken up by a number of English writers on war and peace and woven into quite original tapestries.

22. Johnson, *Quest for Peace*, 91–109; Contamine, *War in the Middle Ages*, 294–96.
23. Quoted in Contamine, *War in the Middle Ages*, 393.

Early Critiques of War—De Bury and Gower

With this background in Continental peace ideas we can now survey the
particular English varieties, which often differed from views that prevailed
in the rest of Europe. In any appraisal of fourteenth- and fifteenth-century
antiwar literature, the point of departure is almost always the escalating
Hundred Years War. No previous conflict had kept the nation in such an
advanced state of military preparedness for so long a time. At first, apologists, like the poet Laurence Minot, wrote in support of Edward's cause,
which presupposed some knowledge of the justification given for the war.
In 1349, on the heels of the victory at Crécy, a bitterly caustic and xeno-
phobic diatribe appeared, written anonymously and in Latin. *An Invective
against France* claimed that traitors had convinced Edward to do homage
to the Valois king Philip VI, which the former had now wisely and fully
repudiated.[24] Considering the immediate social implications of the early
campaigns, and the gathering resistance among the commons, it is not
surprising that such instances of "spontaneous" patriotism ebbed significantly by the 1360s. The balance tipped in favor of the emergent complaint literature, and the government quickly began to develop more sophisticated means for raising support. Soon, however, the rising political,
economic, and military toll, punctuated by rare victories (albeit spectacular
ones), created a proportional sense of hopelessness and weariness. In such
a context peace could have been thought of primarily as an idyllic state,
and there is strong evidence that the war did give rise to a revived genre of
pastoral literature patterned after Virgil.[25] But the realistic assessments that
predominated indicate a new level of discussion over the place of warfare
in a Christian society. Traditional methods for eliminating its scourge
(prayer, avowed justice of cause, peace negotiations, truces, and so on)
seemed ineffectual as the war dragged on; this created an incentive to re-
evaluate the process of war and to focus on preferred alternatives.

At the very start of the Hundred Years War, between 1337 and 1340,
the government fell deeply into debt. The first sustained antiwar sentiment
was closely tied to popular opposition to the new taxes exacted to finance

---

24. Laurence Minot, *The Poems of Laurence Minot, 1333–1352*, ed. Thomas Beaumont
James and John Simons (Exeter: University of Exeter, 1989), 26–56. Appendix 2 includes an
English translation of *An Invective against France*, along with some other patriotic verses
from the time. Barnie, *War in Medieval English Society*, 54.

25. See Helen Cooper's *Pastoral: Medieval into Renaissance* (Ipswich, Eng.: D. S. Brewer,
1977).

the initial campaigns, especially the confusing levy of 1340. The "Prophecy," written by John of Bridlington around 1349–50, severely criticized both Edward's prosecution of the war and the high taxes, which were causing tremendous suffering among the people.[26] An English version of the satirical "Vows of Heron" appeared that went further than the French original by condemning war on a broad scale. It also included trenchant attacks on Edward's supposed betrayal of vows, the scandalous behavior of chivalrous knights, and the horrors of battle. Two other early poems, "On the Times of Edward II" and "Against Taxes," "put these themes in the vernacular of protest." Both works complained about the inequities of tax levies where the rich pay less or are able to avoid paying altogether. The writers, probably clergymen, charged corruption in the reading of assessments. Although such works of protest were not widely circulated and could only pretend to a national audience, they probably give some indication of popular opinion. Again, the class divisions are apparent and can be traced to the earliest years of the war. Evidence also suggests that many clerics made up their minds about the war based more on social and economic considerations than on official opinions rendered by their estate's leaders.[27]

Perhaps the earliest major critique of war among England's intelligentsia came from an unsuspecting source—Richard Aungerville (also Richard de Bury), bishop of Durham and probable tutor to Edward III, who finished his *Philobiblon* in 1345, the year he died. Primarily interested in books and their preservation, Aungerville, in the chapter "The Complaint of Books Against War," voiced his opposition to war through the unusual perspective of books which come into physical danger. These volumes cry out: "Almighty Author and Lover of Peace, scatter the nations that seek after war, which harms books beyond all pestilences. For wars, which lack a ground in reason, make furious assaults upon all that is opposed to them and, discarding the governance of reason, proceed without discreet judgment and destroy the vessels of reason."[28] Not only was the bishop skeptical of just wars, but he found them utterly irrational. He credited war with having caused the long-standing disappearance of those works of Aristotle which have been "subjected by the most unjust laws of war to a vile hire-

---

26. Waugh, *England in the Reign of Edward III*, 234–39.
27. Ibid., 235–36.
28. Richard de Bury, *The Philobiblon*, ed. Archer Taylor (Berkeley and Los Angeles: University of California Press, 1948), 41; N. Denholm-Young, "Richard de Bury (1287–1345)," *TRHS*, 4th ser., 22 (1937): 139.

ling soldier!" In his conclusion, if one did not know that books were
speaking, the same lament could have been made by many soldiers and
civilians alike: "For by wars we are dragged away to foreign lands, are
killed and wounded and frightfully disfigured, are buried beneath the
earth, drowned in the sea, burned in the fire, and slain by every kind of
death." And, because of these losses they humbly ask the Ruler of
Olympus that he "may insure peace, remove wars, and make the times
tranquil under His own protection."[29] In using the device of speaking
through books Aungerville may have been making a sharp criticism of the
Hundred Years War during its earliest stage. Had he been more direct
surely he would have had much to lose, with all of his preferments (including high ecclesiastical and administrative positions) having come at the
hands of his former pupil, Edward III. The bishop's reference to peace was
undeveloped and imprecise. He did not reveal a "deeply Christian concern
for the whole commonwealth nor a philosophic interest in the discovery
and the control if possible of the basic causes of war."[30] His determined
dislike for war, however, and the destruction that accompanied it helped
set the stage for more penetrating and moralistic critics like John Gower.

As already described, Gower, like Aungerville, put little faith in *jus ad
bellum* arguments. But early in his career he had supported Edward III's
claim to the French throne. He began to exhibit doubts first in 1369 when
he sided with a group of prelates who opposed further taxation because a
truce with France had just been broken. Gower felt that taxing the clergy
was a disastrous method for winning wars and saw Edward's readiness to
do so as further proof that he had come under the counsel of greedy flatterers, chiefly Alice Perrers. The parish priests could ill afford another
back-breaking excise, especially when England appeared deliberately to
have destroyed the peace.[31] In his opinion, it was nothing more than greed
and selfishness that propelled kings and soldiers once again into battle.
Over the next twenty years Gower turned completely against the war and
in both major works of the period, *Vox clamantis* and *Confessio amantis,*
condemned the bloodshed on strictly moral grounds. In the latter work he
maintained that peace was the natural condition of humankind, since God
forbade homicide in the Decalogue and the angels proclaimed peace at
Christ's birth. War does nothing but destroy this favorable situation and

29. Bury, *Philobiblon,* 41–45.
30. Adams, "Pre-Renaissance Courtly Propaganda," 439–40.
31. Gardiner Stillwell, "John Gower and the Last Years of Edward III," *Studies in Philology* 45 (1948): 454–56.

therefore hurts the public welfare, which should be founded on love not contention:

> After the law of charity,
> There shall no deadly war be:
> And each nature it has defended
> And in her law peace commended,
> Which is the chief of man's wealth,
> Of man's life, of man's health.
> But deadly war has his cousin
> Of pestilence and of famine,
> Of poverty and of all woe,
> Whereof this world we blame so,
> Which now the war has underfoot,
> Til God Himself thereof does bote [make better].[32]

Gower went on to say that whatever good God bestows on the earth will be disrupted and damaged by war, including the Church, clergy, families, and livelihoods. The "possessioners" among the secular clergy were a common target of antiwar polemicists of the late fourteenth century, including Gower. Here, Genius, the opponent of war, rails against a Church that has become so perverse in coveting worldly goods that it seeks bloodshed and manslaughter rather than peace. Such acts are against Christ's law of charity and natural law as well. Even heathens should be spared, since they have souls that need to be saved: "A Saracen if I should kill, I kill the soul forth with all, and that was never Christ's love." Genius concludes by addressing another common concern of the day when he tells Amans of the danger posed by flatterers who would push the king toward war. When the Israelite King Ahab sent flatterers to Judah's king Jehosophat and the latter ignored prophetic warnings, he is defeated in battle and his kingdom divided.[33]

In his earlier *Vox clamantis* Gower had extended his concern for the public well-being to a condemnation of those who self-indulgently go to war out of cupidity. His harsh words for another segment of the clergy, the warrior clerics, have already been documented. Here he railed against the

---

32. Gower, *Confessio amantis*, lines 2261–72, in *Complete Works*, vol. 2, bk. 3, p. 287.
33. Ibid., bk. 4, lines 1679–81; bk. 7, lines 2662–63; Russell A. Peck, *Kingship and Common Profit in Gower's "Confessio Amantis"* (Carbondale: Southern Illinois University Press, 1978), 91, 146.

abandonment of their calling, which is to care for souls — a peaceful activity: "If those who ought to restore peace practice war, I do not know how
one can safely enter upon the path of peace."[34] For Gower, peace was a
societal good that could be attained if each person acted according to his
or her proper station in life. Most members of each estate, however, have
instead chosen to forgo their duty and think only of themselves. His main
attack on the knights stemmed from their greed and lust:

> Outwardly, the greedy lords deal in the blessings of peace, but in-
> wardly, wars still stand first with them. As long as it can store up
> more loot through war than through peace, avarice does not know
> how to love the good things of peace. And envy does not permit
> you to conduct yourself peaceably toward me, for my tears are
> laughter in your ear. It is nothing to you if the downtrodden people
> bewail their sufferings, provided that the general misfortune brings
> in money to you.[35]

At other times Gower accepted the just-war concept even though he believed it had been abused terribly. He asserted that knighthood had been
established for three purposes: to enhance the common good, to defend the
orphan and widow, and to protect the Church, all of which can be incorporated within the boundaries of legitimate warfare; but in all three cases
avarice has diverted knights from their duty and led them to become less
rigorous in their assessment of cause.[36]

Since Gower, therefore, believed that some wars were legitimate, he upheld a version of the just war that laid emphasis on *jus in bello* restraints.
He wanted knights to serve as what might be the modern-day equivalent
of United Nations peacekeepers. Their role was to maintain order and
tranquillity, perhaps even fighting when absolutely necessary to ensure that
greater good. The conditions under which he was writing, however, indicate that a just war was an extraordinary and extremely rare occurrence.
Gower was in fact making a just-war argument *against* Edward's claim to
France. His king's policy was self-aggrandizing in a way that harmed the
vast majority of the English people. In taking this kind of position, the
poet was arguing for peace not war, and yet basing it on a kind of moralistic inversion of the just-war concept itself.

34. Gower, *Vox clamantis*, in *Major Latin* Works, bk. 3, pp. 125–26.
35. Ibid., bk. 7, lines 31–40, pp. 254–55.
36. Barnie, *War in Medieval English Society,* 121–22.

In later years, Gower became even bolder and extended his criticism to include royal neglect of the common good. He enjoined the king to protect the nation and its welfare, which was impossible when flimsy pretexts were continually dragging him into another phase of a never-ending war. One of the "official" charges made against Richard II after his capture at Conway Castle was that in at least eight instances he had "violated his official promise to keep peace toward clergy and people" and given himself over to evil counsel. Gower agreed with this assessment and so came to throw his support behind the Bolingbroke usurpation in 1399.[37] His accession address to Henry IV was an unabashed panegyric to peace that promised the new king great glory and honor if he would only make peace with France. Gower was able to laud Henry for keeping peace while still implying that the king might not always be so inclined.[38] Keeping good relations with France was the obvious policy choice, for it could help usher the rest of Christian Europe into a golden age united in peace:

> Peace is the chief of all the world's wealth;
> And to heaven it leads each the way;
> Peace is the soul and life of man's health
> Of pestilence and war it does away.
> My liege lord, take heed of what I say,
> If war may be avoided, take peace to hand,
> Which cannot be without God's son.[39]

Gower warns, however, that there are those who appeal to peace for their own ends and fool others into thinking they are sincere:

> The peace is as it were a sacrament
> In the sight of God, and shall with words plain,
> Without any double intent [meaning]
> Be treated, for the truth cannot feign;
> But if men within themselves are vain,
> The substance of the peace may not be true,
> But that every day it changes anew.[40]

37. George R. Coffman, "John Gower, Mentor for Royalty: Richard II," *PMLA* 69 (1954): 953–64.

38. James Dean, "Gower, Chaucer, and the Rhyme Royal," *Studies in Philology* 88 (1991): 265.

39. Gower, "Address to Henry IV," in *Political Poems and Songs*, 6.

40. Ibid., 13.

The only test of whether true peace is the ambition is to determine whether the motive is love. As early as the *Mirour de l'omme* he warned the knights: "Thou shalt receive good or evil according to the intent thou hast, for God looks into thy heart. Even in a just cause, thou canst do wrong." Gower has objectified completely the right-intent principle and placed the burden of responsibility on the individual soldier.[41] Such a test may sound reminiscent of Augustine's condition for a just war, but Gower has made it rather a stipulation for a *just peace*. Love for others will prevent wars, not make allowances for them. Pity keeps war far away and promotes charity.[42] In this small way Gower moved away from the earlier position that war is endemic to human society to the contention that peace is the more natural state.

It has been suggested recently that Gower's pacifism "is both broad ranging and thoroughly developed."[43] Certainly one cannot read the poet's entire corpus without feeling that peace was a major preoccupation for Gower; and his talents as a poet are becoming more recognized, especially through his creative use of the rhyme royal in his address on peace to Henry IV. Clearly, he would not have composed this work in such a fashion unless he felt particularly passionate about the subject.[44] On the actual content of his didacticism, however, Gower's pathway to peace was much too simple and unrealistic, despite his incisive thoughts on the practice of war in his day. He has no faith in the common people, and as one scholar has put it, "his social gospel presupposes no social equality but is limited to fostering honesty and integrity within established society by all members of it."[45] But it would be unfair to expect him to fantasize about ideas too far outside the intellectual climate and discursive framework in which he wrote. The contributions he did make, by helping introduce a language of peace into contemporary political and social discourse, are very significant. He understood that peace was too precious to be left to the designs of corrupt knights. His organic view of society was not new, but his em-

41. Yeager, "*Pax Poetica*," 104.
42. Dean, "Gower, Chaucer, and the Rhyme Royal," 267.
43. Yeager, "*Pax Poetica*," 108.
44. Dean, "Gower, Chaucer, and the Rhyme Royal," 265.
45. George R. Coffman, "John Gower in His Most Significant Role," in *Elizabethan Studies and Other Essays in Honour of George F. Reynolds* (Boulder: University of Colorado Studies, 1945), 53; Janet Coleman, *Medieval Readers and Writers, 1350–1400* (New York: Columbia University Press, 1981), 140; R. B. Dobson, *The Peasants' Revolt of 1381* (London: Macmillan, 1970), 97–98.

phasis on the relationship between love and common profit was.[46] In discussing war, Gower developed from the Augustinian stress on charity a nascent peace ethic that stopped with encouraging a right relationship among the estates. War can no longer be viewed as inherently good or benign, since the greater good of the public welfare is always hurt and disrupted by it. Gower may have been overly moralistic with his solution to the problem of war but he helped expand the parameters of discourse as, among a number of celebrated literati, respect for contemporary war justifications continued to decline.

Ricardian Politics and the Prosecution of War

Before going further, we should address briefly the often complex political developments that characterized English government in the last quarter of the fourteenth century and which became grist for the mill of literary complaint. The death of the Black Prince before his father, left the throne to the deceased heir's son, Richard II (1377–99). The new reign was fraught with trouble almost from the start. Edward's final years had witnessed the revival of the war after 1369 when the Gascon nobles rose up against English rule and were quickly joined by Castilians who resented the Black Prince's invasion to depose a French claimant to their throne in 1367. It appears the king was becoming increasingly senile so that at Richard's accession a declining war effort had left the English with little more than Calais and the area surrounding Bordeaux.[47]

Just before the old king died an outburst against the war's mismanagement erupted in the "Good Parliament" of 1376. The king's mistress, Alice Perrers, was temporarily driven from court, and certain other members of the court party were impeached. Inheriting the throne at the age of ten, Richard was first dominated by his powerful uncles, John of Gaunt, duke of Lancaster; Edmund Langley, duke of York, and Thomas of Woodstock, duke of Gloucester, as well as the influential earls of Arundel, Warwick,

---

46. Arthur B. Ferguson, *The Chivalric Tradition in Renaissance England* (Washington, D.C.: Folger Shakespeare Library, 1986), 38; John H. Fisher, *John Gower, Moral Philosopher and Friend of Chaucer* (New York: New York University Press, 1964), 135–203.

47. James Sherborne, "John of Gaunt, Edward III's Retinue and the French Campaign of 1369," in *Kings and Nobles in the Later Middle Ages: A Tribute to Charles Ross*, ed. Ralph A. Griffiths and James Sherborne (New York: St. Martin's Press, 1986), 41–61.

and Nottingham. With the war effort continuing to deteriorate and the
Commons still forced to raise support for it, social discontent swelled
against poll taxes levied by Parliament since 1377, eventually inciting the
infamous Peasants' Revolt of 1381. Gower had predicted something of this
sort in his *Mirour de l'omme*. Other causes of the Peasants' Revolt were
also related to the war effort. Just before the outbreak of the revolt, panic
swept the Kentish coast that the French were about to attack. There was a
general feeling that the government was indifferent to the danger. There is
also evidence that since the late 1370s fewer people were willing to serve
in the infantry and that increasing numbers of men-at-arms and archers
were deserting.[48] Other religious and social issues tended to dominate the
"demands" of the rebels, and Richard coolly and forcefully dealt with
them.

During the years that followed, the king began to replace traditional
courtiers and officials with his own favorites, most notably Michael de la
Pole and Robert de Vere, thereby engendering tremendous resentment
among the older, established aristocracy. Political shake-ups were accompanied by foreign policy struggles during this period, from 1383 to 1388.
De la Pole, now the earl of Suffolk, promoted peace, and while he was a
constant target of the "Lords Appellant,"[49] who finally removed him from
the chancellorship during the Merciless Parliament of 1388, his assessment
of the conflict with France was becoming more accepted. The monk at
Westminster wrote of reports that the king had offered in 1387 to renounce his claim to France, except for Aquitaine, for an indemnity, and to
do homage to the French king, since "if he [Richard] was going to have to
maintain a ceaseless state of war against the king of the French, he would
inevitably be compelled to be for ever burdening his people with new im-
posts, with damaging results for himself."[50] By this time the Castilian situation was settled, and only Gloucester and Arundel remained opposed to a
truce with France. Although the king came under the sway of the Appel-
lants from 1388 until 1397, his peace policy triumphed and there was
virtually no war party during those years. Even though most of those in

48. Close Roll, 4 Richard II, memb. 36 [C.54/220]; Dobson, *Peasants' Revolt*, 20–21, 94–
98; Gower, *Mirour de l'omme*, in *Complete Works*, vol. 1, lines 26487–26506.

49. Rather than impeach de la Pole and de Vere, the magnates, including Arundel, Warwick, Nottingham, Gloucester, and Lancaster's son, Henry Bolingbroke, appealed to the
House of Lords to accuse Richard's party of treason. While Suffolk and de Vere were exiled,
others faced imprisonment or execution.

50. *The Westminster Chronicle, 1381–1394*, trans. L. C. Hector and Barbara F. Harvey
(Oxford: Clarendon Press, 1982), 205.

power accepted the rationales behind the truce, they also found ways to divert much of the tax revenue collected in the late 1380s into their own coffers. The outcry against such corruption induced the Commons to demand an accounting of revenues received in 1388.[51]

The relations between England and France were practically cordial at the end of Richard's reign. The poet Jean Creton visited the court in the spring of 1399 and was given remarkable freedom to observe. He and at least four other visiting scholars wrote glowing assessments of the king and his court, which would have hardly been possible had there been any serious tension between the two countries. The 1390s were also the years when Mézières was attempting to garner support for a final peace that would enable France and England to cooperate in a crusade against the Muslims.[52] Despite the real outward amity there were forces working hard to reignite the war. Charles VI's brother, Louis, duke of Orléans, was not well disposed to peace; and since he hoped to carve out a kingdom for himself in Italy in the face of English opposition, he made an alliance with Bolingbroke, who was by early 1399 facing confiscation of his property along with other heavy-handed threats and indignities from Richard. Orléans also feared that lasting peace would bring an end to the Schism, as Mézières had dreamed, and his objectives in Italy depended on a still divided Christendom.[53] His actions finally ruptured the peace after 1399, bringing a new king to the throne of England and a renewed plea from Gower that the peace be kept.

The Subtleties of Fiction — Langland and Chaucer

Richard's reign is often noted for the first great flowering of English vernacular literature that accompanied it, and many have argued that this was due partially to the rejection of the French language in the midst of a longstanding war.[54] But much of this writing, especially the didactic works, may have also been spurred by a greater interest in larger political and

51. J.J.N. Palmer, *England, France and Christendom, 1377–99* (Chapel Hill: University of North Carolina Press, 1972), 137–40.

52. His two major works on this theme, *Le Songe du vieil pèlerin* and *Epistre au roi Richart II* were written in 1389 and 1395.

53. Palmer, *England, France and Christendom*, 222–26; A. R. Myers, *England in the Late Middle Ages* (Harmondsworth, Eng.: Penguin Books, 1952), 31–36, 44–45.

54. Janet Coleman, "English Culture in the Fourteenth Century," in *Chaucer and the Ital-*

religious issues, as well as more opportunities for public discourse. We have already seen where Parliament was taking on a much greater role in determining public policy during these years — achieving a power that would not last beyond the war. Perhaps most significant, from Gower to Hoccleve, there was an uninterrupted chain of relations and associations among all of these writers, which regularly put them into contact with each other across the printed page and obviously promoted cross-currents of ideas. Despite the multiple genres and styles employed, there was a corporate sense of public duty that each of them felt party to, although some to a greater extent than others. As "spokesmen" for the poor and the just, they turned to existing national problems, including the destructiveness of armed conflict and the reasons behind it, and applied their Christian ethics with great resolve.

By the late fourteenth century a less direct attack on the Hundred Years War, but a no less powerful one, appeared in the early vernacular poetry of Geoffrey Chaucer and the minor cleric William Langland. The wider circulation of both *The Canterbury Tales* and *Piers Plowman* (albeit in a pre-print culture) meant that these works could hardly criticize openly the war policy of Edward III.[55] With both writers, however, there was a strong indictment of the French campaigns, and even though there was not a corresponding disaffection with all war, their stinging observations presented a new and compelling case for peace as a preferred alternative to destructive and immoral wars.

As is the case with Gower and most other disaffected writers surveying the progress of the Hundred Years War after the initial campaigns were over, Langland, in his *Vision of Piers Plowman,* looked at contemporary society critically and blamed those people and institutions that were most responsible for the war's multitude of ill effects. Directing much of his recurring anger against clerical corruption, the author was especially horrified at the Great Schism, and in passus 19 he criticized the pope "who should help all people, and sends men to kill those that he should be saving."[56] Most of this allegory, however, bemoaned England's social and political predicament, attributing much of the problem to Edward's war policy.

---

ian Tricento, ed. Piero Boitani (Cambridge: Cambridge University Press, 1983), 33–63; Elton, "English National Self-Consciousness," 133.

55. Lee C. Ramsey, *Chivalric Romances: Popular Literature in Medieval England* (Bloomington: Indiana University Press, 1983), 209–10.

56. B-text, passus 19, 426–27, quoted in Basil Cottle, *The Triumph of English, 1350–1400* (New York: Barnes & Noble, 1969), 61.

The view of war found in *Piers Plowman* is most interesting for the variances one finds in the A and B texts. In both, passus 3 opens with Lady Meed (personifying reward), the king, and Conscience at court in Westminster. The disastrous expedition referred to in this section may be that of John of Gaunt into Auvergne during the winter of 1373, even though the actual circumstances mentioned do not correspond with complete accuracy to this campaign.[57] Most scholars, however, seem to hold to an earlier date for its composition, probably in the late 1360s.[58] Even though Lady Meed, as Alice Perrers, levels a scathing assessment of the campaign, she is criticized as well for diverting the king away from his duty to lead the armies into France himself. In the A text Conscience complains of "Meed the maid" before the king, advising him not to marry her:

> She is frail in her faith, fickle in her speech;
> She makes men misdo many score times;
> To hold onto her treasure she injures full many.[59]

Lady Meed counters by blaming Conscience for damaging the king even more when in Normandy Edward was convinced to "hibernate" during the cold winter while his men plundered rather than fight for their lord's honor.[60] The worst accusation comes when she holds Conscience responsible for the king's buying peace and thereby selling his claim to the French throne:

> Cowardly, Conscience, you counseled him thus,
> To leave his lordship for a little silver,
> Over the richest realm that rain hangs over![61]

Lady Meed continues by stating that meed, or reward, is necessary for all of society to function, including the soldiers who fight the king's wars,

57. William Langland, *Piers the Plowman, A Critical Edition of the A-Version,* ed. Thomas A. Knott and David C. Fowler (Baltimore: Johns Hopkins University Press, 1952), 87; B. F. Huppé, "The A-Text of *Piers Plowman* and the Norman Wars," *PMLA* 54 (1939): 37–55.

58. See William Langland, *Piers Plowman, An Edition of the C-Text,* ed. Derek Pearsall (London: Edward Arnold, 1978), 9, 103.

59. Langland, *Piers Plowman,* A, passus 3, lines 109–11, p. 87.

60. Ibid., lines 173–81, p. 89.

61. Ibid., lines 190–93, pp. 89, 160–61. As part of the terms of the Treaty of Brétigny (1360), Edward was to receive three million gold crowns as ransom for King John II of France.

as long as it is received for valor on the battlefield. Conscience rejoins by describing to the king two types of meed: "God's meed and his mercy," and the worldly meed that magistrates desire. He ends the discussion by retelling the Old Testament story of Saul, who was commanded by God (through Samuel) to make war on Agag of Amalek, but to "covet not his goods." By disobeying he brought disaster on the Israelite nation, a lesson Langland probably hoped was not lost on Edward III. A new age is hoped for, one in which "Kind Wit shall come together with Conscience" and love will reign.[62]

Here passus 3 ends in the A-text. The disapproval lodged against the war effort is hardly veiled, and there is some hint that war itself can be transcended with the ideal world posited at the end. The most significant aspect of the A text section, however, may be the open criticism of Edward III's ruinous French campaign, predicated on the failure to keep the peace as spelled out in the Treaty of Brétigny. Conscience represents the treaty's position, which included Edward's renunciation of his claim to the French throne. His tone regarding the king's "heritage of France" gives it a spurious character when spoken of by Meed. She, always looking for the material reward for herself and her retinue at court, castigates Conscience for robbing others, including the poor French people, who had recently made a down payment on the indemnity at Calais. The resumption of war had led to expensive English defeats, and the king, now under the insidious influence of Alice Perrers, had refused to take personal, active command. One recent study has concluded that not only was Langland "descrediting the war as a greedy and unscrupulous affair," he was also condemning the "policy [including support of Edward's 'just cause'] which Meed and her bought retinue would advocate at court."[63] At this early stage there was already great cynicism over how government policy was made at court. By the next reign, the politics of aristocratic faction and the outcry against royal "flatterers" interested in their own gain led to a severe crisis in government and eventually to the usurpation of the crown itself.

But the skepticism Langland displayed toward Edward's claims in France do not indicate a lack of belief in the just war. Still, he demonstrated how easily kings resort to war and on very shaky foundations, and often with ulterior motives. The story of Saul and Agag is a good example of this. In the A text, there is hope that Edward's heir will correct the mistakes of his

---

62. Ibid., lines 223–24, 245, 272–73, pp. 90–92.

63. Anna P. Baldwin, *The Theme of Government in Piers Plowman* (Cambridge: D. S. Brewer, 1981), 36–37.

father and usher in a period of peace: while Saul refers clearly to Edward, David seems to represent the Black Prince, who "will be crowned and will gain final victory and lasting peace."[64] This exemplary knight holds out the promise for a better future for England in the war if the abuses which characterized the expeditions are eliminated.

In the B text, however, which was completed in the late 1370s, during the reign of Richard II and after the scandals of the Good Parliament (1376), all optimism of this kind is gone. The passus continues from the last line of the A text with fifty-one more lines, adding to the description of the ideal future to come. Langland's hope now rested solely on the coming reign of Christ himself who will usher in a new age. When this happens, and swords are converted into *productive* plowshares, "such love, peace and honesty of life will arise among the people" throughout the world:

> All who bear weapons of war — daggers, broadswords, lances, axes, or hatchets — will be condemned to death unless they have them hammered into sickles and scythes, or coulters, as Scripture says: "They shall turn their swords into ploughshares." Every man will be actively engaged, with plough, pickaxe, or spade, or else spin-ning, or spreading manure on the fields.[65]

Clergy will also concern themselves again with pastoral duties instead of "hunting." One justice will rule throughout the realm. "There will be no more battles; no one will carry arms. And if anyone pays a smith to forge them, he shall be smitten to death with his own blade! As Scripture says: 'Nation shall not lift up sword against nation.'"[66]

For Langland, then, war was a practical and necessary activity, even heralded as good when fought properly and in the interests of peace or justice. Peace itself was an ideal, relegated to the millennium, along with an end to all other human miseries. His attack on war is limited to how it is prosecuted and the motives behind it. Honor should not be sacrificed, hence the criticism of Edward's renunciation of his claim to the French throne. But like Gower, he held that the effects of war on the people and

---

64. Huppé, *"Piers Plowman,"* 44–54.

65. William Langland, *Piers Plowman: A New Translation of the B-Text,* trans. A.V.C. Schmidt (Oxford: Oxford University Press, 1992), 32; Cottle, *Triumph of English,* 66–68.

66. Langland, *Piers Plowman,* B, 32–33. This "peace" coda found in the B-text is included also in the C-text, which was completed by 1387. Langland, *Piers Plowman,* C, passus 3, lines 453–98, pp. 84–87, 142.

the hardships they endure must also be taken into account, and thus, that war should not be prolonged. A strong, effective foreign policy, therefore, was needed. The implication that theory alone cannot justify a war was founded on this heartfelt belief that war was in no sense a noble activity, if only because one must be sensitive to its reality, that is, the destruction it causes, a condition which became impossible to ignore after the post-1367 defeats. This lower-order cleric passionately desired a powerful, Christian monarch who would introduce lasting peace into England (and Europe), but unlike similar hopes detected in Dante or Marsilius, he and his English contemporaries framed theirs around particular political, social, and economic exigencies of the time, eschewing broader, more theoretical formulations.

Langland understood war to be a societal illness rooted in individual sinfulness; and because he found that ideal societies cannot be created in the premillennial age, the poem is truly pessimistic about any reform occurring before Christ's return and the defeat of the Antichrist. Chaucer, who also believed war to be a consequence of personal sin, differed from Langland by holding out some hope for regeneration. This outlook is readily evident in his "Tale of Melibeus," which is a sweeping indictment of war, and the only complete story in *The Canterbury Tales* related by the author himself, Geoffrey the pilgrim. The tale is based on a French version of Albertanus of Brescia's thirteenth-century *Liber consolationes et consilii,* which had been translated into many vernacular languages, testifying to its popularity.[67] Chaucer probably wrote it intentionally to throw in his lot with Langland's and Gower's opposition to Richard II's war and its "perversion of justice."[68] A friend of Gower's who was ransomed after his capture during the expedition of 1359–60, Chaucer did not reveal directly his views regarding the war. Although he appears to have been a silent supporter of Richard's pacifist policy early on, he nevertheless had to be careful in his criticisms, for as a minor government official political involvements had most likely already cost him several promotions.[69] Chaucer

67. Renaud de Louen, *Le Livre de Mellibee et Prudence,* in *Sources and Analogues of Chaucer's Canterbury Tales,* ed. W. F. Bryan and Germaine Dempster (New York: Humanities Press, 1958), 568–614.

68. William W. Lawrence, "The Tale of Melibeus," in *Essays and Studies in Honor of Carleton Brown* (New York: New York University Press, 1940), 100–110.

69. Because of his association with Sir Simon Burley's "court party" Chaucer may have lost two controllerships of customs at the time of the 1386 baronial purge. Being a court poet also made him necessarily more cautious in expressing political views. Barnie, *War in Medieval English Society,* 132–33; Cottle, *Triumph of English,* 71–75.

became involved in negotiating peace treaties and trade pacts later in his career, though to what extent is still a mystery.[70] A growing sense of disillusionment with his king, however, may have led him to resurrect a story that, with adaptations, bore striking parallels to the Ricardian government of his day. For this reason, it is worthwhile to look at the story in detail, keeping in mind that in all of *The Canterbury Tales,* this is the only one told by Chaucer himself.

Most of the "Tale" revolves around the question of whether Melibeus should go to war against three "old foes" who came to his home one day while he was in the field, beat his wife Prudence and severely wounded his daughter Sophie. Calling his friends together for advice, the older and wiser professional men (surgeons, physicians, and lawyers) advise him to avoid war or at least to take time to consider seriously such an action.[71] The "young fold," however, scorn this advice and exhort Melibeus

> that while the iron is hot men should strike, rightly so, for men should right wrongs done to them while they are fresh and new. And so with loud voices they cried, "war! war!"

One old man then offers his experienced insight:

> My lords, there are many men who cry "war! war!" that know full little what war amounts to. . . . But once war begins there are many children . . . that shall starve while young because of the war, or else they will live in sorrow and die in wretchedness. Therefore before they start any war men must take great counsel and deliberation.

The opposition cuts him off, and since the majority counsels war, this is the plan adopted by Melibeus.

At this point Prudence speaks up and warns against acting too hastily. After a philosophical discussion with Melibeus about taking advice from women, she offers her own view of what constitutes good counsel, emphasizing that "it is no folly to change counsel when the thing is changed, or else when the thing seems otherwise than it was before."[72] She advises that

---

70. V. J. Scattergood, "Chaucer and the French War: *Sir Thopas* and *Melibee,*" in *Court and Poet: Selected Proceedings of the Third Congress of the International Courtly Literature Society (Liverpool 1980),* ed. Glyn S. Burgess (Liverpool, Eng.: Francis Cairns, 1981), 294.

71. Geoffrey Chaucer, "The Tale of Melibeus," in *The Canterbury Tales,* in *The Complete Works of Geoffrey Chaucer,* ed. Walter W. Skeat (London: Oxford University Press, 1931), 505–7.

72. Ibid., 508–10.

in choosing his own counselors Melibeus should first "meekly beseech the Most High God that He will be your consellor," and then that the others be "without ire," while avoiding flatterers. She tells him further that his present council includes too many "strange folk, and young folk, false flatterers, and enemies reconciled, and those that show you reverence without love."

Melibeus's wife then turns to the all-important topic of war. She argues like the physicians that "vengeance is not conquered by another vengeance," "but certainly, wickedness shall be conquered by goodness, discord by accord, war by peace. . . . You shall understand that the vengeance you propose is of great consequence," in that it will bring retaliation and war, and "damages without number, of which we are not aware at this time."[73] Noting Cicero's wisdom and patience, Prudence asks her husband if his vengeance is not merely willfulness, a carnal desire to fight for material goods and family. The Roman authority cautioned against battle, believing that love for others is a trait that cannot be stolen, needs no defense, and by promoting forgiveness and compassion precludes appeals to just causes and "proper authority." Prudence contends that the crime against Sophie was due to Melibeus's neglect of Christ and that he has not defended himself adequately against the three enemies of flesh, fiend, and world. Melibeus agrees finally, especially since vengeance can harm good men, but still worries that if none is taken then the perpetrators will continue in their crimes. Here Prudence counsels patience once again and blames her husband for being too concerned with his wealth. For by trusting in riches "you would stir up war and battle. I counsel you to begin no war to keep your riches, for they are not worth wars to maintain," since no man is ever satisfied with what he has. Prudence concludes: "For there is great peril in war, therefore a man should flee and eschew war, as much as is possible."[74]

Taking his wife's advice to make peace, Melibeus still hesitates, asserting that since they are guilty, his adversaries should make the first move. But Prudence quotes Solomon: "For while another man causes dissension reconciliation begins with yourself." She calls the three foes together and "wisely shows them the great good that comes from peace and the great harm and perils that accompany war." Shocked and moved, they respond

73. Ibid., 510–18.
74. Ibid., 517–25.

favorably to her desire for peace and ask for "mercy and pity." Melibeus, however, still wants to disinherit them of their possessions and banish them forever. Prudence asks him to appeal to reason, for such an action would be perceived as covetousness. Finally, he completely forgives them and outwardly hopes that his example will be repeated in many other places, declaring that all men are sinners but that God is merciful.[75]

The issues discussed in this story are timeless and clearly applicable to the political and military situation under Richard II. Ever since the resumption of hostilities following the breakdown of the Treaty of Brétigny in the late 1360s, the Hundred Years War had become utterly ruinous for England. Most of the French territory was lost, and nearly every military expedition had met with failure. Chaucer was giving voice to this jaded feeling, probably found among many of the English, through the old man's complaint that those who cry for war do so with no understanding of the tragedy that can result. Furthermore, in Prudence's challenge to her husband that he choose counselors who are godly, older, friends (not former enemies), without anger (not predisposed toward war), and not flatterers, Chaucer was definitely describing the Ricardian court and remarking possibly on the youth of the king himself. In addition, Prudence's admonition that changing events and perspectives should encourage one to seek different counsel, could possibly be the author's way of questioning the motive behind the Hundred Years War in the 1380s and 1390s.[76]

Prudence's real-life ally for peace would have been Michael de la Pole, the earl of Suffolk, who shaped England's peace policy after 1384, between the time of the disastrous Norwich Crusade of the previous year and Richard's resumption of nominal control after recovering power from the Gloucester faction in 1389. As the king's favorite and before his ouster in 1388, Suffolk had worked for a permanent peace with France, which he declared in a speech at the opening of Parliament in 1384. But de la Pole was unable to convince Parliament that the threat of French invasion (which lasted well into 1385) was nonexistent. Chroniclers, such as Thomas Walsingham, record that in 1387 Richard wanted to return to France all Continental holdings. Sensing the growing sentiment for this position, Gloucester arranged a three-year truce with France beginning in 1389, which the king later renewed for four additional years. After his

75. Ibid., 525–29.

76. Gardiner Stillwell, "The Political Meaning of Chaucer's *Tale of Melibee*," *Speculum* 19 (1944): 433–37.

marriage to the seven-year-old French princess Isabella in 1396, Richard believed that peace with France would become permanent.[77]

Chaucer seems to have been part of the royal faction at this time and was clearly in favor when Richard's party was ascendant. Yet he was critical of the king's choice of young and inexperienced counsel, which he saw as responsible for the ultimate failure of the sincere efforts at peace. The king appeared to be in over his head and was thus unable to take charge of a conflict that had spread its destruction over a large territory, even if he did want peace. Chaucer's version of "The Tale of Melibeus" is fascinating for its suggestion that peace must come from a private ethic of selflessness toward one's fellow beings. Melibeus may represent the king in this instance or he may represent the nobles who were ultimately the ones engaging in war and ready to take up arms in private acts of vengeance. And in using the more expansive term — war — the author would not permit a violent act of retribution even if the wronged party had a right to it.

Lynn Staley Johnson has offered the possibility that in the "Tale of Melibeus" Chaucer was constructing a "reversed hierarchy" that "signals a shift from strict justice and the harsh laws of war to merciful adjudication and diplomacy." In doing so, Chaucer hoped to awaken Richard II to his primary responsibility as king, of ensuring peace and domestic harmony, which meant working within established institutions of government, including Parliament and the council of nobles. Richard's abandonment of Westminster in 1387 on the eve of the Merciless Parliament was an abdication of proper rule and verged on a declaration of war against the nation. In this tale, then, Chaucer may have been condemning two wars: the one between England and France, and the one between England and the king. Chaucer admired Richard's desire for international peace but found him working at cross-purposes in sowing seeds of strife within the realm itself. Since we have stated that the restoration of concord and tranquillity were major components of the medieval peace idea, it is no surprise that these two configurations operate in tandem in Chaucer's critique of the political and military situation of his day and demonstrate how that aspect was still the overriding emphasis in a post-plague England, where economic recovery was still insufficient to make commercial considerations paramount.[78]

In "The Tale of Melibeus," Chaucer created the strongest challenge yet to war in his day. He appealed to considerations for the public well-being

77. Ibid., 437–38.

78. Lynn Staley Johnson, "Inverse Counsel: Contexts for the *Melibee*," *Studies in Philology* 87 (1992): 137–45.

(like Gower and Langland) and agreed that wars produce economic and political disarray; but by questioning the relevancy of just causes he went much further. The ability of war to redress material wrongs is no longer beneficial enough to compensate for the destruction (spiritual and material) it may bring in its wake.[79]

"The Tale of Melibeus" measures Chaucer's overall attitude toward war. There are, however, other parts of *The Canterbury Tales* that provide vivid portrayals of war's perpetrators, the knights. A lively debate has taken place over the past several years concerning the extent of Chaucer's antiwar position. Much of the disagreement centers around the image of the knight in both the prologue and "The Knight's Tale," and what message Chaucer may have intended by making him less than the epitome of chivalry. The most thorough evaluation of "The Knight's Tale" is found in Terry Jones's *Chaucer's Knight: The Portrait of a Medieval Mercenary* (1980), which rejects the traditional view of the tale as a "courtly, philosophic romance" in which the knight is "an idealized Christian warrior." He counters that Chaucer's mercenary soldier only "pretends to the dignity of knighthood," basing much of this conclusion on the status of mercenaries in the fourteenth century, the author's inclusion of "The Tale of Melibeus" in *The Canterbury Tales,* and the discrepancy between the tale and the original story—Boccaccio's *Teseida*—upon which it is based.[80]

While historians have found much to recommend in this understanding of Chaucer's knight (especially in the context of his other antiwar leanings), Elizabeth Porter, in a 1983 article, argued for a return to the original position. Much of her evidence is forced, however, such as when she uses his poetical descriptions of brutality in war as tacit approval for such behavior. She claims that neither "The Tale of Melibeus" nor Gower's "Address" on Henry IV's accession can be construed as "pacifist in the modern sense of the word" and should therefore not be read as antiwar statements.[81] Her logic is flawed in that it creates an either/or interpretation of these works on the position of war and peace. A fuller reading of what they wrote does indicate "a war-weariness and disquiet felt by men who could see no end to the conflict between England and France," but this tentative position soon expanded into a more extensive critique of war. They ac-

79. Yeager, *"Pax Poetica,"* 117–21.
80. Terry Jones, *Chaucer's Knight: The Portrait of a Medieval Mercenary* (Baton Rouge: Louisiana State University Press, 1980), 141–47.
81. Elizabeth Porter, "Chaucer's Knight, the *Alliterative Morte Arthure,* and Medieval Laws of War: A Reconsideration," *Nottingham Medieval Studies* 27 (1983): 57, 63, 77–78.

cepted the just war but much of their complete body of work suggests a
deep cynicism about its application. The concept's current usage appeared
more and more contrary to their understanding of Christian morality.
Much more likely is Maurice Keen's suggestion that Chaucer's character
was idealized in the hope that real knights would aspire to his example.[82]
But even this understanding seems to skirt the full weight of Chaucer's
writing on the subject.

Let me turn to two other examples in *The Canterbury Tales* that support
the contention that Chaucer parodied chivalry and held to strong antiwar
views. First, in "The Parson's Tale" when the parson sermonizes on one of
the seven deadly sins, anger, he preaches that

> Of Ire comes these stinking products: first hate, that is old wrath;
> discord, through which many a man forsakes his old friend that he
> had loved a long time. And then comes war, and every manner of
> wrong a man can do to his neighbors, in body or in cattle. Of this
> cursed sin of Ire comes all manslaughter.[83]

Once again, personal behavior has consequences that, with only slight hy-
perbole, can lead to unfathomed societal turmoil and sin. Here, in the last
tale before going into his retraction, Chaucer made no apologies for any
kind of violence, seeming to insist that only by *patientia* can adversaries be
overcome, using Christ as a model of long-suffering and forgiveness.[84]

The other example is less direct but in its own way very telling about
Chaucer's criticism of late fourteenth-century knighthood. Just before
going into "The Tale of Melibeus," the author begins "The Tale of Sir
Thopas"; but after only a few lines he breaks it off because the story is
tedious and "doggerel rhyme."[85] Sir Thopas is a Flemish knight who embodies to absurdity the chivalric ideal of Chaucer's day. His exaggerated
sense of honorable and noble conduct, through an extreme asceticism, en-
hances a myth that can be ridiculed easily.[86] It is no accident that the paci-

82. Maurice Keen, "Chaucer's Knight, the English Aristocracy and the Crusade," in *En-glish Court Culture in the Later Middle Ages,* ed. V. J. Scattergood and J. W. Sherborne (New York: St. Martin's Press, 1983), 45–61.

83. Chaucer, "The Parson's Tale," in *The Canterbury Tales,* 694.

84. Karl Heinz Göller, "War and Peace in the Middle English Romances and Chaucer," in McGuire, *War and Peace in the Middle Ages,* 137.

85. Chaucer, "The Tale of Sir Thopas," in *The Canterbury Tales,* lines 2099–2108, p. 504.

86. Ramsey, *Chivalric Romances,* 210–13.

fist Dame Prudence follows this aborted attempt at a good, old-fashioned chivalric romance.

A final argument for Chaucer's incipient animus against chivalric pretensions stems from his translation of Boethius's *Consolation of Philosophy,* which he never retracted and which he thanked God for allowing him to complete. In this work Chaucer added "pacifist" commentary in Metre 5 of Book 2, castigating excessive chivalric behavior that goes to wars to avenge wrongs when it is clear that no "rewards come from bloodshed."[87]

Recently a few scholars have wondered if perhaps there is not a much more thoroughgoing pacifism to be found in Chaucer.[88] Their point of departure is the linguistic similarity between the authorial voice of the "Thopas-Melibeus" pair and Chaucer's "Retraction" at the end of the *Canterbury Tales.* Only in these sections is the writer speaking directly to the reader, using the first person, and only here are the deeply personal themes of guilt and need for forgiveness so paramount. In "Melibeus" Prudence asks her husband to forgive his enemies in order to prevent war, and Chaucer himself seeks God's forgiveness as he reflects on his own past actions and works "of worldly vanitees." In addition, the author added to "Melibeus" pacifist language missing in Albertanus's original story. How else might someone in Chaucer's position best include in his works thoughts that "weighed heavily on him," when the political climate made more overt expression imprudent or even dangerous? Whether or not this evidence is enough to imply that Chaucer was "a man of peace by inclination," who rejected war more out of personal disposition rather than observed abuses (as Gower did), there is little doubt that he rejected war from an ethical standpoint and viewed it as a manifestation of gross human sin.[89]

Without a doubt, then, the three best known and talented poets of fourteenth-century England — Gower, Langland, and Chaucer — all spoke out forcefully against a conflict that had stretched the entire course of their lives: the Hundred Years War. Their cultural milieu witnessed a widespread erosion of support for the war, especially after 1360, for which they served as a voice and a clarion.[90] It would be wrong to picture any of them as

87. Chaucer, *Consolation of Philosophy,* bk. 2, metre 5, lines 24–32, in *Complete Works,* 149; Göller, "War and Peace," 132.
88. Yeager, *"Pax Poetica,"* 108–21; Göller, "War and Peace," 131–45.
89. Yeager, *"Pax Poetica,"* 117–21.
90. Barnie, *War in Medieval English Society,* 117–20.

pacifist in the modern sense, since they made no indiscriminate judgment from which they could not retreat, although Gower and Chaucer came perilously close to condemning the practice of war outright. But most of the English literati who complained about the Hundred Years War were still bound by the moral conventions of their day, which accepted war as a flawed but necessary response to sin. These three, however, put that commonplace to the test by trying the French war and the elites who made it in the court of Christian principle. Langland retained a millennial hope that once Christ returned and defeated the forces of evil, He would usher in an age when peace reigned; and Chaucer was nearly as idealistic in believing that human nature could be so forgiving of wrongs perpetrated. In both cases, peace was just beginning to be understood as a possibly permanent solution to the problem of war. Because they found true peace to be merely a repository for changed individual attitudes, however, their ability to conceptualize it into a policy or realizable societal condition would be necessarily limited.

4

PEACE DISCOURSE DURING THE HUNDRED YEARS WAR

Clerical and Later Literary Responses

The Christian outlook that each writer has projected so far onto the subject of war is no coincidence in a time when religion permeated every aspect of society. The Church was more than a handmaiden to a bellicose crown. While much of the upper clergy supported the French war, rumblings of opposition were heard by the late fourteenth century. Indeed, there is every possibility that most of the parish clergy (especially those in lowest orders, such as Langland perhaps) were very critical of the war, if only for financial reasons. The disapproval among the more learned and beneficed, however, tended to be ideological and philosophical; and what is most curious is that both orthodox and heretical opinion on the matter was very similar.

As discussed in Chapter 2, it is difficult to fathom fully the social alignments that produced either cooperation with the war effort or bitter opposition to it. Many of the attacks on warfare were directed against the pope's encouragement of the French war and what was assumed to be his support of the enemy. But more deeply, there was a growing resentment among many English people (and clergy) against the rampant materialism among some ecclesiastics and their violent means for obtaining greater wealth, all of which tarred the Church with a warring character lacking any moral basis. As a result, contemplating peace became a more focused activity, as remedies for relief naturally would have to explore the full range of peaceful alternatives.

Orthodox Clerical Contributions

The virulent anticlerical mood of the fourteenth century has been well covered. The ingredients go beyond differing political objectives among nationalist and papal interests, although they must not be viewed in isolation from them. The bulk of the war's costs were falling unduly on the commoners, and as the costs became heavier, questions arose over whether the clergy or lay lords were paying their fair share. The rebels of 1381 clearly believed the poll tax was only another device to protect the wealthy. Factions developed among the clergy over who had the right to tax them, king or pope. Friars supported the crown "as long as they could channel the consequences against the endowed clergy and away from themselves." By the 1370s the battle lines were drawn; and satire against friars and debates over the theory of dominion made for some pretty strange bedfellows. Both the archbishop of Armagh Richard Fitzralph, one of the leading churchmen in Britain, and Wyclif sided more with the secular clergy and attacked the friars for their presumptuous claims. As Fitzralph defined it, "all dominion rests on divine grace. Those not in a state of grace, because of sin, have no dominion." To assert dominion one must own the property over which to exercise it. By professing poverty the mendicants-friars are not involved in pastoral care, since this is a "form of civil lordship," and therefore should not claim any jurisdictional or property rights.[1] This clerical dominion debate raged throughout the 1370s and 1380s. Uthred of Boldon, a Benedictine, was the chief defender of the monks against attacks by the secular clergy, but his entanglements in papal politics and tributes hurt his credibility and forced fellow Benedictines, like Adam Easton and Thomas Brinton, also to get involved in defending the regulars.[2]

The net effect of these celebrated controversies over clerical dominion and possession fanned the flames of both governmental and popular anti-clericalism as the Church seemed clearly at odds with what many believed

1. Katherine Walsh, *A Fourteenth Century Scholar and Primate: Richard Fitzralph in Oxford, Avignon and Armagh* (Oxford: Clarendon Press, 1981), 377–406.
2. Wendy Scase, *"Piers Plowman" and the New Anti-clericalism* (Cambridge: Cambridge University Press, 1989), 6–7, 11–12, 19.

to be its rightful spiritual and pastoral role. The Lollard Nicholas Hereford summarized much current opinion when he delivered his famous, condemnatory Ascension Day sermon at Oxford in 1382, at the chancellor Robert Rygge's request. Hereford took up Wyclif's recent attacks when he denounced the greed for material goods exhibited by the whole of the clergy, possessioners and friars alike—all to the detriment of the poor commons. A few years earlier, in 1376, Brinton had pleaded with his fellow bishops to become voices for reform by putting aside their ambition and covetousness.[3] Post-plague England was witnessing an unprecedented number of individuals and movements calling for reform and deeper spirituality. Many openly blamed the Church for the succession of disasters that had befallen them, including war. Such misgivings did not lead to heresy for most people, but rather to a number of sincere exhortations to peace and love among Christian peoples on both sides of the Channel. Evidence also suggests that like the literary moralists renowned churchmen took it upon themselves to act as spokesmen for the disadvantaged victims of incessant war. Both Brinton, as bishop of Rochester, and Fitzralph were alarmed at the voracious appetite for violence with which their lay contemporaries went into battle. By insisting that Christian morality be heeded here, perhaps they, and others like them, hoped to regain respect for their offices by becoming an ethical voice for the nation. Much of their rhetoric tends in that protonationalist direction, where the soul of England itself appears at stake. Returning companies of soldiers were sometimes "hired" by local lords to help them intimidate "shire and hundred courts, sheriffs and even royal justices." The great age of livery and maintenance was about to begin, as private armies of retainers attached to powerful nobles insisted on having their way in local areas, to the great consternation of the inhabitants.[4] The pulpit could be a powerful voice of chastisement and reform amid such conditions, and there is evidence that some priests and bishops took this pastoral role most seriously.

A number of years ago G. R. Owst presented evidence that "pulpit denunciations" against prevailing injustices provoked vocal dissatisfaction or even revolt against current social conditions. He may have exaggerated their influence when one considers the pervasive cries for reform that are

3. Anne Hudson, "Wycliffism in Oxford, 1381–1411," in *Wyclif in His Times,* ed. Anthony Kenny (Oxford: Clarendon Press, 1986), 69–70; Thomas Brinton, *The Sermons of Thomas Brinton, Bishop of Rochester (1373–89),* ed. M. A. Devlin, Camden Society, 3d ser., vol. 75 (London: Royal Historical Society, 1954), 2:315–21 (Sermon 69).

4. Anthony Steel, *Richard II* (Cambridge: The University Press, 1962), 168.

common to most sermons. But just because the famous couplet echoed during the 1381 revolt—"When Adam delved and Eve span / Who was then the gentleman"—was a commonplace that can be found in fourteenth-century literature, including the works of Brinton and the Dominican John Bromyard, does not mean it was inconsequential. What is more certain, however, is that these preachers attacked all forms of clerical and noble vice. That they may have believed they were the voice of the people is further suggested in their singling out those classes most condemned during the revolt, including bishops, monks, greedy nobles, and war profiteers.[5]

All that said, it may be that a more modest explanation is in order for what united a wide range of churchmen against certain or all aspects of the conflict with France. Brinton, Bromyard, Fitzralph, Wyclif, and lesser-known priests simply may have been proclaiming their own personal distaste for the Hundred Years War and were willing to use whatever means at their disposal to broadcast their opinions. While this may not have been their only motive, the passion with which they preached against the war at times could easily lead one to make that assumption; and if we keep in mind the nature of the war, such views had to have been popular ones by the 1380s. Conflict with the warring nobility, then, could have been inspired by any one of a number of reasons, from lust for social and political power, or wealth, to a desire for moral uplift and overall stability, as well as economic differences and considerations. But in the end it may be conscience that played the greatest role.

How did the clergy explain the degeneration of the present war into uninhibited killing sprees and greedy quests for plunder? A look at some contemporary homilies, sermons, and injunctions support the medieval commonplace that characterized social sin as an extension of personal vice, much like in Chaucer's "Tale of Melibeus." In a late medieval homily book, expanded from the *Ayenbite of Inwyt*,[6] there is a typically medieval description of how personal dispositions can lead to tragic endings:

> When the fiend [Satan] sees love and peace among good men, he has thereto much envy and does all that he can or may, and with the fury of ire he stirs their hearts to discord and strife.

5. Ibid., 71–74; G. R. Owst, *Literature and the Pulpit in Medieval England,* 2d ed. (Oxford: Basil Blackwell, 1961), passim.

6. Written by Dan Michel of Northgate in 1340, this work is mostly a translation of the French treatise, *Le Somme de vices et de vertues* (1279).

Strife leads to chiding and then disdain, which incurs

> cursings and threatenings, which stir men's hearts to ire so that
> melées and wars begin among them and do not cease until the ton
> of them are avenged of the other.[7]

Without reading too much significance into these words—which echo
Chaucer's Prudence—their appearance in a book of worship may indicate
that the English church was sensitive to the potential for great sin in wars
as they were currently being launched and fought. If so, the movement
away from only official prayers for victory in war, which had served as a
major function of the medieval church, surely has some roots in the growing tide of clerical sentiment against the Hundred Years War. As early as
1346, Fitzralph, then archbishop-elect of Armagh (and close friend of de
Bury), preached a sermon in London concerning the conflict. He exhorted
the people to pray for the king's person, that he receive "prudent and sane
counsel," and "that he may obtain a just and happy issue" in his military
campaigns. This may all sound rather predictable but Fitzralph's independent mind is demonstrated as he goes on:

> Wherefore men pray improvidently that he [the king] may over-
> come his enemies, and also slay in battle. For those who pray thus
> in their praying offend God, in acting contrary to his command—
> 'Thou shalt love thy neighbour as thyself' (Matt. 22) . . . . They
> hinder the king, withdrawing from him their *spiritual* petitions.

To pray that God would "pour out the blood of their adversaries" violates
the way of prayer, which tells us "that each shall seek and pray for *all* men
that which they would desire to be done to them by others."[8] Fitzralph
underscored the persistent stigma that existed in the English church with
regard to killing in combat. To pray for bloodshed against your enemy is
to disobey God's command that each person love his or her neighbor, even
if circumstances made bearing the sword permissible when sanctioned by a
just cause. By declaring further on in the sermon that it is even wrong to
pray for any victory in battle, the archbishop-elect was disavowing just

---

7. Owst, *Literature and the Pulpit*, 458–59.
8. Landsdowne MS 393, fol. 26b, 48; Aubrey Gwynn, "The Sermon-Diary of Richard
FitzRalph, Archbishop of Armagh," *Proceedings of the Royal Irish Academy* 44, sec. C
(1937–38): 22–32; Owst, *Preaching in Medieval England,* 203–4.

those procedures that the crown had built up and depended on to gather support for its war policies:

> But prayer is to be made that [the king] may obtain a just peace, that we . . . may live a quiet and tranquil life, . . . and that so we may live piously and chastely. . . . And indeed less learned men often err greatly when they pray for the king and his nobles, demanding from God that he give them corporal triumph in battle over their foes.[9]

Despite the challenge inherent in this statement, Fitzralph hedged and proved he was ever the loyal Englishman when he concluded with an acceptance of war's place in society and the need to pray for the armies involved (but again, not for victory): "The Law of Nature requires that we pray for the king, and also support our troops — *in facultatibus;* for he is the protector and defender of the people." And he declared the French war to be a just one, not only because it was not an offensive war, but also because England and France were really one kingdom.[10] As already seen, Fitzralph was a leading exponent of dominion theory, which held that only rulers in a state of grace were true authorities. Although he himself was completely loyal to the crown, such ideas clearly undercut a crucial foundation of just-war theory — proper authority. In fact, the archbishop-elect had great difficulty "in reconciling the patriotic sentiments . . . with his own calling as a priest and preacher."[11] Being concerned primarily, however, with the spiritual welfare of those involved in conflicts, as well as of those urging war and victory, Fitzralph was able to confine his criticisms of war to the spiritual level.. He neither evaluated specific campaigns nor left himself open to a charge of disloyalty.[12]

Thomas Brinton, bishop of Rochester from 1373 to 1389, was another fourteenth-century critic of war, who while much more outspoken than Fitzralph, was careful to couch his peace rhetoric in personal and spiritual terms. A former Benedictine monk at Norwich, he became royal confessor

9. Aubrey Gwynn, "Richard Fitzralph. Part III," *Studies* 23 (1934): 404; Owst, *Preaching in Medieval England,* 204.

10. Owst, *Preaching in Medieval England,* 204.

11. Walsh, *Fourteenth Century Scholar,* 228–30, 251.

12. Fitzralph preached two other sermons between 1346 and 1347 that dealt with the French war, and which came on the heels of the victory at Crécy. He elucidated in these the same position by calling on parishioners to pray for a happy conclusion to the war and not for the shedding of blood. See Gwynn, "FitzRalph, Part III," 404–5, and Walsh, *Fourteenth Century Scholar,* 251.

and gave Richard's coronation sermon. He was one of the four bishops selected to counsel the knights of the shires in 1376. Brinton enjoyed the wide respect accorded few others of his profession, even among lower-order clergy like Langland. The latter lived near St. Paul's in London and attended regularly the sermons delivered at the outdoor pulpit at Paul's Cross where Brinton often preached. There are striking similarities between the two men. In the B text of *Piers Plowman* Langland incorporated verbatim parts of Brinton's sermons, including large portions from one he gave on 18 May 1376 introducing the "rat parliament," and against Alice Perrers. Both men encouraged the public to express its discontent with national policy during the crisis of the Good Parliament in 1376. And on the issue of the war, each had a great deal to say about the corruption and class-based greed with which it was riddled.[13]

While Brinton accepted the chivalric law of arms in theory, he blamed its ineffectiveness on the violations of its membership. Criticisms of this kind often had an impact that went beyond the original intent of the author. In this case, as the reprehensible behavior of knights was catalogued and the ideal restated, some could assume that properly fought wars were a practical impossibility. The critical words, therefore, of medieval preachers were especially vulnerable to a more inflammatory interpretation than perhaps originally intended by those among the commons who opposed the war.

Brinton and some of his contemporaries did make it difficult to believe that scrupulous circumstances in practice could be met and honorable wars fought. In 1374 he preached in favor of the traditional, chivalrous knights, whose origins he traced to ancient Rome. He deemed their calling a high one involving much labor because of their oath to obey their lord, to "never desert the field, to protect the life of princes, and not to refuse death for the common weal." The knight should also show respect to the clergy, "maintain peace and order, shed blood for his fellow-countrymen in time of need, injure no man's property, and live of his own."[14] In 1378, after the death of Edward III, Brinton delivered several sermons on the lamentable state of a kingdom reduced to poverty and susceptible, through defeats in war, to foreign control of the Church. The theme of peace as an alternative way of life formed the basis of at least two of these sermons.

---

13. Brinton, *Sermons*, 1:xxi–xxxi; Sermon 69, 2:315–21; Steel, *Richard II*, 30–31. Brinton borrowed a great deal from John Bromyard's *Summa praedicantium* also in this sermon, especially from "Ordo clericalis" and "Dominatio."

14. Brinton, *Sermons*, 1:167–68; Barnie, *War in Medieval English Society*, 121.

Brinton continued to bewail humanity's sins, which he determines to be the only cause of war — transgressions that can be atoned for by living like Christ, who came to bring peace among people as well as with God.[15] In the sermon, *Pax vobis,* taken from John 20, the bishop quoted many New Testament passages demonstrating that it is God's intent that Christ bring peace, ending with the benediction from Philippians 4:7: "'And the Peace of God, superior to all knowledge, tends our hearts and minds' so that temporal and eternal peace are finally attained."[16]

The following year, in another sermon, an anonymous preacher echoed these sentiments of Fitzralph and Brinton in admonishing the people to pray for those besieged in Brittany, not that the war would be won but that peace would result, regardless of how it comes about:

> But, I pray you, who shall go to pray for peace? Truly, Christian
> men, I see three things that God has taken great vengeance on; and
> if we will look to this land of England this time, I fear that these
> three sins are overmuch reigning. But what is the cause that we
> have no peace these days, no peace as we were wont to have? Cer-
> tainly sin is the cause; for whereas this land was once full of good-
> ness and holiness in living, now this goodness has grown into great
> malice and shrewdness, and holiness has turned into sinful wretch-
> edness.[17]

As was typical of medieval prelates, wars were understood as God's scourge for a nation's sins. In the case of Brinton and the preacher, the English did not necessarily have a just cause for fighting; they were being forced into combat because they had turned away from righteous living. If pressed, both of them probably would have tendered a very loyal acknowl-edgment of Edward's (or Richard's) claim to the French throne, but their

15. Brinton, *Sermons,* Sermon 60, *De sancta Maria Magdalena* (22 July 1375). See also Sermon 7, *Uno ore honorificetis. Ad Romanos 19* on the "beauty of peace" (1:16–17).

16. Ibid., Sermon 73, *Pax vobis* (Spring 1378), 2:336–39. Cf. Sermon 70, which follows up the archbishop of Canterbury's request for prayers for peace in 1376 (2:322–26); David Wilkins, ed., *Concilia Magnae Britanniae et Hiberniae, a Syndodo Verolamiense,* A.D. *446–1717* (London, 1737), 3:100.

17. Royal MS 18 B, xxiii, fols. 123b–126; Woodburn O. Ross, ed., *Middle English Sermons,* EETS OS, no. 209 (London: Humphrey Milford, Oxford University Press, 1940), 212; Owst, *Preaching in Medieval England,* 205–6; C. T. Allmand, "The War and the Non-Combatant," in *The Hundred Years War,* ed. Kenneth Fowler (London: Macmillan, 1971): 175–76. This sermon, "Sermo pro pace," was delivered in English "by a good and stirring preacher of God's Word" and is based on the text "Quis ibit ad rogandum pro pace?" found in Jeremiah 15:5.

rhetoric could have been easily heard another way. As would be the case right up into the sixteenth century, to blame wars on this kind of reasoning is to view them as punishment and to undermine further their legitimacy by those claiming just cause. The alternative of peace is steadily becoming an overwhelming preoccupation, but in the fourteenth century it is still unable to stand on its own without at least some martial encasement.

A final example of contemporary orthodox opinion expressed against the war is found in the ambitious and well-respected *Summa prædicantium* (Notes for preachers) of Dominican John Bromyard. This work is divided into many topics to assist preachers in preparing sermons. The issue of war comes up under the sections "Lex," "Nobilitas," "Militia," "Pax," and "Bellum," and in each case, the author offered a caustic attack on late medieval warfare. Bromyard found much wrong with war in all of Europe, from the Guelf-Ghibelline struggle in Italy to the role played by mercenaries in the French war. While not a pacifist, he was perhaps, excepting Wyclif, the harshest critic of war in his day.[18]

Bromyard's exhaustive treatment of the subject may be what is most exceptional about it. At one point he bemoaned the neglect of knights toward their true profession and the consequent increase in the power of heathen nations:

> For battles have been raised well nigh in every land of Christendom with the shedding of Christian blood continually, great and huge. . . . The lordships of Christian men decrease and go downward, and the lordships of heathen men grow upward and increase.[19]

Comparing himself to a prophet, like Brinton he called on the English to forsake their sins, especially the plundering by soldiers, since, as a result, all virtue has been destroyed. Bromyard credited the popular admiration for "Charlemagne, Roland, Oliver and other knights of antiquity" and participation in tournaments for the degeneracy of knighthood into an overwhelming predilection for bloodshed. He then claimed that as soon as knights are dubbed they immediately turn against their vows to protect the Church, uphold true religion, avenge evildoers, and protect the poor:

18. "Bellum," "Lex," "Militia," "Nobilitas," and "Pax," in John Bromyard, *Summa prædicantium* (Venice: Dominicum Nicolinum, 1586), 1:92–100, 410–44; 2:23–26, 107–11, 191–201; Allmand, "War and the Non-Combatant," 176; Allmand, *Society at War,* 38; Owst, *Literature and the Pulpit,* 174.

19. Royal MS 18 B, xxiii, fol. 139; Owst, *Literature and the Pulpit,* 330–31.

For to-day, as soon as they are decorated with the belt of knight-hood, they rise up against their fellow Christians, rage violently against the Patrimony of Christ, plunder and spoil the poor subject to them, afflict the wretched pitiably and pitilessly, and fulfill their extravagant wills and lusts.

These soldiers march and have their fun not at the king's or their own expense "but at the expense of the churches and poor, whom they spoil in their path," such that they "seemed to be going to a feast rather than to war."[20]

The most unusual of Bromyard's broadsides is his sharp renunciation of the nationalist sentiment he astutely perceived to be growing during the war. He called nationalists "citizens of the Devil's State," who "divide others from them on the score of country, race or language, provoking them in an attitude of wrath and tumult," and who contradict the Scrip-ture, which declares that in Christ there is no Jew nor Greek:

For we bid and pray each day in holy church — all manner of priests and other men also — for to have peace. But the greater harm is that we have evermore strifes and debates, each man well nigh with the other that there is no peace in their hearts. For no man loves an-other. And outwardly, as we all know, we are in war against many lands on each side, and they against us.[21]

Bromyard's awareness of the increasingly popular nationalist rationales for wars is unique but his other views were rather commonplace. Fitzralph, Brinton, and he are all critical of the nobility's conduct in wars, and the national sins which caused them, and each bears an abhorrence for any conflict among Christians. For them peace is also an ideal, predicated on a reformation of personal behavior that can then be extended to all of soci-ety. The peace they desired would restore a disordered commonweal to the harmonious state that they believed had existed before the war had de-stroyed it. It would lessen civil strife, since the poor are the chief victims of war. Peace, therefore, serves as a panacea or an alternative to war, bringing with it a desired end that can be apperceived and realized only in relation to the consequential ideal it represents. By the terms of such reasoning,

20. Bromyard, "Bellum," in *Summa prædicantium*, 1:92–100, quoted in Owst, *Literature and the Pulpit*, 333–38; Allmand, *Society at War*, 38–39; cf. Additional MS 21253, fol. 105.
21. Royal MS 18 B, xxiii, fols. 65, 167; Owst, *Literature and the Pulpit*, 563–64.

peace as an actual societal condition can never be contemplated fully and, hence, will always remain outside the realm of possibility.

Yet this assessment of the antiwar discourse that runs through the fourteenth and fifteenth centuries has tried to show that with each discursive and ideational twist a new dimension is added to the various political and religious *langues* in which writers discussing the problem of war were engaged. These included the *jus armorum,* scholasticism, Christian allegory, and even what was a clear though developing language of personal morality founded largely in the Bible. At the same time a sublanguage of peace itself was being fashioned and shaped by the interaction of more pacifistic *paroles* (and peace idioms) with these current, ultimately unstable languages.

Heterodox Clerical Contributions

The unique circumstances of a long, drawn-out war provided fertile ground for a burgeoning body of literature on the subject, one that was never in danger of expiring as long as the war continued. Of all the critics, however, the most radical treatment of war and peace comes from John Wyclif, the heretic who did most to disrupt conventional wisdom and discussion on this topic. Unfettered by the need to conform to established opinion, especially that which had been developed and taught by the Church, he went beyond what was acceptable. Along with the Lollards who followed him, Wyclif came closest to rejecting war entirely as a means for settling disputes among nations, no matter how virtuous the cause or how legitimate the authority. The only allowance he made was in acknowledging his revered master Augustine's reliance on proper intention. A war fought for charitable reasons might be legitimate, but for Wyclif such a war would almost always constitute a contradiction in terms.

Before discussing Wyclif's beliefs in this area, we must first return to the ecclesio-political context in which he lived, preached, and wrote. His early career at Oxford was supplemented by important government service in the 1370s. Aside from the major debate over clerical taxation there also erupted a controversy regarding papal appointments (provisions) to higher ecclesiastical offices in England by the end of Edward III's reign. On the former issue, the wealthy secular churchmen, or "possessioners" were increasingly coming under attack as the war burden increased the need for subsidies. Popes had collected taxes from them since the Fourth Crusade (1199) but had not imposed any levies during the first phase of the war, between 1337 and 1360. When they were revived by Gregory XI in 1372, all monies collected were to go to Avignon to fight the pope's Italian war, with Edward receiving no share. This action came on the heels of a large grant to the king made in convocation a year earlier. With the support of king and council, the clergy refused to contribute to the papal exaction; but the problem of provisions was more complex, since it tended to pit one cleric against another. Native aspirants and patrons came to despise the papal interference in the choice of candidates for vacant benefices. Under the leadership of William Courtenay, bishop of Hereford, the convocation of 1373 refused to allot the king any more taxes until some remedy was made. Wyclif was one of seven English ambassadors sent to treat with the pope on this issue.[22]

The events of the next five years find Wyclif in government service, slowly becoming more heretical and making enemies among bishops and other clerics who were offended by his attacks on the Benedictines, two of whom, Courtenay and Brinton, were now sitting in high office. Whether out of disappointment for his own lack of preferment, despite promises to the contrary, or because he truly came to find corruption everywhere, Wyclif continued in his heresy and took every opportunity to hammer away at fellow men of the cloth. With this background it is easier to see the various strands of Wyclif's antiwar discourse and how they were caught up in deep-seated attitudes toward those in society who seemed to profit from such orchestrated bloodletting.

In his treatise *On The Seven Deadly Sins*,[23] Wyclif returned to the familiar postulate that finds the root of war in the sin of anger, for "ire is full contrary to the fellowship and charity that should be in the people." In the Old Testament men fought as directly commanded by God. But since that time God has told men to beat their swords into ploughshares and commanded, through Christ and the apostles, that men behave toward one another with love (charity): "For Saint Paul bids that all our deeds be done in charity; and by God's law we should love our enemies, and so make them friends by the strength of charity." Since we are not fighting to

---

22. K. B. McFarlane, *John Wycliffe and the Beginnings of English Nonconformity* (London: English Universities Press, 1952), 25–45.

23. While this work cannot be positively attributed to Wyclif, it is both contemporaneous with and consistent with other writings that are clearly his. For lack of evidence to the contrary, it will be assumed that Wyclif is the author.

avenge God's injuries at His leading or with charity as the motivation, "it is a known thing that men should not now fight."[24] With one fell swoop Wyclif completely eliminates just cause, proper authority, and right intention as justifications for war. In theory they may be tenable but in the real world they are meaningless and irrelevant. (Both Wyclif and the Lollards upheld Fitzralph's theory of dominion, and the bishop became somewhat of a hero to them.)[25] This theoretical attack on war is then followed by further evaluation of right motive and a condemnation of the traits that actually bring men to blows: selfishness and hatred. The culprit here, found also in his more direct *De officio regis,* is the warrior clergy led by the Antichrist in Rome (or Avignon). The pope teaches that if Christians do not fight their enemies they will be destroyed by them, "and damn their own souls. And thus out of love we chasten them, as God's law teaches us." But Wyclif, who was a careful student of the Bible, discovered a different scriptural command — that each one love his enemies and never kill them: "And wise men of the world hold their strength and thus vanquish their enemies without any stroke; and men of the gospel vanquish by patience, and come to rest and to peace by suffering death." It is incumbent upon the Christian to renounce everything for love in the interest of fellow humans, even if that means losing all of his or her earthly possessions. "And if we fight thus for love, it is not love of charity; for charity seeks not proper good in this life but the common good in heaven by virtuous patience." And while many may use the excuse that they are fighting for charity, they will be uncovered on Judgment Day (Domesday).[26] Wyclif identified love with peace and associated war with anger or hatred. These stark observations make one condition spiritually desirable and the other clearly unacceptable. Echoing Gower and Chaucer, an element of pity and forbearance characterizes Wyclif's understanding of love such that the good of others becomes the paramount consideration for all actions.

Having set up the problem of war as a spiritual condition, Wyclif put the blame for its popularity squarely on the shoulders of the Church, which exhorts soldiers to kill but should know better. In one passage he indirectly faulted the knights themselves when he criticized their lifestyles

24. [Wyclif], *On The Seven Deadly Sins,* in *Select English Works,* chaps. 12 and 13, pp. 134–37; Daly, *Political Theory,* 141, 150.

25. McFarlane, *John Wycliffe,* 86; Anne Hudson, "A Neglected Wycliffite Text," *Journal of Ecclesiastical History* 29 (1978): 263. For a full discussion on the links between the orthodox Fitzralph and his Lollard progeny, see Walsh, *Fourteenth Century Scholar,* 452–68.

26. [Wyclif], *On the Seven Deadly Sins,* chap. 14, pp. 137–38.

as without virtue and given over to vice. He saw no honor in killing with such a selfish spirit, declaring that a butcher has more charity killing animals than a knight has for those he slays, but adds that the chivalry are led to this lifestyle by the evil designs of the pope. On the issue of proper authority, Wyclif argued that just because the pope enjoins men to fight in crusade does not mean he is right. Paul said that even Peter sinned after he was filled with the Holy Ghost, and so "why might not the antichrist sin? He is the antichrist, who by hypocrisy reverses Jesus Christ in his false living." The pope's interest in wealth betrays his calling to service and poverty. Clergy are also guilty for consenting to the pope's sin by defending it or by helping carry it out: "For if manslaughter among secular persons is odious to God, much more so among priests who should be Christ's vicars. And clerks consent through preaching and supporting his cause, and in cowardly dumbness for a foul love, and secular persons in many ways consent to this sin."[27] So far then, this late medieval heretic has taken on the most inviolable aspects of medieval warfare by eradicating the bulwarks that fortify it. By denying the Church's authority to proclaim just wars, he deprived the individual soldier of any spiritual cover for his actions. The Church may have always condemned excessive violence and plunder, but by promising pardons and granting indulgences for fighting in "just wars," a soldier's cruelty and robbery appeared to have little effect on his salvation. With Wyclif the knight could no longer be so sure, and it is for this reason that the responsibility rested so heavily on the clergy, whose job it is to reconcile sinners to God.[28]

For Wyclif, it seems the Norwich Crusade in 1383, which utterly disgusted him and which glaringly demonstrated the falsity of the Church's teachings on war, was the last straw. He wrote a flurry of tracts in the 1380s in which he systematically set out to discredit the entire range of clerical offices, from curates and prelates to priests and monks. In each diatribe he at some point sought to discredit the office by focusing on its holder's involvement in the unholy practice of war. The prelates, who make most of the decisions and are responsible for what is taught about war, came in for more sustained abuse. As "enemies of peace, counselors and maintainers of war . . . their prayers are cursed." They want wars to help perpetuate simony, hypocrisy, covetousness, and "the robbery of their

27. Ibid., chaps. 15–16, pp. 139–42.
28. Lange, *Histoire de la doctrine pacifique*, 198.

poor tenants." But, Wyclif asserted, "if they were the true procurers of peace, they should gladly and joyfully give up all their worldly lordships and their flesh and blood and bodily lives to make peace and charity among Christian men." It is their duty to teach about the benefits of peace through sermons, confessions, and counseling. These worldly prelates, however, are the most warmongering of all men, full of pride and covetousness, who "maintain many men or arms to kill Christian men in body and they themselves kill many thousands in soul and body."[29] Wyclif accused clerical possessioners (that derisive name for monks and friars who wrongly sought temporal dominion) of inciting wars also, so they can "maintain their possessions and worldly lives." The curates teach men to go to war "to get worldly honor and a little dirt by false warring outside of charity." And the priests were accused of encouraging wars through their offer of pardons.[30] In each case, Wyclif's major complaint was that these clerics, by warring, leave the people without spiritual guidance and so mislead the flock that "certainly no tongue in this life may tell how many souls have gone to hell by these cursed captains and by the antichrist's jurisdiction and censures."[31]

By undercutting the authority of the Church to sanctify war and with a rigorous biblical scholarship, Wyclif challenged the very basis for late medieval warfare. Yet even he acknowledged that some wars of conquest were licit if they were clearly commanded by God. (How this was to be determined without papal authority he did not discuss.) He may have been extremely doubtful that such wars were possible, especially in the purified sense which made love the sole motivation, but he leaves an opening nonetheless. The intellectual respect he paid to Augustine on this point, however, did not mean as much to those who followed after him. The Lollards were even more thorough in their denunciations of war. What they had in common with Wyclif was their rejection of papal authority on this issue, but also the feeling that peace was crucial because it was inextricably wrapped up in an individual's eternal destiny. The "orthodox" clerics may decry immoral wars that strain English resources to the breaking point, but they are really hypocrites who would quickly engage in bloody conflict

29. Wyclif, *Of Prelates*, in *English Works*, 52–54, 73, 90–91. See Barnie, *War in Medieval English Society*, 123–24.
30. Wyclif, *Of Clerk Possessioners, The Office of Curates,* and *The Order of Priesthood,* in *English Works*, 132, 147, 176.
31. Wyclif, *Of Prelates*, 100.

if it padded their purses and increased their power and prestige. In effect, if they were really men of peace (or of the gospel) they would categorically condemn war and the aggrandizement that sustains it.

Lollardy is such an interesting movement precisely because it crossed all class boundaries. There were variances of opinion on many doctrinal issues, but men and women from all walks of life were essentially the same in their unorthodoxy on the issue of war and peace. Their internalization of Wycliffian antiwar sentiment is unique and remarkable for its depth. The outspoken early Lollard leader, Nicholas Hereford, mirrored Wyclif's judgment when he said: "Jesus Christ, duke of our battle, taught us the law of patience and not to fight bodily."[32] In his attack on the "possessioners" during the 1382 Ascension Day sermon, a year after the Peasants' Revolt, Hereford argued that the king could lessen the tax burden of the laity by reforming the monks, friars, and other wealthy clerics.[33] The meaning here is clear: without the grasping lifestyle and sycophancy toward the pope exhibited by these churchmen, wars would not be stirred up and the levies would be unnecessary. Another leading heretic, William Swynderby, was charged in the courts of the bishops of both Lincoln and Hereford in 1390. Given a safe conduct to refute the indictment the following year, he did so, and then went into hiding. After being sentenced he made his appeal in a letter sent to Bishop Trefnant of Hereford, including in it his reasons for holding pacifist views: "For whereas Christ's law bids us to love our enemies, the pope's law gives us leave to hate them and to kill them, and grants men pardon to war against heathen men and to kill them. . . . Whereas Christ's law teaches peace, the pope with his law assails men for money and gathers priests and others to fight for his cause." Swynderby argued from Scripture much as the early church fathers did, claiming that Christ came to give life not to take it, and that by ungirding Peter, He had condemned the use of the sword. In Wycliffian manner the defendant excoriated clerics who fight, since they are called to be shepherds, not warriors.[34]

Two Cambridge professors gave the official response to Swynderby's pacifism, declaring: "To go to war in a just cause or against infidels is holy and licit, and to say otherwise is erroneous." They based their conclusion

32. Contamine, *War in the Middle Ages*, 293–94.
33. Scase, *"Piers Plowman,"* 6–7; Hudson, "Wycliffism in Oxford," 69–71.
34. *Registrum Johannis Trefnant, episcopi Herefordensis*, A.D. *1389–1404* (Hereford, Eng.: Wilson & Phillips, 1914), 238–70. The translations from the Latin in this section are mine.

on Aquinas's and Augustine's defense of just wars.[35] That same year, before the same court, Walter Brut offered a defense of his pacifist views, which found much in common with Swynderby. Aside from the biblical allusions, Brut contended that everything about war went against the spirit of the gospel and the way of love:

> From this it should be evident that Christ, the king of peace and savior of humankind, came to save, not to condemn, and by giving the law of charity to the faithful, taught us to show respect, not anger, and not to hate our enemies, nor to repay evil with evil, but to resist evil. For all these things promote peace and destroy those things not devoted to healthful peace and love. But the Roman pontiff promotes wars and the killing of men in war, not just against our enemies who are clearly infidels, but also against Christians, all in exchange for earthly goods.

Brut made no distinction between wars against infidels and wars against fellow Christians; both were evil since they sprang from the same ill humor of hatred and a willingness to do harm to others, rather than from the biblical spirit of humility and patience.[36] These positions of Swynderby, Brut, and other Lollards went to the heart of an ideological vulnerability in Wycliffian, and later Anabaptist, New Testament christology. According to Allmand, their "opinion holds that Christians cannot freely and forcefully defend themselves against injuries aimed at them, nor against bodily attacks, nor against violence of other kinds. Such an opinion is against the good of the general peace, against all order of government and against all reason."[37] Such a complete rejection of war was so out of the mainstream that it was never taken seriously. To expect Christian charity to permit all kinds of wrongs seemed anarchic in any realm of activity except the strictly personal. The divergence between Lollard idealism and established opinion is most clearly brought out in the Twelve Conclusions presented by the Lollards to Parliament in 1395 and in the subsequent charge brought against them by the bishops. The tenth conclusion dealt with the issue of war, indicating its central position in overall Lollard "dogma." It is worth quoting in its entirety for its great similarity to Wyclif, but also because of its concern for war's effects on the commons:

35. Ibid., 369–70.
36. Ibid., 309–16.
37. Allmand, *Society at War*, 20–21; Allmand, "War and the Non-Combatant," 175–76.

The tenth conclusion is that manslaughter by battle or pretending a temporal or religious just cause without special revelation is expressly contrary to the New Testament which is a law full of grace and mercy. This conclusion is openly proved by the example of Christ's preaching here on earth which mostly taught one to love and to have mercy on his enemies, and not to kill them. The reason is that for the greater part where men fight, after the first stroke, charity is broken; and whosoever dies outside of charity follows the highway to hell. And beyond this we know well that no clerk can find by scripture or by reason any lawful punishment of death for one deadly sin and not for another. But the law of mercy that is the New Testament forbids all manslaughter. In the gospel is the same law found in the Old Testament, "thou shalt not kill." The corollary is that it is a holy robbery of the poor people when lords purchase indulgences to escape punishment and guilt for those that serve in his armies, by gathering them together to kill Christian men in foreign lands for temporal goods, as we have seen. And knights who run toward heathenness to get themselves a name for killing men, displease much the King of Peace; for by meekness and suffering our belief is multiplied, and fighters and manslayers Jesus Christ hates and warns: "whoever kills by the sword, dies by the sword."[38]

The Wycliffian emphases on loving one's enemies, the falsity of the Church's teachings, and the abuse of indulgences are all here, along with the resolve that persecution only strengthened their belief. It is also interesting that the Lollards went further than Wyclif and suggested that a war could only be permitted when there is a special revelation ordaining it. This may not solve the dilemma over proper authority but it pretty much lays to rest the notion of an unerring power to make war, while advancing individualistic ethical tendencies that Wyclif broached only tentatively.

The bishops responded to the Lollard conclusions with sixteen points of their own. Number fifteen charges the heretics with believing "that it is not lawful to kill any man, neither in dome [the course of legal judgment] nor out of dome, neither Saracens, nor other enemies by battle, as knights did when they assailed the holy land, because it is said in the gospel that

38. Anne Hudson, ed., *Selections from English Wycliffite Writings* (Cambridge: Cambridge University Press, 1978), 27–28; Geoffrey F. Nuttall, *Christian Pacifism in History* (Oxford: Basil Blackwell, 1958), 23–24.

you should not kill."[39] No self-respecting Lollard would dispute this accusation in the least. The emphasis on their opposition to crusades against Muslims and pagans may have been a shrewd move to insinuate their heresy, but they would have subscribed to the above position wholeheartedly. These two contradictory positions, both so boldly put, indicate clearly just how alien complete pacifism was to late medieval society, much as it continues to be today. The tremendous and enduring Lollard passion against war finds expression in records of court proceedings against them in Norwich between 1428 and 1431. In just that short amount of time forty-five cases of heresy were tried. Thirteen of these, nearly twenty-nine percent, included charges for opposing either killing or fighting. Both going to war for one's country and capital punishment were denounced by the defendants, who contested that "every man should remit all vengeance only to the sentence of God."[40] Other Wycliffite tracts and sermons argued the same position, fearful that men would die in their sins and be damned, with no hope for repentance.[41] Such a depth of feeling on the problem of war may have exerted marginal impact, but it could not be ignored, since Lollardy was recognized as a dangerous heresy.

A number of years ago K. B. McFarlane wrote an influential book that assumed the existence of certain "Lollard knights" at Richard II's court, basing his conclusion on statements made to that effect in the contemporary chronicles of Henry Knighton and Thomas Walsingham. What is most intriguing about McFarlane's study is its assumption that these knights were protected by the crown and that they had an association with Chaucer, who may have also harbored Lollard sympathies.[42] Since the book's publication a few scholars, despite McFarlane's full array of evidence, have found these notions too unlikely and have attempted to refute them. But the thesis has been far from demolished.[43] Critics are probably

39. Hudson, *Selections*, 20, and *The Premature Reformation* (Oxford: Clarendon Press, 1988), 367–70.

40. Norman P. Tanner, ed., *Heresy Trials in the Diocese of Norwich, 1428–1431*, C4S, vol. 20 (1977), 11–15, 142.

41. See Jack Upland, *Friar Daw's Reply and Upland's Rejoinder*, ed. P. L. Heyworth (Oxford: Oxford University Press, 1968), 55; Anne Hudson, ed., *English Wycliffite Sermons* (Oxford: Clarendon Press, 1983), 1:416–17; *An Apology for Lollard Doctrines*, ed. James Henthorn, Camden Soc., vol. 20 (London: J. B. Nichols & Son, 1842), 87.

42. K. B. McFarlane, *Lancastrian Kings and Lollard Knights* (Oxford: Clarendon Press, 1972), 177–85; V. J. Scattergood, "Literary Culture at the Court of Richard II," in Scattergood and Sherborne, *English Court Culture in the Later Middle Ages*, 38–41.

43. Maurice Keen, "The Influence of Wyclif," in Kenny, *Wyclif in His Times*, 132–34; Hudson, *Premature Reformation*, passim.

more on the mark when they question the cohesiveness of the knights as a group or whether they can be considered Lollards in the full sense of the word. The king was no lover of heretics, and only one of the knights, Sir Thomas Latimer, was ever formally charged with being one; but William Nevill, as constable of Nottingham Castle, did protect Hereford for a time, and there is evidence that Sir John Montagu also gave refuge to suspected Lollards. McFarlane convincingly argued that regardless of how many knights there were, until Sir John Oldcastle's disastrous revolt in 1413, many Lollards believed they had friends in high places.[44]

The most literary and one of the least heretical of this group was Sir John Clanvowe, who had a vast career serving the government as soldier, diplomat, and chamber knight for Edward III and Richard II. He fought in France in the 1360s and 1370s but was part of the team sent to negotiate peace in 1385. A friend of the "court party" who lost favor when the Lords Appellant took control in 1386, he appears to have stood by the king and later negotiated a truce with France in 1389. Even though Clanvowe joined in a disastrous crusade against the Moors in 1390, he was treating with France again early the next year. Two of Clanvowe's works survive, and one of them, *The Two Ways,* does show an affinity for some Lollard ideas. While not overtly polemical or heretical — he does not challenge transubstantiation or other doctrines — the book contrasts two ways of life. The life of the average, hard-working commoner is morally preferable to the violent noble whose wealth and lifestyle is based on destroying that of others. Clanvowe lamented the fact that the latter people are most highly regarded in his society: "For the world holds them worshipful that are great warriors and fighters and that destroy and win many lands, and waste and give much good to them that have enough." Those who live simply and "suffer patiently wrongs that other folk do and seem to them satisfied with little good of this world" are scorned and called "lollers [idlers], fools and shameful wretches."[45] While in this passage Clanvowe did not condemn war, he seriously questioned its practice among Christians. *The Two Ways* indicates sympathy with the Wyclif/Lollard emphasis on Christ-like behavior (*imago Christi*) and the overall mercy that people should exhibit toward each other, but there is nothing in it that could be construed as heretical. If his friends were of the same mind, perhaps these

---

44. McFarlane, *Lancastrian Kings,* 198–99, and *John Wycliffe,* 130–32.

45. John Clanvowe, *The Works of Sir John Clanvowe,* ed. V. J. Scattergood (Cambridge: D. S. Brewer, 1975), 9, 19–27, 70. Clanvowe died in Constantinople in 1391, and this work was probably composed near the end of his life.

"Lollard knights" were more attracted to "pietistic and moralistic" attitudes of the early Lollards rather than specific sacramental, doctrinal beliefs.[46]

An opposition to war (for some, a particular war) had permeated all layers of society by the end of the fourteenth century and it is to be expected that there would be extremes on both ends of the issue. But as with other writers already discussed and among those to come, there is a cumulative pull in an antiwar direction with each new interpretation of the problem and a readiness to entertain new conceptions of peace. The "popular" literary and poetic figures that wrote during the first years of the new century approached the issue of war with less reticence than their predecessors. They may not have been as caustic as Gower or Wyclif, but they wrote in an atmosphere less worshipful of the roles that institutions such as knighthood or the Church played in establishing both the *jus ad bellum* and the *jus in bello*.

"Popular" Literature and War ca. 1400

In his recent study of war and social order in medieval England, Richard Kaeuper remarks that the growing "popular"[47] complaint literature, mostly poetry, that appeared after 1370,

> moving away from the romance convention of glorifying war, shows an acute awareness of the horrors and destruction inseparably linked with war. Thus, the evidence of literature dovetails with other indications that many in England associated war with oppressive financial burdens and with exacerbated problems of internal justice and order; it also suggests that a few thinkers had yet more basic objections.[48]

46. J. Anthony Tuck, "Carthusian Monks and the Lollard Knights: Religious Attitude at the Court of Richard II," in *Studies in the Age of Chaucer. Proceedings, No. 1, 1984: Reconstructing Chaucer,* ed. Paul Strohm and Thomas J. Heffernan (Knoxville, Tenn.: New Chaucer Society, 1985), 149–53. McFarlane believed Clanvowe was a trusted councillor to Richard II and a friend of Chaucer and described *The Two Ways* as a "pacifist tirade." See McFarlane, *Lancastrian Kings,* 197–206.

47. Since it is virtually impossible to determine how many people had access to this literature, the term "popular" here (with quotations marks) refers to the more simple and doggerel style of writing that also appealed to less educated tastes.

48. Kaeuper, *War, Justice, and Public Order,* 340.

The validity of this assessment has been borne out convincingly by the evidence already presented, but the question remains whether this burden of war was constant enough to have created a fundamentally dynamic antiwar sentiment among a noticeable part of the population, before an apparent concomitant rise in nationalist feeling helped rehabilitate eroding support for martial activities. When did complaints over war taxation metamorphose into critiques of warfare itself as it was being practiced? A decisive answer to this conundrum may be all but impossible to reach; it is almost certain, however, that even the celebrated English victories under Henry V were unable to stem the tide of cynicism that accompanied the entire war effort. There is evidence as well that English nationalism at this time was confined largely to creating cultural unity, and that the accompanying xenophobia was more isolationist than confrontational.[49] Perhaps it is because the fiscal demands and security fears became so unendurable for the commons that a "popular" element in the antiwar crusade became more apparent in English vernacular poetry after 1370.

One of the earliest examples, *Wynnere and Wastoure,* may date from as early as 1352. In this work the unknown poet dreamt of two armies (both are Edward III's), one led by Wynnere (including the pope, lawyers, friars, and merchants) and the other by Wastoure ("men-at-arms, bold squires of blood, bowmen many"). Each side at odds with the other, the poet hoped that the Black Prince would "come to keep them at peace." At the king's bidding, the son does reprove them for their dissension, and so, both armies present their pleas to the crown. Wynnere accuses Wastoure of "spending all the hard-earned wealth of thrifty people. Wastoure's lands lie idle; he is apt to bring the country to ruin," all because of "revelry and rioting."[50] Wastoure rejoins by charging Wynnere with being stingy and neglecting the poor. The king decides to permit Wastoure to go on to London and spend money while Wynnere must go to the papal court until summer, at which time he will be summoned and expected to help in the war with France. The king, therefore, seems to sanction Wastoure's argument and lifestyle because his soldiers are allowed to cheat people in London "of their purses," since their private lives do not concern him. By contrast, Wynnere and his forces must be managed, since they are angry

49. Neillands, *Hundred Years War,* 190.

50. *Wynnere and Wastoure,* ed. Israel Gallanz (Oxford: Oxford University Press, 1920; reprint, Cambridge: D. S. Brewer, 1974); Gardiner Stillwell, "*Wynnere and Wastoure* and the Hundred Years War," *English Literary History* 8 (1941): 241–42; Coleman, *Medieval Readers,* 97.

about paying more than their fair share in the war, much of which is wasted by the knights. The poet's description, therefore, of those forces involved in making war policy indirectly blamed the king for the reckless autonomy of the knighthood to wreak havoc on the rest of the nation. It may also be true that the poem simply reflects the growing dissatisfaction, not with war in the abstract, but with a specific war's misconduct and expense.[51]

The meaning and purpose of *The Alliterative Morte Arthur*, also written between 1350 and 1400, has undergone reevaluation recently. The work is being interpreted now as an anti-romance, part of a genre that criticizes and satirizes the incongruity between romance and contemporary society. According to Karl Heinz Göller, "The poet seems particularly interested in unmasking the trivialised and romanticised form of literary portrayal of war and heroes, by confronting it with the moral and physical results of real war."[52] Gawain is the chief figure among the knights, but far from heroic, his faults are clearly identified, especially his arrogance, temerity, and thirst for power. In *The Alliterative Morte Arthur* the monstrous nature of war is starkly held up against romanticized fiction. Arthur's battle of Sessoyne is strikingly similar in its effects to what happened to Edward III's army at Crécy. The earlier king's battle with the giant of Mont St. Michel is a parody of chivalric combat. It is reckless, sloppy, and inconclusive on Arthur's part. Without feeling, the damsel in distress (the duchess of Brittany) is not rescued but slain by the giant and with great cruelty. "Arthur's humour and irony, the emphasis on bawdy and grotesqueness, all this turns the episode into a burlesque *adventure*." By making it such a violent, ignoble mess, the poet uses knightly combat to eradicate any romantic notion among his readers concerning the true nature of war. The laments for Arthur's slain men are tragic and graphic in the way they describe the bloody details surrounding the soldiers' demises. At the poem's beginning, Arthur wants to be sure that the war is legitimate, but his council rebuffs his concern by stating that revenge is enough of a reason. Swayed by the knights, the king never questions war again.[53] There may have been, then, a morbid fascination with the brutal activities associated

---

51. Stillwell, "*Wynnere and Wastoure*," 242–47; Kaeuper, *War, Justice, and Public Order*, 339.

52. Karl Heinz Göller, "Reality versus Romance: A Reassessment of the *Alliterative Morte Arthure*," in *The Alliterative Morte Arthure: A Reassessment of the Poem*, ed. Karl Heinz Göller (Cambridge: D. S. Brewer, 1981), 15–17; *The Alliterative Morte Arthure*, trans. Valerie Krishna (Washington, D.C.: University Press of America, 1983).

53. Göller, "Reality versus Romance," 18–28.

with war among the people (this was written in post–Black Death England), but the sense of tragedy that goes along with these descriptions in
The Alliterative Morte Arthur makes this poem more than a story of daring adventures designed simply to entertain.

The same may be said for quite a few other Middle English romances,
such as *Libeaus desconus, Ipomydon,* and *Sir Perceval of Galles.* All three
depict scores of hapless victims whose lives are constantly plagued by chaotic injustices, confusion, and the violent whims of powerful knights. The
authors blame this morass of disorder on leaders too weak to stop wars
they have started and on the inability of war's victims to act in their own
behalf. The earliest extant manuscript of the popular *Golagros and Gawain* dates from 1470, but the alliterative romance in surely much older.
The poem displays a "critical, at times even sceptical, attitude towards the
knightly code of honour — but also towards chivalric combat and war." By
the end, Arthur realizes that all his conquests and daring exploits mean
little when measured against the true rewards of loyalty and friendship.
Awntyrs of Arthur reflects similar sentiments when a ghost from purgatory
exposes the vanity of the world, its denouement in war, and the consequent suffering by the poor. Pity and concern for the commons is the pervasive message, along with the virtue of mutual love and respect.[54]

The turn of the century witnessed a further flurry of anonymous poems
expressing doubts about the benefits of war. One already considered,
Dives and Pauper, questioned the legitimacy of contemporary wars being
fought according to just-war formulas that were being abused continuously and without remorse.[55] The poem "Mede and Much Thank" (ca.
1400) also takes the form of a dialogue between a rich man and a poor
man (a common device!), who this time meet in the forest. The wealthy
man brags that he enriches himself through flattery and supporting wars
while common soldiers fight and suffer distress; but he will live to an old
age making merry with his gains. The wiser poor man rebukes him for
profiting from and thus perpetuating war:

> Your wicked speech came from afar.
> Evil you speak, worse do mean.
> You would ever more there were war,
> (for profit and pillage you might glean,)
> Christian blood destroyed clean,

54. Göller, "War and Peace," 120–30.
55. *Dives and Pauper,* vol. 1, part 2, pp. 13–49.

And towns burnt in glede [fires].
Your conscience is full lean;
You would not come there but for meed.[56]

This poem typifies a shift in the romantic poetry of the later Middle Ages. It is candidly cynical about war and its glories, whereas earlier poetry distanced the reader from the horrors of battle through a "rhetoric of heroism."[57] In another example, "Treuth, Reste, and Pes" (1401), the poet exalted truth, justice, and obedience to laws in order to keep the commoners from rising and reducing the realm to waste and ruin. He prefigured men like John Fortescue and, in the next century, Richard Morison, when he included rebellion in the category of war and called for a stable, trustworthy government to maintain peace and prosperity both at home and abroad:

Also is written in the gospel
A word that God Himself chose:
Rather than fight, a man should go sell
Any of his clothes, and buy himself peace. . . .

An old saying was spoken of yore:
What is a kingdom treasury?
Beasts, corn stuffed in store,
Rich commons, and wise clergy;
Merchants, squires, chivalry
That would be ready at a rising,
And a chivalrous king in wits high,
To lead in war, and govern in peace.[58]

While the writer still found much to admire in a "chivalrous king," it is a ruler's discernment to know when to go to war and when to keep the peace that is most desirable. And at home he should quench the seeds of malice before they consume and lead to war, "so the more you will live in rest and peace." A good king has wise councillors, and "God's will is

56. "Mede and Muche Thank," in *Twenty-Six Political and Other Poems (Digby 102)*, ed. J. Kail, EETS OS, no. 124 (London: K. Paul, Trench, Trübner, 1904), lines 65–72, p. 8.

57. Coleman, *Medieval Readers*, 96–97.

58. "Treuth, Reste, and Pes," in *Twenty-Six Political and Other Poems*, lines 53–56, 65–72, p. 11.

locked up when men's counsel make peace."[59] That peace should be the objective of all government action is emphasized in this very political poem through the device of ending each of the twenty-one stanzas with the word "peace."

One of the more overt pleas for peace, which has by now become the focus of antiwar discourse, is found in another poem, "How Man's Flesh Complained to God against Christ," composed between 1400 and 1421. The conflict that exists here between the soul and the body is reminiscent of Augustine's two cities and the spiritual, idealistic connotations given to real peace. But this poem reads more like a lament, an appeal to God as a last resort, since earthly authorities are unresponsive to the writer's pleas:

> Thus my soul, my body slays
> With great anguish and torment.
> She tells, Jesus died for peace;
> But from his school she is gone;
> Between us war does increase.
> Her sword is drawn, her bow is bent.
> She says but, "fleshly lusts, seize"!
> We men are dead, and both are shent [disgraced].[60]

Mum and the Sothsegger (ca. 1403–6) closely resembles *Piers Plowman* in both style and subject matter. A poem about Richard II's deposition, it paints a panoramic picture of the state of the realm plagued by wars while envisioning a new role for the aristocracy in a political rather than military arena.[61] Humanist writers of the English Renaissance would find this idea particularly attractive as the mirrors and advice manuals to courtiers become prevalent modes of political expression over the next two centuries. Many of these works stress the need for the nobility to create a new relevance for itself by elevating its members above the brutality of warmaking.

The foregoing discussion of "popular" (or "populist") poetry is far from being either exhaustive or systematic; but the most significant contributions it makes do not require such an approach for our purposes. It is sufficient to know that there is now suggestive evidence that antiwar sentiment may have had a following among the population at large, since most

59. Ibid., lines 64, 95–96, pp. 11–12.

60. "How Man's Flesh Complained to God against Christ," in *Twenty-Six Political and Other Poems,* lines 89–96, p. 92.

61. *Mum and the Sothsegger,* ed. Mabel Day and Robert Steele, EETS OS, no. 199 (London: Oxford University Press, 1936); Powicke, *Military Obligation,* 130.

of this literature was written either by or for the less educated reader. Add to this the evidence of Lollard pacifism and regular protests against war taxation, and it would be naïve and negligent to believe that English people were generally unaffected or uninterested in overseas conflicts. And perhaps most significant of all, it is in this complaint literature (along with Gower's works) where the first signs of "peace" discourse emerge. This is important because by changing the focus of the discussion from the problem of war to the alternative of peace, the latter idea can begin to function as an independent concept. When this happens, as will be shown in the contemporary works of Thomas Hoccleve and John Lydgate tentatively, and definitively once Erasmian humanism comes to England, the finer gradations of what peace can mean in a public setting (as opposed to a generalized personal virtue) allow peace to become a factor in official policy by the mid-Tudor period.

Developing "Peace" Discourse in the Fifteenth Century: From Hoccleve to Ashby

Thomas Hoccleve, born around 1368, worked as a clerk in the office of the Privy Seal for most of his life, about thirty-five years, constantly complaining of poverty even after receiving an annuity in 1399. A writer of many poems, Hoccleve's greatest, *Regement of Princes,* was written around 1412 and dedicated to Prince Hal, the soon-to-be Henry V. Hoccleve's work was patterned after earlier advice manuals to princes, but he offered his own particular emphases. The last three sections particularly stand out in the context of our discussion. Section 13 treats the topic of prudence and 14 the importance of good counsel. In both Hoccleve relies heavily on Chaucer's moral tales for guidance, such as in the latter section when he warned against flatterers, greedy men at court, and advice from the young. In section 14 he also, somewhat abruptly, recalls for the reader that Chaucer had written on a similar theme in the "Tale of Melibeus" and pauses to exalt his hero's literary talents. Some manuscripts even include a miniature portrait of Chaucer at this point, with an exhortation by Hoccleve for readers to look on it as one would an image in church and think about this great author. That Hoccleve admired the writer of *Canterbury Tales* is not surprising, but it is significant that he praises Chaucer for that portion of *Canterbury Tales* where Chaucer's views on war are most apparent.[62]

In fact, in the very next, and last, section of the *Regement*, Hoccleve focused exclusively on war and its evils. His descriptions were quite conventional, arguing that the practice is unchristian and unreasonable, as well as an economically unprofitable means of settling international disputes.[63] He began by relating how peace would reign in the home if men would sometimes swallow their pride and listen to their wives (a reference to Chaucer's Prudence?). Then, consolidating the previous discussion on flattery and counsel, Hoccleve brought it to bear on the need for peace in the country as a whole. Most wars are unjust and caused by ambitious "flatterers and avaricious courtiers."[64] He questioned the motives and therefore the justice of the French war when he proclaimed that it was being fought merely to gain wealth, as Alexander coveted gold in ancient times. Wealth of this world is temporary, so one should be storing up treasures in heaven, including the virtue of peace. One way to achieve this is for the two kings to come to terms quickly, most preferably through a marriage between Prince Henry and the French princess, Katherine, which would bring, "by matrimony peace and unity."[65] The writer seems honestly to believe that all strife will then end and England and France will remain in a state of true concord. For most late-medieval writers unity was an inextricable side effect of true peace.[66]

In discussing the alternative to war, however, Hoccleve broke some fertile ground. Peace is still the product of personal virtues practiced on a wider scale, this time, "conformity with God, humility and tranquility with neighbours." Yet one can be misled and tricked into embracing a false peace:

> The kiss of Judas is now widespread,
> Tokens of peace exist, but small love is had. . . .

62. Jerome Mitchell, *Thomas Hoccleve: A Study in Early Fifteenth-Century English Poetics* (Urbana: University of Illinois Press, 1969), 1–2, 24–29; E. F. Jacob, *The Fifteenth Century, 1399–1485* (Oxford: Clarendon Press, 1961), 660.

63. Hoccleve decried the ruin engendered by France's internecine wars.

64. Mitchell, *Thomas Hoccleve*, 29.

65. Thomas Hoccleve, *The Regement of Princes*, in *Hoccleve's Works*, ed. F. J. Furnivall, EETS ES, no. 72 (London: Kegan Paul, Trench, Trubner, 1897; reprint, Millwood, N.Y.: Kraus Reprint, 1973), lines 5335–41, 5363–66, 5386–90, 5394, pp. 192–94.

66. Mitchell, *Thomas Hoccleve*, 29.

> Many a honey word and many a kiss
> There is; but wait on the conclusion,
> And private gall [bitterness] all turned upside down;
> There is left wicked dalliance.[67]

Written three years before Agincourt and addressed to Prince Henry, this passage in the *Regement of Princes* may refer to the despair surrounding the numerous truces that had been broken, including the most recent one of Richard II, ended in 1401 by Henry IV. For Hoccleve, peace was the result of godly behavior, including sincere attempts to achieve it and a love for the enemy who would benefit.[68] Normally peace comes after exhaustion in war, but God wants peace now and always:

> When you have strained and fought your fill,
> Peace follows moot, but what good is it then
> That peace were had? What lust have you left to spill?
> The blood that Christ with his blood bought, when
> He on the cross died? . . . .

Hoccleve discovered in peace a standard by which all human relations could be defined, not just the individual's relationship to God, even though that is important as well. By distinguishing between true peace and the temporary peace that comes from being worn down by prolonged wars (or from a need to revise strategy and move forces into a more advantageous position), he has removed peace from the hold of idealistic moralists and from the temporary considerations of time and space. His bifurcation of peace helped create a tougher standard for those who complain and offered, with some reservations, realistic hope for a change in policy that would ensure lasting peace. The assumption is that truces for tactical purposes, as had been the custom, did not bring true peace, while the marriage between Henry and Katherine would indicate a more sincere willingness to come to terms with the differences between the two Christian nations. Both responses were seen by Hoccleve as the product of two dif-

---

67. Hoccleve, *Regement of Princes*, lines 5081–89, pp. 181–83; Adams, "Pre-Renaissance Courtly Propaganda," 441–42.

68. Hoccleve, *Regement of Princes*, lines 5195–5201, p. 187; V. J. Scattergood, *Politics and Poetry in the Fifteenth Century* (London: Blandford Press, 1971), 99–100.

ferent ways of behavior, either continued anger (ire) or love for fellow Christians — real concord, real peace.[69]

Of all the fifteenth-century poets, John Lydgate, a one-time court poet and monk of Bury St. Edmund's from about 1382 to 1449, may have exhibited the strongest and most personal affection for peace. Deeply disturbed by the Hundred Years War, which reached the centennial of its existence during his adulthood, Lydgate had a "continuing preoccupation with the theme of war and peace" and wanted a permanent cessation of hostilities. He admired Henry V for his participation in fashioning the Treaty of Troyes (1420), and in his *Troy Book* (1420) he reflected Hoccleve's hope and the promise of the treaty that with the marriage of Henry and Katherine:

> I mean thus, that England and France
> May be all one, without variance,
> Out of hurt's old rancor to drive away.[70]

The *Siege of Thebes* (ca. 1420–22) goes even further. In the Epilogue, there is a heated debate between Jocasta, who prefers settling disputes through negotiation, and Adrastus's council, which promotes the use of force. By the end Jocasta's view becomes the basis for a forceful rejection of war, supported by biblical passages and commonsense arguments. War only destroys things, like the walls of Thebes, and encourages the vices that cause it, such as greed and ambition. A final prophecy of peace between France and England ("peace and quiet, concord and unity") includes language taken directly out of the Treaty of Troyes.[71] Like Hoccleve, Lydgate hoped that careless leaders would not treat these words as rhetorical flourishes that simply served to placate both parties at one particular moment. The closing lines of the *Siege of Thebes* illustrate this concern and the hope for a peaceful age to come:

69. Hoccleve, *Regement of Princes,* lines 5195–5201, 5321–27, 5377–81, 5386–90, pp. 187, 192, 194. Hoccleve held that until all the world is under the rule "of heaven's bliss, that is endless, to which you bring the author of peace," war between Christians and heathens would occur (lines 5433–39, p. 196).

70. John Lydgate, *Lydgate's Troy Book,* ed. Henry Bergen, EETS ES, no. 97 (London: K. Paul, Trench, Trübner, 1906), bk. 5, lines 3411–13; Scattergood, *Politics and Poetry,* 100–101.

71. Derek Pearsall, "Lydgate as Innovator," *Modern Language Quarterly* 53 (1992): 14; John Lydgate, *Lydgate's Siege of Thebes,* ed. A. Erdmann and E. Ekwall, EETS ES, no. 125 (London: K. Paul, Trench, Trübner, 1920), lines 3655–4703; Derek Pearsall, *John Lydgate* (London: Routledge & Kegan Paul, 1970), 155–56.

But the venom and the violence
Of strife, of war, of contact, and debate,
That make lands bare and desolate
Shall be proscribed and voided out of place.[72]

Suffusing his vision of true peace is its link with the common good, and it is here that Lydgate made his most profound critique of war. Many of his shorter poems continue this theme, as in where he states unequivocally: "The common weal (rem publicam) you must of right prefer / Always considering that peace is better than war."[73]

By emphasizing the connection between the public welfare and peace, Lydgate completed a process that stood the basic Thomistic rationale for warfare on its head. The theologians (and Vegetius) had permitted going to war if it would benefit the commonweal, but Lydgate put the ox back before the cart and faulted wars for creating the need to restore peace (and the commonweal) in the first place. His *Praise of Peace,* written after Henry V's death, between 1422 and the peace negotiations of 1443, is a virtual paean to peace. With the rumblings that would lead to the Wars of the Roses already apparent, Lydgate went beyond pleas for peace with France and demanded an end to all war. After beginning the poem with a play on the letters PAX, he describes the difference between inward tranquillity and outward peace. The king was still held up as the example and the repository of real peace through his own behavior.[74] After citing numerous biblical, mystical, and historical situations wherein peace is proclaimed the only sure protector of the commonweal, he ends the poem with one of the most categorical pronouncements against war in his day:

All war is dreadful, virtuous peace is good,
Strife is hateful, peace the daughter of pleasure,
In Charlemagne's time there was shed much blood,
God send us peace between England and France;
War causes poverty, peace causes abundance,
And between both might it the more increase,

---

72. Lydgate, *Siege of Thebes,* lines 4690–93; Scattergood, *Politics and Poetry,* 100–101.

73. John Lydgate, *The Minor Poems of John Lydgate. Part II: Secular Poems,* ed. Henry N. MacCracken, EETS OS, no. 192 (London: Humphrey Milford, Oxford University Press, 1934), 556; Allmand, *Hundred Years War,* 154.

74. Lydgate, "A Praise of Peace," in *Minor Poems,* 786–87; Scattergood, *Politics and Poetry,* 100–101.

Without feigning, fraud, or variance,
Between all Christians, Christ Jesus, send us peace.[75]

Incorporating Hoccleve's distinction between true peace and pretended peace, Lydgate provides here the classic distillation of what war was doing to the educated elites of England by the 1430s. A systematic transformation of the discourse on the problem of war had gradually and almost imperceptibly taken place over the past century. A new intellectual climate had formed on the issue, expanding the critique into a more generalized condemnation of war, which is easily seen in much of the literature being produced. The evidence of political interest and challenge to prevailing policies cannot be undervalued, even if it was cast in acceptable genres and rhetorics. Vernacular writers identified "the production of knowledge with the interests of a particular time, place, and political community," in this case, war-weary England. Both Gower and Lydgate understood the possibilities for language, especially rhetorical theory, as "a key articulation of the possibilities of applied political discourse; they imagine a rhetoric that is . . . assigned to the service of civic discourse."[76] The fifteenth century, like much of the late fourteenth century, found its most respected literary figures (especially Hoccleve and Lydgate) casting their lots with the anti-war rhetoricians of the age. By encasing their opinions in practical terms they were laying the groundwork for a rhetorical tradition in England that would affect the debate on war tremendously over the next century.

As discussed throughout this study, intellectual change is invariably connected to larger historical developments that were inextricably linked themselves. In the political realm, the growing isolation of Henry VI's government from the desires of the people produced tremendous cynicism with regard to the war and its prosecution. Henry's coronation in Paris in 1422 was in name only. Events before and since demonstrated how ineffectual the English were at both governing any part of France and subduing areas still loyal to the dauphin. Disarray and weakness at court and within the military served to encourage opposition to Lancastrian rule and

75. Lydgate, "A Praise of Peace," lines 117–84, pp. 788–91.
76. Rita Copeland, "Lydgate, Hawes, and the Science of Rhetoric in the Late Middle Ages," *Modern Language Quarterly* 53 (1992): 63, 67; Pearsall, "Lydgate as Innovator," 14–15, 22. Pearsall argues that Lydgate was a royal propagandist by the 1420s, and as such, less oppositional than other vernacular writers. It might be further argued, however, that in crediting the king with a peaceful and stable reign, the poet was identifying the evils of war and the need to avoid them in the future, thus clearly helping to define a specific role for Henry VI's government in maintaining "profitable peace."

to identify those nobles directly involved in the war as corrupt and self-serving. Once again, the war's progress witnessed a concomitant realignment that by its end found most social classes, to include a large portion of the nobility, opposed to continuing the war and calling for large-scale reform. The justice of the war's cause was debated with increasing openness by lay and clerical writers who acted as the conscience of the nation on this issue; and far fewer people were making the case for Henry's claim to the French throne. Most important, by the time of Lydgate, the English, regardless of status, came to find common cause in predicating peace on the needs of the commonwealth. The organic whole of society, with its class-based notion of mutual responsibility, was in danger if the financial and political costs of war were not addressed adequately. Among the French, there was little attention to similar concerns, and since the war was portrayed by many there as promising national unity (by expelling the English) rather than threatening to destroy it, and since Charles VII proved to be a much more effective ruler than the English king, fewer candid and penetrating arguments for peace appeared in France. In England, however, since peace held the greatest chance for reform and economic vitality, pacifist expressions multiplied during these years, and the mood of the nation seriously challenged the nature of contemporary warfare in a way that had never been seen before.

The political problems that continued to beset the national government during the reign of Henry VI (1422–60) obviously helped focus the problem of war more on the need to establish good and effective rule. Here the associated notion of concord (agreement) became fully incorporated into the peace idea much as tranquillity (calm order) became a constituent element during the barrage on knightly behavior. The former introduced a further conceptual turn built on a natural acceptance of the latter. Concord denotes a resolution of differences that suggests long-term considerations, a skill to be developed to prevent the more rash and self-interested from continuing to foster violence and disorder. New diplomatic horizons were dawning, and their exploration by early modern governments would become a significant factor in international relations by the next century. In England, the goal of a safe, sustainable, and mutually beneficial peace would characterize much of the work of embassies during that time. But here, in the fifteenth century, the institutional framework of the past, including the functions of the estates in promoting the common good, were undergoing tremendous change. New roles for king and nobility were being espoused as the New Learning made its first inroads into England by mid-century. War became more of a corporate decision among king, magnates, and commons, and its place circumscribed by the dictates of national security. The absence of original, substantive political theory, except for that advanced by Sir John Fortescue, during this period may not be due just to the abandonment of the clerical intelligentsia,[77] but rather also to a particularly English predilection for pragmatic solutions to specific problems. On the issue of warfare, the middle of the fifteenth century seems to signal decisive movement in a direction that would become a hallmark of Tudor government—the emphasis on advice and consent in national policymaking, from trained bureaucrats, humanists, and Parliament.

Perhaps the utter incompetence displayed by the last Lancastrian king permitted or encouraged greater license among concerned subjects who searched for solutions. As has been shown, an antiwar literature had existed for quite some time, but it may have reached critical mass only after Henry's debacles and losses in France. Fortescue, who had disapproved of Henry V's pretext for war even though it led to English victories, would have found very little to admire under the rule of his son. Many, like Bishop John Stafford in his address to Parliament in 1433, were associating peace with justice and the ability of the estates to carry out their functions in society without threat of harm or impoverishment.[78] The anonymous *Tractatus de regimine principum ad regem Henricum Sextum,* written about 1436–37, was one of a growing number of advice treatises addressed to the king offering strategies for reinstituting strong government and regaining the respect of the English people. The work also indicates that the establishment of peace with France was becoming a precondition for achieving these goals. Echoing a familiar theme, the author referred to the angels proclaiming peace at Christ's birth and to the reconciliation between man and God which His death brought. Chapter 3 in book 1 ends with a plea and a hope that the war with France might end, and that men will come together in Christian peace and unity.[79]

Another important work, which appeared anonymously in 1436–37, *The Libelle of Englyshe Polycye,* and which provided a strong argument

77. Jean-Philippe Genet, "Ecclesiastics and Political Theory in Late Medieval England: The End of a Monopoly," in *The Church, Politics and Patronage in the Fifteenth Century,* ed. Barrie Dobson (New York: St. Martin's Press, 1984), 23–44.

78. C.M.D. Crowder, "Peace and Justice around 1400: A Sketch," in *Aspects of Late Medieval Government and Society: Essays Presented to J. R. Lander,* ed. J. G. Rowe (Toronto: University of Toronto Press, 1986), 53–81.

79. *Tractatus de regimine principum ad regem Henricum Sextum,* in *Four English Political Tracts,* ed. Jean-Philippe Genet, C4S, vol. 18 (1977): 67–71.

for peace, made its case not from a philosophical or theoretical standpoint but for reasons of state, having more in common perhaps with Machiavelli than Augustine.[80] The work came out just after the duke of Bedford's death, at a time when the English war effort was languishing. There was great pessimism over the duke of Burgundy's abandonment of the English alliance and his help in the French siege of Calais in 1436. However, just after the arrival of the English sea forces, the twenty-day siege ended. The poet was tremendously moved by this potential for English power, and addressing his didactic verse to the lords of the Council, he exhorts them to build up a strong navy so the nation will never be threatened by this kind of war again.[81] In what is a very early explication of the doctrine of deterrence, the writer insists that the growth of sea power is unrelated to maintaining a war policy. In fact, war is pictured as detrimental to effective government and the public welfare. Yet only by using the sea as its "wall of defense" can England intimidate other nations enough to reduce the probability that it will have to go to war.

Peace is the natural complement to deterrence in the *Libelle*. The writer gave tranquillity among nations a quantitative as well as a qualitative value. If England controlled the surrounding seas, in order for trade to continue and flourish, nations would need to be at peace with it, especially Flanders:

> But many lands would seek peace out of need;
> The sea well kept, it must be done for dread [out of fear].
> Thus will Flanders need to have unity
> And peace with us, and it will not be otherwise
> Within a short while, and ambassadors
> Will be here soon to treat for their succor [relief].
> This unity is pleasing to God,
> And peace after the wars variance;
> The end of battle is peace surely,
> And power causes true, lasting peace.[82]

Despite this emphasis on the economic benefits of peace, a very medieval idealistic quality remained:

80. Adams, "Pre-Renaissance Courtly Propaganda," 444.
81. *The Libelle of Englyshe Polycye,* ed. Sir George Warner (Oxford: Clarendon Press, 1926), xv–xviii.
82. Ibid., lines 1082–91, pp. 54–55.

That as for anything that is without,
England were then at ease without a doubt,
And thus should every land, one with another,
Commune together as brother with his brother,
And live together warless and in unity
Without rancor in true charity,
In rest and peace to Christ's great pleasure,
Without strife, debate and variance.

A final appeal to the Sermon on the Mount and the teaching "blessed are the peacemakers" proved that Christ came to bring peace and unity and, therefore, that these should be the goal of all men.[83] The *Libelle,* a curious poem, with a backward glance as it predicts the future, remains completely consistent in its promotion of peace and total disregard for "legitimate" warfare, despite its nationalistic tone.

Lydgate was still writing political poems at this time, and because of "verbal correspondences between the two poems" he probably knew the writer of the *Libelle.* His own response to Burgundy's attack on Calais was similar in that he declared the attack denoted, not a need for escalation of the English war effort, but rather an even greater need for peace. The poem, "Debate of the Horse, Goose, and Sheep," which refers to the attack on Calais, was written soon after 1436. In it the horse and sheep promote peace, but the former demonstrates the ill effects of war on the wool trade and how commercial greed can be a cause for war, since Burgundy wanted to close Calais to English wool exports. The literary network at this time continues to suggest a certain self-consciousness and unity of purpose regarding the war among writers. Not only was Lydgate familiar with the author of the *Libelle* but he alluded to Chaucer in significant ways. The "Debate of the Horse, Goose, and Sheep" evokes the *Parlement of Foules,* and in the prologue to Lydgate's *Fall of Princes* there is specific reference made to the "Tale of Melibeus." In other places the monk clearly admired Chaucer "as a purveyor of general moral truth."[84] Lydgate was extending therefore a tradition of moralist critique on public issues that happened to place increasingly greater attention on the multiple failures of the French war.

There is evidence that the "Debate of the Horse, Goose, and Sheep," along with some other short poems of Lydgate, had a substantial circula-

83. Ibid., lines 1098–1105, 1131–36, pp. 55–56.
84. Pearsall, *John Lydgate,* 64, 200–207.

tion in manuscript and were especially "popular" among the commons for
their "low style." The majority of people in England had become thoroughly fed up with the economic toll the war had taken. By the 1430s, not
only were they exasperated by the tax burden but the effects on trade had
a ripple effect that had only added to the misery of the population at large.
As early as 1378 the Commons petitioned the king to curtail his use of
merchant ships for the royal navy (and to provide recompense), since
many vessels had been destroyed and trade lost as a result. In both England and France debates raged over the rights of merchants to exact retribution. Mézières argued against permitting reprisals, known as letters of
marques, since he believed they would inhibit trade and exacerbate tensions. But what about the losses inflicted? Public protests became more
common as the government seemed to remain indifferent to the suffering.
The town of Beverley reacted fiercely against a loan demanded in 1435,
and its inhabitants wrote a letter to Robert Rolleston, wardrober and pro-
vost, indicating their feelings. Corruption was endemic by this time. More
armies were raised through contracts with the crown, and the subsequent
encouragement to economize made opportunities for plunder and personal
gain even greater. The nobility continued to be vilified but so was anyone
else associated with the military or the complex logistical apparatus
through which it operated. Government clerks, especially those sitting in
the exchequer, who were in charge of purveyance for the army and navy,
and administrators of war treasuries easily succumbed to the spoils emanating from their positions, and for that reason, were particularly hated.[85]
When the war finally ended (in 1453) in ignominious defeat and without a
treaty that might have offered some reward for so much suffering, the
English people were under the growing perception that not only had good
government been a cost of the war, but quite clearly the integrity of the
whole social and economic order.

The complications which the Wars of the Roses brought to the crown's
malfeasance in France led not only to clashes between the noble families of
Lancaster and York, but also to much more serious popular unrest, such as
Cade's Rebellion in 1450. Fearing a total collapse of government, much of
the popular poetry and other literature addressed itself to the prince's need
to abandon his corrupt counselors, to quell riots and rebellions, and to

85. Ibid., 200; Allmand, *Society at War*, 141–42, 159–62; Mézières, *Songe du vieil pèlerin*, 2:421; M. M. Postan, "Some Social Consequences of the Hundred Years' War," *Economic History Review* 12 (1942): 1–8.

bring peace in war.[86] While there was a great deal of political propaganda directed to the battle for the crown, writers like Fortescue, regardless of which side they took, were often willing to switch to the other for the sake of order and peace. George Ashby, Clerk to the Signet to Queen Margaret, wrote poetry while in the Fleet between 1460 and 1463, and/or during the Readeption of 1470. The "Active Policy of a Prince" was written as advice for Edward, Prince of Wales, and is divided into three parts, examining the past, present, and future, with accompanying opinions of philosophers.[87] The poem begins by lauding "Masters Gower, Chaucer, and Lydgate, premier poets of this nation," with the author hoping that he will some day join their elite company.[88] After complimenting the royal family, Ashby mourned the wars of recent days, full "with such great battles dispiteous." His praise for Edward included many of those qualities sadly missing in the prince's father: circumspection, living of his own (that is, without resorting to extra parliamentary grants), choosing advisers wisely, staying in charge over everything, paying debts, acting quickly and decisively, and listening to wise counsel. Then Ashby warned against repeating past mistakes:

> I would fain you would keep in remembrance
> To be right well advised by good sadness,
> By discreet prudence and faithful constancy
> Before you begin a war for any riches,
> Or out of fantasy or simplicity.
> For war may be lightly commenced,
> The doubt is how it shall be recompensed.[89]

Writing at a time when the chivalric romance was reviving, Ashby may have been attuned to the mythical attributes being bestowed on the knights of yore. He did not want the reality of war and its consequences to be overshadowed by the fanciful delusions of a nonexistent past. In addition, contrary to the Arthurian idea of chivalric honor, backing down from battle is not cowardice:

86. See Scattergood, *Politics and Poetry,* 173–217.
87. George Ashby, "Active Policy of a Prince," in *George Ashby's Poems,* ed. Mary Bateson, EETS OS, no. 76 (London: Kegan Paul, Trench, Trubner, 1899), v–vi, 12–13.
88. Ashby was a great admirer and imitator of Lydgate. See Margaret Kekewich, "George Ashby's 'The Active Policy of a Prince': An Additional Source," *Review of English Studies* 41 (1990): 533–35.
89. Ashby, "The Active Policy of a Prince," lines 674–80, p. 34.

> I mean not for unthrifty cowardice,
> Which is in all realms abominable,
> But out of willfulness people to surprise [attack],
> For that which might otherwise be recoverable,
> By just means and to God acceptable.
> For man knows not what he begins,
> How fortunes of destructive war ends.[90]

Ashby was one of the few literary figures of the Wars of the Roses to comment so definitively on the problem of war. He tied his hopes and plans for England's government to its ability to incorporate peace into its policies. There are no "coherent pacifist ideas" here, and clearly he "urged that princes should cultivate the arts of peace because peace was usually a wise expedient";[91] but Ashby was one of that new breed of antiwar polemicists who saw history as functional in determining future actions. The pedantic moralism of earlier discussions on war and peace left the burden of decision to God and his chosen vessels, be they popes, kings, or knights. By the end of the fifteenth century, these issues had divided and rent the nation for too long to be left to questionable and diffuse power bases. The only sure way to prevent another military nightmare like the one that occurred between 1337 and 1498 was to involve the commonweal and to place these concerns under the firm direction of a revived and reformed government, which through the expanding role of Parliament and the royal council also became more inclusive by the middle of the sixteenth century. In this guise the more complex peace idea, including tranquillity and concord, could become a regular part of national debates on the issues of war and good government.

A New Typology of Peace

Since the last half of the Hundred Years War peace came to take on different meanings depending on the various situations and purposes for which it was used. First, there was the oldest and most deeply embedded understanding of peace as a spiritual quality that redounds almost exclusively to the individual Christian, who was required to love his or her enemy and

90. Ibid, lines 681–87, p. 32.
91. Adams, "Pre-Renaissance Courtly Propaganda," 445.

demonstrate mercy. As already discussed, this Augustinian position actually came to form the basis for the just war by relegating peace to a restricted arena and not extending it to society at large. Such a personalized view of peace is usually associated not only with the related idea of charity but also with mercy, piety, sufferance, and patience. The last term especially indicates the attitude of personal forbearance that became an essential element of this strictly spiritual ethic.

We have seen that the Crusades and prolonged dynastic wars that kept Europe locked in nearly uninterrupted combat for more than three hundred years, led in England to an unavoidable erosion of faith in both the just war and the law of arms as means for controlling violence. The commentators on Gratian and the decretalists attempted to delineate more concretely when wars were legitimate by expanding the *jus ad bellum* (right to make war), while the theologians put renewed emphasis on right intent on the part of individual soldiers. The knights were castigated on every front for unchivalric behavior, and works by Honoré de Bonet, Christine de Pisan, and Nicholas Upton hoped to restore the *jus armorum* by expanding the code to which its adherents must give allegiance. The breakdown of protective social institutions to which this situation gave rise provided the context for the second manner in which peace was invoked by the 1380s. Here peace meant the restoration of order and stability along with an end to knightly lawlessness and corruption. Tied inextricably to societal conditions and relationships, this meaning of peace invoked associations with order, quiet, rest, concord, and law. Gower, in his *Confessio amantis,* complained vehemently about the use of the just war by the nobility and "greedy lords" to amass great wealth in a criticism that would become standard over the next century. The exhortations of Bromyard, Fitzralph, and Brinton also concerned themselves with a return to order, law, and peace. These are but a few of the countless critiques of the "chivalry" that appeared by late century.

Closely related then to these couplings between peace and order or peace and tranquillity were the renewed emphases on peace as a rigorous Christian ideal that reflected the *imago Christi* in everyday life. For Chaucer, Wyclif, the Lollards, and many unquestionably orthodox thinkers who were enamored of this understanding of peace, the ability to live piously and chastely depended on the absence of war. This added dimension, which would not relegate peace to a primarily spiritual realm, also contradicted the personalized ethic of Augustine even as it included a similarly heavy concentration on charity, sufferance, mercy, and holy living. Peace with God, however, could only truly exist if people were at peace with their neighbors, which was a virtue in itself, not dependent necessarily on the particular temporal position of good and evil, which could suggest and promote a just recourse to war. Since the Scriptures plainly stated that Christ came to earth as the angels proclaimed peace, opposition to war must be a matter of conscience for all true Christians. Those who stressed this aspect of "Christ-like" peace usually found themselves confronting the Church, by arguing that its pastoral calling was being neglected for worldly gain through war. Wyclif assailed the clergy most stridently in this regard, and many of his works take up this theme with great relish. Because he doubted any charitable intent in warfare, he declared that men should now leave off fighting. All clerics, from the pope to the parish priest, were guilty of leading men to perdition by teaching them to kill rather than serving God and one another.[92]

The Lollards followed closely this line of reasoning when in article 10 of their Twelve Conclusions they declared that war went against the New Testament, since Christ taught us to be merciful to our enemies.[93] For them, peace was a matter of consistent Christ-like behavior among all people, even between Christians and heathens. It must be suffused with a heartfelt love for others and a willingness to sacrifice personal desires for God's kingdom of both spiritual and existential peace. This is an important shift, for the Lollard kingdom was not simply a hope of heaven after death, but one that existed in the here and now. This same belief would hold true as well for many English humanists and Protestants of the sixteenth century.

The final context for the emerging peace discourse of the later Middle Ages focuses on the practical benefits brought about by an end to war. In conjoining peace with the related ideas of prosperity, wealth, profit, and health, its more moralistic and ideological connotations or bases are muted and a concentration placed on its benefits to the nation. There are obvious similarities with those who argued for a restoration of stability and order, but "practical peace" writers came to the fore later and provided a more sophisticated, enduring, and profound understanding of the many possibilities of peace.

Lydgate, Hoccleve, the writer of the *Libelle of Englyshe Polycye*, as well as others who argued for peace from more pragmatic stances, appear for

92. [Wyclif], *On the Seven Deadly Sins*, chaps. 12 and 13, pp. 134–38; Wyclif, *Of Prelates*, 52–54, 73, 90–100.
93. Hudson, *Selections*, 27–28.

the most part in the early fifteenth century. A notable exception to this is Gower, who, possessing a fascination with peace that may have been somewhat superficial, early on did delineate with resolve the deleterious impact of war on English society. But Gower usually preferred to speak in platitudes, despite his very deep concern that destructive wars end. Hoccleve, however, as we have seen, penetrated further into the implications of peace, considering its abuse to be just as responsible for harming society as war. For him, peace was the result of godly behavior; but he went further, claiming that there were tangible advantages for the nation in loving one's enemy and called particular attention to the social disintegration that had accompanied the civil war in France.[94]

Employing peace in much the same manner as Hoccleve, Lydgate may have exhibited the strongest and most personal affection for its practical aspects, clearly emphasizing the connection between it and the public welfare. *The Libelle of Englyshe Polycye* does much the same with its advocacy of deterrence as a means to promote economic growth and security. All three writers together demonstrate the complexity of the peace idea as it came to be expressed in the early fifteenth century, when it was located increasingly in the language of political economy and less according to scholastic definition. Scholastic discourse could not incorporate fully the growing number of peace paradigms, and even though it still functioned as a valve to stem illicit warfare, the conceptual categories and linguistic forms it offered were too far removed from real events and concerns. The theologians had sanctioned warfare if it benefited the commonweal, a casuistry that varied only slightly from the cruel-necessity argument found in Augustine. Lydgate's approach, which would have much in common with those writing on war and peace in the next century, laid bare the speciousness of such reasoning by blaming war for creating the need to restore a harmony that would exist already if peoples and nations lived in peace.

While emphasizing economic well-being, these writers nevertheless assimilated other notions that stressed the personal and orderly characteristics of peace. A restorative quality is intrinsic to all four "types" of peace, and again, except for the first, which focuses more on the spiritual aspect, they are predicated on bringing an end to war (temporarily or completely) and all other violent conflicts among men. Depending on particular situations and concerns, the rhetoric itself changed and shifted emphasis. Those times when brigandage and military setbacks predominated, writers tended

---

94. Hoccleve, *Regement of Princes*, lines 5336–41, p. 192.

to bemoan the corruption and lack of discipline among soldiers, longing for an orderly peace that protected life and property. The Wycliffian critiques followed times when there were enhanced perceptions that the papacy favored France in the war, which in turn led many to call for reform of those Church teachings and practices that seemed to promote war at the expense of spiritual concerns. When commercial and agricultural troubles became acute or when severe conditions began to improve, as they did in the early fifteenth century, the discourse associated peace more directly with economic vitality and security, including ancillary ideas like deterrence. The reign of Henry VI witnessed the confluence of all of these conditions, and this precipitated a most vigorous discussion about the possibilities for peace. The ongoing war and the virtual collapse of royal government yielded an outcry against a conflict that was sapping the realm of its lifeblood and destroying the commonweal. While the nation did not find itself in such dire straits the following century, there were moments of rebellion and war when similar conditions existed and fears of a return to that inglorious past once again emerged. During those times a transformed peace discourse helped attune the nation once again to the overwhelming problem of war and violent conflict while attempting to direct energies to more productive outcomes.

Conclusion

These evidences of antiwar literature in late medieval England have been compiled to emphasize the growing aversion to the Hundred Years War and to trace the simultaneous development of early peace discourse. As has been shown, just-war theories and reliance on the law of arms to legitimize war had their limits and were substantially discredited in their application by the fifteenth century. England's constitutional system, which included some degree of consent before overseas military ventures were undertaken, made it easier to debate the problem of war itself.

It is difficult to know what the nation at large thought of the French war. News was hard to come by, and most people probably concerned themselves primarily with their own realm of work, family, and illness, rather than with a war going on far across the Channel. But as stated earlier, complete isolation from these events was rare. Some artisans, such as smiths, armorers, and shipbuilders benefited, as well as "purveyors and victualling officers." Taxation and continuing states of emergency made it virtually impossible for most people to ignore the war.[95] Many echoed the concerns of the critical literati. Sir Thomas Gray, who had been a prisoner in Scotland proclaimed: "Peace in itself is the earthly possession most to be coveted by all reasonable natures as the sovereign blessing of the age." Sir John Mandeville, after returning from his travels, lamented that "since the time of my departure, our two kings . . . have not ceased to war with destructions, depredations, ambushes and slaughter." In 1391, Walter Brut, describing himself as a "sinner, layman, farmer and a Christian" denounced all war as against the Bible. And Lollards throughout the realm could concur with Nicholas Hereford's contention that "Jesus Christ, duke of our battle, taught us [the] law of patience, and not to fight bodily."[96] Without too much exaggeration it can be said that a true movement, albeit an uncoordinated one, swept across England in the later Middle Ages, determined to end the war with France and tending toward a reevaluation of the whole practice of war itself.

With each writer who took up the challenges of advocating and preaching peace, some new, if very small, addition to the discourse was introduced. And each concern — whether it be for the common good, reform of government, reform of Church, or redirection of aristocratic activity — added an important dimension to the overall antiwar argument. New conceptualizations of peace began to affect contemporary modes of discourse and expand the vitality of those languages which were adaptable to peace paradigms, most notably the emerging discourses of political economy and Christian humanism. Once the war was over the lessons were not quickly forgotten, and the cumulative weight of these opinions found a haven in the overarching government policy of Henry VII and in the optimism of Erasmian pacifism.

95. Hewitt, *Organization of War,* 154–63.
96. Ibid., 133; Allmand, "War and the Non-Combatant," 175–76; Contamine, *War in the Middle Ages,* 294.

5

HUMANISM, WAR, AND AN EMERGING PEACE ETHIC

While the protracted wars which plagued late medieval England continued to enhance the value of peace, a context in which true peace could be envisioned came only with the arrival of the New Learning. It is mistaken, of course, to view the Renaissance as occurring within a dispassionate intellectual vacuum or in isolation, and it is precisely because medieval commentators had so tilled the ground that some humanists were able to reap the ideal of peace as a virtue above all others. If war was a sign of human depravity according to Gower, Lydgate, or Wyclif, it was even more so to those who possessed a greater optimism about the possibilities of human will, reason, and personal endeavor. For many educated people, then, by the early sixteenth century, achieving peace became the supreme test of humankind's ability to overcome a disposition toward barbarity—which if passed, would clearly separate it from the ignorant and brutish beasts that did not possess the benefits of reason and Christian teaching.

From a Medieval to a Humanist Peace Discourse

The actual impact of the burgeoning medieval peace discourse on the humanists is immensely difficult to assess. If we look at the external evidence by way of the publication record, we see that new editions of Gower's *Confessio Amantis* were published in 1483, 1532, 1544, and 1554, including an edition by Caxton and two others by the royal printer Thomas Berthelet. Lydgate's works experienced even more continued popularity. Of those which include a large peace component, ten new editions were published between 1494 and 1559.[1] At the same time Robert Crowley was reprinting Wyclif's *Pathway to Perfect Knowledge* (1550) and the peace-laden B text of *Piers Plowman* (twice in 1550).[2] While these figures in themselves are inconclusive, they do suggest a significant readership for respected medieval authors, unhampered by the so-called humanist disdain for their didactic moralism. As Elizabeth Eisenstein has so well described the impact of printing on early modern literate culture: "Increased output directed at relatively stable markets, in short, created conditions that formed new combinations of old ideas at first and then, later on, the creation of entirely new systems of thought."[3] While the development of the peace idea can hardly be called a new system of thought, it was, nevertheless, significantly transformed by humanists, who considered it such a valuable concept in all of its manifestations, that they fashioned it into an ethic with which all Christians should clothe themselves.

The access to medieval works by virtue of printing which humanists and Protestants enjoyed, and the "knowledge explosion" this access brought about, had an effect that while not easily determinable was crucial all the same.[4] The printed word in itself might have contributed to an elevation of the peace idea by encouraging debate and thereby proffering a dialogic means for two adversaries to come to terms. According to Walter Ong, "the word moves toward peace because the word mediates between person

---

1. *The Fall of Princes* (1494, 1527, 1554 [twice]); *Troy Book* (1513, 1555); *Proverbs* (two editions published ca. 1510); *The Serpent of Division* (1535, 1559).

2. J. R. Thorne and Marie-Claire Uhart, "Robert Crowley's *Piers Plowman*," *Medium Aevum* 55 (1986): 248–53; John N. King, "Crowley's Editions of *Piers Plowman*: A Tudor Apocalypse," *Modern Philology* 73 (1973): 346–48.

3. Elizabeth L. Eisenstein, *The Printing Revolution in Early Modern Europe* (Cambridge: Cambridge University Press, 1983), 43–44.

4. There is a danger in viewing the advance of printing as a cause or even indicator of social and cultural outlooks. Most dissemination of ideas continued to occur through oral channels, but here printing still could have had an enormous effect by broadening the information base of orators, especially preachers. Denis McQuail, *Mass Communication Theory*, 2d ed. (London: Sage, 1987), 182–83; R. W. Scribner, "Oral Culture and the Transmission of Reformation Ideas," in *The Transmission of Ideas in the Lutheran Reformation*, ed. Helga Robinson-Hammerstein (Dublin: Irish Academic Press, 1989), 83–104.

and person. No matter how much it gets caught up in currents of hostility, the two persons keep talking, despite themselves they are not totally hostile."[5] It is precisely this need to "civilize" or "rationalize" the problem of war that motivated men like Gower, Hoccleve, Wyclif, and Lydgate to devote so much of their literary output to the cause of peace, even before the advent of printing. Lydgate was especially attracted to the possibilities of eloquent language "in reforming men and creating order." To him, the poet civilizes the human animal and has a duty to set out instructive examples in a way that convinces as well as delights the reader. The *Fall of Princes* portrays the destructiveness of Fortune, contrasting it with poetry, all in the service of humanity's highest good and the commonweal, which includes peace.[6]

The humanists were actually not so different from these late medieval writers and certainly practiced a moralism all their own. Considering their lack of plagiarism from medieval works and a predilection for the rediscovered classics, perhaps their borrowings are more of a reformist or ideational form, springing from a natural adoption of the interpretive traditions of their predecessors when similar contexts emerged. While Chaucer could find Cicero's emphasis on mercy useful for his discussion of war in the "Tale of Melibeus," Erasmus was able to argue that peace came from recognizing that all people are bound by universal laws, thus rooting his pacifist position more firmly in Stoic presuppositions.[7] We can definitely conclude that the sixteenth century was a dynamic age, an age of innovation and recombination, and temporal peace with its many delicate and practical virtues caught on as the century progressed. If we look then at the internal evidence, we find that the lines of argument differ little between 1440 and 1540 even if the idioms of expression do.

5. Walter J. Ong, S.J., *The Presence of the Word: Some Prolegomena for Cultural and Religious History* (New Haven, Conn.: Yale University Press, 1967), 192–95. See also Roger Caillois, *Man and the Sacred,* trans. Meyer Barash (Westport, Conn.: Greenwood Press, 1980), 177, which contrasts the hostile nature of oral culture with the peace norm that exists in typographic societies.

6. Lois A. Ebin, *John Lydgate* (Boston: Twayne, 1985), 16–18. For Ebin, Lydgate's genius lies in the way he helped to embed these values in English culture. "A Praise of Peace" "moves toward the realm of artifact . . . in its distillation of permanent values from impermanent events" (p. 91). On Gower's and Lydgate's application of rhetorical theory within a larger, purposeful civic discourse, see Copeland, "Lydgate, Hawes, and the Science of Rhetoric in the Late Middle Ages," 57–82, and Frank Grady, "The Lancastrian Gower and the Limits of Exemplarity," *Speculum* 70 (1995): 552–75.

7. Erasmus, *Panegyricus ad Philippum Austriae Ducem,* in *CWE,* trans. Betty Radice, 27: 54–56.

It is a belief in the expanding possibilities of peace through literary device that ultimately connects the medieval moralists and the Erasmian
humanists.

But humanists had scant respect for scholastic technique and exhibited
an outright disdain for the detached moralism that often accompanied it.
Their enchantment with antiquity tended to preclude the serious consideration of emergent ideas, even peace, which could be found in any product of medieval discourse. Erasmus and his coterie of "pacifists" harkened
back rather self-consciously to ancient Rome and adopted the classical humanism of Stoic philosophy as their vehicle of social and political expression. For them, of course, the difference was that now in the Christian era
there existed even a greater moral obligation and opportunity for bringing
about *concordia* and *pax* among all people.[8]

Early imperial Rome appeared to many humanists a golden age; the *pax
Romana* ensured effective government, economic prosperity, and social
tranquillity as the world had never witnessed before or since. Erasmus,
Thomas More, Richard Pace, and Juan Luis Vives all admired the Stoic
teaching that stressed the kinship of humanity and adherence to those natural laws which led reasonable creatures to live at peace and treat one
another with love and kindness.[9] In both *De beneficiis* and *De otio,* Seneca
taught patience and toleration rather than retaliation or anger in the face
of injury. But he and Epictetus typify the ancient Stoic bias that caused
them to call upon their fellow citizens to restrain their passions against the
enemy as a "great soul" or "noble man" rises above his inferiors. The
victory over evil is largely an internal one, where the soul is uplifted and
baser feelings of revenge are mastered.[10] The Renaissance humanists, however, were also Christians and tended to view all humans as part of God's
creation and equally deserving of the benefits of peace in an external sense.
Along with Scripture, classical *sententiae* denouncing wars were habitually
used by humanists in England to convince readers of the morally superior
condition of peace. Some of the more notable examples include "pax op-

8. John C. Olin, "The Pacifism of Erasmus," in *Six Essays on Erasmus* (New York:
Fordham University Press, 1979), 17–31.

9. Gilles D. Monsarrat, *Light from the Porch: Stoicism and English Renaissance Literature,* Collection études anglaises no. 86 (Paris: Didier-Erudition, 1984), 15–16, 72–76, 85–
89, 99–101; Lange, *Histoire de la doctrine pacifique,* 190–91.

10. Seneca, *De beneficiis* 7.30.2, 5, and *De otio* 1.4; Epictetus, *Discourses* 1.25.29,
2.13.11; Ronald G. Musto, *The Catholic Peace Tradition* (Maryknoll, N.Y.: Orbis Books,
1986), 17.

tima rerum, quas homini novisse datum est,"[11] "dulce bellum inexpertis,"[12] and "pax iniusta utilior est quam iustissimum bellum."[13] Overall, the writings of Seneca, Epictetus, Pliny, Sallust, and Silius informed much humanist opinion regarding war and peace, but it was Cicero's *De officiis* that became the prescribed standard by which princes should rule and conduct relations with one another, at least until late in the century.[14] In England alone this work was translated and reprinted continuously in the first half of the sixteenth century, sometimes twice in one year, and as the premier example of civic oratory, the writer was by far the most quoted expert on politics of the day. Yet despite his arguments for humane behavior, integrity, and a larger vision of common humanity, Cicero also argued in favor of the just war. Augustine had found his arguments little more than subtle casuistry to defend previous Roman conquests. Erasmus, however, emphasized Cicero's humanitarianism and connected it with similar emphases he found in the New Testament.[15]

11. "Peace is the best of all things given to man by nature." Silius, *Punica* 11.592–93; referred to by Pace, in *An Oration on Peace,* publ. 1518, in J. G. Russell, *Peacemaking in the Renaissance* (Philadelphia: University of Pennsylvania Press, 1986), 235, and found in Erasmus's *Querela pacis,* in *CWE,* trans. Betty Radice, 27:299, and in the anonymous, Erasmus-inspired poem, *A Pretye Complaynt of Peace* (London, John Byddle, [1538], sig. C1r.

12. "How sweet is war to those unfamiliar with it." Originally taken from the Greek poet Pindar's proverb *glukus apeirois polemos,* this saying served as the title of Erasmus's most antiwar adage (*Adagiae* 4.4.1). See also Pace, *Oration,* 237; Richard Taverner, *Proverbes or Adagies with New Addicions Gathered Out of the Chiliades of Erasmus* (London, 1539); and George Gasciogne, *Dulce bellum inexpertis,* in *The Complete Works of George Gasciogne,* ed. John W. Cunliffe (Cambridge: Cambridge University Press, 1907–10), 1:142–84.

13. "The worst peace is preferable to the best (or most just) war." Cicero, *Epistulae ad Atticum* 7.14, and *Epistulae ad familiares* 6.6.5. Perhaps the most common of all antiwar slogans, Lydgate repeated it (see Chapter 4), as did Erasmus in *Querela pacis* (pp. 310–11) and *Panegyricus* (*CWE,* 27:55); Colet in a celebrated sermon preached around 1513 (John B. Gleason, *John Colet* [Berkeley and Los Angeles: University of California Press, 1989], 256–59]; the writer of the advice manual, *The Institucion of a Gentleman* (London: Thomas Marshe, 1555, sigs. F2v–F3v); and Stephen Gardiner in two of his letters written during the wars of the 1540s (no. 86, to Paget, 13 November 1545, and no. 117, to Somerset, 28 February 1547, both in James A. Muller, ed., *The Letters of Stephen Gardiner* [Cambridge: The University Press, 1933], 189, 265).

14. Cicero, *De officiis* 1.53–56, 100, 107, 2.32; Seneca, *Epistulae morales* 91.17–18, 94.61–69, 113.27–31, and *Quaestiones naturales,* bk. 3; Sallust, *Bellum Catilinae,* 1–3, 9, and *Bellum Iugurthinum,* passim.

15. Adams, *Better Part of Valor,* 7–8; A. C. Lloyd, "Emotion and Decision in Stoic Philosophy," and I. G. Kidd, "Moral Actions and Rules in Stoic Ethics," in *The Stoics,* ed. John M. Rist (Berkeley and Los Angeles: University of California Press, 1978), 233–58; Matthew 5:9, John 14:27, 16:33, 1 Peter 3:11, Hebrews 12:14.

Henry VII and the Vestiges of Chivalry (1450–1509)

Before considering the impact of humanism we must first turn to the cultural context of early Tudor England. The cult of chivalry was experiencing a last gasp beginning about 1450 before expiring (in its traditional guise) by the 1530s. Technological and tactical innovations, especially more powerful guns and revived cavalry shock action, had given brief respite from the massive siege and counter-siege action that characterized the final stages of the Hundred Years War, but which returned after the 1530s.[16] During these intervening years with their renewed emphasis on prowess, Henry VIII was most active in trying to revivify the glories of field action, even as "firearms effectively ruined the battle as a chivalric exercise."[17] Yet until Henry's wars, which began in the 1510s, England had generally tried to withdraw from commitments and situations that might entangle it in foreign conflicts. The civil war that followed the long French conflict left the nation weary and impoverished both politically and economically. As already shown, Edward IV did attempt another invasion of France in 1475 but only with great difficulty could he muster the necessary forces. In fact, there is good reason to believe these troops were woefully unskilled and unprepared because the growing unpopularity of military careers had led to a shortage of suitable soldiers. Edward, and his surrogate, the bishop of Durham, made eloquent pleas for support in the Parliament of 1474, even associating a renewed war with the maintenance of peace and prosperity at home. Perhaps they were responding to the counterarguments of men like Lydgate, who had found war in the previous reign to be the cause of social, political, and economic ills. The saber-rattling did not lead to battle, largely because of the duke of Burgundy's lack of support, so Edward resorted to a practice that would also be popular with the first Tudor king: leave France with a large indemnity and annual pension.[18] In the end, both Edward IV and Henry VII eschewed war, aiming instead to unify and strengthen the realm bureaucratically and judicially by extending royal administration relentlessly into local areas.

On the Continent, however, rulers generally did not have the luxury of withdrawing behind protected boundaries. Learning a different lesson in

16. Vale, *War and Chivalry*, 171–74.
17. Ibid., 173.
18. Lander, "Edward IV's 1475 Campaign," 82–83, 91.

the war with England, French monarchs sought greater security by creating a professional standing army between 1445 and 1448.[19] War would become an ineradicable fact of life for France, Spain, and the Holy Roman Empire throughout the early modern period, while England could choose whether and when to become involved in foreign dynastic struggles. Yet a skeleton of chivalry prevailed among the English nobility until the gradual humanist transformation of education shifted the focus away from prowess and more toward letters. The late fifteenth century witnessed a growing uneasiness with the attributes and products of knightly codes but there was no satisfying alternative. Critics of war maintained a "chivalric frame of reference" that even went so far as to champion the true calling of the knight as peacemaker.[20] But this incipient movement to give knighthood a relevance beyond its traditional and feudal setting proved instrumental in creating a uniquely English evolution of knight into gentleman, and ultimately a more practical understanding of his role within the commonweal.[21]

Without attaching too much meaning to this metamorphosis, recent research has nonetheless offered some intriguing insights into how the developing concept of gentleman-statesman in England directly challenged martial values prominent in the education of medieval knights. Philippe Contamine recently made a study of the difference between gentleman and *gentilhomme,* two ideas that emerged in the later Middle Ages. The latter concept refers to a "quaint and faintly ridiculous" figure, courageous and respectable, while the former "evokes a more active figure, open and receptive to changing times and habits." England's production of "gentlemen-bureaucrats" and "merchant gentlemen" was unique in Europe, and in France especially, it was harder for nobles to redefine their primary roles in society.[22]

Henry VII's reign provided a suitable environment that permitted a weaning of the noble away from the main activity of fighting, while ushering him into a newer role that made use of other, more functional talents in government, rather than martial valor. The story of the king's shrewd ability to unite a kingdom fractured by civil war has become almost legendary in its retelling; and it therefore may seem obvious that he avoided war

19. Ibid., 147.
20. A. B. Ferguson, *The Indian Summer of English Chivalry* (Durham, N.C.: Duke University Press, 1960), 107, 129.
21. Ibid., 118–19; Ferguson, *Chivalric Tradition,* 40–42.
22. Philippe Contamine, "France at the End of the Middle Ages: Who Was Then the Gentleman?" in *Gentry and Lesser Nobility in Late Medieval Europe,* ed. Michael Jones (New York: St. Martin's Press, 1986), 212; Jean-Marie Constant, *La Vie quotidienne de la noblesse française aux XVIe and XVIIe siècles* (Paris: Hachette Littérature, 1985).

at least in part because it would have not allowed him to create a strong political nation. Yet Henry seems to have been genuinely opposed to war as an activity, especially after the Yorkist defeat at Exeter in 1497.[23] He was something of an early exponent of *realpolitik,* more concerned with the political and economic rather than the spiritual benefits of forsaking war. The celebrated foreign policy intrigues that pacified Ireland, France, Spain, and Scotland (the latter two through marriage treaties) served to make England just as serious a player in international affairs as any war could have.[24] According to S. B. Chrimes, Henry VII's most noted modern biographer, he abandoned the quest for a greater English empire in France because "mediation and the encouragement and preservation of a balance of power, not aggression or conquests, were his objectives, as befitted a realist who realized the limitations of his power. The influence he sought to wield was financial rather than military."[25]

Contemporary evidence paints a similar picture. Robert Fabyan offered this eulogy to the king:

> Of whom sufficient laud and praise cannot be put in writing, considering the continual peace and tranquility which he kept this his land and commons in, with also this subduing of his outward enemies of the realms of France and Scotland, by his great policy and wisdom, more than by shedding of Christian blood or cruel war . . . but all Christian princes hearing of his glorious fame, were desirous to have with him amity and alliance.[26]

Polydore Vergil's chronicle of Henry's reign includes three specific references to the king's dislike for war and love of peace. The use of peace as both policy and a defense can be found in this description of his foreign affairs: "It was indeed a great ambition of Henry's to be in friendship and peace with neighbouring monarchs, and specially with King James [IV of Scotland]; so that his English subjects, knowing there was no refuge or place of safety for rebels in neighbouring lands, would the more readily be

23. Gilbert Millar, *Tudor Mercenaries and Auxiliaries* (Charlottesville: University Press of Virginia, 1980), 8.

24. See S. B. Chrimes, *Henry VII* (Berkeley and Los Angeles: University of California Press, 1971), 272–93, 318–21; also A. F. Pollard, *The Reign of Henry VII from Contemporary Sources,* vol. 1, *Narrative Extracts* (London: Longmans, Green, 1913), lii–lx.

25. Chrimes, *Henry VII,* 321.

26. Robert Fabyan, *The New Chronicles of England and France in Two Parts,* ed. Henry Ellis (London: F. C. and J. Rivington; T. Payne; Wilkie and Robinson; Longman, Hurst, Rees, Orme; Cadell and Davies; J. Mawman; and J. Johnson, 1811), 678.

kept in obedience."[27] In other places Vergil remarked that "Henry was a lover of peace," and that "he was most fortunate in war, although he was constitutionally more inclined to peace than war."[28] The king's pairing of peace with economic prosperity is readily evident in a perusal of the royal proclamations issued during his reign. Those which announce or renew peace and "free trade" with Austria, Burgundy, Denmark, and the Holy Roman Empire were predicated on a desire for an "abstinence of war, increase of merchandise, and amities be had" and an interest in "very firm and perfect amity."[29] Yet Henry's proclamations of peace were constructed legalistically, more as contracts, especially when compared to those of his son and grandson.[30] That he viewed the maintenance of peace as a practical value can be found even in his will, when he admitted his desire that the princess Mary marry the archduke of Austria (later Charles V) to ensure "peace, profit, and commodity . . . universally and particularly for our said realm and subjects."[31]

If the above evidence appears overly rhetorical or circumstantial in presenting Henry as a monarch devoted to peace, a look at how he viewed his own military may shed greater light. "Indifferent toward training," he did not feel the need to compel a hesitant nobility into fulfilling its military obligations. Thus, no military procurement policy emerged, indicating that he was "reluctant to go the whole way in military matters." Again, it may ultimately have come down to money, as Henry was always careful to weigh in the balance (and on the balance sheet) the expenses for his government.[32] That he found it too costly to fund a military that would bind local magnates to himself surely suggests that he found the production of any kind of war machine to be a very low priority.

27. Polydore Vergil, *The Anglica Historia of Polydore Vergil,* A.D. *1485–1536,* ed. and trans. Denys Hay, Camden Soc., 3d ser., vol. 74 (London: Royal Historical Society, 1950), 29.
28. Ibid., 101, 147.
29. *TRP,* no. 18 (1489), 19–20; no. 21 (1490), 22; no. 23 (1490), 24.
30. For example see no. 29, "Announcing Peace Treaty with France," 12 December 1492: "The king our sovereign lord Henry, by the grace [of God] King of France and of England and lord of Ireland, doth you to understand that good, sure, and firm peace, union, and amity is made and concluded betwixt the king our said sovereign lord and the right high and mighty prince his cousin of France." Ibid., p. 31. This construction is found in Henry VIII's announcements until around 1525 when more emphasis is placed on the value of peace as a proper condition between states. This trend becomes even more pronounced by 1543 and into the reign of Edward VI.
31. Henry VII, *The Will of King Henry VII,* ed. Thomas Astle (London: Printed for the Editor, 1775), 41.
32. James R. Hooker, "Notes on the Organization and Supply of the Tudor Military under Henry VII," *Huntington Library Quarterly* 23 (1959–60): 20–31.

In associating peace more naturally with economic vitality, Henry was also reflecting the genuine convictions and concerns of his own merchants, especially those in Calais and Bruges, who wanted to ensure that the wool staple in Flanders continued its profitable growth. The Cely family wool merchants felt they had a great deal to lose if Flanders were attacked by the French and the trade interrupted. In 1484 they worried that "schrowyd tornys" (annoying injuries) by the English could lead to war, while six years earlier, the elder Richard wrote to son George at Calais that he hoped Christ would show them "great mercy" and "send them a good peace in the Duke of Burgundy's lands, or else there will be no foreign buyers forthcoming."[33] The customs revenues were important to the king's overall plan to make the crown as self-sufficient as possible, and as such, it found common cause and mutual interest with England's merchants abroad.

There has been a small trend recently to portray Henry's foreign policy as less one-dimensional, and this includes reducing the emphasis usually put on his peacemaking. One historian has gone so far as to claim that the king's successes in diplomacy were based on his brilliant warmaking and military skills.[34] These and other arguments, however, do not detract from or contradict what Polydore Vergil and other contemporaries maintained about Henry's innate desire for peace; they only expand the foundations on which his peace was constructed. At the same time, other scholars have emphasized the practical nature of the king's maintenance of peace. A recent study of the Anglo-Scottish Treaty of Perpetual Peace (1502) provides a case in point. The agreement's central tenet, the marriage between Henry's daughter Margaret and Scottish king James IV, came out of a long, painstaking process of negotiation between the two nations that originated under Edward IV. With this pact Henry was able to reduce significantly the threat of a revivified "auld alliance" between Scotland and France. Only after his son's ascension to the throne in 1509 did the peace

33. *The Cely Letters, 1472–1488,* ed. Alison Hanham, EETS no. 273 (London: Oxford University Press, 1975), letter 24, 218; pp. 29, 215–16.

34. Ian Arthurson, "The King's Voyage into Scotland: The War that Never Was," in *England in the Fifteenth Century: Proceedings of the 1986 Harlaxton Symposium,* ed. Daniel Williams (Suffolk, Eng.: Boydell Press, 1987), 1–22. See also Steven Gunn, "Chivalry and the Politics of the Early Tudor Court," in *Chivalry in the Renaissance,* ed. Sydney Anglo (Suffolk, Eng.: Boydell Press, 1990), 107–28; and Richard Glen Eaves, *Henry VIII's Scottish Diplomacy, 1513–1524: England's Relations with the Regency Government of James V* (New York: Exposition Press, 1971), 25.

begin to deteriorate and to break down finally in 1511. It is unlikely the
elder Henry would have permitted that to happen.[35]

The various components of Henry's "pacifist" policy are difficult to
measure. Most likely, the king was primarily interested in maintaining political and economic security at home and saw wars as distractions and
drains on the treasury. That overtly pragmatic approach to foreign policy
was a bit anomalous for the age and probably owed little to any personal
devotion to the moral superiority of peace which the late-medieval writers
had argued; but even if this were the case it does not preclude the possibility that unintentionally Henry was identifying with and even supporting
newer outlooks that promoted peace as an indicator of enlightened society.

Perhaps the most important correspondence between these two configurations of peace (pragmatic and moral) and a growing decline in martial
activity can be found in the penetrations which the New Learning made
into England by the turn of the sixteenth century, with its emphasis on a
new nobility and the virtues of peace. As early as 1497, in his commentary
on Romans 12, the dean of St. Paul's, John Colet, strongly criticized the
effects of war while praising the health that comes from peace:

> Hence we ought to aim as much as possible at goodness, in order to
> conquer evil; and at peace and forbearance, to overcome war and
> unjust actions. For it is not by war that war is conquered, but by
> peace, and forbearance, and reliance on God. . . . Sooth to say, the
> Christian warrior's prowess is his patience, his action in suffering,
> and his victory, a sure trust in God.[36]

This gloss on Paul's discussion concerning the powers of government authorities was a critical exercise that renders pacific chivalric imagery and
reveals Colet's early rejection of Thomist just-war arguments and his belief
that no good could ever come from such an evil thing as war.[37] This attitude would continue into the next reign and would place him in a much
more adversarial position with respect to actual government policy.

35. David Dunlop, "The Politics of Peace-Keeping: Anglo-Scottish Relations from 1503 to
1511," *Renaissance Studies* 8 (1994): 138–61.
36. John Colet, *Ioannis Coleti enarratio in epistolam S. Pauli ad Romanos,* ed. J. H. Lupton (London, 1873; reprint, Ridgewood, N.J.: The Gregg Press, 1965), 86–88.
37. Robert P. Adams, "The Literary Thought on War and Peace in English Literature of
the Renaissance," *American Philosophical Society Year Book 1955* (Philadelphia: The American Philosophical Society, 1956), 274.

Also in 1497, an interlude was presented at court entitled *Fulgens and Lucres,* written by Henry Medwall, chaplain to Cardinal Morton, and based on Bonus Accursius's Ciceronian-inspired *De vera nobilitate* (1428), which had been published in an English translation by Caxton in 1481.[38] The scene is of a humble humanist, Gaius Flaminius, who wins the hand of a refined Roman woman, Lucres, because of his virtuous honor and for being a valuable and "loyal servant of the state."[39] In rejecting his rival, a more traditional knight named Publius Cornelius, Lucres exclaims:

> That a man of excellent virtuous condition,
> Although he be of a poor stock born,
> Yet I will honor and commend him more
> Than one that is descended of right noble kin
> Whose life is all dissolute and rotted in sin.[40]

The expanding definition of true honor to include activities other than martial expertise and the courtly love to which it gave rise further enabled the mid-Tudor English gentleman to create a new identity for himself which had clear antecedents in the changing nature of public service during the reign of Henry VII and perhaps even earlier. In providing a humanist education for his heirs — Arthur and then Henry — the king understood the value of letters for capable rule in a modern prince. Henry VIII's schooling, however, lacked some of the practical wisdom of his father, especially in financial matters; and in the area of war, it re-created problems that mercifully had been spared the realm during the first Tudor's reign.

A Return to War (1509–1514)

A full discussion of how humanism helped to introduce a noticeable shift in aristocratic self-awareness will come later in this chapter. At this juncture it should be pointed out simply that the growing value of education for gentlemen became strongly apparent by the 1510s. Some were still

38. The Caxton edition included John Tiptoft, the earl of Worcester's, translations of Bonus and Cicero's *De amicitia* and *De senectute.*

39. Mervyn James, *English Politics and the Concept of Honour, 1485–1642. Past and Present,* Supplement, no. 3 (1979): 59.

40. Henry Medwall, *The Plays of Henry Medwall,* ed. Alan H. Nelson (Woodbridge, Eng.: D. S. Brewer, 1980), pt. 2, lines 789–93, p. 86.

reluctant, however, to consider book learning a knightly skill. There is the well-known story related by the diplomat Richard Pace in 1517 of an unknown gentleman who remarked: "It becomes the sons of gentlemen to blow the horn nicely, to hunt skillfully, and elegantly to carry and train a hawk. . . . The study of letters was for rustics. . . . Rather my son should hang than he be educated."[41] In France, the older chivalric upbringing was still predominant, but in England a new aristocracy and gentry, often connected to commerce, business, or law came to the fore, and many were educated in the universities. Influenced by humanism, they looked not to find their place in a specifically defined social continuum but to use their divinely bestowed faculties to discover God's purposes in the world and their place within them. The person of the prince was necessary to keep proper balance and order for this integrated, organic hierarchy, which, while in need of reform, was still not to be disturbed in any fundamental way. At the apex of the social structure, the prince provided an example of both wisdom and moderation. He was to be just, selfless, and generous, the antithesis of the tyrant. He was also to act as the guarantor of peace, which was the fundamental means for ensuring stability. Reminiscent of the arguments posited by Marsilius and Dante, humanists often tended toward utopian visions of reform that depended on the abilities and ethics of princes.[42] In this outlook, the traditional knights held no special place, civil service superseded military service, and the gentleman who served the prince should display all the characteristics of virtuous, godly, and loyal behavior.[43]

Did Henry VIII measure up to this lofty princely ideal? Some of the most celebrated humanists in Europe at the time hoped he would. Between 1509 and 1519, Colet, Thomas More, and Erasmus (the so-called Oxford reformers) all felt that the king might usher in a new progressive age for Europe — one that included an end to war. Basing their beliefs on the Stoic optimism of Cicero and Seneca, they viewed humans as perfectible beings who, through education, could use their God-given abilities to follow

41. Richard Pace, *De fructu* (Basil, 1517), preface cited in *Early English Meals and Manners,* ed. F. J. Furnivall, EETS OS, no. 32 (London: Kegan Paul, Trench, Trübner, 1868), xii–xiii. J. H. Hexter, "The Education of the Aristocracy in the Renaissance," *Journal of Modern History* 22 (1950): 2.

42. Johnson, *Quest for Peace,* 111–12, and "Two Kinds of Pacifism: Opposition to the Political Use of Force in the Renaissance-Reformation Period," *Journal of Religious Ethics* 12 (1984): 39.

43. Paul N. Siegel, "English Humanism and the New Tudor Aristocracy," *Journal of the History of Ideas* 13 (1952): 452–67.

Christ's example and live according to God's law (natural law). For human progress, however, the humanists insisted on the absence of war, which they held to be the most reprehensible of sins. Those attributes of chivalry which contributed to anything less than total aversion to bloodshed were similarly excoriated.[44] Determined soon after his succession, however, to demonstrate expertise in the art of war, Henry would prove less than the ideal role model for princes. Yet the fact that his overseas ventures were sporadic and that he openly supported humanists of the pacifist persuasion (such as Colet, Vives, and Erasmus) kept the latter's hopes alive, at least until the failure of the Treaty of Universal Peace (1518).[45]

The king's first foray into Continental politics came in November 1511 when he joined the Holy League against France, despite a peace treaty made by his father that was still binding. The following year, Thomas Grey took a force to assist Ferdinand of Spain's invasion of Guienne. The Venetian consul in London reported that the Privy Council opposed the campaign, and so Henry worked to put Louis XII in the wrong with an insincere and bogus peace initiative that the French king summarily rejected.[46] The resulting, full-scale expedition to France was the first for England in Europe since the Hundred Years War had ended in 1453, and the soldiers demonstrated their inexperience by retaining the longbow rather than using the newer handgun. But the 24,000 troops sent in 1513 were able to capture the towns of Thérouanne and Tournai, and to win the Battle of the Spurs on August 16. Peace came in 1514, and Henry kept the towns, for a time, along with a pension. The simultaneous victory over Scottish king James IV at Flodden by the earl of Surrey seemed to indicate that these early military ventures were brilliant successes that boded well for the future.[47]

Even in the midst of martial euphoria, however, there was a prominent dissenter. Colet's famous sermon against war, delivered on Good Friday

44. Robert P. Adams, "Designs by More and Erasmus for a New Social Order," *Studies in Philology* 42 (1945): 133–39; Stanley Windass, *Christianity versus Violence: A Social and Historical Study of War and Christianity* (London: Sheed & Ward, 1964), 65–66.

45. A. G. Dickens and Whitney R. D. Jones, *Erasmus the Reformer* (London: Methuen, 1994), 66–68.

46. *Cal. Ven.* 2:11; C. G. Cruickshank, *Army Royal. Henry VIII's Invasion of France, 1513* (Oxford: Clarendon Press, 1969), 1–6.

47. Corelli Barnett, *Britain and Her Army, 1509–1970* (London: Allen Lane, 1970), 3–13; C.S.L. Davies, "The English People and War in the Early Sixteenth Century," in *Britain and the Netherlands,* ed. A. C. Duke and C. A. Tamse (The Hague: Martinus Nijhoff, 1977), 6:2; J. J. Scarisbrick, *Henry VIII* (Berkeley and Los Angeles: University of California Press, 1968), 21–25.

(March 27) 1513,[48] did come when England's prospects for victory were quite low, but it is indicative of his long-standing opposition to wars on moral and religious grounds. Within the past year he had quoted in a previous sermon Cicero's adage that the most unfavorable peace was preferable to the most just war.[49] The bishop of Rochester at the time, Richard Fitz-James, and other enemies of Colet were aware of this and looked for a chance to use it to discredit him. The Good Friday sermon on the victory of Christ provided just that opportunity when the dean of St. Paul's repeated the Ciceronian maxim and supported it with his own passionate commentary.[50] Erasmus recounted most of what he preached, describing how at one point Colet expounded on the infrequency of just wars:

> For they, he said, who through hatred or ambition were fighting, the bad with the bad, and slaughtering one another by turns, were warring under the banner not of Christ but of the Devil. At the same time, he pointed out to them how hard a thing it was to die a Christian death; how few entered on a war unsullied by hatred or love of gain; how incompatible a thing it was, that a man should have that brotherly love without which no one would see God, and yet bury his sword in his brother's heart.[51]

Considering the residual medieval criticism that found its way into much of the antiwar discourse of the day, Henry may have feared that the sermon could engender a lack of nerve among his soldiers, and so he called Colet to meet with him the next day at Greenwich, where they talked in the garden for one and a half hours. What the dean said to reassure the king is not known but Henry was impressed, and, to the dismay of Colet's enemies, publicly drank to him: "Let every man have his own doctor, and

48. Colet's most recent biographer doubts the sermon was given until 1515 when the war was essentially over and England in retreat. Erasmus, who was there at the time, provided the details that for lack of any contradictory evidence, should be upheld. Erasmus's statement that "no one dared attack Colet" after the king's support was given may be a reflection of hindsight when enemies were noticed even before October 1514. Wolsey's assumption of the chancellorship the following year seems to me an irrelevant basis for dating the sermon. Gleason, *John Colet,* 256–57.

49. See note 13.

50. J. H. Lupton, *A Life of John Colet* (London: G. Bell & Sons, 1909), 188–89; Desiderius Erasmus, *Lives of Johan Vitrier, Warden of the Franciscan Convent at St. Omer and Jean Colet, Dean of St. Paul's, London,* ed. and trans. J. H. Lupton (London: George Bell & Sons, 1883), 41–42.

51. Erasmus, *Lives of Vitrier and Colet,* 43–44.

every one follow his liking; but this is the doctor for me."[52] It is unlikely that Henry made Colet see the error of his ways (or vice versa), for six years later, a letter from a canon of Mainz to the dean praised him for a recent antiwar speech he had given: "You treated the topic with such great authority that I might truly say that the power of Christ shone out of Colet. By His power you safely dispersed the darkness of your treacherous adversaries; you conquered, by almost apostle-like composure, men raging against the truth; and you quietly turned aside their insane onslaughts."[53]

Colet and his colleagues continued to castigate the just war throughout their various antiwar writings. The cynicism over weary excuses for selfish conquest and bloodlust evolved from the earlier critiques made by their medieval forebears, even if they were loath to acknowledge it. But for the humanists the intellectual climate had clearly shifted in their favor, and they felt no compulsion to counter scholastic and legal arguments point by point, since those constructs were themselves too divorced from the real world and common sense. Yet by reducing the issue of war to a call for sensible reason and the example of Christ, the Erasmian "pacifists" may have been just as negligent as their medieval counterparts in appealing to unreal notions to discredit all wars. The humanists, however, did have an impact on the development of peace rhetoric, not just in their significant contributions to the sheer volume of antiwar complaint, but also by creating an accepted value for peace that would grow eventually into a new ethic that rejected war both as a moral good and as the natural means for settling disputes among nations. By looking at the early wars of Henry VIII and the tremendous amount of peace rhetoric that accompanied them, we can perhaps better appreciate just how much the focus did move away from the value of glorious victory in war to the diplomatic skill involved in making a true peace—even if at this stage, peace was more of a tool of statecraft than an actual ethic.

52. Ibid., 44–46; Cruickshank, *Army Royal*, 6–7; Lupton, *Life of John Colet*, 190–93.

53. Marquardus de Hatstein to Colet found in *Epistolae aliquot eruditorum virorum* (1520) and quoted in Edward Surtz, *The Praise of Wisdom* (Chicago: Loyola University Press, 1957), 272–73. Here I must once again differ with Gleason who believes that Colet preached a retracting (or conciliatory) sermon to appease Henry at some later date. The only evidence for this is an unsubstantiated statement made by Matthew Parker many years later. Keeping in mind this letter from Mainz and his Bible commentaries, Colet's commitment to an antiwar stance is unequivocal, and it is doubtful he would have begun compromising at this late stage in his life. More than likely he just let pass Henry's suggestion that he clarify his views at some later time (which is a vague request anyway), hoping the king would become too preoccupied with other matters. Gleason, *John Colet*, 258–59.

While Colet may have been the most notable and pointed critic of Henry's first war, he was hardly alone. Erasmus had written his famous *Praise of Folly* in 1509 and, four years later, *Julius Excluded from Heaven,* which condemned the bellicose actions of Julius II in forming the Holy League. His English friends protested more cautiously and tentatively. Archbishop William Warham opened the Parliament of 1512 by stating that the sins of rulers and peoples were responsible for wars.[54] As late as December 1514, the Spanish ambassador gave an instruction for Ferdinand that acknowledged Henry's warmongering while remaining confident that "his Councillors can be influenced through their dislike of war" to accept peace.[55] Despite the war, however, Henry's shine had lost little of its luster in the eyes of the most committed antiwar humanists. Since the English king had made peace while Spain and France remained at war, Henry seemed to have taken the higher ground, even if, in truth, it was the expense of two simultaneous campaigns that had provided the heeded counsel.

The Emergence of Erasmian Pacifism (1514–1518)

The peace treaty concluded with Louis XII in 1514 gave rise to great expectation among many humanists that Europe could now unite in peace and prepare to launch a crusade against the Turk. For these men, Christian nations were exhorted to follow the example of Christ and to live peaceably among themselves; heathen lands were, of course, to be denied participation in this glorious quest. Between 1509 and 1520, according to one historian of this group, "by critical analysis (books, pamphlets, sermons, letters, etc.) they strove to discern anew the nature of war, the peaceful potentialities of human nature, and the problems whose solutions were most urgent if peace and social reforms were to be achieved in practice."[56]

Erasmus, with his international reputation, was the moral leader and the most prolific of these writers. In 1515 he produced an edition of his *Adages* that included *Dulce bellum inexpertis,* a straightforward yet stinging attack on early modern warfare. This particular adage was published

---

54. Adams, "Designs by More and Erasmus," 140; Russell Ames, *Citizen Thomas More and His Utopia* (Princeton, N.J.: Princeton University Press, 1949), 82.

55. *LP,* 1(2): 3524. Those who favored a peace policy were not as dominant at court by this time. David Starkey, *The Reign of Henry VIII: Personalities and Politics* (New York: Franklin Watts, 1986), 48–51.

56. Adams, "Literary Thought on War and Peace," 275.

separately as *Bellum Erasmi* two years later and became an immediate
"best-seller." Translated into English in 1533, the work went through thirteen editions (including Latin, English, and German) before the author's
death in 1536 and was thereafter reprinted at least once every two years
throughout the rest of the sixteenth century.[57] *The Education of a Christian
Prince* (1516), which was written for Archduke Charles and presented to
Henry VIII in 1517, followed similar themes in chapters devoted to treaties,
the arts of peace, and on beginning wars. Published the same year as Machiavelli's *Prince,* Erasmus presents a model in this work which contrasts
sharply with the martial character Machiavelli recommended for the ideal
Italian prince.[58] The most thorough and lucid of the Dutchman's "peace
works," *The Complaint of Peace* (*Querela pacis*), appeared in 1517 while
he was in England[59] and during a time when the prospects for universal
peace seemed to be once again falling apart. It is an angry, cynical work that
attacks not only war but also nationalism, political corruption, and lack of
proper education.[60] Erasmus's final major contributions toward the peace
effort of the late 1510s (and into the early 1520s) are found both in his
satirical colloquies, which were published between 1518 and 1528, and
which included "The Soldier's Confession," "The False Knight," and "Fish-
Eating," and in the prefaces to the gospels in his New Testament paraphrase
(1522–23). Full of disillusionment and pessimism, the dialogues depict the
"follies of his age," the most glaring being that of war.[61]

The impact of Erasmus's works in England may have been greater than
those of any Englishman during this time. Oxford bookseller John Dorne
compiled a list of books sold in 1520, and it indicates a preference for
Erasmus even over Aristotle. Of two thousand total books sold, one hundred and fifty were authored by the humanist. Most popular were the
Enchiridion militis Christiani and *Adagiae,* yet there were also significant

57. Adams, "Designs by More and Erasmus," 140–41; Sidney Anglo, *Spectacle, Pageantry and Early Tudor Policy* (Oxford: Clarendon Press, 1969), 125–26.
58. Adams, "Designs by More and Erasmus," 141; Desiderius Erasmus, *The Education of a Christian Prince,* trans. Lester K. Born (New York: Columbia University Press, 1936), 154, 205–14, 238–57; Anglo, *Spectacle, Pageantry and Early Tudor Policy,* 138–39.
59. Erasmus had spent almost the entire time from 1509 until 1515 in England as well.
60. Adams, *Better Part of Valor,* 165–67.
61. Adams, "Designs by More and Erasmus," 142; Bainton, *Christian Attitudes,* 134–35; Desiderius Erasmus, *The Whole Familiar Colloquies,* trans. Nathan Bailey (London: Ham-ilton, Adams, 1877), 38–40, 258–90, 329–34, and *The First Tome or Volume of the Para-phrase of Erasmus Upon the Newe Testamente* (London: Edward Whitchurche, 1548); Windass, *Christianity versus Violence,* 68. "A Soldier's Confession" is one of Erasmus's most thorough attacks on the *jus armorum.*

sales of his more controversial *Dulce bellum inexpertis, Moriae encomium* (*Praise of Folly*), and the unacknowledged *Dialogus Julii*.[62] His popularity, combined with his radical views on war and peace, make it crucial that we consider him carefully and look at what lasting contribution he may have made to the establishment of a peace ethic in Tudor England.[63]

Despite the overall congruity of thought in Erasmus concerning war (except perhaps for a letter written near the end of his life, which will be examined later) there are certain theoretical problems that have plagued scholars who have studied his works closely. Chief among them is whether Erasmus, upon close scrutiny, was a true pacifist in the early Christian or Anabaptist sense. Recent opinion has assumed generally that he was not, yet without begging the question, one could argue that this particular distinction concerning the humanist's approach to peace is largely irrelevant. Because he was not trying to create a pacifist ideology based on an airtight system of moral logic, we should not be looking for such. What was logical about war? As stated earlier, humanists like Erasmus wanted to strip away the over legalistic, technical, and abstract veneer that had characterized the discussion of war since the Middle Ages. They preferred a return to common sense and reason which could be expanded and inculcated in all people through proper education, wherein one's natural propensity for peaceful behavior would be developed.[64] With this understanding of their purposes then, we can see properly that their programs were hopeful and idealistic. It was, however, an idealism based on a simple, natural desire that all people live in harmony with one another and behave in an appropriately Christ-like manner in their everyday lives. For this reason, it was unnecessary for Erasmus and others to be complete pacifists in order for them to be instrumental in moving the issue under discussion away from war and onto a new ethic centered on the value of peace. Ignoring the pitfalls of theory, they were, above all, interested in affecting behavior and in creating a new way of living. The presupposition that human nature was "perfectible" was all that was needed for the ideal to become the possible.[65]

62. McConica, *English Humanists*, 88–90. See H. R. Plomer, *Hand-Lists of English Printers 1501–1556*, pt. 2 (London: Blades, East & Blades, 1896), for more on the English publication history of Erasmus's works.

63. Dickens and Jones, *Erasmus the Reformer*, 216.

64. Erasmus, *Querela pacis*, 295; Adams, *Better Part of Valor*, 239; Windass, *Christianity versus Violence*, 70.

65. Jean-Claude Margolin argues that this particular moralistic contribution of Erasmian pacifism is by its nature of lasting impact. Jean-Claude Margolin, *Guerre et paix dans la*

Without a doubt Erasmus introduced a new approach to the problem of war at the beginning of the sixteenth century. It rested on the actions of the newly emerging nation-state as personified in the power of the prince. An idea already noticed in Chaucer, Erasmus held that war was merely an extension of personal behavior into the realm of political policy, and so in this way, "spiritual peace" was the foundation of all other types. Therefore, the decision to go to war is a human act of the princely will, as is the decision to end it. Since all discord is a violation of reason and the law of nature, so is war; therefore, it is an individual (as opposed to the more impersonal idea of state) who is to blame for breaking the peace and, by implication, God's law.[66] The divine endowment of reason separates humans from the animals and gives them the unique capacity to avoid warring against one another.[67] With these assumptions, it is no wonder that Erasmus's pacifist circle placed so much hope in Henry VIII. He seemed the ideal prince, one who had been educated in the New Learning and who supported its growth throughout England. In 1514, he had also *chosen* to make peace and thus set the example for the remainder of Christian Europe. To Erasmus, the prince was all-important in bringing about the peaceful world to come. "A good and wise prince will make an effort to preserve peace with everyone but especially with his neighbors." Rather than focusing on the arts of war, the ideal prince will develop the arts of peace so as "to preclude any future need for the science of war."[68] War is not only morally wrong but also destructive to the nation. It is a "useless extravagance" that brings poverty in its wake. Therefore, "when the prince has put away all personal feelings, let him take a rational estimate long enough to reckon what the war will cost and whether the final end to be gained is worth that much — even if victory is certain, victory does not always happen to favor the best causes."[69] This distinctly unprovidential

pensée d'Erasme (Paris: Aubier Montaigne, 1973), 9. A similar conclusion is drawn in Olin, "Pacifism of Erasmus," 27–28. Because of perceived theoretical problems in Erasmian pacifism, J. A. Fernandez-Santamaria finds the less idealistic Spanish neoscholastic school more credible. See J. A. Fernandez-Santamaria, *The State, War and Peace: Spanish Political Thought in the Renaissance, 1516–1559* (Cambridge: Cambridge University Press, 1977), 122–44, 155–59.

66. Erasmus, *Querela pacis*, 298–99.

67. Ibid., 291–95; J. A. Fernandez, "Erasmus on the Just War," *Journal of the History of Ideas* 34 (1973): 204–15.

68. Erasmus, *Education of a Christian Prince*, 205, 239.

69. Ibid., 244–50; Erasmus, *Erasmus Against War*, ed. J. W. MacKail (Boston: Merrymount Press, 1907), 60; "Dulce bellum inexpertis," in *The Adages of Erasmus*, trans. Margaret Mann Phillips (Cambridge: The University Press, 1964), 323–24; and *Querela pacis*, 316–18.

view of success in war is about as far removed from a medieval understanding as one can get. Yet Erasmus went further, unafraid to tackle even
the once sacrosanct theory of the just war, which still provided kings with
rhetoric to justify nearly any sort of violence they wished to wage.[70]

To Erasmus and other like-minded humanists, the hollowness of just-
war rhetoric was self-evident, and it was merely their task now to hold it
up to its deserved ridicule. They were quick to echo Colet's and Cicero's
assertion that an unjust peace was preferable to the most "just" war. It is
better for a king to "buy peace" than to increase his territory through war.
Erasmus found the Church's "just-war tradition" to be the product of its
"swallowing a gobbet of civil laws" which contradict the laws of Christ.[71]
Once justified, wars are declared glorious simply at the whim of a prince,
"be he child or idiot." They are fought over trifles, such as a pretended
title of long ago or a tiny transgression or omission in "a treaty covering a
hundred clauses." "We will not attempt to discuss whether war is ever
just; who does not think his own cause just? . . . Among so many treaties
and agreements which are now entered into, now rescinded, who can lack
a pretext — if there is any real excuse — for going to war?"[72] As Wyclif had
railed over a century earlier, the clergy who support wars (and the popes
who initiate them) are to be chastised particularly for betraying their rightful calling. *Praise of Folly*'s portrait of an ailing, old, warmongering Julius
II is laughingly pathetic on the surface and yet meant to engender remorse
and sadness over the pontiff's destructive imprint on the face of Christendom.[73] Most of all, however, "the just war could be nothing but a myth
because all the doctrinal assumptions behind it, as harsh empirical evidence clearly demonstrated, were invalidated by the reality of man's behavior."[74] In the colloquy "Fish-Eating" (1526), the fishmonger tells the

70. Adams, "Literary Thought on War and Peace," 276.
71. Erasmus, *Querela pacis*, 313; Dickens and Jones, *Erasmus the Reformer*, 69–70.
72. Erasmus, *Querela pacis*, 305, and *Education of a Christian Prince*, 251. J. T. Johnson
contends that for Erasmus a just war "in the *jus in bello* sense" was unimaginable, and that
he came "extremely close to denying the possibility of *jus ad bellum* justice as well." Johnson,
Quest for Peace, 159–60. If we follow this reasoning, then perhaps it is in their failure to
recognize that the *jus in bello* could never be eliminated, but only controlled, which left the
Erasmians with simply an ideal in their approach to war and peace. Erasmus also wrote
several early letters condemning "just wars." See *CWE*, vol. 2, no. 288, and vol. 4, nos. 541
and 566.
73. Desiderius Erasmus, *Moriae encomium*, in *CWE*, trans. Betty Radice, 27:138–40; *Education of a Christian Prince*, 251; and *Querela pacis*, 308–11, 313; Windass, *Christianity
versus Violence*, 68–69; Bainton, *Christian Attitudes*, 131–33; James D. Tracy, *The Politics
of Erasmus: A Pacifist Intellectual and His Political Milieu* (Toronto: University of Toronto
Press, 1978), 27.
74. Fernandez, "Erasmus on the Just War," 217.

butcher that if he were the emperor, he would release the then-captive king of France and admit that it is only because of fortune that the war went well for him and not for his enemy.[75] With this exchange, along with other writings, it is clear that Erasmus wanted not only to de-institutionalize warfare but to demystify it as well.[76] For all his idealism, he was probably most logical and successful in this particular humanist endeavor to show war for what it really was.

In combining then the languages of classical (Stoic) humanism with the Christian, New Testament gospel, Erasmus's view of a universal humanity under Christ more securely located *concordia* as the essence of *pax* and the foundation for peace in personal behavior, as a social and political corrective, and as the basis for a people's prosperity (*publica utilitas*): "What is there in the whole of existence, better and sweeter than friendship? Absolutely nothing. But what is peace, except friendship among many? Just as war is nothing else but a private quarrel extended to others."[77] By blending these various conceptions of peace into a plea for the virtuous life, the Erasmians went beyond the more primitive and experiential medieval conceptions and not only fashioned peace into a personal ethic but also predicated it on more earthly and existential grounds.[78] No longer did fear of government collapse or anarchy alone lead people to consider publicly the benefits of societal unity and agreement, nor did ruinous wars that drained the nation in every respect become necessary before social critics stressed

75. Erasmus, *Colloquies*, 267. In his New Testament gospel dedications (Matthew to Charles V, Mark to Francis I, and Luke to Henry VIII), the Continental protagonists came under a thinly veiled criticism for pursuing wars that hurt the poor and destroy the commonweal. Henry, however, was praised for his pursuit of philosophy and learning instead of wasteful knightly pastimes. Erasmus, *Paraphrase Upon the Newe Testamente*, preface, sigs. 1r–7v.

76. Erasmus was an early critic of nationalism, as can be seen from this colloquy as well as from a passage in the *Querela pacis* where he declared that "the Englishman is enemy unto the Frenchman for no other cause but that he is a Frenchman. . . . The place doth separate and divide men's bodies but not their minds." Erasmus, *Querela pacis*, 314–15. This position is not surprising considering Erasmian humanism's debt to Stoicism and the platonic belief in the unified spiritual progression of humankind. See also Alistair Fox, "English Humanism and the Body Politic," in *Reassessing the Henrician Age*, ed. Alistair Fox and John Guy (Oxford: Basil Blackwell, 1986), 38–39, and Philip C. Dust, *Three Renaissance Pacifists: Essays in the Theories of Erasmus, More, and Vives*, American University Studies, vol. 23, ser. 9 (New York: Peter Lang, 1987), 49–62.

77. Erasmus, "Dulce bellum inexpertis," 322; Olin, "Pacifism of Erasmus," 27.

78. E. Vernon Arnold, *Roman Stoicism* (Cambridge: Cambridge University Press, 1911), 408–36; J. M. Rist, *Stoic Philosophy* (Cambridge: Cambridge University Press, 1969), 22–36, 97–111; André Bridoux, *Le Stoicisme et son influence* (Paris: J. Vrin, 1966), 191–238.

order and calm—*tranquillitas*. The interrelationships were becoming more inseparable and unified into a single, more nuanced idea of peace.

Finally, the question of whether Erasmus retreated from this seemingly full-blown pacifist position must be addressed briefly. It is true that much later, in 1530, he wrote a letter on the subject (*Utilissima consultatio de bello Turcis inferendo*) at the request of jurist John Rinck, wherein he acknowledged the legitimacy of wars against the Turks. In a Europe, however, where toleration was unimaginable among Christian sects, much less for Muslims, such an apparent inconsistency is to be expected even from someone as peace-minded as Erasmus. Erasmus's idea of peace was essentially a Christian one, predicated on a society devoting itself more fully to obeying the commands of the Bible and to imitating Christ.[79] Those peoples who had not the privileges and joys of Christian living were missing the key to maintaining a peaceful world. Thus, Erasmus is consistent in elevating his value of peace as a standard for all Christian people, even if it cannot be fully expressed and appreciated until all the world acknowledges Christ's authority and teachings. This argument, however, is not simply a slickly repackaged just-war idea in the Augustinian vein. For Erasmus never calls for crusades per se and he always believed that true conversion could only come from peaceful persuasion.[80] But it provides a window into a major drawback of Erasmian pacifism, that is, the culturally contained, unequivocal sense of right which its adherents believed they possessed. It is this devotion to a particular kind of contented, Christian, moral and tranquil society based on education that perhaps provides the key to understanding why Erasmus's greatest humanist contemporary, Thomas More, could acknowledge his friend's love for peace, while at the same time, openly permit, and even expand on the rights of his Utopians to make war.

Before discussing *Utopia* we should look at an important reinterpretation of Henry's first French war and the attitudes expressed toward it by Erasmus and More. As early as 1505–6, with Erasmus in England and More translating Lucian's satires, it was becoming evident that part of the

---

79. Erasmus, *Querela pacis*, 299, 303–5, 310, 319, and *Education of a Christian Prince*, 256; Jean-Claude Margolin, "Erasme et la guerre contre les turcs," *Il pensiero politico* 13 (1980): 3–38.

80. Erasmus, *Querela pacis*, 319; Michael J. Heath, "Erasmus and War against the Turks," in *Acta Conventus Neo-Latini Turonensis*, ed. Jean-Claude Margolin (Paris: Vrin, 1980), 991–99; Bainton, *Christian Attitudes*, 133. See also Ronald G. Musto, "Just Wars and Evil Empires: Erasmus and the Turks," in *Renaissance Society and Culture: Essays in Honor of Eugene F. Rice, Jr.*, ed. John Monfasani and Ronald G. Musto (New York: Italica Press, 1991), 197–216; Maria Cytowska, "Erasme et les Turcs," *Eos* 62 (1974): 311–21.

humanist attack on contemporary society would include the repudiation of tyranny and empty military glory by centering on particular perceptions of socialization and education. Both men came to believe that original sin operated largely "through the agency of inherited social forms," which included chivalry — an idealized code of behavior that in reality gloried in bloodlust and greed. Echoing a medieval critique of the *jus armorum,* these humanists, however, related their condemnation of war to issues of public concern and political motivation. In one of the Lucian dialogues, *Cynicus,* More highlighted the conflict that *consuetudo* (habit) and *appetitus* (appetite) have with "rational judgment" and suggested that blind passion and social custom carry people along with such force that few think through carefully the consequences and morality of accepting what has always been.[81]

Erasmus was so appalled by the 1513–14 campaign that he immediately launched a barrage of invective against the heroic tradition that justified such unholy slaughter. More went further when he wrote against the French patriotic poem, *Chordigera,* exposing in horribly graphic detail the barbarity of "noble war," much as the *Alliterative Morte Arthure* had done a century earlier.[82] The condemnation of chivalry would continue throughout the century, and later we will turn to particular contexts when others, like Vives and Sir Thomas Elyot, would offer important new insights on this theme. But here, in the 1510s, we can determine a concrete example when humanists found the law of arms contributing to an unnecessary conflict, and so need to recognize the sincerity of their early efforts to end war among Christian nations and princes. The rejection of chivalry and the espousal of peace were evidently more than rhetorical ideals for either Erasmus or More.[83]

In considering then More's *Utopia,* first published in December 1516, we need note that it appeared at a time when the author and his fellow humanists were most optimistic about all nations uniting in an accord of amity and peace. There were reasons for such hope. Despite the victories in the previous war, English treasury disbursements plummeted from £700,000 in 1513 to £50,000 in 1518. Tournai had been ceded back to

81. Thomas More, *Translations of Lucian,* ed. Craig R. Thompson, in *CW,* vol. 3, pt. 1 (New Haven, Conn.: Yale University Press, 1974), 21–23, 167–68; Dominic Baker-Smith, "'Inglorious Glory': 1513 and the Humanist Attack on Chivalry," in Anglo, *Chivalry in the Renaissance,* 129–32.

82. Baker-Smith, "Inglorious Glory," 140–41; Germanus Brixius, "The *Antimorus* of Germanus Brixius," ed. Daniel Kinney, in *CW,* vol. 3, pt. 2, appendix B, 469–547.

83. Baker-Smith, "Inglorious Glory," 137.

France for an indemnity, and only Calais remained in English hands. "Peace and renunciation of continental ambitions were the key elements in More's ideal of the right and good foreign policy for England." He thought that since Henry was no longer ostensibly committed to pursuing Continental territorial goals, the king would turn to domestic policy and deal severely with rich oppressors within England. More joined the Council, perhaps for this reason, in 1517.[84] But in *Utopia*, the international situation is less settled and Hythlodeus's objections to serving the king of France are not overcome. This is evident when he remarks in Book 1: "Almost all monarchs prefer to occupy themselves in the pursuits of war — with which I neither have nor desire any acquaintance — rather than in the honorable activities of peace, and they care much more how, by hook or by crook, they may win fresh kingdoms than how they may administer well what they have got."[85] As with Erasmus, More's aversion to war was most passionate in his hatred of mercenaries, whom he referred to as robbers. After describing their corrupt nature, also in Book 1, More echoed the humanist position that war is not endemic or ineradicable, but that "you never have war unless you choose it, and you ought to take far more account of peace than of war."[86] All mention of war in Book 1 mirrors the pacifist beliefs of his contemporaries, especially his cynicism regarding the motives of kings who were at present engaged in it.[87]

Book 2 presents more of a problem. The Utopians are skeptical about treaties, much the same as Erasmus was, since "mutual good feeling which *nature* causes to spring up in all men is better than any mere treaty."[88] There is also the initial acknowledgment that "war, as an activity fit only for beasts and yet practiced by no kind of beast so constantly as by man, they [Utopians] regard with utter loathing. Against the usage of almost all nations they count nothing so inglorious as glory sought in war."[89] From this point on, however, More related how, why, and in what circumstances the Utopians justifiably go to war. He focused on four just causes: defense of country, expulsion of hostile foreign invaders from friends' lands, rescue

84. J. H. Hexter, *More's Utopia, The Biography of an Idea* (Princeton, N.J.: Princeton University Press, 1952), 154–55; J. A. Guy, *The Public Career of Sir Thomas More* (Brighton, Eng.: Harvester Press, 1980), 6–7.
85. Thomas More, *Utopia*, ed. Edward Surtz and J. H. Hexter, in *CW*, vol. 4 (New Haven, Conn.: Yale University Press, 1965), 57; Guy, *Public Career*, 9–10.
86. More, *Utopia*, 65.
87. Ibid., 87–93; Ames, *Citizen Thomas More*, 11.
88. Surtz, *Praise of Wisdom*, 301; Erasmus, *Education of a Christian Prince*, 238–39.
89. More, *Utopia*, 199, 201.

from tyranny, and revenge for injuries. The second and third reasons might be connected to the expressed desire in More's day for Christians to unite in a crusade against the Turks. All four, however, can be reduced essentially to two kinds of just war — to protect the good life in Utopia and to extend it abroad, where other people want peace rather than tyranny and war.[90] The Utopians will not fight over money matters but will act to protect one of their own citizens who is harmed in another land: "If the guilty persons are not surrendered, they cannot be appeased but forthwith declare war." Despite their celebration of valor and even bloodshed in a just war, "their one and only object in war is to secure that which, had it been obtained beforehand, would have prevented the declaration of war."[91]

The readiness to use mercenaries and see them killed, along with the sanctioning of political assassination and propaganda, describe a totalitarian state which is determined to protect its superior way of life at all costs.[92] This perfect state cannot permit change or allow itself to be corrupted. As Shlomo Avineri has aptly observed: "Those people, who are outside of the Utopian establishment of perfection, are, by definition and nature, base and wicked: had they been otherwise, they would necessarily become part of Utopia. Thus if they refuse the Utopians' offer to live with them in one commonwealth they may be exterminated, as their very unwillingness to accept membership in the perfect republic attests to their moral corruption."[93] If this interpretation is correct, it would explain the Utopian deviation from strict Erasmian pacifism's near total rejection of just war. Whereas Erasmus awaited the rewards of a proper education, More could only see humanity's corruption and the need to preserve what is good.[94] Working within a just-war tradition which permits the righting of wrongs in certain instances, he more astutely perceived the struggles involved in putting the humanist program into action, fearing that any progress may be lost if not protected. His hierarchy of values, therefore, cannot position peace at the top, because in the case of Utopia, any form

90. Adams, *Better Part of Valor,* 149; Surtz, *Praise of Wisdom,* 277–81.

91. More, *Utopia,* 203.

92. Ibid., 205–17; More, *Translations of Lucian,* 79–127.

93. Shlomo Avineri, "War and Slavery in More's *Utopia,*" *International Review of Social History* 7 (1962): 289. See also Fritz Caspari, "Sir Thomas More and *Justum Bellum,*" *Ethics* 56 (1946): 303–9.

94. Alistair Fox, "Facts and Fallacies: Interpreting English Humanism," in Fox and Guy, *Reassessing the Henrician Age,* 32; Adams, *Better Part of Valor,* 144–49; Michael Howard, *War and the Liberal Conscience* (New Brunswick, N.J.: Rutgers University Press, 1978), 13–18.

of tyranny would be worse than war. As with Erasmus, the prince is the crucial figure in bringing about a universal peace, but only a just, godly king can guarantee all of the good things for a society. Thus, it becomes paramount that Utopia not be corrupted by the reaches and effects of foreign tyranny, and all means are permitted to ensure that such does not occur. Although More accepted the Stoic premises of the other humanists, he also comprehended a basic fact of human nature — that people usually seek "pleasure before virtue, justice, and the common welfare." He always tempered his optimism with a large dose of stark reality, despite the risk of inaction that often accompanied such a tendency.[95] His use of the just-war model, albeit one uniquely constructed and argued, demonstrates the continued efficacy of strictly controlled wars to reduce grievous social and political sin, which can never be eliminated absolutely.

But even here, given the impossibility of definitively and exhaustively interpreting *Utopia,* More may have been at his satirical best. His opening lines, which mention the "invincible king of England, Henry" and "His Serene Highness, Charles, Prince of Castile," should be compared with Erasmus's adage *Scarabeus aquilam quaerit* (another antiwar statement) in which "both *invectis* and *serenissimus* are listed among the 'magnificent lies' that must adorn royal titles," since they really connote senseless war and destruction. All of this rings, again, of the humanist distaste for social conventions and deferences that were indisputably irrational, unwise, and harmful to society.[96]

The Peace Movement in Eclipse (1518–1529)

More himself, who seemed to waver between hope and despair, finally entered wholly into the king's service in the spring of 1517. He probably genuinely expected that Henry would adhere to a peace policy, especially with the rumors of a general peace so strong throughout Europe. Erasmus was skeptical that his friend could serve the king and still be an independent voice for reform. Henry appears not to have relied on More at all in making foreign policy, including decisions concerning war. Wolsey's secret diplomacy helped bring about the long-awaited Treaty of Universal Peace,

---

95. Adams, "Designs by More and Erasmus," 144; Brian Bond, "The 'Just War' in Historical Perspective," *History Today* 16 (1966): 113–14.

96. Baker-Smith, "Inglorious Glory," 143–44; Erasmus, *Querela pacis,* 290, and "Scarabeus aquilam quaerit," in *Adages,* 234.

which was signed on October 2 by England, France, the Holy Roman
Empire, the papacy, Spain, Denmark, Portugal, Hungary, the Italian states,
the Swiss Confederation, and the Hanseatic towns. The English signatories
included More, Tunstall, and Mountjoy.[97] Colet immediately responded by
preaching another sermon on peace at St. Paul's before Henry, Wolsey, papal
legate Campeggio, and the French ambassadors. The royal secretary, Richard Pace, who had assisted in bringing the nations together also delivered an
oration on peace there to celebrate the coming to terms.[98] The speech reso-
nates with a sincere desire that universal concord and tranquillity among all
Christians be accomplished. Drawing on classical and biblical sources, Pace
catalogued the evils of war: "unbounded greed for possession . . . ; monstrous and barbarous cruelty; insatiable thirst for human blood and mutual
slaughter; spoliation of poverty; overthrow of towns and cities; in a word,
instant ruin of piety and religion beyond anything that can be described."[99]
Pace borrowed heavily from Erasmus, even quoting from *Dulce bellum
inexpertis,* and lauded peace as "the heap and accumulation of all good
things." Henry and Wolsey received praise for "you applied all your heart
and all your mind . . . to the initiation of universal peace among all Christian
princes," and thereby brought "all thoughts to health-bearing peace."[100]
Pace used *concordia* and *pax* interchangeably in his oration, revealing his
belief that both terms represented equally the desired absence of strife, war,
and even personal turmoil as reason and harmony prevail among Christians. Other humanists when writing in Latin likewise often refused to make
any distinctions between these two terms.[101] Most assuredly this oration was
printed and promulgated for its propagandistic value, but this does not
detract from what appears to be Pace's own sincerity about what he was
saying. He was a humanist who embraced the *vita activa* in a way More was
unable to, finding fulfillment as an agent for peace and reform through his
diplomatic roles.

97. Lange, *Histoire de la doctrine pacifique,* 212–14.
98. Jervis Wegg, *Richard Pace: A Tudor Diplomatist* (New York: Barnes & Noble, 1971),
115–40.
99. J. G. Russell, *Peacemaking in the Renaissance,* 15–16, 234–36; Guy, *Public Career,*
8–12. The oration was published in Latin in December 1518 by the King's printer, Richard
Pynson. The English translation in Russell, *Peacemaking in the Renaissance,* is used here.
100. Pace, *Oration on Peace,* 236–39. Pace uses the adjectives "healthful" and "health-
bearing" several times when referring to the virtue of universal peace.
101. Pace, *Oration on Peace,* 235. He also quoted Sallust here: "nam concordia parvae res
crescunt, discordia maxime dilabuntur" [for peace makes small states grow, while discord
harms the greatest empires]. Sallust, *Bellum Iurguthinum* 10:6.

This peace of 1518 that brought Pace so much joy gave birth to great expectations. A few days after the signing a meeting between the kings of England and France was announced. These next few years, between the treaty's signing and the Field of the Cloth of Gold (June 1520), were a heady time for the Erasmian "peace party," even though the agreement came under tremendous strain almost from the start. Still Henry's, and even Wolsey's, reputation had been enhanced, for both Erasmus and More found in England a "genius above all others in Renaissance Europe." On the surface, the meeting between Francis I and Henry in Calais kept hopes raised for the immediate future, with the English king making an unrecorded oration to peace while there. The Venetian emissary to France, however, proved more perceptive in his assessment of the event and of the state of Europe in 1520: "These sovereigns are not at peace. They adapt themselves to circumstances, but hate each other very cordially."[102]

In fact, for both personal and dynastic reasons, Wolsey continued his intrigues on the Continent, involving himself directly in the Hapsburg-Valois rivalry with the intention of becoming the arbiter of Europe. The result, however, was an end to peace and a disastrous new English incursion into France between 1522 and 1523. Wolsey would have preferred further diplomacy to outright war but councillors Suffolk and Norfolk prodded the king into launching the campaign.[103] Once hostilities broke out, Wolsey was quick to lend his political and diplomatic skills. But as soon became evident, England had neither the tax base, the manpower, nor the materiel to support a long-term occupation force. By the second year there was less agreement on the validity and wisdom in continuing with the war. Thomas Cromwell, a lesser-known M.P. at the time, drafted a speech for Parliament in which he argued the foolishness of a war with France, especially considering England's military stature and the impossibility of conquest in an age when French unity and nationalism were on the rise.[104] The chronicler Edward Hall observed that after Wolsey's own

---

102. *Ven. Cal.* 3:119; Adams, *Better Part of Valor,* 158, 172–85; Anglo, *Spectacle, Pageantry and Early Tudor Policy,* 135–169; Adams, "Literary Thought on War and Peace," 267.

103. J. S. Brewer, *The Reign of Henry VIII from His Accession to the Death of Wolsey,* ed. James Gairdner (London: John Murray, 1884), 2:50; Ames, *Citizen Thomas More,* 66–67; Barnett, *Britain and Her Army,* 14.

104. *LP* 3(2):2958; J. R. Hale, *War and Society in Renaissance Europe, 1450–1620* (Leicester: Leicester University Press, 1985), 33; Barnett, *Britain and Her Army,* 14; Ames, *Citizen Thomas More,* 66. Cromwell's arguments against war rested on practical considerations such as the uncertain exit of bullion, danger to the king's life, impoverishment of the realm, and the perpetual threat of invasion through Scotland. Thus he makes the brazen

parliamentary speech in April 1523, heated debates over taxation erupted before reluctant support was given to the French campaign. Another contemporary, Elis Gruffydd, found the war beneficial only for king, nobility, gentlemen, and professionals. To almost everyone else it offered no cause for joy, as the soldiers themselves "were thinking of their wives and children and husbandry and those cowardly men with bare hearts who would rather go home to their mothers and fathers, some to plough and thresh, others to follow the cart and hedge and dig and live niggardly, these were unwilling and were angry with anyone who talked about staying there during the winter." The English forces in France became lazy, refusing to build huts and make fires to keep dry and warm. At one point they threatened mutiny, when during a battle they shouted "home, home" and turned an orderly retreat into total chaos.[105]

Whether the complaints of Parliament and soldiers were part of a more pervasive attitude toward the war cannot be fathomed fully. But there is some interesting evidence that reveals a division within the upper ranks of government. In March 1524, for example, Louis de Praet, Charles V's ambassador, believed that the English nobles desired peace, and Hall indicated that there was such expectation that "men hoped that peace should ensue" when a papal emissary arrived the following month.[106] Other English people thought that had the imperial victory at the Battle of Pavia not disrupted the balance of power, "surely the king of England, would have had peace with the French king."[107] Henry had enjoined his countrymen and -women to support the war out of respect for his honor, which Francis had offended by breaking so many of his promises.[108] But the very tenuousness of the alliances in the 1520s also made it difficult to rally opinion in favor of the war, including an invasion of France. G. W. Bernard has described the failure as one of poor planning overall:

---

declaration that "it is simpleness for us to think to keep possessions in France, [which] is severed from us by the ocean sea." Roger Bigelow Merriman, *Life and Letters of Thomas Cromwell,* vol. 1 (Oxford: Clarendon Press, 1902), 27–46. See John Guy, "Wolsey and the Parliament of 1523," in *Law and Government Under the Tudors,* ed. Claire Cross, David Loades, and J. J. Scarisbrick (Cambridge: Cambridge University Press, 1988), 15–16.

105. Edward Hall, *Hall's Chronicle* (London: J. Johnson, 1809), 661; Elis Gruffydd, "Suffolk's Expedition to Montdidier, 1523," *Bulletin of the Faculty of Arts, Fouad I University,* ed. M. B. Davis 7 (1944): 41; G. W. Bernard, *War, Taxation and Rebellion in Early Tudor England* (Brighton, Eng.: Harvester Press, 1986), 5–6.

106. Hall, *Hall's Chronicle,* 678; Bernard, *War, Taxation and Rebellion,* 6.

107. Hall, *Hall's Chronicle,* 691.

108. Bernard, *War, Taxation and Rebellion,* 7.

The propaganda campaigns against the French in 1523 and 1525 were much too *ad hoc,* somewhat defensive, with an air of protesting too much. The list of lapses by Francis seems as much the basis for a deal as a justification of war. The fluidity of alliances played its part in the failure of the government to secure the financial support of the country for an invasion of France in 1525. The projected campaign that year was not the culmination of a sustained process but the sudden . . . response to a single event.[109]

These are very important considerations in understanding the apparent apathy or dissatisfaction with this war. Had the temptation of true, lasting peace which many hoped for between 1518 and 1522 so completely dissipated just because the government declared that fresh transgressions by Francis necessitated renewed hostilities? Ever since the Hundred Years War there had existed a heightened sensitivity to the practicalities of wars and the purposes behind them. Could it be that many people found very little reason for this war, suspecting that next time France would be the ally and Charles the enemy? And what did England have to gain from involving itself in what were essentially Continental dynastic conflicts?

Nothing distanced the English from their government more than the wartime requests for subsidies. Wolsey was almost universally hated for his continued attempts at this time to squeeze money from the people. More was put in a very uncomfortable position, when, after his election as Speaker of the House in 1523, he was forced to give tacit approval to the king's war and even to become one of the collectors of that year's levy, which had encountered a great deal of opposition.[110] Wolsey's Amicable Grant of 1525,[111] however, proved to be the catalyst for the first major public outcry against a Tudor war. Even if the opposition was centered mostly in Kent, it is significant that here soldiers were stationed before being sent to France. The most telling evidence of the hatred for this tax is found in a remarkable 1525 letter from Warham to Wolsey. The archbishop was the commissioner of the Amicable Grant for Kent, but he admitted the futility of most of his efforts, as "the people sorely begrudge and murmur, and speak cursedly among themselves as far as they dare;

109. Ibid., 11.
110. Guy, *Public Career,* 14–23; Ames, *Citizen Thomas More,* 66–67.
111. According to Hall, the Amicable Grant demanded "that the sixth part of every man's substance should, without delay, be paid in money or plate to the King, for the furniture of his war." Hall, *Hall's Chronicle,* 694. See also Henry Ellis, ed., *Original Letters Illustrative of English History,* 3d ser., vol. 1 (London: Richard Bentley, 1846), 367.

saying that they shall never have rest of payments as long as some [i.e. Wolsey] liveth, and that they would rather die than to be thus continually handled." Warham asked Wolsey "to send me your counsel in writing what shall be best for me to do." The people do not believe the grant will be repaid since the previous loan is still owed. To take away the wealth of the nation to support the war means that "the King's Grace must coin copper and brass for gold and silver is spent and gone, which should be to the great reproach of this realm." The great impoverishment of the land that results, in turn, only enriches France. And whatever England gains in France will soon be lost again anyhow, so that "the King's Grace long continuance there would be to the great decaying and desolation of this realm."[112]

While Warham cannot be considered a completely disinterested party, since he was known to have opposed the 1512–13 campaign, if even only a hint of what he reveals were true, it would testify to a cynicism about the justice of the war that permeated by this time down to the people themselves. But he went even further to declare, in an incredible passage, that they would have rather had peace even than victory:

> I have heard say moreover that where the people are commanded to make fires and tokens of joy for the taking of the French king, diverse of them have spoken that they have more cause to weep than to rejoice thereat. And diverse (as it has been shown to me secretly) have wished openly that the French king were at his liberty again, so as there were a good peace, and the King's Grace should not attempt to win France. The winning whereof should be more costly to England than profitable: and the keeping thereof much more costly than the winning.[113]

The men of Kent also reminisced about the peaceful policies of the previous king, who "lacked no riches or wisdom to win the kingdom of France if [he] had thought expedient," yet who by eschewing war, still left England with as much territory in France as the present ruler, who had spent enormous sums on campaigns. Another letter to Wolsey from the duke of Norfolk shows that Norwich was reluctant to pay the grant as well, even though there may have been more overall support for the invasion there.[114] According to Hall, the hostility was felt throughout England,

112. Ibid., 371–72.
113. Ibid., 374.
114. Ibid., 376–81; *LP* 4(1):1295, 1323, 1329.

such that "burden was so grievous, that it was denied and the commons in every place were so moved, that it was like to have grown to a rebellion."[115]

In Kent and throughout much of England during April and May, people claimed poverty so as to avoid paying the Amicable Grant, and at least one commissioner—Warham—found the excuse valid.[116] By 1525, clearly, princely (noble) honor as a pretext for war had lost much of its appeal. With the expense of battle resting more on the people at large rather than the knights, popular involvement continued to expand as it had since the early fifteenth century. Peace was being inextricably linked with economic vitality, and war with poverty. Peace was becoming a cherished value irrespective of its Christian foundation and more a practical consideration. It was beginning to emerge as a condition in its own right—not just the idealistic and unreal (in a fallen world) alternative to just wars or to chivalric codes to temper violence.

The extent to which this new value for peace had pervaded English culture is not found simply in a few examples of popular protest, but the symbolism to which it gave expression can be seen dramatically in the court ceremony that accompanied the "peace" of 1527. On November 10, after mass, jousts, and an enormous supper (of eighty dishes!) in the banqueting hall, Henry took the foreign ambassadors and other members of court into the disguising chamber where they viewed a dramatic performance organized by Wolsey. Drawing on eyewitness accounts, Sidney Anglo presented the setting:

> At one end of the hall an artificial arbour symbolized the amity between England and France. It consisted of a fountain running with perfumed waters, behind which an olive tree, alluding to Universal Peace, grew from the floor to ceiling. On either side was a tree, signifying the makers of that peace: a hawthorn decorated with the arms of England and the insignia of St. Michel; and a mulberry tree with the arms of France within a garter.[117]

The drama itself portrayed contemporary European conditions and centered on a beleaguered Church and an imprisoned pope whom Wolsey rescues by getting the French and English kings to act together against his captor. When Henry and Wolsey threaten the Holy Roman Emperor,

115. Hall, *Hall's Chronicle*, 697.

116. In a letter dated 15 April to Sir Thomas Boleyn and Sir Henry Guildford, Warham, concluded that "in good faith, I think there is a great poverty in Kent and lack of money as has been seen in many years." *LP* 4(1):1266; Bernard, *War, Taxation and Rebellion*, 111–12.

117. Anglo, *Spectacle, Pageantry and Early Tudor Policy*, 232.

Charles V, who kept Francis's two sons captive, "the Emperor's Chancellor came forward to conclude a peace, and the two princes were released."[118]

The change in alliance may be argued to have allowed Wolsey the chance to use Charles's breaking of the peace (of the Church) as a pretext for beginning a new war. Nevertheless, the Peace of Amiens (1527) was used by the cardinal (through pageants) to create an image of himself as the great pacifier of Europe—the one to lead the world into a Virgilian golden age of perpetual peace.[119] By contrast, just four years earlier, the tone of the pageants celebrating the emperor's visit in May 1523 were shrouded in the trappings of Mars, such as when Charles and Henry were equated with Samson and Hercules. Yet there were paeans to peace even then. During the parade in London, Hall described one scene along their progress:

> They came to the stocks [meat market] where there was a quadrant stage where on was an arbor [flower garden] full of roses, lilies and all other flowers curiously wrought, and birds, beasts and all other things of pleasure. And about the arbor was made the water full of fish, and about it were the elements, the planets and stars in their places, and everything moved, and in a type [image] on the top was made the Trinity with the Angels singing, and the Trinity blessed the king and the emperor, and under his feet was written, *behold the lover of peace and concord.*[120]

Pope Clement's escape from imperial captivity in January 1528 provided Wolsey with the opportunity to throw another sumptuous feast for all the ambassadors at court, which included performances of Terence's *Phormio.* The dining hall had at its head a large decorated garland of box, on the front of which was written in gilt, *Terentii Phormio.* On the sides were the inscriptions *Cedant arma togae* [they lay down their armor] and *Foedus pacis non movebitur* [the treaty of peace will not be shaken]. Under the garland was inscribed *Cardinalis Pacificus,* and other sayings of peace, such as *Pax cum homine et bellum cum vitiis* [peace with humankind and war with sin], were found along the sides of the hall. After the performance of *Phormio,* "three richly clad girls appeared, representing Religion, Peace, and Justice. They complained that they had been expelled from

118. Ibid., 233; Hall, *Hall's Chronicle,* 734–35.
119. Anglo, *Spectacle, Pageantry and Early Tudor Policy,* 229.
120. Hall, *Hall's Chronicle,* 638–39.

well-nigh all of Europe by heresy, war, and ambition." After cataloguing the evil actions of the enemy, they appealed to "their most generous Father" for deliverance. Finally, a boy came out reciting a Latin oration that gave thanks for the pope's release.[121]

These overblown, self-indulgent court entertainments may have been little more than a charade, yet they do reveal an important transformation was taking place in that the greater value was being placed on peace as a state of being or condition of humankind. Pageants lauding peace with such pomp would have been unthinkable one hundred or even fifty years earlier. What was different was that now there was a clear recognition that peacemaking had become the ideal activity for statesmen, as opposed to (or at least commensurate with) glorious exploits or deeds of war. Wolsey was appealing to his peers and embodying a popular desire. He could easily support and even promote wars if his king so desired, but he wanted Henry and himself to be remembered more as peacemakers, not as Caesars or Alexanders, regardless of possible hidden agendas. He had labored tirelessly for "universal peace," which, for him, "was the supreme aim of a diplomatic career."[122] When war seemed again possible in 1529 (this time against the Holy Roman Empire), there was no enthusiasm for it in England. It is debatable whether an army even could have been raised. Now out of the loop of negotiations leading to the Peace of Cambrai (1529), and unable to obtain the pope's permission for the king's divorce from Queen Catherine, the pageantry of 1527–28 reflected not the legacy Wolsey had desired but rather a tragic end to a career confounded by a mixture of self-aggrandizement and good intention, with the former now weighing much heavier than the latter.[123]

The Idea of the English Gentleman in the 1530s and 1540s

The chivalric ingredient in the court celebrations of the Tudor period, whether it be the jousts in Wolsey's pageants or the Elizabethan Accession-Day tilts, served as important means for communicating the prince's sovereignty by emphasizing his or her isolation at the top of the feudal pyramid.

121. Anglo, *Spectacle, Pageantry and Early Tudor Policy,* 235–36.
122. J. G. Russell, *Peacemaking in the Renaissance,* 93–132, 233.
123. Barnett, *Britain and Her Army,* 15.

As the modern nation-state became an established entity in the sixteenth century, and the symbols of suzerainty were no longer so essential, the chivalric images—which remain in royal coronations and weddings to-day—testified more to the continuity of English institutions than to the survival of the values they once might have embodied. But by the time of Henry VIII, even with such a martial prince at the helm, the military significance of chivalric exercises had began to wane, with the Elizabethans realizing their near total impotency.[124]

This discussion has emphasized so far the critique of just wars made by Erasmians, who wanted to offer an ethic of peace in place of arguments to legitimize war. Beside these *jus ad bellum* explanations, however, the other major obstacle to such an ethic came from continued *jus in bello* attempts to circumscribe behavior in war through a particular code of conduct. As we have seen in Chapter 2, the traditional forms of chivalry began to erode during the mounting chaos of the Hundred Years War. The sixteenth century, affected by Renaissance humanism, stepped up these attacks on "bloody chivalry" and offered an enhanced political role for the nobility, something of which we have already seen in the governments of the first two Tudor kings, but to which we must now turn and examine in greater detail.

The sixteenth century witnessed two notable chivalric revivals. The first, under Henry VIII, began around 1513 with the coming of the French war and the appearance of a popular English life of Henry V, which made numerous comparisons between the two monarchs. Lord Berner's translation of Froissart was published during the 1523–25 campaign, and the popular romances of Bevis of Hampton, Guy of Warwick, and the "Seven Champions of Christendom" retained their hold on the popular imagination. The stories of Arthur and other romantic legends continued to be part of English chronicles even up to the time of Holinshed and Stowe. Yet it is significant that there was almost no new literature celebrating English feats of arms, which may indicate that the revival was not very deep-seated. Even the iconography of the king has no counterpart to Titian's equestrian portrait of Charles V in a striking military pose.[125] Without

124. Ferguson, *Chivalric Tradition*, 46–47, 50. For an alternative, New Historicist view, see Richard McCoy, *The Rites of Knighthood: The Literature and Politics of European Chivalry* (Berkeley and Los Angeles: University of California Press, 1989), which is challenged in Ben Lowe, "The Role of Peace in Elizabethan Military Strategy, 1572–1593: A Look at the Manuals," *Fides et Historia* 24 (1992): 3–14.
125. Davies, "English People and War," 13–16; Ronald S. Crane, *The Vogue of Medieval*

question, humanism militated against any strong insistence that martial exploits were a sign of a prince's or nation's greatness — and this was probably most obvious in England. As already noted, the humanist rejection of the chivalric ethos was based on a multifaceted dislike for deleterious social convention as well as on personal morality, the product of a vibrant confluence of Stoic and Christian ideas.[126] Erasmus's Christian knight "was to be clearly a hero in the wars of the spirit, not of the world." Most of his fellow humanists detested the chivalric romance and its glorification of violence. Wars, as such, affronted more the Christian aspect of their worldview than the classical outlook; however, the Middle Ages were viewed as having corrupted both traditions through an ignorance that had led to a bellicose, prodigal society.[127] As much as possible, these men attempted to eliminate from their world all martial values found in medieval chivalric culture, and by so doing, created a situation that made future revivals purely romantic in nature.[128]

Central to the humanist attack on chivalry was the new sense of citizenship, based on the Ciceronian ideal of public service, that Erasmus, More, and Vives believed exhorted one to a personal devotion to the commonwealth. Knowledge of history, the Bible, and classical literature was necessary to improve society, while romances diverted the true "citizen" from just such vital learning. After the failure of 1518, the next round of attacks on chivalry came with Vives's own scrutiny of popular heroic romances. In Chapter 5 of his *Instruction of a Christian Woman*, written for the princess Mary in 1523, he waxed eloquent on which books should be read by the person who desires to become truly educated. He bemoaned the fact that "there is in use nowadays, worse than among the pagans, books written in our mothers' tongues that are made but for idle men and women to read, and have no other matter but of war and love." If the handling of armor is questionable for men, is it not worse for women "to look upon

Chivalric Romance During the English Renaissance (Menasha, Wis.: George Banta, 1919), 8–9; *The First English Life of King Henry the Fifth, Written in 1513 by an Anonymous Author Known Commonly as the Translator of Livius,* ed. Charles L. Kingsford (Oxford: Clarendon Press, 1911).

126. Nicholas Orme, "The Education of the Courtier," in Scattergood and Sherborne, *English Court Culture*, 63–85.

127. There had been a clear, though probably minority, tradition against reading romances, however, since the later Middle Ages. William of Nassington expressed a not-so-unusual clerical position when he bragged that his book of religious instruction contained "no vain speaking of deeds of arms nor of amours" and that romances in general were "nothing but vanity." Scattergood, "Chaucer and the French War," 291.

128. Ferguson, *Chivalric Tradition,* 55–56.

them" and "be conversant among them with heart and mind"?[129] In *The Office and Duty of a Husband,* he became even more strident in his hatred for romances, finding in them the root cause of all sorts of vice: "These books do hurt both men and women, for they make them wily and crafty, they kindle and stir up covetousness, inflame anger, and all beastly and filthy desire."[130] Upon his arrival in England, where he remained from May 1523 until November 1528, Vives presented a just-completed translation and commentary on Augustine's *City of God* to Henry VIII, to whom he had also dedicated the work. A relative latecomer to the humanist debate on war, the Spaniard not only criticized the chivalric romance but also entered into the debate over just wars and peace. His glosses of book 19, chapters 11 and 13, reveal a mind so dedicated to a vision of European peace that it neglected totally the just war as espoused by the early church father. He noted that "Peace is the chief good and war the chief evil," and followed with,

> The whole goodness of peace, and of that especially which Christ left us as his full inheritance, is gone, all but for the name and imaginary shade thereof, all the rest we have lost: nay we have made a willing extrusion of it, and expelled it wittingly, and of set purpose, imagining our whole felicity to consist in the tumults of wars and slaughters. And oh so we brave it, that we have slain thus many men, burnt thus many towns, sacked many cities! Founding our principal glories upon the destruction of our fellows. But I may begin a complaint of this here, but I shall never end it.[131]

Here, Vives chose not to acknowledge the Augustinian notion of just war but rather to stress the more pacifist sections of his thought in order to argue against wars that are wittingly engaged in, unnecessarily, and which

129. Juan Luis Vives, *A Very Fruteful and Pleasant boke callyd the Instruction of a Christen woman, made fyrste in latyne, by the right famous clerk mayster Lewes Vives, and tourned oute of latyne into Englysshe by Richard Hyrde* (London: T. Berthelet, 1541), sigs. D1v–D2r. Hyrde's English translation includes an introduction that also warns against reading romances. Crane, *Vogue of Medieval Chivalric Romance,* 11; Ferguson, *Chivalric Tradition,* 57; Robert P. Adams, "Bold Bawdry and Open Manslaughter," *Huntington Library Quarterly* 23 (1959–60): 36–37.

130. Juan Luis Vives, *The Office and Duetie of an Husband,* trans. Thomas Paynell (London: John Cawood, [1550]), sigs. O5v–T3v; Crane, *Vogue of Medieval Chivalric Romance,* 11–12.

131. Juan Luis Vives, ed., *Saint Augustine, of the Citie of God: with the Learned Comments of Io. Lodovicus Vives,* trans. J. Healey (London: G. Eld and M. Flesher, 1620), 719, 723.

could be avoided. As with Erasmus and More, this humanist understood the decision to go to war as a personal one.[132]

By the 1530s, however, with England at peace with its neighbors, the peace rhetoric shifted away from skepticism about just wars to a constructive peacetime political role for the nobility. Perhaps as further indication of the imprint ideas of peace were having on the nation, the ruling class found itself uncomfortable with serving the state in primarily a military function, especially when newer members often owed their elevations to nonmilitary forms of service. The attack on chivalry in the 1530s and 1540s was imbued both with a strong Protestant element (to be examined in Chapter 6) and with the overwhelming restlessness and enhanced sense of duty that elites exhibited as they fashioned new roles for themselves within the English commonweal.

Vives's rejection of romances for their lack of edification may be understandable, but he probably need not have worried so much about their glorification of violence. Even within traditional chivalric handbooks that proliferated among the noble laity, the emphasis was already shifting away from bloody feats of arms to blazonry and guides to fashioning the proper lifestyle for established gentility. Wynkyn de Worde, Caxton's successor, reprinted the *Book of Hawking, Hunting and the Blazing of Arms,* first published after the battle of Bosworth (1485) and commonly referred to as the *Book of St. Alban's.* This immensely popular work was a compilation "devoted to the pursuits and interests of a *generosus,* in this case a country gentleman." Interestingly enough, the longest selection included came from Nicholas Upton's *De officio militari* and the English *Book of the Lineage of Coat Armour,* both dating from the early fifteenth century.[133] These books, which dealt with civil conduct among the upper classes, helped to encourage emerging notions that true nobles were to serve the nation and act with equanimity in all affairs so as to maintain good government and peace throughout the land. Even more fascinating is the fact that this softening of the martial instinct was built on vestiges of the *jus in bello,* which appears to have remained vibrant and continued to influence codes of behavior even among a class that was constructing new and less bellicose roles for itself.

Humanist learning facilitated a shift in emphasis from the knight's military duty to the gentleman's civic responsibilities. Whereas in the Middle

132. J. G. Russell, *Peacemaking in the Renaissance,* 13–14.
133. Jacob, *The Fifteenth Century,* 660–65.

Ages arms and chivalry could not be separated from the aristocratic class, now gentlemen found new opportunities and invested more of their energies in other activities. Roger Manning has shown that a ritualized form of poaching acted as a "symbolic substitute" for war in Tudor and early Stuart England, giving aristocrats all the accoutrements of battle (challenges, oaths of loyalty, displaying armor, "capturing trophies of battle," and so on) without the disruptive violence of private combat or large-scale war.[134] As peace became valued and financially preferable, the nobility had more time to pursue a greater variety of interests[135] and grew to have a stake in preventing new wars—especially prolonged ones. To serve one's country came to mean not just providing ready military assistance but achieving expertise in a variety of political offices and being more devoted to serving the nation in times of peace.[136] Between 1501 and 1601, twenty-nine books were published with the purpose of resurrecting martial values, which each author found in sore decay, and to reiterate the need for military-trained gentlemen. But most of these works were written by soldiers—many of them careerists—and they indicate, more than anything else, the terrible apathy or even hostility that was being directed by this time toward the "ideals" of chivalry.[137] In *Utopia*, More derided "the whole range of chivalrous-aristocratic values and practices." The Utopians consider war a royal sport that the common folk are driven to "by the madness of princes."[138] Even someone with an affinity for Caxton, like John Skelton, more often employed classical allusions in speaking of knights than the language of chivalry. In his play *Magnyfycence* (ca. 1515–16) the character Adversyte actually admits that there is much folly in knightly behavior:

> And some I make in a rope to totter and walter [swing];
> And some for to hang themselves in a halter;
> And some I visit with battle, war, and murder,

134. Roger B. Manning, "Poaching as a Symbolic Substitute for War in Tudor and Early Stuart England," *Journal of Medieval and Renaissance Studies* 22 (1992): 185–210.

135. "The essential material base for a shift in the significance of 'peace' was a greater variety of occupations and honours; estate management, region administration, court service and diplomacy." Hale, *War and Society*, 97.

136. Ruth Kelso, *The Doctrine of the English Gentleman in the Sixteenth Century* (Urbana: University of Illinois Press, 1929; reprint, Gloucester, Mass.: Peter Smith, 1964), 45–46, 49; Kenneth Charlton, *Education in Renaissance England* (London: Routledge & Kegan Paul, 1965), 81.

137. Kelso, *Doctrine of the English Gentleman*, 43–45.

138. Hale, *War and Society*, 29, 38; Ferguson, *Chivalric Tradition*, 52–53.

And make each man to slay the other;
To drown or to slay themselves with a knife—
And all is for their ungracious life.

Later, fun is made of the bold idiocy of Crafty Conveyance and Cloaked Collusion, who, full of bluster, challenge each other over who is the tougher. In the end, the noble attribute that best represents Magnyfycence is majesty rather than chivalry.[139]

Perhaps the two men most responsible for engrafting the new, unchivalric image of the English gentleman onto the national consciousness were the Protestant humanists Sir Thomas Elyot and Roger Ascham. Elyot's *Boke Named the Governor* (1531), which he dedicated to Henry, was concerned primarily with educating the aristocracy to serve the Public Weal "which is disposed by the order of equity, and governed by the rule and moderation of reason."[140] Headed by a strong sovereign the Public Weal has many concerns, and to avoid chaos and discord (again, echoes of Erasmus) it becomes the duty of "wise men of the realm" to take on some of the many tasks of government as delegated by the king. The nobles are most suited to this vocation since they have the means to pursue a rigorous education from early childhood.[141] As Elyot turned to the methods of upbringing within his class, he acknowledged the virtues of physical exercise, although some types, such as hunting, hawking, and dancing must be engaged in only with care. He found that "shooting in a long bow" is the most profitable physical activity of all, not because the skill may be needed in battle, but because it trains both the body and mind.[142]

Elyot's greater challenge to the older order of noble behavior, however, is seen in his definition of honor, which comes not from adherence to a military code but from applying learning in service to the state or commonwealth, much in the Ciceronian and Aristotelian mode.[143] In the introduction to his *Preservative against Death*, Elyot pursued this idea with clarity and conviction:

---

139. John Skelton, *The Complete English Poems,* ed. John Scattergood (New Haven, Conn.: Yale University Press, 1983), 194, 201–4; Fox, *Politics and Literature,* 236–40; Ferguson, *Chivalric Tradition,* 53–54.

140. Thomas Elyot, *The Book Named the Governour,* ed. Arthur T. Eliot (Newcastle-upon-Tyne, Eng.: John Hernaman, 1834), 1.

141. Ibid., 8–22.

142. Ibid., 50–89.

143. Ibid., 95–101; James, *English Politics and the Concept of Honour,* 60–61; Audrey Chew, *Stoicism in Renaissance English Literature* (New York: Peter Lang, 1988), 152–56.

A knight has received that honor not only to defend with the sword Christ's faith and his proper country, against them, which impugns the one or invades the other: but also, and that most chiefly, by means of his dignity (if that be employed where it should be, and esteemed as it ought to be) he should more effectually with his learning and wit assail vice and error, most pernicious enemies to Christian men, having thereunto for his sword and spear his tongue and his pen.[144]

Similarly, in his comments in the *Boke* concerning proper attitudes for the true gentleman, he stressed the virtue of placability. Wrath is "a vice most ugly, and most distant from humanity." Men should seek reconciliation rather than revenge and promote good laws, which could be used to avoid the injustices of blind "wrath and cruel malignity."[145] This point, to which many who have studied Elyot have not given due attention, indicates a certain incorporation of a peace ethic into an institutional framework, which if effected, would contribute toward reform of the commonweal. Laws become a means, in this case, for keeping peace and, thus, for perpetuating a preferred condition in society that can contribute to its future health and prosperity.

All values, then, even those shared with the chivalric tradition, are being placed in a new context of the commonwealth. Even though the idea of commonwealth still carried much of the medieval cast, which emphasized organization, hierarchical society, and mutual obligations to maintain good order and peace, by the 1530s, this became more universally interpreted as the body politic. Escalating social change enabled men such as Elyot to conceive of government as an agent of positive reform that offered fresh approaches to new and growing problems. Elyot's Public Weal, or *respublica,* had become a concept alien to the chivalric tradition, with the aristocracy no longer viewed just as local protectors or knights-errant. And a simple, personal loyalty to the king was being replaced by a more complex socioeconomic concern for the nation embodied in service to the monarch.[146]

The distinctive nature of this new English gentleman becomes even clearer when comparing him to his contemporary Italian prototype. Cas-

144. Thomas Elyot, *A Preservative Agaynste Deth* (London: Thomas Berthelet, 1545), sigs. A2v–A3r.
145. Elyot, *Book Named the Governour,* 113–25.
146. Ferguson, *Chivalric Tradition,* 59–61.

tiglione's *Courtier* (1528; English version, 1561) depicts a knight-become-
courtier, whose "courage was accomplished rather than learned" and who
gloried in feats of arms in a manner that would have been very unfamiliar
to Elyot.[147] Most of all, greater attention is given to specific behaviors and
manners that should characterize the modern, educated gentleman, including the development of a "gentle and pleasing manner in his daily conver-
sation," temperance in food and drink, and learning to participate in
courtly banter with great wit.[148] By concentrating on court etiquette, however, Castiglione is no less devaluing the place of martial activity in even a
precariously defended Italian society. He does not push the knight as forcefully into a position of public service, as do the English writers, and considering the chaotic state of Italian statecraft, probably could not; but he
must be included in that expanding group of Renaissance thinkers who
believed that "society by now ought to have grown out of warfare."[149]

Ascham's *Toxophilus* (1545) bears a striking affinity to Elyot's *Book
Named the Governor*, even if it is primarily concerned with archery. Dedicated to Henry VIII but written "to all gentlemen and yeomen of England," the work is divided into two parts. The first book deals with the
reasons for learning and practicing shooting while the second one discusses
particulars on how to shoot well. Ascham followed Elyot in his insistence
that the learned gentleman develop his body as well as his mind. Archery
was the best physical exercise because it "hinders little or nothing at all,"
and through it, scholars are able "to maintain their health and studies
withal."[150] While Ascham realized the periodic need for archers in wartime,
he warned against depending upon physical strength to win battles, which
would be a tragic waste of a gentleman's skills, time, and energy. Ultimately, the Prince, who leads by example, "in his heart must be full of
mercy and peace, a virtue most pleasant to Christ, most agreeable to man's
nature, most profitable for rich and poor."[151] He goes on to cite the great
tragedy found in war, even though it is sometimes required to ensure a
peaceful future: "There is nothing worse than war . . . through which great
men be in danger, mean men without succor, rich men in fear, because they

147. Ibid., 62; Charlton, *Education in Renaissance England*, 82.
148. Baldesar Castiglione, *The Book of the Courtier*, trans. Charles S. Singleton (Garden
City, N.Y.: Anchor Books, 1959), 109, 135, 169–76.
149. Hale, *War and Society*, 97–98.
150. Roger Ascham, *English Works*, ed. William Aldis Wright (Cambridge: The University
Press, 1904), 3–4, 11.
151. Ibid., 32.

have somewhat, poor men in care, because they have nothing. And so every man in thought and misery."[152]

With Ascham, we have an example of a humanist who has adopted the Erasmian peace ethic that takes no glory in war but who has begun also to move away from the near complete idealism of the Dutchman and some of his contemporaries. The use of war to bring about a better future condition is a last resort and is not really based on any just-war idea that legitimizes violence for the sake of the public welfare. On the contrary, for Ascham, mercy has replaced justice as the desired nexus of human intercourse, and so instead of looking for restitution and revenge (in the name of the commonwealth or not), he would seek pacification and forgiveness of injuries—a needed skill for a society still forging the implements of compromise in diplomacy. Like Elyot, the new gentleman here is to pursue those activities which have a positive, salutary effect on society. The "compleat gentleman" of the 1530s and 1540s had come to accept a good deal of the humanist value for peace, as part and parcel of his new understanding of and participation in the Tudor commonwealth.

This discussion of the changing perceptions and roles for aristocratic men, while interesting for its affinities with certain aspects of Erasmian humanism, is also significant for what it says about the changing dynamic within contemporary peace discourse. As pointed out in the previous chapter, one of the primary attacks made by critics of war in the later Middle Ages revolved around the excessive appetite for brutality and bloodletting that had come to characterize the noble warriors. As England suffered political and social dislocations of the worst kind during the Hundred Years War, the outcry for orderly peace and the restoration of strong government reached peak level by the middle of the fifteenth century. The monarchy constructed by Edward IV, Henry VII, and Henry VIII had muted these criticisms and made them nearly obsolete. Kings now dealt with maverick nobles and their retinues swiftly and with little mercy. When rebellion and costly wars again threatened the nation's stability, there emerged renewed calls for civil order, as we will see in Chapter 7. For the most part, however, the changing nature of aristocratic vocation that characterized the sixteenth century signaled a greater focus on practical peace concerns that dealt largely with economic issues and which incorporated the commonwealth idea more fully. With larger armies and costlier campaigns threatening, the fears of lawlessness were less pronounced; but

152. Ibid.

there was nevertheless a heightened awareness of threats to trade, national income, and purveyance, among others, to compensate. In short, English monarchs had heeded the calls for orderly peace and a restrained nobility, and humanist values simply made it easier for a new group of "gentlemen-bureaucrats" to emerge. Domestic peace and tranquillity had been secured for the most part, and many English people reveled in it. But the attention to the benefits of peace did not dissipate or languish, as threats continued to surface. The nation's newfound political strength and the security that accompanied it would encounter no new major peril from renegade, uncontrollable nobles, but rather from renegade, indomitable religious partisans and petty dynastic jealousies that threatened economic growth and vitality.

Conclusion

To recognize the new role for the aristocracy being sketched by Ascham and Elyot is not to say that a great ideological and social transformation occurred overnight in England. But evidence indicates clearly that the future was moving in their direction.[153] Lest too facile a linkage be made between this newer perception of public service and an abhorrence for war, it is important to remember that it was immensely difficult if not impossible to conceptualize the problem outside some kind of just-war framework, even if that framework was being criticized and consequently changed over time. As long as that remained the case, the debate on war operated beyond evolving professions and humanist training. The overall impact of an increasingly pacified aristocracy during this period, however, did contribute to some taming of the martial spirit even as just wars continued to be supported and valorized. While greater diversity of opinion with regard to war and peace policies was surely a by-product of the expansion of public roles for the English ruling class, there remained a powerful, albeit dwindling, cadre of traditional family elites who continued to know only war and who lent generous support to Henry's Scottish and French campaigns throughout his reign. Heroic commands and victories could still lead to individual advancements while the nation itself might be

---

153. See Hexter, *Education of the English Aristocracy.*

moving toward defeat and bankruptcy.[154] The Howards even had poet lau-
reate John Skelton immortalize their exploits on the field at Flodden and in
France.[155] Yet after the 1512–13 campaign, military service to the king
through noble retinues began to fall off substantially. Whereas mercenaries
and auxiliaries made up over one-fifth of the total army in 1513, they had
increased to one-third in Suffolk's of 1523, one-fourth of all forces in
1546, and constituted one-half of the 30,000 soldiers commanded by
Hertford in 1546. The hirelings, while reviled and ridiculed almost everywhere, did possess a better knowledge of and a wider experience in modern warfare, in which the "quasi-feudal" English army found it more and
more difficult to compete. By the 1540s a division had opened up between
the supportive nobility, who, still existing as a military elite, accepted soldierly duty to Henry, and much of the rest of England, which had probably "lost any illusions about the glory of war by the 1520s." The recruit-
ments of the 1540s were no longer carried out through pressing feudal
obligations but by a "national system," which was so thorough that it left
"the reign of Henry VIII as the last in which military service was the nation's most conspicuous duty."[156]

All of this is not to say that a decline in chivalric values led to more
overt pacifism or to a noticeable opposition to warfare in the abstract. The
English (and all other Europeans) as a whole continued to accept that war
was an ineradicable part of life and even necessary for the security of states
and societies that might be threatened by foreign aggression. The expanded roles of upper-class civil servants to include a wider range of responsibilities and tasks connected with diplomacy and peace, simply gave
evolving peace discourse a professional character and authenticity, which
facilitated its incorporation into the upper echelons of government where
policy was being made. Wars would still be undertaken during these years,
and with great purpose, but their prosecution and resolution would be
influenced increasingly by the multiplicity of peace positions that had
emerged fully by the sixteenth century.[157]

154. Helen Miller, *Henry VIII and the English Nobility* (Oxford: Basil Blackwell, 1986),
144.

155. Skelton, *Complete English Poems*, 113–21. Greg Walker, in *John Skelton and the
Politics of the 1520s* (Cambridge: Cambridge University Press, 1988), 5–34, questions this
traditional view.

156. Miller, *Henry VIII and the English Nobility*, 157–61; J. J. Goring, "The Military
Obligations of the English People, 1511–1558" (Ph.D. diss., University of London, 1955),
270–73, 279–80.

157. Hale, *War and Society*, 97–99. The just war was given renewed attention also at this

The purpose of this chapter has been to demonstrate the leavening effect
of Christian humanism on an incipient late-medieval peace value. The resulting peace ethic has been viewed then in terms of the specific ways in
which it intersected with English wars and the rhetoric that accompanied
them between 1485 and 1530. Finally, the impact these new ideas of peace
had on a burnt-out code of chivalry and a new emerging political role for
the upper classes has been examined. In the end the two languages of
antiquity employed by humanists—taken from a humanitarianism found
in both classical Stoicism and the Christian gospel—helped to extol the
value of peace, and in turn, the ideas of peace also broadened and transformed the range of expression available to the users of these languages. A
discourse of peace was developing that eclectically combined a number of
linguistic conventions to match the political and economic contexts that
had necessitated a greater concentration on peace as an idea, and now also
as a matter of state. Throughout all, what has been made most clear is that
the way of peace was being embraced, even in its idealistic form, in such a
way that it was becoming a part of the national consciousness.

The absolute necessity for peace felt by many humanists conforms to a
recent assessment of the ideology of Renaissance warfare by Michael
Howard: "Perhaps the most significant of all the developments that occurred in the early modern period . . . was the virtual abandonment of the
just war. War became accepted as a natural, if not indeed necessary, element in international politics, and its conduct was molded by pragmatic
necessities rather than by abstract principles."[158] At this early stage when
the Ciceronian and biblical guidelines for achieving peace seemed applicable and possible, Erasmians determined war to be unnatural. They did,
however, reject much of the intellectual tradition that justified war, realiz-

time by the Spanish neoscholastics (Victoria, Suarez, Gentili, Sepulveda, and de Castrillo),
who revived Thomistic justifications in support of colonial conquests and to counter Erasmian "pacifism." While they proposed a stricter *jus in bello* and took into account the possibilities of peace among nation-states, these schoolmen differed from the English writers, who
were wary of most just-war arguments. English humanists also possessed a more complex
notion of commonwealth (see Chapter 7). To men like Elyot, Cromwell, More, and Hugh
Latimer, commonwealth was a positive ideal as they came to recognize the power of the state
in generating ongoing reform, which included maintaining the peace. The neoscholastic view
comes across as more conservative, protective, and restrictive, as if change must be avoided
and war used to preserve the status quo (or to preempt disruptions to the status quo). The
Thomists appear to have generated little interest in England, and only Gentili's works were
published there during the sixteenth century. For more on their ideas, see Fernandez-
Santamaria, *State, War and Peace,* 122–43.

158. Howard, "Constraints on Warfare," 3.

ing that wars were endemic to most (non-Utopian) human interaction, and
arguments always could be marshaled to favor them. For this reason,
Erasmus especially, saw the need to posit peace as a countervailing force to
the just-war idea. He and others like him hoped that if peace's ethical
worth were made paramount, it would temper scholastic just-war arguments that might be strong logically, yet devoid of the moral philosophical
underpinnings that humanists believed should condition all human behavior. Even if war no longer needed to be legitimized in the abstract, the
Renaissance witnessed a concomitant rise in attitudes that opposed war as
an institution. Without rejecting its utility on occasion, many people came
to believe that on largely practical grounds, it was not a constructive
means for achieving political and social stability or economic prosperity,
that is, the highest good. The combination of biblical scholarship, humanist education, and overall interest in commonwealth reform encouraged a
number of sixteenth-century English Protestants to problematize issues of
war and peace within a real-world context and to take the emergent peace
ethic and find effective ways to implement it.

In a simultaneous development, J. R. Hale, the preeminent authority on
Renaissance warfare notes the new attention given to peace as a result of
the civilianization process Europe underwent in the sixteenth century,
wherein the highly regarded professions, such as the law, ranged far from
the traditional education noblemen received in the Middle Ages: "Perhaps
the most important factor of all—after state moderation of persistent un-
ruliness—was the notion of peace itself, peace which, in spite of the dis-
trust we have noticed, was now more generally seen as a positive, attainable, prolongable, above all profitable and interesting phase of national
life." Henceforth, any military revolution was accompanied by one "in the
connotations of peace"; in this case that meant becoming an idea no
longer understood simply as a pause between fighting or an ideal unattainable in this world. A whole range of martial pastimes and activities either
disappeared or became much less important. With the clergy helping to
inculcate this new approach to peace into society at large (as we shall see),
peace was seen more as an "attractive alternative to the perpetual preparation for recurrences of violence."[159]

This role of the Church points to one area that has yet to be explored in
this discussion, the Christian, or more specifically after 1534, the mostly
Protestant contribution to English understandings of peace. The implica-

159. Hale, *War and Society,* 96–97.

tions of religious attitudes in this area are enormous for their scope and attention to the common person, all of which made it incumbent upon religious and political leaders of the mid-Tudor period to remove ideas of peace from the safe and sheltered world of the ideal and place them into the present daily struggles of spirit and society.

6

EARLY PROTESTANT NEGOTIATIONS OF WAR AND PEACE

Protestants interpreted issues of war and peace through the language of biblical exegesis, which basically attempted to apply the literal meaning of Scripture to existing personal and social concerns. Believing that the Bible was the ultimate source of truth and that it should serve as a guide for determining proper behavior, they often employed expressions from the Bible in much the same way that humanists employed classical *sententiae*. In the early modern world, received truth from recognized authorities carried extraordinary weight, and for many Protestants, conflicting moral stands resulted from following those in authority who had misappropriated — purposely or not — the Bible. They believed humanity's distance from this font of religious truth had done great injury to the Christian commonwealth. In England, even among the more conservative Anglican clergy, there was a heightened attention to the precise meanings of certain scriptural passages, as a proliferation of expository sermons and commentaries exhorted the faithful to greater godliness. Fearing both the militancy of the pope and those faithful Catholics determined to bring the nation back to the "true faith" by violent means if necessary, English churchmen, especially after 1533, became less respectful of interpretive traditions associated with the Roman church. As a result, the evangelicals' alternative trust in the king's power to foster harmony and right faith generated an "obdurate belief in non-resistance" toward temporal authority, even though Henry VIII persecuted them from time to time.[1]

Scholars interested in the role of resistance theory in developing political thought have emphasized instances where Protestants argued in favor of the armed, coercive force of the state to protect the faith from papist minions, who would extinguish it altogether; and how in those areas where the state persecuted rather than protected, especially in Calvinist enclaves, true Christians (through the lower magistrates) had a right and responsibility to serve God rather than man, and thus resist. Most prominently in France and Holland some did interpret Calvin in this manner, and their spiritual kindred among the English Puritans and Scottish Presbyterians made similar contentions,[2] but even their message did not unilaterally favor war except in dire circumstances when they believed Protestantism was imperiled. Overt challenges to legitimate authorities were the real danger posed by resistance theorists, not their promotion of wars, which they believed should be fought only as a last resort. In fact, there was a wide range of evangelicals who spoke out on issues of war and peace, most of whom were not very radical and who proved to be very loyal subjects of the crown. Many reformers ardently supported patriotic causes but they did not, as a group, clamor for Protestant crusades.

It is important to recognize the great diversity of opinion and not to misunderstand the biblical hermeneutics that informed their beliefs or to caricature an evangelical message that had its foundation in Scripture. Here Protestants grappled, often existentially, but certainly dogmatically, with Christ's promised blessings for peacemakers. A number of English Protestants who found allusions to the preferable "way of peace" throughout the Bible and in the writings of the early church fathers whom they admired came to reject war as a sinful activity, the product of a general apostasy that included human greed and lack of Christian charity.[3] Because of their determination that war was simply the result of sin, fewer of them

1. Whitney R. D. Jones, *The Tudor Commonwealth, 1529–1559* (London: Athlone Press, 1970), 75.

2. Christopher Goodman, George Buchanan, John Knox, John Ponet, and a number of seventeenth-century Puritans. Quentin Skinner, *The Foundations of Modern Political Thought*, vol. 2, *The Age of Reformation* (Cambridge: Cambridge University Press, 1978), 189–348.

3. Stanley L. Greenslade, *The English Reformers and the Fathers of the Church* (Oxford: Clarendon Press, 1960), passim; John E. Booty, *John Jewel As Apologist of the Church of England* (London: SPCK, 1963), 58.

elevated it to the status it received in canon law, as a means to right wrongs and advance the kingdom of Christ. It is also significant that English evangelicals were often humanists and therefore affected to some degree by the classical (Stoic) discourse that appealed to Erasmus and More, as well as by their critical approach to biblical texts.

But the Protestant Reformation also presented a natural challenge to social and political conventions that were no longer serviceable in an age where reform and renewal were the watchwords. The "purification of language" that accompanied regeneration of religion included dispensing with the antiquated features of some concepts with the intention of redefining them. In discussing how ideas of law, liberty, authority, and tradition underwent such a process during the development of early modern resistance theory, Donald Kelley could have been talking just as easily about the problem of war, where likewise, "as always large social conflicts were accompanied by struggles for language, and so the process of 'politicization' exemplified by the Reformation was implied from the beginning in the arguments of the theologians and scholars."[4] Among evangelicals the Bible was the hermeneutical handbook *par excellence,* the measure for separating the relative (and adiaphoric) from the imperative. Many of those who attempted to abide by such a rigorous standard came to place peace in the latter domain. When their arguments became infused with a strong dose of the pragmatic, as was the case in England, the politicization of peace into policy was almost effortless, and perhaps even a bit surreptitious, as we shall see when turning to the events of the 1540s.[5]

In looking at Protestant contributions to Tudor thought on war and peace, one must not demarcate too broadly between these and other current strains of discourse that shared many of the same assumptions. In the 1530s England officially became a Protestant nation in the most general sense of the word, but the values and concerns that energized the religious reformers took their time to germinate and were far from prevalent, especially among the more traditional-minded. Most of the Protestants examined in this chapter, however, were of that evangelical stamp which characterized Luther, Calvin, and all others who upheld a strict adherence to scriptural authority, the necessity of individual regeneration through faith

---

4. Donald R. Kelley, "Ideas of Resistance before Elizabeth," in *The Historical Renaissance: New Essays on Tudor and Stuart Literature and Culture,* ed. Heather Dubrow and Richard Strier (Chicago: University of Chicago Press, 1988), 48.

5. G. R. Evans, *Problems of Authority in the Reformation Debates* (Cambridge: Cambridge University Press, 1992), 37–69, 80–85.

in Christ, and a strong desire to lead a Christ-like life, and who, in the case of England, submitted to an erastian church. By concentrating on the mid-Tudor period (ca. 1530–58), it is difficult to assign clear confessional labels to several of the men discussed in this chapter. What may have kept divines like Roger Edgeworth, Cuthbert Tunstall, and John Longland in the Henrician camp was their instinct for survival, but also perhaps an initial advocacy of the erastianism which led them to speak out against papal corruption, including the pontiff's propensity for self-aggrandizing wars. Even though these men were doctrinally conservative, their interest in a broader spectrum of reform distinguishes them from the pre-Reformation clergy (*pace* Christopher Haigh), including the most Catholic of all—Edgeworth. It is among the more evangelical, as we shall see, with their emphasis on conscience and concrete change that the parameters of peace as an ethic expanded. It must always be kept in mind, however, that much cross-pollination of ideas existed and that most early Protestants were humanists, even if with varying degrees of emphasis and fervency.[6] Yet, as they rejected the authority and traditions which had distinguished the Roman church for centuries, they expected Christians to exercise new and different degrees of responsibility with respect both to their personal spiritual journey and in how they reflected Christ in the world about them. Even as many Protestants found biblical passages that denounced war and conflict, in certain circumstances they acknowledged that wars would be necessary for maintaining right belief. Early Protestants, therefore, often found themselves confronted by a New Testament and humanistic ethic of peace on one hand and the possible need to defend their religion on the other. In England, where these alternatives were perhaps most pronounced, the struggle that resulted proved creative in expanding peace discourse to include more realistic and less idealistic notions and contingencies. As we have seen, the recourse to war was never an easy one. Throughout the Middle Ages, however, there were institutional authorities, such as Church and king, who legalized ethical questions regarding just warfare.[7] For English Protestants, while allegiance usually was fixed more squarely on the king, individual conscience played a greater role than ever, as moral issues

6. See Ferguson, *Indian Summer*, 94–95. Ferguson makes the point that Protestants, like humanists, were nonchivalric in temperament, connecting that tradition with medieval Catholicism. While humanism helped to create the social ideal of commonwealth that saw war as barbaric, it was within the "Anglican Reformation" that it "achieved some sort of domestication in English culture."

7. Russell, *Just War*, 306.

were no longer so easily categorized or definitively grasped. In building a more complex idea of peace, then, Protestants might try to assess pertinent biblical passages as straightforwardly as possible and attempt to apply them to contemporary society as their own best judgments and consciences dictated. This process, when performed, did result in new conceptualizations built on medieval and humanist foundations. Novelties appeared where emphases differed and as the ideas on war and peace of the major Continental reformers were incorporated into a particular intellectual and religious milieu.

Many Protestants adopted a few leading, albeit qualified, assumptions of Erasmian humanism. Most important, both movements respected the original meanings of biblical texts as the foundation for all ethics and considered warfare among Christians as a form of apostasy, contrary to the way of Christ. But for Protestants, *knowing* the truth was not enough. There had to be a practical way to translate the truth into purposeful action. In a 1548 letter to the duke of Somerset, for example, Calvin blamed England's troubles "not from the lack of preaching, but from failure to enforce compliance with it."[8] If conflict was unavoidable and love the primary motivation—not an easy determination for most of them— then it was incumbent upon Christians to bring it to an end as soon as possible and find a realistic way to usher in the benefits of peace.

The ethical quandaries thus engendered relate closely to Reformed Protestantism's focus on human depravity, an inescapable condition that includes a penchant for selfishness and therefore greedy wars. While this was a concern among medieval theologians, the additional burden of conscience was particularly heavy for Protestants also educated in humanist moral philosophy.[9] To make war moral was exceedingly difficult; the first step was a careful and strict legitimation of cause. Protestants therefore approached the *jus ad bellum* in just such a manner, trying to find ethical rationales that went beyond medieval formulations for redressing injuries and recovering honor or territory. If all else fails and Christ would be glorified by going to war, then it should be fought as humanely as possible. Both soldiers and citizens must exhibit love toward the enemy, avoid cruelty, and live holy lives indicative of a just cause (where responsibility for the war rests with the ungodly enemy). This last aspect was important so

8. Jones, *Tudor Commonwealth,* 10.
9. Paul Oskar Kristeller, "The Moral Thought of Renaissance Humanism," in *Renaissance Thought and the Arts: Collected Essays* (Princeton, N.J.: Princeton University Press, 1990), 57–60.

that Christians avoided war, which many Protestants viewed as divine judgment because of the consequent harm it inflicted on the commonwealth. Conversely, if people would attend to the virtues of peace—gifts from God—destructive conflicts among nations could be mitigated, despite the sinfulness of human nature, and social harmony, predicated on holy living, might prevail.

Lutheran and Reformed Contributions to the English Reformation

To a great extent Erasmian humanism's appeal within intellectual circles determined the nature of religious reform once Continental Protestant ideas began reaching England.[10] Most students of this period are familiar with the connection between northern humanism and religious reform; but not all reform movements owe the same debt to their humanist predecessors. For this reason we need to recount the introduction of both Lutheran and Reformed theology into the English Reformation in order to establish points of contact between Continental Protestant opinion on war and peace and the discourse that arose in England on this subject at the same time.

Martin Luther's immediate notoriety and theological stature after his Ninety-Five Theses were publicized led scholars at both Cambridge and Oxford to read him as early as 1518. Initial disciples included William Tyndale, Miles Coverdale, Hugh Latimer, Robert Barnes, and Thomas Bilney. The first two, who were responsible for the earliest printed translation of the Bible into English, signal the most important legacy of Lutheranism in England—putting vernacular Scriptures into the hands of the people. Otherwise, Luther's appeal was limited. Henry VIII was never fond of the German reformer, having written against his sacramental views and in return receiving the title "Defender of the Faith," from Pope Leo X in 1521. The years of Thomas Cromwell's and Anne Boleyn's ascendancy, however, did see some overtures being made to the Lutherans. Current scholarship demonstrates the clear evangelicalism of those in power during the 1530s and their effectiveness in controlling patronage and influencing govern-

10. Maria Dowling, *Humanism in the Age of Henry VIII* (London: Croom Helm, 1986).

ment policy.[11] But the setbacks of the Schmalkaldic wars for the German Protestant princes, the failed marriage to Anne of Cleves, and the execution of the chief minister put an end to any thought of rapprochement with the Lutherans. Luther's adamant refusal to sanction Henry's divorce was not irrelevant to this turn of events. Any confessional influence on the English church would have to enter subtly at first, and then only in the trail of strong support for the royal supremacy.[12] By the end of the 1530s, Tyndale, Bilney, and Barnes had been burned as heretics, Latimer had resigned his see at Worcester, and Coverdale was lying low. Meanwhile, among the staunchest of the royal supremacists serving the king, such as Cuthbert Tunstall and Stephen Gardiner, a particular distaste for Lutheran dogma had manifested itself, as they, like many others, equated it with Lollardy, which was seen as radical and subversive.[13]

The ties to the Continent though were never severed and, in fact, remained quite strong, with religious ideas usually finding their way into England along trade routes. German and Swiss cities, such as Basel and Strasbourg, were connected by commerce to the English wool staple at Antwerp, where Tyndale himself went into hiding just before his capture. The conservative reaction in England by the early 1540s prompted some of the more evangelical Protestants to go into exile, and almost all of them preferred Zurich and Strasbourg to Wittenberg, which had always been less accommodating to foreigners and shunned the ostensible internationalism of the Swiss movements.[14] Heinrich Bullinger, Zwingli's son-in-law and successor in Zurich, not only welcomed these visitors but kept up a lively correspondence with many of them after they had returned home. John Hooper became a particularly close friend and would play a large role in the reform movement of the next reign. After 1540 it was clear that Swiss models of reform were proving more attractive to English reformers, and the commonalities were most obvious in tendencies toward moral legalism, iconoclasm, and doubts about the real presence in the Eucharist.

11. Susan Brigden, "Thomas Cromwell and 'the Brethren,'" in Cross, Loades, and Scarisbrick, *Law and Government under the Tudors*, 31–49; Retha M. Warnicke, *The Rise and Fall of Anne Boleyn: Family Politics at the Court of Henry VIII* (Cambridge: Cambridge University Press, 1989), 131–62; G. R. Elton, *Reform and Reformation: England, 1509–1558* (Cambridge, Mass.: Harvard University Press, 1977), 170–73.

12. Diarmaid MacCulloch, "Two Dons in Politics: Thomas Cranmer and Stephen Gardiner, 1503–1533," *Historical Journal* 37 (1994): 17–18.

13. R.A.W. Rex, "The English Campaign Against Luther in the 1520s," *TRHS*, 5th ser., 39 (1989): 85–106; David Loades, "Martin Luther and the Early Stages of the English Reformation," in *Politics, Censorship and the English Reformation* (London: Pinter, 1991), 156–57.

14. Diarmaid MacCulloch, "England," in *The Early Reformation in Europe*, ed. Andrew Pettegree (Cambridge: Cambridge University Press, 1992), 173.

Lutherans did not consider these matters quite as important and held different views from their English and Swiss counterparts.[15] Thus a combination of political expediency, economic ties, and common interests in reform served to turn eyes more squarely on events and ideas coming out of Zurich. As discussed below, the penetration of Erasmian humanism into both lands may have also aided in bringing the two together ideologically.[16]

Recent research has shown, however, that despite the Swiss connection, English Protestants did not adopt foreign ideas unaltered. Tyndale, a visitor to Wittenberg, always treated Luther as one source among many for his beliefs.[17] There is a good deal of evidence to suggest that still-prevalent Lollard opinions also affected how some doctrines were received and interpreted.[18] For example, most Lollards were opposed to the real presence, and a residue of this may be found in the unique views of the sacrament offered by John Frith, Hooper, and Latimer. Interesting links between humanism, Lollardy, and Protestantism can be found both in the careers of Bilney and Tyndale.[19] Even the allegedly reformist Ten Articles, drafted in 1536 after the death of the first two queens, carved out uniquely English positions, most noticeably by repudiating Luther's solifidianism and in including charity as also necessary for salvation. The more restrictive Six Articles, enacted in 1539, although commonly interpreted as a return to Catholic dogma even as the nation remained virulently anti-papal, was still not a wholesale reaction or return to the past. The king continued to depend on the least radical evangelicals for support of the supremacy, and the appointments to bishoprics between 1532 and 1536, in which nine of eleven went to their kind, demonstrate their strong erastian inclinations. A committee organized in 1540 to produce a fuller guide to proper belief included, therefore, a wider range of theological opinion than has been often recognized—from Cranmer's evangelicalism, to the humanism of Thomas Robertson and John Redman, to the Catholicism of Roger Edge-

---

15. Ibid., 172.

16. Erasmus was quoted as an authority for reform by several English Protestants, including John Hooper (on images) and Thomas Becon (on living a godly life in prayer). Dickens and Jones, *Erasmus the Reformer*, 200–202.

17. Loades, "Martin Luther and the Early Stages of the English Reformation," 152–53.

18. R. G. Davies, "Lollardy and Locality," *TRHS*, 6th ser., 1 (1991): 191–212; Hudson, *Premature Reformation*, passim.

19. J. F. Davis, "The Trials of Thomas Bilney and the English Reformation," *Historical Journal* 24 (1981): 775–90; Donald Dean Smeeton, *Lollard Themes in the Reformation Theology of William Tyndale* (Kirksville, Mo.: Sixteenth Century Journal Publishers, 1986); Loades, "Martin Luther and the Early Stages of the English Reformation," 154.

worth. The result was the so-called King's Book, passed by Parliament in 1543 under the Act for the Advancement of True Religion. But even in the most conservative acts of late Henrician ecclesiastical policy, there was some equivocation on transubstantiation (but not the real presence) and numerous statements in support of scriptural authority.[20] (After all, Scripture had been the basis of Henry's case for divorce in the first place.)

The Henrician settlement, however, was not fluid enough for most evangelicals, and doctrinal deviance met with the severest of punishments. The choice of Tunstall to preach the Palm Sunday sermon at Paul's Cross in 1539, with its strong anti-papal rancor and defense of traditional ceremonies, marks the government's position over the next seven years. As a result, the migrations to Reformed centers on the Continent continued undiminished until the king's death in 1547.[21] All of this changed drastically with the succession of the boy-king Edward VI (1547–53), whose education, along with that of the princess Elizabeth, Henry had entrusted to tutors of advanced Protestant opinions, such as John Cheke and Roger Ascham. According to G. R. Elton this decision was not without effect: "With the help of other 'Erasmians', these men created for Edward and his sister Elizabeth a humanist school which put the pedagogic precepts of Erasmus and Vives into practice and attracted as pupils also the offspring of several court peers."[22] The returning exiles and underground Protestants, however, came to have a greater and more abiding impact than the young king's humanist upbringing. Not only would the influences of Bullinger and Martin Bucer, reformer of Strasbourg, be felt, but those of a more recently heralded reformer in Geneva as well.

At this point it might help to look more carefully at the actual connections that existed between Erasmian humanism and Reformed theology before assessing the impact of the latter on English Protestantism.[23] The Reformed theology that first appeared in Zurich and then, with a few alterations, in Geneva was greatly indebted to Renaissance humanism. The techniques of Erasmus and his followers in finding or producing accurate texts, especially of Scripture, and then applying critical methods of analysis became a vital element of Zwingli's, Bucer's, Bullinger's, and Calvin's re-

20. Richard Rex, *Henry VIII and the English Reformation* (New York: St. Martin's Press, 1993), 155–59.
21. Ibid., 154–55.
22. Elton, *Reform and Reformation*, 318.
23. Most of the following discussion is taken from Alister McGrath's lucid *Intellectual Origins of the European Reformation* (Oxford: Blackwell, 1987), 32–68.

form programs. The effect of Erasmus's moral philosophy on Swiss humanism, and on Zwingli in particular, even led to a strong interest in pacifism between 1516 and 1519. No other reformer mirrored Erasmus's views about reform as closely as Zwingli. His adoption of the *philosophia Christi* and Scripture principle in the early 1520s as part of an overall educational reform demonstrates these leanings. Lutheran emphasis on exact doctrinal definition and theological subtlety was relatively foreign to the Swiss.[24] By the end of his life, however, Zwingli used the Stoic Seneca to challenge the optimism of Erasmus, feeling that human society was completely unregenerate and would hopelessly remain so without special divine intervention. He lost faith in the ultimate success of humanist studies to educate morally. His successor, Bullinger, retained Zwingli's pessimism, and those English Protestants who were in close contact with Zurich and had become students of its institutionalized reform picked it up as well.[25]

Second-generation Reformed theologians who subscribed to basic Zwinglian tenets introduced their own unique insights into the nature of reform. The notion of adiaphora, that there is no particularly correct position one must take in some areas of doctrine or practice, evolved out of Erasmian humanism into the theology of Martin Bucer. Bucer received a humanist education and read the Dutchman intensively, coming to a similar "emphasis upon the tropological sense of Scripture — in other words, upon the ethical application of the scriptural text to the specific historical situation of the reader."[26] Bucer may not have written about war and peace but he believed passionately that ethical behavior was the foundation of the truly regenerate Christian, and in so stressing the example of Christ's life, downplayed the Lutheran accent on faith.

Recent Calvin studies have stressed his humanist roots and their persistence even as he became fully evangelical theologically.[27] For example, his *Institutes of the Christian Religion,* first published in 1536 and then revised periodically until a final edition appeared in 1559, includes a discussion of natural theology that shares many similarities with Cicero. Both believed "that man possesses inconclusive, fragmentary and inconsistent knowledge of God," but while Cicero considered this detrimental, Calvin

24. Ibid., 46, 49.
25. Ibid., 51.
26. Ibid., 52–53.
27. William J. Bouwsma, *John Calvin: A Sixteenth Century Portrait* (Oxford: Oxford University Press, 1988).

thought it advantageous, thus furnishing the basis for his views on predestination and the authority of Scripture. Adherents to Reformed theology
depended on the superior knowledge and sovereignty of God to compensate for their own lack of complete understanding. Predestination was only
one of several doctrines that the mature Christian had to believe because
they were in the Bible, even in the face of all their terrible antinomy. The
Bible was the only sure source for truth in this world, and so for Calvin, it
must be sought for guidance in any moral dilemma — and the reformer
held that moral dilemmas were the overriding fact of day-to-day Christian
living.[28]

English reformers recognized and reflected some of that painful reality
in their struggles with issues relating to war and peace. The evangelicals,
preoccupied with a number of ethical issues, were frustrated by the fact
that the Bible called for particular behaviors and yet original sin and its
consequences seemed to preclude their perfect achievement. Rather than
remain awash in either speculative optimism (like Erasmus) or pessimism
(like More), however, as with Calvin, they attempted to work out their
problems with "fear and trembling." Utopia was heaven but Calvinist-
inspired reformers believed that they had nevertheless a calling to labor
unceasingly to create a godly kingdom on earth. Peace would not be ultimate, everlasting, or universal, but it could be had on some level and this
is what Christ commanded. The combination of this cautious Reformed
hope with English concerns for maintaining a just and vigorous commonwealth, produced some of the most interesting and unique ideas yet about
peace.[29]

The government of Protector Somerset permitted this and other debates
over a whole range of issues when, soon after coming to power in 1547, it
relaxed considerably the censorship of printed works.[30] Almost everyone
high up in Edward's government was in regular communication with Calvin early in the reign, from Somerset and the royal tutors, to the king
himself. The cordiality of those relationships further moved the English
church along Reformed lines. The earliest evidence of outright doctrinal
changes in this direction can be found in the publication of Cranmer's
Book of Homilies and the requirement that Erasmus's *Paraphrases* of the
New Testament be placed in every English church, culminating in the ap-

28. McGrath, *Intellectual Origins*, 54–59.
29. Euan Cameron, *The European Reformation* (Oxford: Clarendon Press, 1991), 185.
30. Rex, *Henry VIII and the English Reformation*, 159.

pearances of the increasingly Calvinist prayer books of 1549 and 1552.[31] Clearly, by this time the English reformers had found the theology at Zurich and Geneva more congenial. By 1548 Archbishop Cranmer was inviting the leading Continental reformers to England to assist his reform efforts, and the near total absence of Lutherans was indicative. The imposition of Emperor Charles V's Interim in 1548 opened the door to Protestant immigrants and led to the establishment of a number of foreign congregations in London.[32]

During this time, Cranmer and Somerset established closer ties with Peter Martyr and Bucer, who, along with the archbishop, genuinely sought to bring unity to the Protestant world. Both Continental leaders were active in England during Edward's brief reign and found much in common with early Anglican tendencies toward adiaphora or a *via media* on certain doctrinal matters.[33] From Zurich, Bullinger interfered without inhibition in the framing of England's religious settlement during these years. His "Zurich faction" in England, which included John Hooper and the Polish émigré, John à Lasco, while influential, lost important battles over vestments and prayer book revisions. As Andrew Pettegree puts it: "Their failure to prevail represented both an assertion of the role of the state in religious affairs and, in the long term equally significantly, an assertion of the right of the English Church to develop independently of Continental models."[34] Once again, the ongoing adaptation of foreign ideas to English situations proved an enduring practice, even as it contributed to greater frustration among the more confessionally rigid.

Adding to these developments, a flood of foreign, mostly Swiss, religious works continued to enter the country unabated. The freedom English reformers possessed to reflect on social and religious reform, and then to publish their ideas during Somerset's protectorate, was also remarkable, and begs comparison to anywhere else in Europe. Whether or not one retains the notion of a group of "commonwealth-men," there were a number of Protestant writers at this time who freely commented on the social ills of the nation and provided both original and unimagina-

31. A. G. Dickens, *The English Reformation*, 2d ed. (University Park: Pennsylvania State University Press, 1991), 222–26.
32. Andrew Pettegree, *Foreign Protestant Communities in Sixteenth-Century London* (Oxford: Clarendon Press, 1986).
33. MacCulloch, "England," 173.
34. Pettegree, *Foreign Protestant Communities*, 26–30, 75.

tive solutions, especially during the "open" years between 1547 and 1549.[35]

Obviously, there were major concerns about general reform among evangelicals that combined Erasmian pedagogy and Calvinist moral legalism. As will become clear in the next chapter, it was largely these Protestants (such as John Hales, William Thomas, and John Cheke) who commented on peace in the context of government reform, always maintaining a watchful eye on the commonwealth and its social and economic health. The schemes for agrarian reform, poor relief, Christian unity, and "perpetual peace" multiplied throughout the Edwardian years. While many were misguided and abandoned in the wake of the social unrest that ultimately led to Somerset's fall from power, others were more pragmatic and continued to evoke interest during the subsequent Northumberland regency.[36]

Why did such developments occur in England at this time? The fact that evangelicals, who were most enamored of Reformed theology and its Erasmian roots, comprised this reformist group indicates some confessional reasons. But many conservatives genuinely promoted peace between 1535 and 1555 as well, without necessarily calling for more sweeping social and economic changes. Two common threads unite conservative and evangelical thinkers. First, both accepted the royal supremacy. This meant that they vehemently opposed the pope's threat to return England — violently if necessary — to the Catholic fold. Second, early Anglicans across the spectrum feared that unleashed forces of religious division would bring unmitigated disaster, producing not only political instability but also social and economic chaos throughout the land. In either scenario peace had to be maintained within and without. A papal crusade against England could easily rend the commonweal; a commonweal torn by religious division was more likely to attract such a crusade.

How much of a threat either of these posed is difficult to assess, but an inordinate amount of writing and preaching against both rebellion and militant popes during these years suggests that the concern was not minimal. Early Anglican clerics were not suggesting that all war was illegitimate, but some did believe the practice itself was the result of sin and thus

35. Dickens, *English Reformation*, 247–54; Loades, "Martin Luther and the Early Stages of the English Reformation," 154–57; G. R. Elton, "Reform and the 'Commonwealth-Men' of Edward VI's Reign," in *The English Commonwealth, 1547–1640: Essays in Politics and Society*, ed. Peter Clark, Alan Smith, and Nicholas Tyacke (New York: Barnes & Noble, 1979), 23–38.

36. Barrett L. Beer, *Rebellion and Riot: Popular Disorder in England during the Reign of Edward VI* (Kent, Ohio: Kent State University Press, 1982), 195–98.

could not be promoted. The economic motives for peace can be detected in many of their formulations of godly peace, but it was only because, for them, war was the consequence of sin and inimical to the way of Christ. Righteous living produced peace and all of the material benefits that enhanced justice and unity. The conceptualization of war and peace in this way is fundamentally different from that of the Middle Ages, which stressed more the natural cleansing and refining function of warfare, and was at times indifferent to the full range of human suffering it caused. Now, war could still be a form of punishment from God but it was rarely viewed as a moral corrective.

The Protestant Response to Erasmian Pacifism

Until the last decade of Henry VIII's reign, therefore, Lutheranism supplemented by Erasmian humanism exerted the greatest foreign influence on the Reformation in England.[37] By the 1540s, however, those radical English Protestants who had left for the Continent during the time of the Six Articles were returning, bringing with them a newer stream of ideas from Zurich, Strasbourg, and Geneva, the ideas of Zwingli and Bullinger, and then of Calvin, whose theocratic experiment in Geneva was renowned throughout Protestant Europe. The *Consensus Tigurinus* of 1549 brought together Bullinger and Calvin on one of the most divisive doctrines of the era — the Eucharist.[38] Both were unified also in their attack on the radical Reformation of the Anabaptists, with each composing a separate tract to refute their heresies (both quickly translated and published in English).[39] The range of Calvin's and Bullinger's contributions to English Protestant thought concerning war and peace cannot be established fully. In truth, the issue is moot anyway, since evangelicalism was rooted in biblical exegesis, meaning that any similarities among reformers could be easily attributed to a shared hermeneutics. But because of the wide circulation of both the *Institutes of the Christian Religion* and Bullinger's sermons later compiled

37. Carl R. Trueman, *Luther's Legacy: Salvation and English Reformers, 1525–1556* (Oxford: Clarendon Press, 1994), 46.

38. Dickens, *English Reformation*, 222–26.

39. John Calvin, *A Short Instruction for to Arme All Good Christian People Agaynst the Pestiferous Errours of the Common Secte of Anabaptistes* (London: John Day, 1549); Henry Bullinger, *An Holsome Antidotus or Counterpoysen, Ageynst the Pestylent Heresye and Secte of the Anabaptistes*, trans. John Veron (London: Dumfrey Powell, 1548).

in the *Decades,* their overall import cannot be dismissed. Since these men spoke in a universal evangelical language, and their works were generally given freedom of circulation in England (if nowhere else), they need to be considered in any full treatment of English Protestant views on war and peace and the ensuing evangelical language that developed.

What does make English thought unique is the original blend of Christian humanism and evangelicalism into a highly specialized treatment of these issues. As we have seen, despite its compelling and popular nature, a certain inherent idealism came close to consigning to failure from the start any Erasmian blueprint for a European-wide peace. To be engineered by an educated and virtuous prince, and founded on biblical principles and a recognition of universal human affinity, such a peace was predicated on a positive view of human nature and individual perfectibility. Alistair Fox has argued recently that it is this "transcendental bias of Erasmus's humanism, . . . insufficiently concerned with practicalities" that put off English humanists who were most interested in translating "wisdom into political action."[40] Taking Thomas Starkey as his case in point, Fox believes that the appeal of Erasmus's approach to improving society was limited by the focus on what ought to be rather than on the English concern with what actually was and could be.[41] While this distinction may be useful at times, one should not lose sight of the fact that discussions of what ought to be can have an impact on what one considers possible, and so cannot be summarily dismissed. But if the English did possess a more "realistic" understanding of the possibilities for reform, and if Erasmianism was of limited effect, what else might have contributed to the more practical discussions, especially on the problem of war, that characterize the mid-Tudor period?[42] Perhaps by focusing on one curiously neglected avenue of

40. Fox, "English Humanism," in Fox and Guy, *Reassessing the Henrician Age,* 50–51. Fox is reacting to the thesis put forth in McConica's *English Humanists,* which argues for a strong Erasmian influence on Tudor policy. This work is in turn building on W. Gordon Zeeveld's *Foundations of Tudor Policy.* See also Pierre Brachin, "*Vox clamantis in deserto:* Réflexions sur le pacifisme d'Erasme," in *Colloquia Erasmiana Turonensia,* ed. Jean-Claude Margolin (Toronto: University of Toronto Press, 1972), 1:247–76.

41. Fox, "English Humanism," 50–51.

42. While Fox credits the English humanists with a great deal of originality in constructing their own, more "practical" brand of humanism (to which Erasmus contributed in only a minor way), Thomas F. Mayer gives greater credit to the Italian and classicist influences. See Fox, "English Humanism," 34–51, and Mayer, *Thomas Starkey and the Commonweal: Humanist Politics and Religion in the Reign of Henry VIII* (Cambridge: Cambridge University Press, 1989), passim. There is little indication, however, that discussion on the problem of war was derivative of any tradition other than Erasmian, Protestant, and indigenous medieval

study — the Protestant element in the Tudor understanding of war — we can arrive at some answers. While many humanists appreciated the peaceful aspirations of Colet, Erasmus, and More, Protestant biblicism countered any idealism with a strong dose of reality. Yet at the same time, by coupling a more pessimistic view of humankind with the intractable command to love one's enemy, its adherents raised the quandary of how one can pursue peace while admitting the occasional necessity of war.

If, as this study has maintained, humanism introduced a peace ethic into the political discourse of the early sixteenth century, the question needs be whether that ethic remained intact once Erasmian optimism had dissipated in the 1520s. While many English reformers retreated from the Stoic and platonic assumptions held by the Dutchman and his followers, they were nevertheless unwilling to reject the moral imperative of peace itself. Rather than pontificate on the barbarity of war and the quest for universal peace, however, Protestant thinkers centered their message on the morality of limiting wars and on making them more humane.[43]

Throughout the sixteenth century some Protestant clerics became more reluctant to promote wars with the zeal of their medieval forbears. Following the line of attack already sketched by those who wrote against the Hundred Years War, these Protestants were even more taken with New Testament exhortations to peace. They weighed carefully as well the ill effects of fighting on society at large, especially the burden of increased taxation in time of war, which would fall most heavily on them and the poor.[44] On the Continent (and to a lesser degree in England),[45] however, churchmen could easily slide back into a martial stance when circumstances suited them. Much of the royal demand for clerical support rested on the need to counter rebellion. But in England, the safety of the realm

---

critiques (including those of the just-war tradition) that coalesced during the mid-Tudor period. See Skinner, *Foundations of Modern European Political Thought,* vol. 1, *The Renaissance,* 244–48.

43. Some of the most interesting and revealing work on the connections between Protestant morality and remnants of Erasmian pacifism is currently being done by Shakespeare scholars. See, for example, Michael Hattaway, "Blood Is Their Argument: Men of War and Soldiers in Shakespeare and Others," in *Religion, Culture and Society in Early Modern Britain: Essays in Honour of Patrick Collinson,* ed. Anthony Fletcher and Peter Roberts (Cambridge: Cambridge University Press, 1994), 84–101; Theodor Meron, *Henry's Wars and Shakespeare's Laws: Perspective on the Law of War in the Later Middle Ages* (Oxford: Clarendon Press, 1993); and Steven Marx, "Shakespeare's Pacifism," *Renaissance Quarterly* 45 (1992): 49–95.

44. Hale, *War and Society,* 33–35.

45. Nef, *War and Human Progress,* 110–11.

could become just as easily a reason for avoiding wars, and in the end, complete tranquillity throughout the land remained the optimum objective.

For Protestants, with their devotion to biblical authority, the just-war concept raised several ideological problems. Along with the many cautions issued against fighting in unjust wars as being perilous to one's soul, there was still, according to John Hale, "no counter-balancing assurance that to die in battle, even against the infidel, was to increase, let alone guarantee salvation." On the other hand, Catholic chaplains often granted mass absolutions as long as the soldiers had fully examined their consciences.[46] For those reformers—such as Bullinger, Hooper, and a number of Puritan divines—who believed that some wars were required to safeguard the true faith, this circumstance helps explain their precise construction of providential holy war. For Cromwell's New Model Army to be strong and resolute in battle it had to be confirmed beyond a doubt in the righteousness of its cause. As will be seen, while these men did not retreat from war when right religion was at stake, they nevertheless argued against the majority of wars that were fought out of territorial or dynastic interests, or to avenge impeachments of personal honor. Like the critics of the Hundred Years War, a large number of Protestants who went back to the New Testament came to find contemporary warfare seriously flawed and suffused with sinful motivations and activities. The hallmark of faith was a belief in the transforming power of Christ in the lives of individuals, who (in good humanist fashion) could then adopt a restrained postmillennial perspective on the coming era of peace. But even with this end in mind, these thinkers believed that if sin were the cause of war, then only by repentance could wars end. Such reformers incorporated peace into their reluctant acceptance of recurring human conflict, and since the ultimate object was peace, demanded that all remedies short of war first be exhausted.[47] In the event of war, the Christian pleased God most by obeying his sovereign (the only possible means for remaining within grace in the event he shed innocent blood), but also by behaving in a Christ-like manner—even toward the enemy.[48]

46. Hale, *War and Society,* 176–77.

47. Henry Bullinger, *Decades,* ed. Thomas Harding, PS, vol. 7 (Cambridge: The University Press, 1849), 1:376; Thomas Becon, *The New Policy of War,* in *Early Works,* ed. John Ayre, PS, vol. 2 (Cambridge: The University Press, 1843), 251; Bainton, *Christian Attitudes,* 128–29.

48. Hale, *War and Society,* 36–37.

By examining the major Continental reformers on the just war and how they found it delegitimized by papal actions, we can see their further movement away from the *jus ad bellum* toward a greater emphasis on the *jus in bello* nature of warfare. Both Luther and Calvin realized that princes habitually offered traditional just-war arguments, without shame, as pretexts for almost any type of offensive they wished to launch. With an Augustinian pessimism furnishing their view of human nature, they rejected the Erasmian notion that people could end war if provided sufficient education, though they did acknowledge that if people were sufficiently educated, perhaps, the evils of war could be mitigated. Along with Zwingli, these men believed that strife and discord were endemic to human society.[49] Luther sought to circumscribe the parameters of the just war by adopting the Augustinian position of a division between the heavenly kingdom (the Church) and the earthly kingdom (the state), each having its own jurisdiction. It was the job of the Church to be persuasive and the state to be coercive, so that war becomes part of the magistrate's duty to wield the sword as a function of his police power. The Church has no need to wield a sword because there is no evil in the heavenly kingdom.[50] At the same time, however, Luther accepted the view that the object of the just war is peace and the righting of wrongs. But the Church could only employ spiritual weapons. In a strange fit of pique, the University of Paris actually censored him for being a pacifist in 1521 because of his comments on Jesus' command to turn the other cheek, and on Paul's exhortation not to defend oneself, which the reformer said applied to all people. The pope also condemned his interpretation of Matthew 5 and Romans 12. Because Luther held that Christians should bear patiently the Turkish yoke for the sake of the gospel, as well as for other similar comments, the Paris theologians believed he was arguing that God used heathens to reprove erring Christians. In truth, however, he was mostly concerned with attacking papal crusades that were undertaken for personal gain and not preceded by a general repentance.[51] Luther could become quite vehement in his support

49. Fernandez-Santamaria, *State, War and Peace,* 155.

50. Martin Luther, *Temporal Authority: To What Extent It Should Be Obeyed, 1523,* ed. Walther I. Brandt, trans. J. J. Schindel, in *Luther's Works,* gen. ed. Helmut T. Lehman, vol. 45: *The Christian in Society, II* (Philadelphia: Muhlenberg Press, 1962), 123–29.

51. Martin Luther, *On Wars Against the Turk, 1529,* ed. Robert C. Schultz, trans. Charles M. Jacobs, in *Luther's Works,* gen. ed. Helmut T. Lehman, vol. 46: *The Christian in Society, III* (Philadelphia: Fortress Press, 1967), 161–65; Bainton, *Christian Attitudes,* 136–42; W. F. Bense, "Paris Theologians on War and Peace, 1521–1529," *Church History* 41 (1972): 169–70; Johnson, *Just War Tradition,* 52–53; Hans J. Hillerbrand, "Martin Luther and the Bull

for certain kinds of wars, as is most evident in his delayed reaction to the Peasants War of 1524–25.[52] Yet he also reasserted the need for Christians to extend their personal relationship with God into the larger realm of society. It was incumbent upon the Church to set examples of behavior that would encourage all the world to embrace the gospel. At other times, especially during those frequent flashes of anger and despair, we see that Luther was no idealist, but a man of both prayer and action. As stated, whether he helped to inform the English Protestant positions on war and peace cannot be adequately determined, but undeniably, those who wrote on the subject, such as Tyndale and Latimer, must have been familiar with this aspect of his work.

It is ironic that Zwingli, who was so enamored of Erasmus, and early on the most "pacifist" of the major reformers, should be killed while fighting in a religious war. Luther saw his death as divine punishment for a preacher who had taken up the sword;[53] yet, for a time, Zwingli was probably the more optimistic about the possibilities for peace. The Swiss reformer took Luther's delineation of the two kingdoms and stressed "positive Christian involvement in worldly government to help it achieve as close as possible a conformity to the laws of the kingdom of Christ,"[54] thereby eschewing Luther's doubt that a fallen world could attain such postmillennialist bliss. Zwingli's position obviously had implications for how the magistrate morally could wield the sword. Also influenced by the humanists, especially Erasmus, he put great faith and hope in the Christian prince who ruled according to biblical principles and in the kinship of humanity which bound all people together. Early on, such as in *The Fable of the Ox* (1510), he directed his attacks on fighting to the mercenaries who were treacherously hiring themselves out rather than protecting their homeland.[55] His experience as a chaplain during Swiss/French wars in

---

Exsurge Domine," Theological Studies 30 (1969): 108–12. Actually Luther's condemnation pinpoints a major difference between Protestant and Catholic thought on war, since the former clearly *did* believe that God could and would use pagans to punish erring Christians. In this vein Protestants had completely demystified war, here having much in common with the Erasmiam humanists.

52. Luther, *Against the Robbing and Murdering Hordes of Peasants, 1525,* in *Luther's Works,* 46:49–55.

53. Bainton, *Christian Attitudes,* 143–44; Johnson, *Quest for Peace,* 148.

54. Johnson, *Quest for Peace,* 49–51; James M. Stayer, *Anabaptists and the Sword* (Lawrence, Kans.: Coronado Press, 1972), 49–51.

55. Ulrich Zwingli, *The Fable of the Ox,* in *Early Writings,* ed. Samuel Macauley Jackson (Durham, N.C.: Labyrinth Press, 1987), 27–34.

1513 and 1515 "intensified his sense of the devastation of war, and the moral and social cost to his own people."[56] Between 1514 and 1519, Zwingli also came under the spell of the universal-peace "movement" and the Erasmians who gave it life. He wrote a friend in 1519:

> Seek out the pastors in your region and instruct them that they should be friends of peace and preach without ceasing about peace, harmony, and staying at home [from mercenary expeditions]. The blood merchants and wastrels cannot lead anyone compared to the princes in a nation inclined to pleasant harmony.[57]

Even three years later, when he had become more defensive about protecting the reform in Zurich and elsewhere in Switzerland, he lost little of his humanist idealism:

> For the children see themselves born of one and the same mother and nourished in one and the same manner. Aye, the reason why the heavenly Father caused all men to be descended from one man, Adam, was also for the sake of peace, otherwise He might have filled the whole world at once with people. . . . So God created man in his own image, so that just as the three persons, Father, Son, and Holy Ghost are one God, who cannot disagree or quarrel with himself, thus also men's lives might be led in a spirit of concord, peace, and unanimity.[58]

In the end, however, the reformer surrendered to his patriotic instincts and confined his opposition to war to the employment of mercenaries. Once at the helm in Zurich he felt compelled to posit self-defense (including preemptive strikes) as a legitimate pretext for war, thus acknowledging a basic tenet of just-war theory. But even before Calvin's differentiation between the visible and invisible churches, Zwingli abhorred crusades and

---

56. W. P. Stephens, *Zwingli: An Introduction to His Thought* (Oxford: Clarendon Press, 1992), 124.

57. Ulrich Zwingli, *Huldreich Zwinglis Sämtliche Werke,* ed. E. Egli and G. Finsler, 13 vols. (Berlin: C. A. Schwetschke und Sohn, 1904–68), 7:233; quoted in Johnson, *Quest for Peace,* 149.

58. Zwingli, *A Warning against Control of Foreign Lords,* in *Early Writings,* 132. A friend of Zwingli's, Leo Jud, translated Erasmus's *Querela pacis* into German and had it published by Froschauer, the well-known printer in Zurich, during this time. Ibid., 130.

holy wars, since he believed the temporal ruler's jurisdiction in using the sword applied only to the visible kingdom and not to coerce belief. Zwingli seemed to find war an expedient necessary to uphold some higher ideal, all the while hoping it would usher in a lasting peace;[59] but like the other Continental reformers, he was nebulous about what such peace would mean, never looking to the implications of what to do once it came or how to maintain it. The English reformers stand out in their ability to delve into just these areas and in being able to offer valuable suggestions based on their nation's particular political, economic, social, and intellectual experiences.

Zwingli died defending the Reformation in Switzerland, and in so doing, helped draw attention to a problem that especially vexed Continental reformers. The requirements for maintaining the true faith in places where it was threatened led them to tread carefully around the whole idea of holy war. Having clearly rejected the Catholic notion of crusade, which they believed was totally self-interested, many of them simply substituted the holy commonwealth for the *ecclesia imperium.* Calvin's doctrine of the lower magistrates functioned as a means for protecting the established order while preventing Christ's Church from being overwhelmed by a hostile temporal authority. But the Genevan found no easy answers when it came to the issue of war and peace. Believing that only the regenerate would be able to live in peace, he held that Christians alone could claim this the natural order.[60] And although he accepted fully the notion of just wars, his discussion of them is full of limitations, no doubt in some part due to the inspiration of his commentary on Seneca's *De clementia.*[61] If there were any points of contact between the Continental and English reformers on this issue, it would most likely be with Calvin, since both he and the English Protestants gave a great deal of attention to the matter of preventing war. The bulk of the discussion on his views, therefore, will be reserved until we examine the changing nature of the *jus ad bellum* among English reformers, where Calvin's thought is most pertinent.

---

59. Zwingli, *Sämtliche Werke,* 2:478; Johnson, *Quest for Peace,* 149–51. This move to a more qualified peace stance (which still accused the Catholic Church of warmongering) is expressed most vividly in the reformer's *Divine and Human Righteousness* (1523) and *The Shepherd* (1524). These can both be found in Ulrich Zwingli, *Writings,* trans. H. Wayne Pipkin, vol. 2 (Allison Park, Pa.: Pickwick Publications, 1984).

60. Bainton, *Christian Attitudes,* 144–47; Walzer, "Exodus 32," 11.

61. Willem Balke, *Calvin and the Anabaptist Radicals,* trans. William J. Heynen (Grand Rapids, Mich.: William B. Eerdmans, 1981), 66. Seneca's work is concerned with how rulers should exercise mercy and exhibit a concern for the general welfare when governing.

Human Nature and the Basis for War

A renewed emphasis on the *jus in bello* which Calvin and other Protestants explicated derives from the pessimistic view of human nature these evangelicals upheld. Original sin left all people with an ineradicable bent for wrongdoing, including violence, which is contrary to God's plan for peace on earth as revealed in Scripture. (Contrast this with the humanist emphasis on original sin as more social and inherited, but surmountable.) According to the Protestant view, it is impossible to abolish warfare because human discord is an endemic condition that can be mitigated only, not eliminated. Christians should strive to prevent dissension and disunity, which give license to discord and eventually to war.[62] Early on, Tyndale took up this position in his *Exposition Upon the Fifth, Sixth, and Seventh Chapters of Matthew* (1532), when he exclaimed "cursed be the peace-breakers," who sow discord and pick quarrels, causing enmity between people, including "stirrers up of princes to battle and war." These and any (speaking to clergy) who falsely enjoin others to hate and "shed blood wrongfully" through God's word are but "children of the devil."[63] Roger Edgeworth, prebendary of Bristol and chancellor of Bath and Wells,[64] echoed these sentiments in a sermon on 1 Peter when he contrasted God's peace with human peace: "The world can give no peace but will rather drive away peace, and make dissension and debate betwixt God and man, and betwixt man and man." But Scripture still demanded that "not only thou must seek for peace, but also thou must pursue it, run after it, labour and find all means possible to catch it."[65] The recognition that sin will bring about conflict and war at times does not absolve Christians, however, from their duty to work for peace. Inertia is not an option for the true follower of Christ. Cuthbert Tunstall, the conservative bishop of Dur-

62. See John Calvin, Commentary on Micah 4:3, *Minor Prophets,* ed. John Owen (Grand Rapids, Mich.: William B. Eerdmans, 1950), 3:265–66.

63. William Tyndale, *Expositions of Scripture and Practice of Prelates,* ed. Henry Walter, PS, vol. 43 (Cambridge: The University Press, 1849), 26–27. For Tyndale's exposure and connection to Erasmian humanism, M. M. Knappen's *Tudor Puritanism* (Chicago: University of Chicago Press, 1939), 3–30, is still very helpful.

64. "Roger Edgeworth," *DNB,* by Thompson Cooper; ed. Leslie Stephen, vol. 16 (London: Smith, Elder, 1888), 385–86. As was the case with Tunstall, it appears that once the opportunity presented itself, Edgeworth drifted back to a more conservative doctrinal stance, able nevertheless to live with the supremacy and a slower pace of reform.

65. Roger Edgeworth, *Sermons Very Fruitfull, Godly, and Learned, Preached and Sette Forrth by Maister Roger Edgeworth* (London: Robert Caly, 1557), sigs. 217r–v.

ham, in a sermon given before King Henry on Palm Sunday in 1538, also
provided a strong statement to this effect: "Wherefore since as Saint Paul
saith in the xiiii chapter of the first epistle to the Corinthians, that God is
not [a] God of dissension, but of peace, who commandeth by his word
peace always to be kept, we are sure that all those that go about to break
peace between realms, and to bring them to war, are the children of the
devil."[66] As with Tyndale, the sowers of discord and war only increase the
sinfulness of society and therefore must not be true Christians.

This preoccupation with the human propensity for violence and dissension is hardly new; it harks back to the earthly city of Augustine, where
true peace can never be established. The pessimism reflected in humankind's helplessness within a sinful, warring world led the medieval church
to invoke God's mercy for remedy from war's worst ravages and for an
occasional respite of peace. For those who had deemed the Church the
culprit in preventing peace and Christian unity, there were ruminations
about a *renovatio mundi* ushered in by a peace-loving Christian emperor.
This was the hope that Dante argued forcefully in *Monarchia,* and which
Marsilius used in forming his political ideas.[67] Protestant/erastian thinking,
while accepting that one's natural condition was hopeless, and that there
was a vital need to beseech God's succor for peace, doubted the Catholic
Church's sincerity in desiring and working for an end to wars. Such cynicism kept them from simply reverting to the earlier medieval just-war position, which institutionalized war as a means of controlling one's violent
and sinful nature, while still accepting the older dichotomy that medieval-
ists had drawn between the ideal and the real. Because most Protestants
felt that the Roman church was responsible for generating much of the
dissension that had racked Christendom over the past several centuries,
they were less ready to accept its determination of just wars.

As we have seen already, such criticism was vocalized early on and with

66. Cuthbert Tunstall, *A Sermon of Cuthbert Bysshop of Duresme, Made Upon Palme
Sondaye Laste Past, Before the Maiestie of Our Soverayne Lorde Kyng Henry the VIII* (London: Thomas Berthelet, 1539), sig. E3v.

67. *Monarchia* seems not to have been read widely in England; there were no versions of it
printed there in the sixteenth century; therefore, his views on war and peace, if of any impact,
came indirectly from others who read him and published on the subject. Many English
writers would have found Dante's ideas impractical or inapplicable to their circumstances.
The first English translation of *Defensor pacis* was published under the auspices of the crown
in 1535 to give ideological backing to the royal supremacy; but it may have found a following also among those who were interested in Marsilius's views on the subject of peace. Marsilius of Padua, *The Defence of Peace,* trans. Wyllyam Marshall (London: Robert Wyer,
1535), sigs. B3v–B4r. See also McConica, *English Humanists,* 136, 167–69.

great vehemence by Wyclif and his followers in the late fourteenth century, while lesser degrees of cynicism characterize an even wider range of medieval English attitudes toward war. But once the break with Rome was made in 1534, the affinity for warmongering became part of the standard criticism of the Catholic Church. The first part of Tunstall's Palm Sunday sermon blamed the pope's obsession with unrivaled power and jurisdiction as the reason for the wars that divide Christendom. His claim to be Peter's heir and "vicar general" over all the earth as Christ is in heaven, was an "ambitious and pompous objection . . . made by him and his adherents; and hath of late years much troubled the world, and made dissension, debate and open war in all parts of Christendom, and nourished the same."[68] In a somewhat veiled allusion to Reginald Pole's mission on the Continent, Tunstall went on to attribute to the pope an insatiable lust for hegemony over all lands (including England) as the basis for the latter's design that Christian nations invade England. The bishop of Rome, being "moved and replete with furious ire and pestilent malice goeth about to stir all Christian nations, that will give ears to his devilish enchantments, to move war against this realm of England."[69] If such a scenario came to pass, all vices would result, with people (both high and low) being slain, women ravaged, and property destroyed.[70] A homily published in 1540, based on 2 Corinthians 6, to be read on the first Sunday in Lent, adopted Tunstall's language (which echoed Tyndale's)—at times word-for-word— in making condemnation of papal militancy official policy:

> For many years past, little war hath been in these parts of Christendom, but the bishop of Rome hath been either a stirrer, or a nourisher of it, unless it were for his ambition or profit. Wherefore good Christian people for as much as God is not [a] God of dissension, but of peace, who commandeth by his word peace between realms; and to bring them to war are the children of the devil, what holy names so ever they pretend to cloak their pestilent malice withall, which cloaking under hypocrisy no doubt is double devilishness, and of Christ most abhorred, because under His blessed name they play the devil's part.[71]

68. Tunstall, *Sermon,* sigs. C6v–C7r.
69. Ibid., sig. D8v.
70. Ibid., sigs. D8v–E1r.
71. Richard Taverner, ed., *Postilles or Homilies Upon the Epistles and Gospels from Ester Untyll Trinite Sondaye* (London: Richarde Bankes, 1540), sig. Z2r.

These diatribes against the papacy were primarily for propagandistic purposes, but their effectiveness rests on the fact that many English Protestants found papal wars totally without justification and therefore completely immoral.[72] True motives — the quest for personal power and material gain — were cloaked in a transparent toga of just-war legitimacy, most ostensibly the preservation of God's church. The senseless killing and bloodshed were unconscionable to those English people who found the pope a corrupt antichrist, and they began to preach peace and unity in the face of this mounting threat to their own designs for reform and Reformation.

Making War Moral: The Protestant *Jus ad Bellum*

Many Protestants, then, equated war with runaway discord and division and designated the Church of Rome as the main perpetrator. But if human nature left so little room for improvement, what could be done, especially in the face of such a formidable onslaught? Here, Protestant thought diverges most markedly from Erasmian belief that a regenerated, educated society can or will eventually see and correct the error of its ways. In what is essentially a two-pronged attack, some reformers attempted to restructure the *jus ad bellum* by emphasizing moral and ethical justifications for war (incorporating much humanist thought as well) and then by making that determination the basis for a detailed expansion of the *jus in bello,* which focused on ways to limit war and extend periods of peace.[73] Calvin embodies both approaches, which is evident in his Bible commentaries and sermons, in all four editions of the *Institutes,*[74] and in the treatise against Anabaptists (published in English in 1549). Here we will only concentrate on his discussion of the *jus ad bellum.* While adopting the overall Augustinian position on the just war, Calvin nevertheless emphasized the need for a careful scrutiny of cause in his statement that "it is the duty of all magistrates here to guard particularly against giving vent to their passions even

72. William Tyndale, *Practice of Prelates,* in *Doctrinal Treatises,* ed. Henry Walter, PS, vol. 42 (Cambridge: The University Press, 1848), 264; Smeeton, *Lollard Themes,* 238.

73. Johnson, *Ideology,* 75–80. Erasmians were opposed generally to any *jus in bello* considerations since that gave war a tacit legitimacy.

74. Published in 1536, 1539, 1543, and 1559.

in the slightest degree."[75] In his commentary on Luke 3:14 he warned: "But the end of it all must be borne in mind, that princes do not allow themselves to sport with human blood, nor may troops, hiring out their energies for slaughter through greed of gain, rush into savagery, for both parties must be impelled by necessity and regard for the public good."[76] All means for coming to peace should be exhausted before the recourse to arms:

> It is true that a Christian prince ought to search all means for peace, and to buy it dear with losses of his own: and so to do that it come not to the sword, until he has assayed all remedies to avoid this necessity. But when he hath done all that in him lieth, and hath recoiled [retreated] as much as he might, if he cannot otherwise maintain the country which is committed unto him: the last refuge is to use the sword which God hath put into his hand.[77]

In fact the reformer found just wars a rare occurrence in his day, asking: "But are wars nowadays by the authority of God? Have men an eye to the thing that is lawful? Yea, do they tarry till they have commandment from God? Nay, they go to it despite of him; the devil drives them forward."[78] If war is absolutely unavoidable, then it must be fought "ethically." Soldiers should always "manifest a spirit of self-discipline and humanitarianism," acknowledging "our own flesh in every man that is made after our likeness," and the magistrate must employ mercy whenever possible.[79] In a particular swipe at the crusading pretensions of Rome, Calvin declared that war could only be defensive. Military campaigns to propagate the Christian faith and extend God's kingdom, as had been fought by Charlemagne, are deemed unjust, as Peter was told to put away the sword.[80]

Calvin's use of Cicero's dictum that governments must be sure that wars

75. John Calvin, *Institutes of the Christian Religion,* trans. Ford Lewis Battles (Philadelphia: Westminster Press, 1960), 2:1500.

76. Calvin, Commentary on Luke 3:14, *Calvin's New Testament Commentaries,* ed. David W. Torrance and Thomas F. Torrance (Grand Rapids, Mich.: William B. Eerdmans, 1972), 1:125; Balke, *Calvin and the Anabaptist Radicals,* 285.

77. Calvin, *Institutes,* 2:1500–1501, and *Short Instruction,* sig. Diiv.

78. Calvin, Sermon on Deuteronomy 2:1–7, *The Sermons . . . Upon the Fifth Booke of Moses Called Deuteronomie,* trans. Arthur Golding (London: Henry Middleton for George Bishop, 1583), 1:63.

79. Calvin, Sermon on Deuteronomy 19:1–7, *Deuteronomie,* 2:686; Balke, *Calvin and the Anabaptist Radicals,* 287.

80. Calvin, Commentary on John 18:36, *New Testament Commentaries,* 5:166–67.

entered into are just, moral, and of the last resort found similar expressions in English Protestant thought. Tyndale proclaimed that "yet princes, if they will be God's children, must not only give no cause of war, nor begin any, but also (though he have a just cause) suffer himself to be entreated, if he that gave the cause repent; and must also seek all ways of peace, before he fight."[81] Latimer once remarked that princes were burdened with a heavy responsibility in determining the righteousness of a cause, for "to go to war in presumptuousness, without an ordinary calling [by God], such going to war I allow not."[82] Even holy war advocates, like Hooper and Bullinger, made the moral decision over justification of wars the foundation for excusing cruelties that followed once hostilities began. As successor to Zwingli in Zurich, Bullinger exercised a tremendous influence over Reformed thought, and his *Decades*—sermons on the Ten Commandments—were circulated widely throughout Europe.[83] On the commandment, "Thou shalt not kill," he declared unsurprisingly that wars must not be entered into that seek "to sustain the troublesome toil of battle" or "set their minds upon gain or pleasure." "Princes therefore must precisely look into, and thoroughly examine the cause of wars, before they begin or take them in hand."[84] But Bullinger admitted that all men are sinful and guilty of some degree of personal aggrandizement in war, and so "all things must first be assayed, before it come to be tried out by battle," since "it is not lawful to make any war, unless it be against open enemies, and wicked men that are incurable." But if there is "any hope of amendment," fighting must be avoided.[85] By stressing the moral underpinnings of the *jus ad bellum* Bullinger relegated war to a peripheral place in the Christian nation's repository of remedies for dealing with wrong and injustice. Because "war is a thing most full of peril, and draweth with itself an endless troop of mischievous evils," it must not become the path of least resistance for wronged nations.[86]

Hooper, who lived near Bullinger in Zurich and became his close friend

81. Tyndale, *Expositions of Scripture,* 26–27.

82. Hugh Latimer, *Sermons,* ed. George Elwes Corrie, PS, vol. 27 (Cambridge: The University Press, 1844), 416–17.

83. The popularity of Bullinger's sermons on the decalogue grew as the century progressed. In 1586 Archbishop Whitgift required all ministers with an M.A. or LL.B degree to own a Bible, a Latin or English copy of the *Decades,* and a notebook. Johnson, *Ideology,* 110.

84. Bullinger, *Decades,* 1:376, 379–85.

85. Ibid., 379–85.

86. Ibid., 373; Johnson, *Ideology,* 81–84, 110–13.

and student,[87] argued in much the same way when he declared that "the magistrate offendeth when he beginneth or continued any unjust battle." As an example of a righteous king who was still punished for this major transgression, he mentioned Josiah, who "although he was a good man, in making war with the Egyptians, where as honest conditions of peace was offered, was slain for his labour."[88] Hooper's zeal for the Reformation could be quite militant in tone, but it was tempered by a strong biblicism that assailed false motives and corruptions in any activity, including war.[89]

A final instance where the stronger emphasis being put on the ethical foundation of the *jus ad bellum* among Protestant thinkers is revealed in Richard Taverner's *Garden of Wisdom* (1539), a book of moral tales based on the experiences of famous men and heavily influenced by Erasmus's *Adages*.[90] This work devotes a great deal of discussion to the overly ambitious and martial exploits of ancient military leaders, including those traditionally accorded great respect. Taverner derided "the insatiable ambition of Alexander, which esteemed none other function worthy for a king, then to enlarge the limits of his dominion," and his father Philip for embarking on conquests that "put thyself in danger to lose both thine own kingdom and also thy life."[91] The author tapped into a tradition of antiwar discourse that found military ventures responsible for much of the misery that plagued commonwealths. Again, since the repercussions of wars are so devastating, it is incumbent on the ruler that he undertake them only when absolutely necessary, or he will bring God's wrath upon himself.

87. Dickens, *English Reformation*, 271–72; John Hooper, *Early Writings*, ed. Samuel Carr, PS, vol. 20 (Cambridge: The University Press, 1843), iii–iv; Elton, *Reform and Reformation*, 317.

88. Hooper, *Early Writings*, 474–76.

89. Hooper was a great admirer of Erasmus and his "emphasis on Christ as a teacher and example." His visitation book written while bishop of Gloucester (1551–53) instructed priests to include the *Paraphrases* in every church, and indicates a familiarity with the *Adages*. Trueman, *Luther's Legacy*, 51–52.

90. McConica, *English Humanists*, 184–85. Taverner also published his own book of proverbs, which borrowed heavily from Erasmus. On the adage "Dulce bellum inexpertis" he remarked: "Battle is a sweet thing to them that never assayed it. He that listeth [desires] to know more of this proverb, let him go to Erasmus which handleth in his Chiliades this proverb both right copiously and also eloquently." Richard Taverner, *Proverbes or Adagies*, sig. 49v.

91. Richard Taverner, *The Garden of Wysdom Wherin Ye Maye Gather Moste Pleasaunt Flowres, That Is to Say, Proper Wytty and Quycke Sayenges of Princes, Philosophers, and Dyvers Other Sortes of Men* (London: Richard Bankes, 1539), sigs. D1r–v, E7v–E8r.

Making War Humane: The Protestant *Jus in Bello*

The second arm of the Protestant outlook on war, the mitigation of violence itself, stems directly from this primarily moral—as opposed to strictly legal—construction of the *jus ad bellum*. While the notion of a humane war may seem oxymoronic to modern sensibilities, this was not so much the case in the sixteenth century. Wyclif had argued that war was always wrong unless it was motivated by a love for the enemy.[92] While he remained skeptical that such wars were possible, Protestant thinkers, on the other hand, tended to look for ways in which such a motive could be implemented when conflicts broke out. Since wars were inevitable, it was essential that one show love to his foe in the spirit of Christian charity and brotherhood. For some, this type of rationalization helped to circumvent the tension and conflict that arose over whether one could rightfully harm any human being, even if the state required it. Again, it was Tyndale who set the framework for this argument: "When you go to war it is important to love the one you fight as a brother or neighbor," even if you have to kill him. It is not as a Christian brother that you do the deed but as a fallen, repentant vehicle of justice: "For thine heart loved him; and thou desiredst him lovingly to obey, and hast not avenged thyself in that state where thou art a brother: but in the worldly state, where thou art another manner person."[93] Thomas Becon, whose *New Policy of War,* retitled *The True Defense of Peace* (1542), was the only full-length treatise on war and peace written in English during the mid-sixteenth century, spent much time hammering out the implications of this issue concerning the spirit with which armies should approach the enemy. He declared that those who go into battle must never be rapacious or cruel, but careful and hopeful of peace:

> They may not go unto wars as tyrants, whose hearts imagine mischief, whose mouths breathe manslaughter, whose works boast lion-like crudelity [cruelty], whose hands desire to be embrued with blood, whose feet are swift to run into evil, whose deeds bring to pass final destruction; but as charitable persons, which . . . would by no means break the bonds of christian amity with no man, but

92. See Chapter 4.
93. Tyndale, *Expositions of Scripture,* 63; Smeeton, *Lollard Themes,* 237.

rather suffer much injury, than they would be once at displeasure with any man.[94]

If the Christian soldier is to love his enemy then it stands to reason that his own behavior must reflect Christ also. Such *jus in bello* considerations are not so new as they are preeminent in discussions on war by the sixteenth century. Erasmians portrayed war as a barbaric practice alien even to beasts. Their solution was for Christendom to cast off this sinful social convention and, in the spirit of common sense and Christian love, eradicate war completely. Protestants (and many Catholics) would agree up to the last item, at which point they saw it an impossible task ever to banish wars completely from human society. But by making them less violent and by soldiers adopting the *philosophia Christi* in their own lives, God would not condemn those who fought. Additionally, Becon held that soldiers should lead exemplary lives, regularly read the Scriptures, listen to sermons, "give themselves unto fervent prayer," and be unified in purpose and faith. If death should come in those circumstances, it "is precious in the sight of God."[95] But this ardent reformer went on to assign similar responsibilities to civilians if God is to smile on their cause. The evils he railed against — corrupt magistrates, money-grubbing lawyers, dishonest merchants, and covetous and oppressive gentry — were all the result of selfishness: "All seek their own profit, and not that which is Jesus Christ's" (Philippians 2)."Where is the christian charity become, which 'seeketh not her own?' 'Let no man seek his own,' saith St Paul, 'but the profit of other.'" Consequently, if there is no repentance at home, then "the valiance and godly behaviour of the soldiers do not profit so much."[96] Latimer attributed the inadequacies of soldiers in battle to an overall decline in morality. Instead of practicing archery in times of peace, men "have taken up whoring in towns instead of shooting in the fields." Their propensities for gluttony, drunkenness, and gambling are also blamed.[97] Similarly, Protestants contended that it was impossible for mercenaries to fight a just war, for if its legitimacy is based in part on the motive and behavior of the combatant, then the paid soldier is always acting immorally. Mercenaries

---

94. Becon, *New Policy of War*, 251.
95. Ibid., 252.
96. Ibid., 252–53.
97. Hugh Latimer, Sixth Sermon before Edward VI, 12 April 1549, *Selected Sermons of Hugh Latimer,* ed. W. K. Jordan, Folger Shakespeare Library (Charlottesville: University Press of Virginia, 1968), 92–94; John Jeremy Goring, "Social Change and Military Decline in Mid-Tudor England," *History* 60 (1975): 193.

also showed no love of country, which by the middle of the sixteenth century became an important point of reference for many Europeans.[98]

So far, then, we have explored how the Protestant view of human nature and the responsibility to maintain a Christ-like life helped to create new emphases when it came to the problem of war. In some cases, however, concern over the use of force became secondary to the societal condition being threatened, and the sense of moral duty in war led to arguments justifying holy war. As stated, during this period men like Hooper and Bullinger and then, later, ardent evangelicals who felt deeply threatened by "Catholic conspiracies" followed this progression of Protestant thought;[99] by and large though, before the religious wars of late century when levels of militancy rose particularly among Calvinists and the forces of the Counter Reformation, reformers believed that war was a terrible thing. It exemplified the worst in human behavior and as such was so contrary to the teachings of Christ that it was to be abhorred and terminated as soon as possible. And much of this attitude never dissipated in England, even during moments of bitter religious strife. Unlike earlier medieval notions, war was not a refiner's fire, a form of ordeal that arbitrated between right and wrong; it could never be a glorious enterprise launched in an aggressive manner to ensure the triumph of "good" over "evil."

Providentialism: War as Divine Punishment

An important transition — one which had roots in Lollardy and medieval "popular" literature — in how the English began viewing war as a temporal and human vice comes from the Protestant insistence that it was a scourge from God for sin, and that He used it to punish apostate nations. Even heathen armies could be employed to chastise a Christian people. Thus, as Bullinger claimed, in any war, "the victor is not always the right . . . for we must distinguish betwixt religion and the men or persons that keep that religion, which do for other causes suffer the Lord's visitation."[100] In the

98. See Joachim Rogge, *Zwingli und Erasmus: Die Friedensgedanken des jungen Zwingli* (Stuttgart: Calwer Verlag, 1962), 46; André Bieler, *La Pensée économique et sociale de Calvin* (Geneva: Librairie de l'Université, 1959), 35–36, 119–20; Balke, *Calvin and the Anabaptist Radicals*, 285–86.

99. Cf. Johnson, *Ideology,* especially 110–13; Michael Walzer, *The Revolution of the Saints: A Study in the Origins of Radical Politics* (Cambridge: Harvard University Press, 1965), 277–99.

100. Bullinger, *Decades,* 1:375.

funeral oration for Ferdinand I, Edmund Grindal, then bishop of London, agreed with Bullinger when he rebuked those who judged the emperor on his inability to defeat the Turk: "To that I answer that counsels, wars, and other actions are not to be judged by the success, but by the purpose, intent, and prudent disposition towards the same."[101] For all the appeal to heaven found in Protestant providentialism, war, at least, was becoming more of an earthbound enterprise. Human agency determined almost every aspect. The prince was given the weighty responsibility for ascertaining just causes, the behavior of soldiers and civilians further determined God's favor, and defeat could come whether one was in the right or not. In truth, Protestant thinkers found only one avenue for ensuring victory in battle and that was through national repentance, which at its root, depended on a type of collective individual regeneration. The emphasis on personal piety and conscience, as well as one's duty to the state, made these calls for godliness different from those proclaimed by their medieval forebears. Becon devoted the majority of his treatise to cataloguing the sins of the people, which he credited for bringing war, which in turn brought about the discord and disunity of his day: "This is the christian public weal rent and torn, and miserably deflowered. Thus is all good order chased away out of the bounds of Christendom." With war clearly portrayed as an undesirable condition at the root of all ills that plague the "public weal," the focus of Becon and others turned to how a nation can best appease God and prevent His scourge, or even perhaps, how to avoid the sins that lead to dissension and ultimately to wars. Becon looks strictly at public morality: "The occasion of all these cruel wars and other plagues, wherewith we are so miserably oppressed, is the despising of God's word, and the wicked and dissolute manner of living, that is used among them that profess Christ by mouth, but love Mahumet in deed."[102]

Becon's *New Policy of War* (1542) is an important work, for it clearly embodies the major trend of Protestant thought concerning war. Obviously, war is not the preferred recourse for settling disputes among nations, or for establishing God's justice and truth on earth. It is rather a punishment *from* God for sin, or the natural culmination of ungodly living.[103] Although Becon and his fellow clerics believed that war was ineradi-

---

101. Edmund Grindal, *Remains*, ed. William Nicholson, PS, vol. 19 (Cambridge: The University Press, 1843), 13.
102. Becon, *New Policy of War*, 238, 244.
103. Henry Bullinger, *A Treatise or Sermon of Henry Bullynger, Much Fruitfull and Necessarye for This Tyme, Concernynge Magistrates and Obedience of Subiectes. Also Concernyng*

cable, they exhorted all Christians to do what they could to ward it off by
leading holy lives. Despite the initial title of his treatise, Becon was not
setting out a policy on war, which may explain why he retitled the second
edition (which came out later that same year) *The True Defense of Peace.*[104]
At one point he stated unequivocally that "so little do all the policies and
feats of men's brains avail, where the help of God wanteth." Then after
citing a number of biblical examples, he declared further: "Here see we
that all the policies of war, that the wits of man can invent, are but vain,
and of themselves not able in any point to get the victory." He agreed it
was important to be so well armored as to protect and preserve the "christian public weal," but war is essentially an expedient, a flawed but necessary response to a sinful world.[105] It is so drastic a step, in fact, that some
Protestant thinkers even allowed individual pangs of conscience to excuse
one from fighting in or supporting a particular conflict. Bullinger, in *A
Treatise Concerning Magistrates,* dedicated to Edward VI, reiterated the
need for each Christian to appeal to his conscience, stating that "if it be so
that the magistrates' causes do set upon to slay the innocents and unguilty
persons . . . in this case the magistrates' commandments are not to be
obeyed. Therefore let the magistrates take heed lest they abuse their authority."[106] This statement is a far cry from Stephen Langton's teaching that
loyalty to the king superseded all private concerns and that only an early
withdrawal from battle might be allowed when the conscience is overly
offended. Bullinger's sentiments were echoed by Latimer when in his later
sermons before the duchess of Suffolk he broached the possibility of civil

the *Affayres of Warre, and What Scryptures Make Mention Thereof. Whether Christen
Powers May War Against Their Enemies. And Whither It Be Laufull for a Christyan to Beare
the Office of a Magistrate, and the Duety of Souldiers with Many Other Holsom Instructions
for Captaynes & Souldiers Both,* trans. Walter Lynne (London: William Powell, 1549), sigs.
A5v–A6v.

104. The full title of the first edition, published under Becon's pseudonym Theodore Basille: *The new pollecye of warre, wherin is declared not only how the mooste cruell Tyraunt
the great Turke maye be ouercome, but also all other enemies of the Christen publique weale,
lately deuised by Theodore Basille* (London: John Naylerre for John Gough, 1542). The
second edition's changed title: *The true defence of Peace, wherin is declaredde the cause of all
warres now a dayes, and how they maye be pacified, called before the Pollecye of warre,
deuysed & lately recognised by Theodore Basille. Psal. cxviii. To the vngodly there is no
peace, but to them that loue thy law (o Lord) ther is moch peace, neyther is there ony thynge
that troubleth them* (London: John Nayler for John Gough, 1542). The second edition also
includes at the end a prayer for peace based on Psalm 115.

105. Becon, *New Policy of War,* 244–45.
106. Bullinger, *Treatise,* sigs. A8r–v.

disobedience by allowing subjects to disobey authorities on account of conscience, "but always quietly, passively, without commotion or active rebellion."[107]

Overall, then, for Protestant thinkers, war was a necessary evil — a formulation to which Calvin also subscribed. It is in the nature of war that all kinds of destruction and cruelty follow. By making it the product of sin, the reformers went further in attributing to it an overwhelming number of evils. War leads to that most detestable of conditions — dissension — and eventually to disunity and its consequences, including poverty, corruption, unrestrained violence, political instability, injustice, and irreligion. This theme runs through nearly the entire corpus of English Protestant writing on war. Tyndale viewed warfare as "wasteful of English resources and counterproductive to evangelization."[108] Concerned that social harmony be maintained and each person able to perform his or her proper function, Latimer deemed "that where war is, there be all discommodities; no man can do his duty according to his calling, as appeareth, now in Germany, the Emperor, and the French king being at controversy."[109] Sir John Cheke bemoaned the corrupting effect of war on the soldiers who were returning from the front:

> And after wars it is commonly seen, that a great number of those which went out honest, return home again like roisters [bullies], and as though they were burnt to the wars bottom, they have all their life after an unsavory smack thereof, and smell still toward daysleepers, purse-pickers, highways to ask their alms, whom ye be afraid to say no unto honestly, lest they take it away from you violently and have more cause to suspect their strength, than pity their need?[110]

Taverner chastised military commanders for neglecting their domestic duties and for putting their nations in peril. Discussing the Persian king Darius, he warned "far better it were and also much more godly, to fetch

107. Allan G. Chester, *Hugh Latimer: Apostle to the English* (Philadelphia: University of Pennsylvania Press, 1954), 190.

108. Tyndale, *The Obedience of a Christian Man*, in *Doctrinal Treatises*, 166; Smeeton, *Lollard Themes*, 238.

109. Latimer, *Sermons*, 390–91.

110. John Cheeke, *The Hurt of Sedition* (1549), in Raphael Holinshed, *Chronicles of England, Scotland and Ireland* (London: J. Johnson, 1808), 3:1002.

wisdom out of wise men's books, than to gather wretched prudence with experiments and such hazards as put the whole country in danger."[111]

Perhaps Bullinger best summarized the common complaint concerning war when he declared that "the evil and misery that war bringeth with it sticketh so fast to commonweals and kingdoms, where it once hath hold, that it cannot be removed." Elsewhere he cautioned further against unnecessary wars, for "war is a most dangerous thing and bringeth with it hopes of infinite troubles," including "dearth and utter scarcity of all things."[112] The reformer warned that he who does "not hear the commodities [selfish interests] of war should allure any [find much taken away] from justice and equity" and urged that "just laws no less ought to be kept in the midst of wars as in the midst of cities."[113] As a whole then, Protestant thought portrayed the practice of war in a negative light, as an unsavory exercise that while necessary on occasion, should be avoided at almost any cost. War was treated with such distaste that there were consistent calls for individuals to repent of their sins and to imitate Christ and thus to avoid it. Christians whose consciences were offended by the military enterprises they were enjoined to support were advised that it was better to serve God than man. It was in their questioning of what they considered to be at best a necessary evil that the value of peace was elevated and offered as the proper end of war and the overall preferred state of human society.

Providentialism: Peace as Divine Blessing

The return to an Augustinian emphasis on peace as the goal of war is a hallmark of English Protestant opinion on the subject. Yet these attitudes went beyond traditional formulations by rejecting peace in its idealized, "spiritual" form or as merely a break in hostilities, providing instead a set of conditions through which it could be actualized. The late medieval war-peace dialectic provided a framework for evangelical thought which contrasted the settings characteristic of both situations, and which preached not just a spiritual or rhetorical love for peace, but actually offered enticements for pursuing an end to war by describing the blessings that await the

111. Taverner, *Garden of Wysdom*, bk. 2, sig. C8v.
112. Bullinger, *Decades*, 1:374, and *Treatise*, sig. A8v.
113. Bullinger, *Treatise*, sigs. B2v–B3r, C2v.

peacemaker. This revived and reworked championing of pragmatic peace is found in almost every pronouncement made about war by the middle of the sixteenth century. By turning to the discussions on peace we can more clearly fathom the extent to which, as an ethic, it provided for many a superior alternative to the rewards usually associated with the glories of war.

First, it must be noted that peace could be invoked in two different, though not mutually exclusive, ways. While the exhortation to be at peace with one's neighbor usually restricted such behavior to interpersonal relationships, there was often a natural extension made into the world at large.[114] With the new emphasis on biblical literalism, for some reformers the passages that dealt with loving one's enemies could not be so easily explained away as applying only to how a person treated a fellow human being. This was less of a problem for some than for others. For example, in Tyndale's exposition of the beatitude "Blessed are the peacemakers," Christ is not speaking "of the temporal sword, but teacheth how every man shall live for himself toward his neighbour." The reformer went on then to demonstrate how princes should still be sobered by this verse lest they start unnecessary wars. Embracing the idea that peace should be the goal of all fighting, the monarch could actually be viewed as a peacemaker when he punishes those who break "the common peace of his land and subjects."[115] Others were not so sure. Edgeworth refused to make the distinction between civil and private peace when he said that "not only thou must seek for peace, but also thou must pursue it . . . and hold it, else it will be gone, the world and carnality will have it away from thee."[116] Both editions of the Edwardian Prayer Book (1549, 1552) contain a collect at Evensong that is even less ambiguous, imploring God to "give unto thy servants that peace, which the world cannot give; that both our hearts may be set to obey thy commandments, and also that by thee we being defended from the fear of our enemies, may pass our time in rest and quietness."[117] The easy movement from a personal ethic to a national or societal one demonstrates the importance the English church—and Protestants in general—attached to the behavior and intentions of individuals in creating

114. John R. Hale, "Sixteenth-Century Explanations of War and Violence," *Past and Present* 51 (1971): 9–15.

115. Tyndale, *Expositions of Scripture*, 26–27.

116. Edgeworth, *Sermons*, sigs. 217r–v.

117. *The Two Liturgies, A.D. 1549, and A.D. 1552: with other Documents set forth by authority in the reign of King Edward VI*, ed. Joseph Ketley, PS, vol. 29 (Cambridge: The University Press, 1844), 37–38, 228–29, 406.

a peaceful and godly world. Unlike Chaucer's allegorical *Tale of Melibeus,* where individual virtues are only longingly and indirectly extended to national concerns or are used as clever, literary conventions, English reformers were establishing a direct connection between the two realms and thereby attempting to unify an ethic that had existed heretofore in a divided state.

Protestant emphasis on a more holistic morality for Christians helped to expand the dialogue regarding just wars. The role of individual conscience in determining the legitimacy of foreign conflicts could just as easily extend self-examination beyond the frontiers of warmaking and into the arena of peacemaking. If a proper Christian understanding of peace was centered primarily on living a certain way, then how did the evangelicals interpret peace and fashion it into a practical ethic? Most fundamentally the concept was nearly always set in contrast to that of war through the construction of binary oppositions. While peace brought harmony, prosperity, tranquillity, rest, order, unity, justice, and true religion, war (as already seen) ushered in just the opposite. By examining the pairings of peace with each of those conditions, we can better comprehend the type of peace Tudor clergymen were calling for, and the extent to which the concept was believed to be procurable in that guise.

While peace was not the natural condition of humankind, Christ still taught it as a way of life, and so it must be obtainable in some degree if the Church remains obedient. Holding the middle ground between Augustinian pessimism and Erasmian optimism, Protestant thinkers were not just moralistic in their pleas for peace but also practical. The fuller title of Becon's treatise, *The true defence of Peace, wherein is declaredde the cause of all warres now a dayes, and how they maye be pacified,* bespeaks the author's belief in the attainability of peace for those who truly desire it. The end of the work is full of allusions to those virtues which accompany peace and which benefit the "public weal." Peace is linked often with God's blessings, which will come when Christians live according to His Word. If discord comes from war, then "rest and quiet" are the fruits of peace, and God will, with peace, "increase it [the country] with the abundance of all things, and make it flourish above all other nations."[118] Becon ended on a positive note, stating that if we eschew discord, God will allow England "to enjoy perpetual tranquility, peace, rest, quietness, and to have

---

118. Becon, *New Policy of War,* 260.

our realms abound with all kinds of commodities that pertain unto the prosperous conservation of a public weal."[119]

The role of peace in preserving social order and economic well-being was echoed in other works as well. Latimer was especially afraid that wars would disrupt the good order of the commonweal and so prayed that God would use the prince and his councillors to defeat the enemy and render justice so "that the people may have rest, and apply their business, every man in his calling." He added that when "all men may live quietly and at rest . . . we may the better serve God, hear his word, and live after it."[120] He offered a similar perspective on peacemaking too, associating it not just with ending physical strife but with economic justice, as in landlords being fair to their tenants.[121] The linkage of peace with justice, however, was not unique to Latimer. Becon designated the main role for princes or magistrates as achieving peace in their realms "above all things," along with "the wealth of the poor commonalty" so that "by this means shall then kingdoms well prosper and long continue."[122] Edgeworth was most direct when he declared that God would not listen to those who "keep not these parts of justice afore rehearsed, nor careth for peace, nor will not labor for to obtain it."[123] In their pleas and aspirations for a complete and inclusive peace, therefore, Protestants/erastians continued to expand the concept into a greater number of constituent elements, having accepted a priori the late-medieval composite of peace as spiritual contentment, tranquillity (calm, order), concord (unity), and the basis for prosperity and success.

From Peace to Holy War?

If we take the statements about war thus far discussed and keep them within a clear hermeneutical and religio-political context, how can we explain the easy slide by some Protestants into a revived holy-war argument? A number of studies have looked at late Tudor and early Stuart writing on just war and holy war, mostly within a Puritan context. It is first of all important to remember that there was no monolithic, universal call for

119. Ibid., 261.
120. Latimer, *Sermons*, 390–91.
121. Ibid., 485–87.
122. Becon, *New Policy of War*, 256, 260.
123. Edgeworth, *Sermons*, sig. 217v.

peace in early modern Europe, and that even some peace advocates based their positions on a need for Christian unity in a crusade against an infidel. But what about promoting righteous, holy wars *among* Christians? Was this a new or more pronounced extension of just-war theory by the late sixteenth century? Perhaps we should address briefly the question of how a society that attended to peace ideas more seriously than ever before gave rise to a "revival" of holy-war justification, and whether that argument appealed to more than a few special interests.

The ideological divisions and political situations that led to the bloody wars of religion in Continental Europe slowly came to threaten England by the middle of Elizabeth's reign (1558–1603). Persecuted Calvinists in the Netherlands and France generated a whole genre of literature dedicated to interpreting in new ways, and according to shifting conditions, the reformer's "resistance theory." Chapter 7 gives some attention to how these ideas were found to be relevant and so contextualized within a uniquely English situation during the Catholic interim of 1553–58. The threat of the Counter Reformation to the Reformed faith was quite real and François Hotman, Philippe du Plessis-Mornay, and William of Nassau, among others who felt grave danger, turned to justifications for resisting princes who would try to impose Catholicism on them and other victims of conscience. Since they were being confronted with armies to enforce conformity to the decrees of the Council of Trent, upholding the right to act according to their religious beliefs could entail meeting force with force.[124] In England, these same arguments, after Henry's break with Rome, were made by ardent Catholics like Reginald Pole and William Allen, who felt every bit as threatened as the Calvinists. For all concerned, the fate of true religion was at stake, and when this similar situation occurred among the Israelites of the Old Testament, God led the nation in a holy war against the heathen enemy. Idolatry was the most heinous of all sins.

Without a doubt these same ideas pervaded the thoughts of a number of Anglicans, especially Puritans, who were heavily influenced by Calvin and his supporters on the Continent. But England's cultural and religious traditions mitigated the overly violent forms of holy-war theory that one finds elsewhere. As already mentioned, Bullinger and his disciple Hooper were convinced that some holy wars were necessary to ward off the greater evil of conquest by ungodly, unrepentant nations, whose people were bound for hell through their unrighteous behavior. The soldiers who acted thus as

---

124. Skinner, *Foundations of Modern Political Thought*, 2:302–48.

God's scourge should be merciless in their eradication of evil, even if it meant complete annihilation of the enemy.[125] But as we have seen, this is only half of the story. Bullinger detested war so much that he delineated clear guidelines that made it extremely difficult to justify in most cases. War was itself a sign of how reprobate humankind was and, as such, was more likely to be the cause of great sin than its eliminator. These Protestants did not recognize slights to royal honor or ancient claims to foreign territories as legitimate causes for wars.

By the late 1570s, when the Spanish threat had become pronounced enough to cause grave concern within and without Elizabeth's government, there was once again an outburst of holy-war literature by ex-soldiers, like Barnaby Rich and Thomas Churchyard, and prelates, such as Stephen Gosson and John Stockwood. A more thorough and balanced examination of the literature on war and peace in the second half of the sixteenth century, however, presents an altogether different picture than one gets by reading the works of zealous divines. High-ranking bishops, such as Edwin Sandys, John Jewel, and John Pilkington, spoke out strongly against war and its train of miseries.[126] As for the spate of military manuals that appeared during these years, most were concerned with revitalizing the military profession, indicating that there was probably little enthusiasm for war of any kind. In all likelihood then, the early Puritan or even non-Puritan promotion of holy war was a limited and not very popular phenomenon.[127] Regardless, these theories did not thrive for very long. The queen did not need such apologies to justify any possible war against the Spanish, and neither did most Puritans require them in their efforts for greater church reform. Both parties abhorred violence unless absolutely necessary. There is indeed much more evidence to suggest that England remained a nation committed to peace. The iconography, fiction, pageants, and overall court culture testifies to this very fact.[128]

The rising tide of Puritan polemic inciting holy war has been traced convincingly by John Hale, but even here caution must be used. He lists in his appendix a total of twenty-two "sermons or other works by clerics largely or entirely devoted to justifying war" between 1578 and 1631,

---

125. Johnson, *Ideology*, 110–14, 130–33; Bullinger, *Decades*, 1:370–77.
126. Ben Lowe, "Religious Wars and the 'Common Peace': Anglican Anti-War Sentiment in Elizabethan England," *Albion* 28 (1996): 415–35.
127. Marx, "Shakespeare's Pacifism," 51–60.
128. Lowe, "Role of Peace," 3–14, and "The Emergence of a Peace Ethic in England, 1337–1600" (Ph.D. diss., Georgetown University, 1990), 419–533.

hardly a groundswell. Most of them are bunched around military crises, such as the threat of the Spanish Armada in 1588. And large gaps where no such sermons are recorded, such as between 1598 and 1617, speak volumes. A close look at some of these divines' rhetoric clearly suggests that they were not necessarily calling out for holy wars or even just wars in every case, but were invoking martial language when discussing spiritual warfare (such as Thomas Broade's *A Christian Warre* [1613]). Another militant divine, John Stockwood, actually delivered a sermon that vilified the ancient Roman army and praised the present queen "whose most quiet and peaceable government . . . we have thus long enjoyed."[129] The point here is that a more rounded view is needed to properly understand the cultural forces at work in late sixteenth- and early seventeenth-century England and their impact on war and peace. There is no glaring anomaly between mid-Tudor and mid-Stuart desires for peace; both were founded on a concern for the commonwealth. John Nef has shown that this is what made England unique among European nations.[130] The events of these reigns speak for themselves: Elizabeth, James, and Charles promoted peace, and only Charles's lack of judgment got him involved in Scottish, Irish, and ultimately, civil wars. English governments during this time stayed out of Continental wars by and large, a claim that few (if any) other major powers could make.[131] When the civil war did occur, the English people distrusted the military and refused still to sanction a standing army; and neutralism was a widespread and popular movement.[132]

A substratum of opposition to most wars and a healthy skepticism about warfare in general appears to have been present throughout this period. A scholar of Elizabethan and Jacobean literature recently went so far as to declare that "the dominant Stuart mode of expression might be characterized as a culture of pacifism."[133] The challenge to Charles I's right to wage war against traditional English enemies was a notable rejection of

129. John Stockwood, *A Sermon Preached at Paules Crosse on Barthelmew Day, Being the 24 of August 1578* (London: Henry Bynneman for George Byshop, 1578), 38–44; J. R. Hale, "Incitement to Violence? English Divines on the Theme of War, 1578 to 1631," in *Renaissance War Studies* (London: Hambledon Press, 1983), 487–511.

130. Nef, *War and Human Progress,* 22.

131. C. G. Cruickshank, *Elizabeth's Army,* 2d ed. (Oxford: Clarendon Press, 1966), 16; Barry Coward, *The Stuart Age* (London: Longman, 1980), 106–14.

132. Lois G. Schwoerer, *No Standing Armies: The Antimilitary Ideology in Seventeenth-Century England* (Baltimore, Md.: Johns Hopkins University Press, 1974), 51–94; David Underdown, *Revel, Riot, and Rebellion: Popular Politics and Culture in England, 1603–1660* (Oxford: Oxford University Press, 1987), 148–65.

133. Marx, "Shakespeare's Pacifism," 58.

a major pillar of just-war ideology. After spending three days fasting and praying in April 1648, the New Model Army declared it would defeat the Royalists and then call "Charles Stuart, that man of blood, to an account for that blood he had shed, and mischief he had done . . . against the Lord's cause and [the] people in these poor nations." As Geoffrey Parker has observed, Cromwell's lieutenants accomplished their goal when they explained their own severity against the enemy as necessary to "prevent the effusion of blood in the future."[134] Returning to the time frame of this study, we can see the roots of this hostility toward wars that impoverish and disrupt lives. In fact, as the sixteenth century wore on, and Protestantism's roots grew deeper, the more likely it is that Anglican bishops, like Sandys, Jewel, and Pilkington, who preached peace, were reflecting the common mood of the English people and government, who preferred peace and fewer parliaments demanding subsidies for armies to join in the religious strife of the Low Countries. The conflagration between king and Parliament during the 1640s over "unwarranted" benevolences and taxes eerily echoes some of these earlier concerns. Just-war and holy-war rationales were quite useful when foreign powers were deaf to English peace overtures, resenting that nation's support of Continental and Scottish Protestant movements. But unlike the Hundred Years War, when a long-standing conflict gave birth to a lively peace discourse, by the mid-sixteenth century such extended warfare was impossible to sustain, most people knew it, and peace became more pressing. In this context, then, it was the holy-war discourse that challenged the status quo and threatened to disturb Elizabeth's relatively stable legal and religious polity, in some ways revealing just how far the wheel had turned in favor of "practical peace."[135]

Early modern English society was grappling with major issues related to war and peace that incorporated a panoply of ideas taken from humanist, exegetical, and even scholastic discourse, among others. English writers and activists at this time encouraged a more sophisticated understanding of the peace idiom, and people in power continued to find applications in policy matters. That there were some popular underpinnings for this only

---

134. Geoffrey Parker, "Early Modern Europe," in *Laws of War*, 42–43, 50–51. Barbara Donagan contends that the "holy war" which deposed King Charles was conducted according to "moral rules," which probably produced less bloodshed when compared to similar conflicts of the time. Barbara Donagan, "Did Ministers Matter? War and Religion in England, 1642–1649," *Journal of British Studies* 33 (1994): 129–35.

135. Christopher Haigh, *English Reformations: Religion, Politics, and Society under the Tudors* (Oxford: Clarendon Press, 1993), 175, 226.

indicates one more support that enabled such perceptual developments to occur in the first place.

Protestant Peace Discourse: A Poetical Example

A Pretye Complaynt of Peace, a short poem published anonymously soon after the Pilgrimage of Grace, best represents these many faces of Protestant peace discourse.[136] The work combines Erasmian appeals to a shared humanity and common sense with growing English nationalism in its unequivocal condemnation of war. The poem's popular appeal may be found in its patriotic sentiments and its complete avoidance of the hard questions about times when war could be justified. It is obvious that the author's purpose was to cajole the reader with a passionate call to reason. The affinity this work bears with Erasmus's earlier *Querela pacis* (*Complaint of Peace*) is hardly coincidental; it uses many of the same arguments against war and has as its central character the personification of peace. But the work is tailored to a strictly English audience, especially in its call for the "poorest sort" to consider the state of the commonwealth and the destruction which war brings to it.

In the "prologue to the reader," the author establishes right away the natural coexistence of peace and wealth, a theme that is carried on throughout the poem:

> That to my country I have so good affection
> To show the people, what hurt cometh of dissension

136. The anonymous author's poem was published by John Byddell, who had taken over the press of Wynkyn de Worde in 1534. Byddell printed many works of Erasmus, the first English primer, and Luther's *De libertate Christiani.* Thomas F. Dibdin, *Topographical Antiquities of Great Britain,* vol. 3 (London: John Murray, 1816), 384–85; E. Gordeon Duff, *The Printers, Stationers and Bookbinders of Westminster and London from 1476 to 1535* (Cambridge: The University Press, 1906), 130–39; McConica, *English Humanists,* 168–69. Internal and external evidence suggest that the poem was published in either 1537 or 1538. See Colin Clair, *A History of Printing in Britain* (London: Cassell, 1965), 59–60. The ease with which the poet moves from applying ideas of peace from one arena to another, indicates a contemporary understanding of the term that could be applied to any situation in which the social and political order is substantially disrupted by deliberate violence. A personally edited version of the poem is provided in the Appendix.

> Wherefore it will flourish and excel
> Let Peace and Wealth, in England ever dwell.[137]

The complaint begins with Peace's sorrow over the inability of people to see that he comes for their own profit, and that he does so by commanding truth and obedience "unto their prince, and one to love another / As it beseemeth every Christian brother." Peace then adopts the Erasmian analogy of comparing the peacefulness of beasts—who are unable to reason—with the violent predilections of men who can. Love becomes the leaven that makes reason compassionate, and so it is through showing charity to your neighbor that true peace evolves:

> I will you show a thing [charity] more excellent
> Which should persuade, you froward [away from] ill intent
> To love, which is of Christ the true doctrine
> And ought to be your only discipline
>
> That doctrine only you say you have profit
> Where are the deeds that would it then declare
> Of concord, peace, quietness and rest
> When one with other, to fight still will not spare?[138]

In true Protestant fashion, Peace then launches into an attack on Roman corruption, which he witnessed while in Italy.

Having been expelled from nearly all of Europe, his good friend Wealth persuades him to visit England, where he is sure to find a congenial welcome. At first this proves to be Peace's experience, and he declares that in England "I found all thing, which made me well again."

> There [in London] found I concord which liked me full well
> With true dealing, just weight, and good measure
> Plenty of victual, gold, and great treasure
> And Justyce ruled there most like a king.[139]

---

137. *A Pretye Complaynt of Peace That Was Banyshed Out of Dyvers Countreys & Brought by Welth in to England, & Than Fearing Both to Be Thins Exiled, Made Great Mone, Untyl Prudence Retayned Them Agayne* (London: John Byddell, [1538]), sig. A3r. Notice the similarity to Erasmus's *The Complaint of Peace Spurned and Rejected by the Whole World* (1518).

138. Ibid., sigs. A4v–A6v.

139. Ibid., sigs. A6v–A8v.

The poor commons are allowed to live by the fruits of "true labor" and show genuine love toward one another. But there is word of "Dissension, come in the north country / Which was ever an enemy to me." When Wisdom goes unheeded, war breaks out, and Peace runs away into the countryside to escape. But he can find no refuge and cries in despair: "In all England I saw men did repair / To war, to war, my cruel mortal foe."[140] Soon he meets up with a despondent Wealth, who tells him that they must flee because

> That until we a while have been absent
> And war have made them bare and indigent
> They will not know the great diversity
> Of Peace, and war / wealth, and adversity.[141]

As with other writers of his day on this subject, the author here (and throughout the poem) has constructed a societal dichotomy that clearly allies peace with all that is good, and war with all that is harmful. The work is essentially a moralistic allegory in a genre that would be used with vigor (and with greater sophistication of form) in later Protestant pedagogy. The lesson taught here, while brazenly oversimplified, does reduce the issue to its bare essentials; and this is what made the people who read it or heard it think. As the story continues, Peace asks Wealth what he should do, and the latter encourages him to hide out in a cloister until "the world will turn a better way." But Peace fears the monks just as much, for they are neither holy nor peace-loving. In the end, with Wealth going off to court as "one in favor with the king's counsel," Peace decides to live in the wilderness until Wealth returns to report that Dissension is expelled.[142]

With his one true companion gone, Peace laments the abandonment and the devastation his enemy, War, will bring to the nation:

> Nay nay truly, for if that I poor Peace
> Hence be exiled, then look for poverty
> War nothing bringeth but great calamity
> Ye foolish people, what thing do ye intend
> Your own destruction still followeth at the end.[143]

140. Ibid., sigs. A8v–B1r.
141. Ibid., sig. B2v.
142. Ibid., sigs. B3r–B5v.
143. Ibid., sig. B6v.

Peace then warns the people against rising up for justice because disobedience and war bring only misery. Since this is the crux of the writer's attack on war, and the point in which he connects it to the doctrine of obedience, it is worth quoting a few stanzas:

> Ye seek for ease as men which lack all wit
> And worthy sure, of great reproof and blame
> God hath ordained a king royal and meet
> For to command Justice in his name
> All things to order, to settle and to frame
> Whom that ye ought to honor and obey
> And not to seek by War a foolish way.
>
> War is the cause of great destruction
> It bringeth men to wretched poverty
> And they which are in true possession
> Their very right causeth them to flee
> They are too blind forsooth that will not see
> The great ruin that followeth cruel war
> Where none is made but every man doth mar [spoil].
>
> For many a Duke, Earl, Lord, and Knight
> Which through Peace do live full wealthy
> By force of war, are driven from their right
> And men of substance are brought to misery
> The poor plowman also full woefully
> Which picketh out his living with great pain
> Soweth his corn into the ground in vain.
>
> For War destroyeth both City, Town & Land
> Who can express any wretchedness
> But that in war it ready may be found
> Extreme hunger, but sin with most excess
> Murder, burning, theft, and filthiness
> What Christian man can love that naughty life
> Where they deflower both widow, maid & wife.[144]

144. Ibid., sigs. B7r–B8v.

Following this emotional harangue against the evils of war and its effects on the commonweal, the writer offered the alternative of peace, as the main character reflects on the words of Christ and the apostle Paul. Since Christ "showed by his life and his commandment / That he had Peace, in favor most of price," Peace condemns anyone that "loves war and counts [himself] for wise."[145] Paul preaches peace also, especially in Corinthians, "where he doth me repute / Most worthy praise, which thing should you refute / That favor war, the root of every vice." Isaiah prophesied that Christ would come in peace, and Silius later said that peace was "chief of all things."[146] Since God, therefore, does desire peace and the king is godly, Peace comforts himself that "in England, which so well doth favor me / . . . I again shall come to my degree."[147]

After remaining alone for eight weeks, Peace is rejoined by Wealth, who declares that "Dissension is gone, with all his naughty train," thanks to the good offices of Prudence. Wealth then tells Peace that the king wants the two of them to come to court quickly, and that "Thou are bound for evermore to love / That godly prince, which war doth much reprove." His councillors also favor Peace, meaning that he will always be welcome: "for some of them have per[s]ued the chance of wars / Which know it is the spring of mischiefs all." But both agree that England must be alert to avoid falling into the folly of war again and the pain "that hath ensued of false discord and strife." The poem ends praising the king for defending Peace "abroad and in every place" and for making it the foundation of his rule and closes with a final prayer for the maintenance of this agreeable situation.[148]

While we might have saved this fascinating work to use in a later discussion devoted to the other responses to mid-Tudor rebellions, the manner in which it embodies the main elements of the Protestant views on war and peace make it even more significant in this context. Borrowing much from the medieval *jus ad bellum* and Erasmus, nevertheless, with the additions by Protestants/erastians who were concerned that legitimate temporal powers wield the sword to promote true piety and domestic well-being, *A Pretye Complaynt of Peace* brings together an array of new and old concerns. There is the clearly nationalist tone, the dependence on the sovereign ruler to fend off war and preserve peace, the identification of dissen-

145. Ibid., sig. B8v.
146. Silius *Punica* 11.591.
147. *Pretye Complaynt of Peace*, sigs. C1r–C2v.
148. Ibid., sigs. C2v–C5r.

sion as the cause of war and the consequent troubles that plague the commonweal, the dichotomy inherent in the practices of war and peace, the need to extend personal behavior—especially charity—into society, the condemnation of romanism, the New Testament exemplars, and the association of peace with rest, quiet, concord, and everything else that permits each member of the commonweal to live happily in accordance with his or her particular calling.

Protestantism and the Possibilities for Peace

Peace discourse among mid-Tudor evangelicals was concerned primarily with fostering and maintaining positive, salutary benefits for the commonweal. In a way, all other medieval and humanist types of peace are subsumed by Protestant formulations that expand the discourse dramatically, now that the humanist ethic is fully validated by and incorporated into much of their biblical and reformist language. And there is a clear sense that rest and calm are necessary conditions for a nation to become not only wealthy but also socially and politically stable. In the midst of tranquillity energies are diverted away from bloodshed and costly defenses and invested instead in agriculture, business, spiritual growth, and the devising of good laws. Tyndale was most emphatic in this regard even to the point of blaming bellicose behavior for creating a taste for domestic rebellion.[149] For those reformers who offered ideas and thought deeply about peace, it had to be sought after if one was to please God and be actively involved in furthering the heavenly kingdom. As Becon noted, only repentance and regeneration could end war, but since war creates an environment conducive to greater sin, it would be much more difficult to obey God in the midst of such bloody conflicts. It is in the interests of all citizens to attain peace and to sustain it for as long as possible, never provoking war, because a nation's spiritual maturity in such times becomes the foundation for all other virtues. This is why these certain concerned Protestants were so vehement in their condemnation of those who stirred up dissent and discord. The greatest fruit of peace is unity (within and among nations)— that state where the commonweal is in consonance and the collective aspirations of the people can be focused on loving one another and serving God.

149. Tyndale, *Obedience of a Christian Man*, 166; Smeeton, *Lollard Themes*, 237–38.

On the surface, this outlook may seem strikingly similar to that of the Erasmian humanists, who seemed fixated on the hope for a *renovatio mundi* based on a biblically educated populace and discerning prince. There are crucial differences, however, in the manner in which each understood the possibilities for peace. For one, the reformers fathomed more realistically the nature of the constant struggle between war and peace. Rather than treating either condition as a general state of human conduct that in the abstract seemed respectively either too illogical or obviously sensible, they portrayed the problem as replete with conflicts and tensions, to be precisely argued and rationalized according to any number of situations. The just war (*jus ad bellum*) was based on a more precise and rigorous ethical foundation that included conscience and appeals to biblical authority. In turn, such a configuration meant a greater emphasis on *jus in bello* considerations, since even just wars were the lesser of two evils and so must be fought as humanely as possible, with charity as the motivation. In addition, limitations on war were calculated and supported by a greater desire for peace — a peace that was not simply a platonic or even Christian ideal, but a condition, which when preserved, contributed immensely to the overall well-being of the realm. Perhaps the most important contribution of English Protestantism to the peace idea comes in the unhesitant avowal that it is social sin and the lack of concern for others that devolves into war. Such an understanding clearly puts war — just or not — outside the Christian commonwealth. Peace is harmonious living and the fount of all that is good, as well as an indicator of a nation's godliness. Once again, this is not to say that English reformers eschewed any and all war, only that they came to believe it was not part of God's natural order for the world.

Finally, this dialectic constructed between war and peace, and the struggle of both praxis and ideology, helped to create a war-peace dynamic that found its way into state policy itself. As newer roles were being cast for prince, clergy, nobility, and commons, the dual considerations of peace and organic harmony required a more frequent, periodic retrenchment from warfare, thus further weakening traditional imperatives to seek justice and vindication through battle. The necessity for any foreign campaign was now pitted against a broadened and enhanced notion of legitimacy and the concomitant cognizance of available preferred alternatives. But we cannot permit these noticeable contributions of erastian and evangelical discourse on war and peace to languish in a vacuum. It is perhaps no accident that the debate on the issue in the mid-Tudor period was being carried on more by clergy than statesmen. Be that as it may, the former's ability to "anglicize" (or pragmatize?) Erasmian thought on the subject by using it to build on late-medieval foundations, with the added dimension of an evangelical sensibility, served to make this war-peace dynamic an operative theater of social and political activity.

7

PEACE, COMMONWEALTH, AND THE CONDUCT OF WAR (1535–1559)

A combination of foreign and domestic factors touched off by the break from Rome left England less willing to go to war in the 1530s. For the next three decades, and even beyond, the policy considerations of Tudor monarchs corresponded more than ever to the emerging peace ethic that had arisen out of late-medieval, humanist, and Protestant thought on the problem of war. While fears over possible Catholic crusades against England were rampant, the government also understood the tentativeness of the new religious settlement. Any excessive levies used to defend these changes could potentially sow seeds of discord or, worse yet, social rebellion. As the Amicable Grant debacle of 1525 demonstrated, the English people were beginning to scrutinize justifications for war much more carefully. In addition, during these years, both nobility and crown were noticeably affected by a loosening of traditional roles and responsibilities and their replacement by more exacting obligations toward the commonwealth.[1] The following discussion will examine the changes encountered by

---

1. "Commonwealth," by this time, was coming to refer to the body politic as well as to the older organic, societal relationships among the estates and their productive interconnection for the good of all. This chapter is an expanded version of the essay, "Peace Discourse and Mid-Tudor Foreign Policy," in *Political Thought and the Tudor Commonwealth: Deep*

king and aristocracy and what effect these may have had on the under-standing and prosecution of mid-Tudor military campaigns. It will then be helpful to look at how the idea of commonweal was being transformed and included in the more pragmatic notions of domestic and international peace, as economic issues assumed greater importance. Finally, through an examination of the mid-century wars and the thoughts of those who con-ducted them, we can better grasp the role of peace ideas in determining policy.

The Nobility and Mid-Tudor Military Decline

Of course any shift made in the place of war in international relations would affect the nobility most of all. The 1540s witnessed a remarkable displacement of traditional recruitment patterns — the "quasi-feudal" method of raising soldiers — by a more "national" system that employed commissions and which prefigured the modern professional army. This change was precipitated by the need in 1544 for additional troops to hold Boulogne. The immediate result was the coexistence of two separate sys-tems of recruitment, which until the Militia Act of 1558, created a chaotic situation, full of corruption.[2] This, along with a corresponding dramatic increase in the numbers of foreign mercenaries and auxiliaries employed in Tudor wars, sounded the death knell for the older feudal establishment's prerogative in making war. As already stated, foreigners comprised only about one-fifth of the total army that invaded France in 1513, but by 1546, the proportion had risen to as much as one-half of Hertford's thirty thousand soldiers. The feeble attempts at military reform, even after 1558, were most concerned with increasing efficiency, however, and came at a

---

Structure, Discourse, and Disguise, ed. Paul A. Fideler and T. F. Mayer (London: Routledge, 1992), 108–39.

2. Two acts were passed in 1558 relating to military affairs, one "for the taking of mus-ter," and the other, "for the having of horse armour and weapon." The latter bill, known as the Militia Act, by providing for assessments of military equipment, brought every segment of society into the national recruitment process. There was included also a clause that protected the landlord's right to exact military obligations from his tenants, even though it was rarely invoked. John Jeremy Goring, "Social Change and Military Decline in Mid-Tudor England," *History* 60 (1975): 193–97; Cruickshank, *Elizabeth's Army;* Miller, *Henry VIII and the En-glish Nobility,* 151–59.

time when much of the realm despaired of war and found little glory in the life of a soldier.[3]

By the 1540s, with the decline in the number of great noble families and the repudiation of obligatory military service by tenants, the king had been forced to devise new and largely unsuccessful methods for raising armies.[4] As in any age, youthful exuberance could compensate for the cynicism of an older generation of knights, as in the case of the young Charles Blount, Lord Mountjoy, in his ill-fated attempt at glory and honor in France in 1544. He typified a new and small aristocratic elite that accepted fully its duty of military service, even as on the rung just below, tenant cooperation in war became increasingly difficult to manage and predict.[5] Those men from whom service was requested may have regarded military obligations as archaic as any other obsolete feudal service. In 1542, for example, Derbyshire landowner John Port's tenants refused service because "it was not their duty." Even the City of London contested the crown's prerogative to require it to provide men-at-arms whenever requested.[6] The following year, initial inquiries of able-bodied men were not answered forthrightly, and the whole recruitment process, plagued with administrative problems, exhibited signs of being irreversibly ineffectual.[7]

The first conspicuous signs of military decline came after the disastrous campaign of 1522–23, which had produced little chance for booty, and which had been plagued by chronic food shortages, bad weather, mutinies, and the realization that Continental professional armies were vastly superior. But for Henry the longbow was still the weapon of choice. A proclamation of 1528 that bemoaned the lack of interest in archery as "decayed and in manner utterly extinct" (a sentiment reiterated in the preambles to statutes in 1533 and 1542) blamed the decline on the "newfangled and wanton pleasure that men now have in using of crossbows and handguns."[8] During Somerset's protectorate the need for more troops was so great that many complained that England was no longer able to defend itself adequately. Depopulation became the prevalent explanation, rooted in despair

---

3. Lowe, "Role of Peace," 3–14.

4. Goring, "Social Change and Military Decline," 188–89.

5. Miller, *Henry VIII and the English Nobility*, 159–61; Ian Roy, "The Profession of Arms," in *The Professions in Early Modern England*, ed. Wilfrid Prest (London: Croom Helm, 1987), 184–86.

6. Goring, "Military Obligations," 1–2.

7. Goring, "Social Change and Military Decline," 189–90.

8. *TRP*, no. 121 (4 December 1528), 177–81. 25 Hen. VIII, c. 17; 33 Hen. VIII, c. 6; *The Statutes of the Realm*, vol. 3 (London: Record Commission, 1817), 457–59, 832–35.

over three consecutive inadequate harvests beginning in 1549 and the impact of enclosures. In reality, poverty and vulnerability in defense increased while military commitments expanded unabated.[9] (The succeeding government discovered that once war had ended, the economy could begin to exhibit signs of recovery.) Also, in times of rebellion, most notably in 1536 and 1549, many Englishmen were unwilling to take up arms against their fellow countrymen, making it necessary, in the latter case, to hire German mercenaries to deal with a domestic outbreak of violence.[10] This growing proclivity for foreign soldiers did not rest easy with some of those high in the government. With constant threats of insurrection and foreign invasion on the horizon, Thomas Cromwell took the first steps toward military reform in 1539 by proposing his "Articles for the ordering of the manred." Coming as it did so close to his fall from power, much of what Cromwell had in mind went with him to the grave. But the acknowledgment that some type of reform was necessary remained, and men such as Sir William Pickering, Sir Thomas Wyatt, and Sir James Wilford, all seasoned soldiers, continued to propose new and better means for Henry to raise armies quickly.[11]

Attempts at creating a "national" recruitment policy were fraught with problems from the start. Besides the actual corruption that came from bribes to commissioners in order to avoid service, there were legitimate exemptions allowed as well, which made it impossible to raise armies in any organized, systematic manner. In addition, there were the age-old fears about excessive military power that accompanied any pretensions at creating a professional soldiery. Henry VIII was not prepared to trust his security to a standing army either—even in time of rebellion—and most English people appear to have equated such a thing with creeping despotism. In broaching this subject in the second dialogue of the *Discourse of the Commonweal,* the Husbandman says: "God forbid that even we had any such tyrants come amongst us"; to which the Merchantman replies that standing armies "would rather be occasion of commotions to be stirred than to be quenched, for . . . the stomachs of Englishmen would never bear that—to suffer such injury and reproaches as . . . heard that such used to do the subjects of France which in reproach they call peasants."[12] In the

9. M. L. Bush, *The Government Policy of Protector Somerset* (Montreal: McGill-Queen's University Press, 1975), 59–60.

10. Davies, "English People and War," 8.

11. Goring, "Social Change and Military Decline," 194–95.

12. Thomas Smith, *A Discourse of the Commonweal of This Realm of England,* ed. Mary

towns there was also the expense of quartering soldiers in barracks or in private homes, neither of which endeared the idea of a standing army to the people.[13]

In the 1540s, one of the reasons for disinterest by the nobility in another of Henry's wars went no further than traditional calculations of potential gain, which by this time, seemed less and less guaranteed as restraints in battle (the *jus in bello*) were emphasized more, or as the economic capabilities of aristocratic households declined. The author of *A Supplication to our most Sovereign Lord King Henry the Eight* (1544) wrote that gentlemen, "consuming their goods in vain pride and wanton lusts, [when] called upon by your Grace to serve your Majesty for the defence of this your realm, have not [the means] to do their duty."[14]

On the other hand, there was the new predilection of the aristocracy itself for nonmartial activities. One of the most thorough statements to this effect comes in an anonymous work, *The Institution of a Gentleman*, published in 1555, during a period of protracted peace just before the reluctant campaign that saw the loss of Calais. Although it follows in a long line of advice manuals that demonstrate the new willingness to redefine traditional roles of king and nobility (and which characterize Renaissance humanism), the *Institution* betrays a greater maturity of thought on the issue of war than we find in either Elyot or early Ascham. In the typical fashion of the time, the author drew from classical examples and rhetoric to call on the gentlemen of England to seek reform and take up with renewed vigor the obligations and responsibilities of society incumbent upon them. At the outset he declared, "a right gentleman ought to be a man fit for the wars, and fit for the peace," but then proceeds to show that while Caesar himself was a brave warrior, he was at heart a man of "mercy and pity" and peace.[15] In the section "How a Gentleman may much profit his Country in being a soldier or Captain in the wars," the writer claimed initially that fighting is allowable only when the cause is completely just, in which case, for a gentleman to avoid service would be

---

Dewar (Charlottesville: University Press of Virginia, 1969), 92–93; Millar, *Tudor Mercenaries,* 9; Cruickshank, *Elizabeth's Army,* 286. Cf. More, *Utopia,* 63, 65.

13. André Corvisier, *Armies and Societies in Europe, 1494–1789,* trans. Abigail T. Siddall (Bloomington: Indiana University Press, 1979), 78–82.

14. *A Supplycacion to our most Soveraigne Lorde Kynge Henry the Eyght,* ed. J. Meadows Cowper, in *Four Supplications,* ed. Frederick J. Furnivall and J. Meadows Cowper, EETS ES, no. 13 (London: N. Trübner, 1871), 52–58; Goring, "Social Change and Military Decline," 190.

15. *The Institucion of a Gentleman* (London: Thomas Marshe, 1555), sigs. A4v–B8v.

to abandon his responsibility to seek justice. He quickly turned next to the preferable avocation of making peace, for "to minister justice in the state of peace it is an office worthy of higher commendation: the reason is, wars are nothing necessary, but of necessity must be defended when they fall. And contrarywise peace is a thing not only most necessary, but it is also called the best thing which ever nature hath given unto men." In quoting the "pacifist" maxims of Sallust and Tully (Cicero), the author has adopted the ancient wisdom that rejected the idea that "our forefathers have made a small commonwealth to flourish and become great by means of wars," while agreeing that "an unjust peace [was] better than a most rightful war." It is certainly no coincidence that he followed this section with one titled "How ambassages be most meet for Gentlemen."[16] Without question, one of the most productive and useful vocations suited for the gentleman is to serve his king and people in the interests of peace. At the end of the treatise, an example "of peace" is presented in the person of St. Anthony, who "was a prince all given to peace and tranquility, even so much as he used to say these words. *Honestius est a Cesare unum Civem fervari, quam mille hostes occidi,* that is to say: It is better and more honorable to an Emperor that one Citizen be preserved and kept, than a thousand enemies to be slain."[17] By speaking more directly about the constructive part the aristocracy could play in promoting peace in England, the writer of the *Institution* was elucidating and contributing to a more thoughtful view of the subject. Whenever one weighed the advantages to be gotten through peace against those of military victory, the former was always to be preferred. The author here has treated the issues of war and peace as important subjects in their own right, unencumbered by the heavy layers of chivalric, traditional, and even religious sanction that had commonly been reserved for any legitimate authority's call to arms. Perhaps stirred by Protestant emphases on conscience and a determinate christology, thinking or articulate English people in the mid-Tudor period were reevaluating the issues of war and peace with an increasing amount of fervor and resolve.

One of the reasons why war became the object of study in the sixteenth century is the fact that the practice itself had expanded on a grand scale. The increase in fiercely ideological (often religious) warfare, the deadlier technology in weaponry, and the greater expense and numbers of troops

16. Ibid., sigs. E1v–F3v, F6r–F8v.
17. Ibid., sigs. L2r–v.

required in foreign campaigns meant that war touched the lives of more people directly. But perhaps most significant, the printing press had allowed for a greater dissemination of all ideas concerning war and peace, not just official propaganda. The moral attention brought by Erasmian (and Anabaptist?) pacifism along with the newer attention paid to the "learned soldier," caused educated people to step back and reexamine their position with a noticeably independent, as well as practical, spirit.[18]

Obedience and Resistance in Preserving the Peace

Raising questions about the character of war was nothing new, but by the middle of the sixteenth century it had taken on an added urgency. As the English people identified themselves more closely with "notions of citizenship and nationhood," it was inevitable that a certain tension would arise when reasons of state conflicted with individual beliefs. We have already seen how some Protestants dealt with this dilemma, by focusing on the individual motivation of soldiers going into battle, by allowing those who could not fight in good conscience to withdraw, or in strict matters of conscience, to refuse support altogether. As the century progressed, the latter alternative became less unusual and the whole "doctrine of obedience" came under strong ideological attack from the likes of John Ponet and Chrisopher Goodman. Throughout most of the mid-Tudor era, however, obedience to the state remained one of the most sacred beliefs shared by those who would serve the nation, even if it was eroding a bit around the edges.

The explosion of nationalist literature from the 1530s on can only be explained in relation to the isolation England must have felt after the split with Rome. Already possessing a highly developed sense of self that was unique to Europe, it was not difficult to act defensively and play up that age-old appeal to naked emotion known as patriotism.[19] The incident that did most to encourage this collective pride in country and king was not

18. Hale, "Sixteenth-Century Explanations," 3–4; Frank Tallett, *War and Society in Early Modern Europe, 1495–1715* (London: Routledge, 1992), 232.

19. Patrick Collinson, *The Birthpangs of Protestant England: Religious and Cultural Changes in the Sixteenth and Seventeenth Centuries* (New York: St. Martin's Press, 1988); Joel Hurstfield, *Freedom, Corruption and Government in Elizabethan England* (Cambridge, Mass.: Harvard University Press, 1973), 223–24; J. W. Allen, *A History of Political Thought in the Sixteenth Century*, 3d ed. (London: Methuen, 1951), 121, 125–26; David Loades, "The Origins of English Protestant Nationalism," in Mews, *Religion and National Identity*, 297–307.

intended by its perpetrator to do anything of the kind. Reginald Pole's Continental flitterings and intrigues, eventually landing him in Rome, never posed any real threat to English security; but the book he published, enjoining his countrymen and women to rebel, and all foreign nations to invade England, was so abusive to Henry that it backfired on its writer. In his *De unione ecclesiastica* (1537), the soon-to-be-named cardinal revived the doctrine that elevated the office of pope above prince in all jurisdictions because of the former's more important role as guardian of the soul. Pole was replying to questions regarding the royal supremacy sent to him by his former pupil, Thomas Starkey, who had recently entered the king's service.[20] It was hoped that some accommodation could be reached between Henry and Pole, even if simply that the latter would agree not to interfere with the king's business. The reply was a great disappointment to Starkey and his employer, but negotiations continued into the following year when it became obvious just how active the cardinal had become in plotting insurrection in and the invasion of his native land.[21]

There is a bit of the surreal in Pole's whole approach to the supremacy. He seems to have been completely out of touch with the situation in England, as is witnessed in his contention that "there remain yet whole legions in England of those which have not bowed their knees unto Baal."[22] For Pole, the holy war he was proclaiming had become nothing less than rescuing a land from heretics as pestilent as the Arians of the early church. For this reason, he enjoined the emperor to break off his fighting with the Turk and attack England with full force, for "thou wouldest first help in that part from whence a greater mischief than the Turks is risen toward the Christian commonwealth where as also easy victory without any peril or danger is offered unto you."[23] All along Pole argued that his crusade was for "the health of the Christian commonwealth," choosing an idiom that his fiercest enemy would employ against his brand of sedition. But it is the adjective that precedes it that completely defines his usage. Where

20. Esme Wingfield-Stratford, *The History of English Patriotism* (London: John Lane, 1913), 1:137–38; John Strype, *Ecclesiastical Memorials* (Oxford: Clarendon Press, 1822), 1:445–65.

21. Strype, *Ecclesiastical Memorials,* 1:477–78.

22. Reginald Pole, *The Seditious and blasphemous Oration of Cardinal Pole Both Against God & His Country Which He Directed to Themperour in His Booke Intytuled the Defence of the Eclesastical Unitye, Moving Themperour Therin to Seke the Destruction of England and All Those Whiche Had Professed the Gospele,* trans. with a preface by Fabyane Wythers (London: Owen Rogers, [1560]), sig. B1r; Jean-Pierre Moreau, *Rome ou l'Angleterre? Les Réactions politiques des catholiques anglais au moment du schisme (1529–1553)* (Paris: Presses Universitaires de France, 1984), 263–64.

23. Pole, *Seditious and Blasphemous Oration,* sigs. B1r–B6r.

the health of the commonwealth is concerned, nothing was more vital than an adherence to the true faith: "I call to witness that love of my country which is engrafted in me by nature—that love of the Church which is given to me by the Son of God." Pole held to an older use of the term "commonwealth" that transcended national boundaries, while in England it had become synonymous with the national body politic. Love of country, for Pole, could not be separated from love of Rome, and it was just this kind of divided allegiance that could not be tolerated in his homeland.[24] Pole was arguing against the entire course of English tradition since the later Middle Ages. He was giving credence to every diatribe that depicted papal militancy raging maliciously against a God-fearing nation. Most English people, Protestant or Catholic, would have none of it, and Henry found more than enough ready respondents willing to dispute Pole's lonely interpretation of true patriotism.[25]

The most forceful proponent of the supremacy in terms of love of country was undoubtedly Thomas Becon. Even though his treatise on war is reticent about the actual practice of fighting for king and country, it holds back nothing in its praise of nation. The preface to the work is an extremely passionate panegyric to the debt one owes to his or her country, which he considers the embodiment of all that is moral and inimically opposed to evil. "It engraffeth in us the true knowledge of ourselves, the fear of God, the love of God and of our neighbour, the true faith in God's promises, the unfeigned obedience toward our superiors."[26] This theme pervades the treatise and is a direct answer to Pole and those few others who unabashedly wrote *Roma est mihi patria*.[27] The following year, when he most likely composed one of his more popular works, *The Governance of Virtue*, Becon, in a section against rebellion and disobedience, even more clearly connected love for country with obedience to the king, insisting that those who rebel because they feel "that the magistrates and high powers do not their duty in the right government of a commonweal, but too much cruelly oppress their subjects" risk eternal damnation. For him, there was only one way to peace and prosperity: "But content thyself with thy vocation, labour diligently and quietly for thy living, study to maintain

24. Ibid., sig. B6r; Wingfield-Stratford, *History of English Patriotism*, 1:137–38.
25. Moreau, *Rome ou l'Angleterre?* 263–67.
26. Becon, *New Policy of War*, 232; Collinson, *Birthpangs of Protestant England*, 8, 16.
27. Derrick S. Bailey, *Thomas Becon and the Reformation of the Church in England* (Edinburgh: Oliver & Boyd, 1952), 20–21; Wingfield-Stratford, *History of English Patriotism*, 1:144–46.

peace, pray for the high powers, think that cross to be laid upon those for thy deserts, amend thy life, humbly lament thy cause to God which will not leave thee succourless."[28] Here Becon got close to defining those responsibilities which many of his contemporaries felt existed among the various orders of society, with particular attention given to king and nobility. Thomas Lever, in a sermon given in 1550, made much the same point, when he exhorted "every soul [to] be subject unto the higher powers, for there is no power but of God. Those powers which be, are ordained of God. Wherefore he that resisteth power, resisteth the ordinance of God, but they which do resist, shall receive to themselves judgement."[29] Both men, however, invoke an ideal of harmony that is vague yet full of good intentions. If their designs were meant to be primarily emotional then they were successful, for the power of feeling in their words — as in patriotic harangues today — would have been a valuable tool of any government. But more sophisticated and profound constructions of the commonwealth would have to await the judicious words of those men who intended to reinterpret and perhaps challenge the existing order without questioning the passion for country which formed its basis.[30]

Peaceful Considerations of the Commonwealth: Starkey, Morison, and Cheke

The Pilgrimage of Grace provided an opportunity for many polemicists to publicize their particular versions of why the commonweal had become partially unraveled. As we have already seen, *The Pretye Complaynt of Peace* was a forthright indictment of war written for commoners (and the nobles to a lesser extent), calling for an overall change in policy based on Christian and humanist principles. Other works were less panoramic or artistic and sought to offer more concrete solutions to the problem. Three writers stand out for their attempt to evaluate carefully the state of the commonweal in the 1530s and 1540s. Richard Morison wrote in response

28. Thomas Becon, *The Governance of Virtue*, in *Early Works*, 456–57; Johnson, *Just War Tradition*, 57–58.

29. Thomas Lever, *Sermons, 1550*, ed. Edward Arber; reprinted in *English Reprints*, vol. 6 (London: n.p., 1871; reprint, New York: AMS Press, 1966), 25–26; Jones, *Tudor Commonwealth*, 65–74.

30. Another, but less nationalistic, response to Pole was Nicholas Wise's *Consolation for Christian People* (London: John Waylande, 1538).

to the 1536 uprising, Thomas Starkey attempted to counter the threat of rebellion being fomented by Pole (although the work's appearance at the time of the Pilgrimage was timely), and John Cheke directed his remarks to the rebels of 1549. In each case, the value of peace is found to inform almost the entire discussion. While many who have examined these works see a much more practical emphasis (than in any hopes for peace), one should perhaps avoid the temptation to deny a contingent element of peace or to wrench them out of the social contexts in which they were written. By adopting a Protestant outlook on the need to quell rebellion as a counterpoint to a need for peace, these men were entering the maelstrom of ideological and personal struggle. Restoration of order and concord among the estates brought prosperity also, and neither could be separated from maintaining peace, even if the cost of achieving that peace was unpleasant.[31]

Starkey, probably the most Italianate Englishman of his time, conceived of an England governed in part according to principles drawn from Cicero and civic humanism. In his famous *Dialogue between Reginald Pole and Thomas Lupset* (1535), he made clear his view of the commonweal in defining "policy" as "a sort of political wisdom; and a framework for politics," by associating the concept with learning, justice, prudence, law, and common counsel. These qualities were essential to "good order" and meant that commonweal was essentially the body politic committed to obeying an informed and capable government. The prince's role was crucial in his formulations of the ideal state and in maintaining peace and good order.

In his preface to *An Exhortation to the People, Instructing Them to Unity and Obedience* (1536), Starkey called for the restoration of unity and obedience to the Supreme Head so that "church and congregation shall both in this age live in perfect quietness and tranquillity, and hereafter also, them that shall succeed, leave a quiet commonweal, to the common comfort of all our posterity."[32] Throughout the work there is the consistent linkage of unity and obedience with breeding concord, quietness, and tranquillity. Since we have seen that these terms were invariably associated with peace, Starkey has allowed peace to become an end of policy here, and so it becomes a reason for obedience. There is no *a priori*

31. Arthur B. Ferguson, "The Tudor Commonweal and the Sense of Change," *Journal of British Studies* 3 (1963): 13–14.

32. Thomas Starkey, *An Exhortation to the People, Instructynge Theym to Unitie and Obedience* (London: Thomas Berthelet, [1536]), sig. a4v.

duty to obey removed from its benefits. He was concerned with the Renaissance pursuit of virtue, a moral and fulfilling life, and selfless behavior on behalf of others, which here depended on keeping the peace: "He is not worthy to live in that common policy, nor to be a member thereof, as one that abhoreth from all good civility." Later he added that "we must think that our master Christ descended down from the bosom of his father, to stablish this concord and unity, in the hearts of all them, which purpose to be inheritors with him in his kingdom of heaven everlastingly."[33] In complaining against division, Starkey stated that "there Christ doth not reign no more than light in darkness doth shine."[34] The *Exhortation* was devoted primarily to a defense of the royal supremacy and "Protestant" doctrine and was therefore not as concerned with a thorough examination of the commonweal as Starkey's *Dialogue*.[35] But it is clear that the author was drawing upon an ethic that had elevated peace as the *summum bonum* for a unified and well-ordered commonweal. The difficulty rested in devising means for remaining at peace and in preventing discord, which if allowed to grow, eventually becomes the death of any prosperous and godly commonwealth.

Richard Morison's *Remedy for Sedition* went furthest in constructing a "very and true commonweal" that was serviceable to the crown for its intent to divert people away from rebellion and into constructive activity.[36] The author found that discord and insurrection produced not reform but a rending of the commonweal, the opposite effect of what the rebels intended. Only in times of quiet can progress and substantive change occur, thus the treatise stressed the value of peace:

> Concord made laws, concord builded cities, increased and conserved them. Concord brought in all honest crafts. Concord bringeth riches which by dissension we seek madly. In time of peace wits attain unto learning, virtue, and wisdom. Concord maketh us the friends of God, the inheritors of heaven, partakers of all the joys that God hath prepared for them He best loveth.[37]

33. Ibid., sigs. B4v, C3r.
34. Ibid., sig. D2v.
35. Mayer, *Thomas Starkey and the Commonweal*, 216–19.
36. Richard Morison, *A Remedy for Sedition*, in *Humanist Scholarship and Public Order: Two Tracts Against the Pilgrimmage of Grace*, ed. David Sandler Berkowitz (Washington, D.C.: Folger Shakespeare Library, 1984), 81–83.
37. Ibid., 145.

Throughout the tract, Morison called on the people to put off their selfish complaining and to work instead for the overall good of the realm, under the guiding hand of an evangelical and reforming king.[38] It is the unswerving allegiance to the crown that provided the foundation for Morison's justification for recourse to war at times, even though the king has a duty to listen to his subjects' concerns. In his edition of the ancient Roman governor Frontinus's war manual, which he dedicated to Henry, he praised the king for "devising in time of peace most godly laws, statutes, and proclamations, for the tranquility and quietness of your subject souls."[39] The utilitarian nature of war is stressed here, and the doctrine of obedience provides a way out of the confusion that probably plagued the consciences of men who feared the power of the Roman church on both domestic and international fronts. The king, however, was not omnipotent, and his ultimate duty was in restoring peace and a thriving commonwealth.

The rebellions in the west country and Norfolk in 1549 came while England was at war with Scotland and France. In early July the king answered the rebels in Cornwall and Devon with a blistering attack for their effrontery in diverting the government from securing its interests overseas.[40] In *The Hurt of Sedition,* Cheke, Edward's former tutor, defined rebellion of this kind as a type of war, and an unjust one at that. His arguments, directed toward the commons, were cast in a commonwealth language that suggested some identification with the economic suffering of the people, while unequivocally condemning their odious actions. If war caused great misery, so did rebellion. Echoing Morison's contention that rebellion seriously injured the nation's welfare, he was quicker to emphasize the greater good of maintaining peace in all circumstances. In *The Hurt of Sedition,* he chastised the rebels for claiming to "rise for religion"; such went against Christ's teaching of fleeing or quietly suffering. As we have seen already, Cheke also reiterated the common arguments against war in his day by addressing the immoral behavior it bred among the soldiers and the destruction that naturally followed from that behavior.[41] Going further

38. Morison, *Remedy for Sedition,* 81–83. A. J. Slavin, "'Tis Far Off, and Rather Like a Dream': Common Weal, Common Woe, and Commonwealth," *Explorations in Renaissance Culture* 14 (1988): 1–28.

39. Sextus Julius Frontinus, *The Strategemes, Sleyghtes, and Policies of Warre Gathered Together, by S. Julius Frontinus, and Translated by Rycharde Morysine* (London: Thomas Berthelet, 1539), sigs. a2v–a5v.

40. PRO, SP 10/8, no. 5; *SP Dom., Edw. VI:* 305.

41. John Cheke, *The Hurt of Sedition Howe Greveous It Is to a Communewelth* (London: John Day & Wylliam Seres, 1549), sigs. A4v, E4v–E5r.

than Morison, he condemned war openly, but agreed with Morison that
sedition was the more dangerous threat to the commonwealth, and so
mourned the all-too-common recourse to arms. He closed his tract with a
paean to the virtues of restoring tranquillity:

> O noble peace, what wealth bringest you in, how doth all things
> flourish in field and in town, what forwardness of religion, what
> increase of learning, what gravity in counsel, what device of wit,
> what order of manners, what obedience of laws, what reverence of
> states, what safeguard of houses, what quietness of life, what honor
> of countries, what friendship of minds, what honesty of pleasure,
> hast thou always maintained.[42]

Again we see the hope that peace seems to offer, not as an ideal state or
condition, but as a real situation offering economic benefits and a better
way of life.[43]

An Era of Peace: England in the 1530s

Despite the obvious rhetoric of Starkey, Morison, and Cheke, one might
still contend that their emphasis on peace was only a strategy for contain-
ing rebellious impulses that threatened the nation as they wrote. It might
be argued also, however, and is probably more likely, that they were thinking of England's long-term prospects in a time of accelerating social change
and disruption. In the mid-1500s many men in important positions in the
government were writing about the state of the commonwealth and making arguments in favor of peace from an economic or, more precisely, commonwealth position. This pragmatic understanding of the desirability of
peace dated back to the Hundred Years War, but it did not become the
primary focus of peace advocacy until this period, when economic conditions and foreign policy needs catapulted pragmatic concerns to the fore-
front. It is at this juncture, we will see, that the humanist and religious
discussions regarding the nature of war and peace provided a wellspring of

---

42. Ibid., sigs. H2v–H3r. These same sentiments appear in the duke of Burgundy's apos-
trophe in act V, scene 2 of Shakespeare's *Henry V*, when he refers to peace as that "nurse of
arts, plenties, and joyful births."
43. Ferguson, "Tudor Commonweal," 28–34.

ethical argument when clearly the motivations behind ending wars (or avoiding them) were often less high-minded.

In an important article written in 1942, which later became the basis for his much-heralded book *War and Human Progress,* John Nef offered his seminal thesis that England's by-and-large avoidance of war between 1540 and 1640 provided the necessary conditions for tremendous economic progress and eventually proto-industrialization: "While the continental fields, hillsides, and towns were continually overrun and ravaged by armies — marching, camping, and fighting — England was normally at peace." As a consequence, England did not "waste" its technological energies supporting a wartime economy, but rather channeled them into more fruitful outlets. Nef concluded that it was England's peace policies that stimulated population growth, leading to a greater expansion of industries, which increased the nation's capacity to supply more people with material goods. All of this encouraged the English to adopt a "mercantile outlook on life" by the start of Elizabeth's reign. The upstart, nouveaux riches were especially aware of the harmful impact of war on trade and usually acted in tandem with the crown to promote peace policies.[44]

While in this cliometric age it may be hard to sustain such an overly simplistic view of economic development, the main outline of Nef's argument has hardly been refuted. In fact, much of it still holds great merit. We know that England was opening up new trade routes that depended on peaceful relations with neighbors during these years, and that there were more people, especially after the dissolutions, who were eager to participate in early capitalistic ventures, both in agriculture and commodities. Wars were always threatening the staple at Antwerp, with a major crisis in 1551 exacerbating fears of great financial loss via spiraling political instability.[45] During the 1530s, memories of the last decade's overseas debacles were fresh, and many commons felt their livelihoods would be lost if new wars broke out and they were forced to pay exorbitant taxes to support them. This attitude, coupled with greater suspicion of those in power, especially war profiteers, helped solidify a peace ethic in England that may not have been intellectually sophisticated but did have at root a pragmatic sensibility that was appealing and in many ways quite accurate. And it can

44. Nef, "War and Economic Progress," 13–38.

45. Herman Van Der Wee, *The Growth of the Antwerp Market and the European Economy (Fourteenth–Sixteenth Centuries),* vol. 2, *Interpretation* (The Hague: Martinus Nijhoff, 1963), 183–86; David Loades, *The Mid-Tudor Crisis, 1545–1565* (New York: St. Martin's Press, 1992), 89–90.

no longer be asserted that the commons' interests were strictly parochial, as recent studies have demonstrated that a great curiosity existed about international events, especially those that impinged on government policy.[46] Put quite simply, in a more economically interdependent Western Europe, for most people, war meant bad times and peace meant good (or better) times. While we may be a bit cautious (and even cynical) about the motives of men like Cheke and Morrison when they wax eloquent on the virtues of peace, we should remember as well that through serious reflection they discerned the benefits peace offered the commonweal and would have been eager to promote its establishment even if social chaos had not been looming.

The pragmatic nature of the commonweal idea as it was employed in the mid-Tudor period received tacit encouragement from Henry's chief minister Thomas Cromwell, as well as some inconsistent support from the king himself. The 1530s were a notably peaceful period, with Cromwell conducting a cautiously defensive foreign policy.[47] During this time, he introduced a new peacetime subsidy, arguing that it would enable Henry to extend this era of peace, which even though costly, would yield greater returns than expensive wars. The first of these, in 1534, was followed by the additional grants of succeeding governments in 1543, 1545, 1552, 1555, and so forth right up until the time of the Spanish war (1581–87). According to G. R. Elton, by convincing Parliament of the need for such revenues, "it was Cromwell's point that the renewal of the common weal was the financial business of the nation."[48] Instituting this practice reveals that the value of peace had been internalized as a national good worthy of reward to a king who can keep it, convincingly replacing the older value put on conquests and winning battles. Without reading too much into its impact, we may find some evidence here of the incorporation of the peace ethic into public policy. In a letter to Sir Thomas Wyatt, ambassador at Madrid, written in 1537, Henry himself instructed his emissary to propose peace as the king's idea and to offer his royal services as a mediator. He saw "great extremity" resulting from continuing wars between the emperor and the French king, "to the disquiet and enfeebling of the whole state of Christendom, and to the great danger and peril of both their per-

46. Elton, "English National Self-Consciousness," 135.
47. Davies, "English People and War," 2.
48. G. R. Elton, "Taxation for War and Peace in Early Tudor England," in *War and Economic Development*, ed. J. M. Winter (Cambridge: Cambridge University Press, 1975), 33–45.

sons, realms, dominions and subjects." It was Henry's desire that they "desist from the following of the quarrels by such extreme and dangerous means, and to suffer the same to be finished and compounded between them by some friendly and amicable mediation."[49] There is undoubtedly a bit of the *politique* in his offer, but Henry was building on a reputation he had already found attractive when Wolsey was fashioning the two of them into the great arbiters of peace in Europe. By the late 1530s, however, Henry had much more at stake than his reputation, and by getting into the good graces of the emperor, he was surely hoping that the Habsburg resentment over the divorce and schism would begin to dissipate. He maintained in his letter to Wyatt that there were practical advantages to pursuing a peace policy, especially during those times when war had become unendurable:

> Forasmuch as having ever in our mind the great good of peace, and joining therwithal the perfect and entire love and amity which we bear to both Princes, we think none opportunity is to be passed which might serve either to the conducing of a quiet in Christendom, or to the avoiding from our so great friends and allies the dangerous extremities and uncertainties of the wars.

If the emperor will not admit the need for peace, Wyatt is to show him its advantages and "therunto lay before his eyes the manifold mischiefs and inconveniences of the war, with the uncertainty of the victory."[50]

Henry sent similar letters to Wyatt throughout the period between 1537 and 1539, at a time when Pole was still very active in his campaign for an invasion of England to bring the nation back into the Roman fold. But Pole's mission collapsed in 1539, and soon thereafter Cromwell fell from power and was executed. As the new decade approached, the king began to long for the days of his youth and his victories at Flodden and in the Battle of the Spurs. Henry's chivalric idyll appears to have been a creation all his own, and a lackluster one at that, since it depended on the fits and starts of a monarch and nobility attempting to live in two different worlds. Whatever revival there was during his reign, it was ephemeral and without much conviction. Only the Border ballads, which are not exactly mainstream English literature, popularized contemporary feats of arms. Chron-

---

49. Henry VIII, *The Letters of Henry VIII*, ed. Muriel St. Clare Byrne (London: Cassell, 1936), 181–82.

50. Ibid., 182–83.

iclers such as Hall viewed the wars of the age as administrative problems rather than noble enterprises. As has been noted, the iconography of the time reveals much the same when the portrayals of statesman Henry are compared with those of the more valiant and heroic Charles or Francis.[51]

C.S.L. Davies has attempted to reconstruct the popular perceptions of war in Henry's reign and offers this insight into why, despite possessing less affinity for war in general, the Tudors undertook them without looking back: "The defence of religion, the defence of the nation (and the two were inextricably linked) made war at the very least a regrettable necessity, a serious study for serious-minded men, and helped to heal the schism which was so apparent in the early years of Henry VIII, between honour and morality, between chivalry and practicality."[52] He concludes that nobles were less willing to play along with the king and his martial exploits as they developed new interests and became opposed to going to wars where "princes play (as they say) for balls." Quoting from that early Elizabethan connoisseur of noble attributes, Laurence Humphrey, Davies states that it was becoming acknowledged that "nobles should try to dissuade princes from unnecessary wars, yet in the end they should obey his will, 'for in the prince is composed the realm's safety,' a significantly utilitarian concept, as opposed to that of honour."[53]

If England's king and aristocracy upheld a greater respect for peace and the benefits it conveyed, why did the 1540s and 1550s turn into a period of almost totally uninterrupted war? This is a complex question. First, Tudor writers, clerics, and politicians never suggested that war could be eliminated, but to the contrary, they often found it a necessary expedient for bringing about the greater good of long-lasting peace; but as argued previously, with the peace ethic introduced and developed by humanists and early English Protestants, greater restrictions were placed on the legitimization of wars, not the least of which was opposition to any action that threatened the commonweal. Second, it must be kept in mind that the peace ethic did not stand at the apex of all virtues attended to at the time. A truly worthwhile and "just" cause for war could easily transform a diffident people into an emotional arsenal, in much the same way that modern

51. Steven Gunn, "The French Wars of Henry VIII," in *The Origins of War in Early Modern Europe,* ed. Jeremy Black (Edinburgh: John Donald, 1987), 47; Davies, "English People and War," 15–17.

52. Davies, "English People and War," 17–18.

53. Laurence Humphrey, *The Nobles, or Of Nobilitye* (London: Thomas Marshe, 1563), sigs. N3r–N4v; Davies, "English People and War," 18; cf. Contamine, "Who Was Then the Gentleman?" 212.

wars do. At the same time, however, it had become more difficult to raise widespread support for wars in England, with the benefits of peace extending across class lines in an age when costs were becoming prohibitive and financing alternatives too few and still quite primitive. Finally, there is also the defensive posture, which, in this age of mounting religious strife, permits a nation to claim that it is only protecting itself from foreign domination or perhaps even annihilation, whether it be in the form of popery, dynastic conquest, or broken treaties, by going to war. Many adherents of this philosophy, the "realists" or *politiques,* such as William Paget, disliked contemporary warfare for its indulgent dissipation of wealth and resources. They realized the need to prepare for battle but employed every means at their disposal to prevent any actual coming to arms. It is most telling that the vast majority of the English people exhibited no genuine enthusiasm for any of the nation's mid-century wars, and the Council itself appears to have felt a great deal of pressure to end these unpopular conflicts. By this time even those who acknowledged such fighting as part of the king's prerogative often argued from a "peace posture"; that is, they regarded hostilities as arising from policy failures that had degenerated into warfare, but which might actually include the righting of wrongs inflicted by an even more reprobate enemy. The debates on the subject that ensued were agonizing ones that attempted to align the dictates of conscience with the needs of state. Many polemicists and policymakers perceived the current wars as the unfortunate consequence of ministerial blunders (which were often really royal blunders) that needed to be rectified most immediately by restoring peace. In some very significant instances, the royal ministers responsible for prosecuting wars they had tried to prevent were proclaiming the need for peace — regardless of just cause — and committed to ending destructive conflicts in general.

A Return to Warfare and the Vantage of Peace in the 1540s

The wars of the 1540s and 1550s were fought in Scotland and France, each theater being inextricably linked to the other. The failure of the Scots to honor the Greenwich marriage contract between Mary of Scotland and Edward of England formed the pretext for the Scottish conflict after July

1543.[54] It was Henry's intention that the two crowns become united under English hegemony in order to deny the French and other potential invaders of England the use of Scotland as a beachhead. Raids were launched into Scotland by the duke of Norfolk in 1542 and the earl of Hertford in 1544 (including the burning of Edinburgh) in retaliation for the breached treaty, even though they served foremost as preemptive strikes intended to keep the Scots off guard while England invaded France.[55] Thus began the period known as the "rough wooing," which lasted until the peace of 1550. Turning to his other hand, in June 1542 Henry sent the bishop of Westminster to Emperor Charles to work out plans for a joint invasion of France the following year. Immediately, preparations were made and ships, weapons, and new revenues were collected. The largest army up until the time of William III was assembled in Kent — a situation that caused Becon, then in hiding, to write his treatise on war and peace.[56] Of the 48,000 troops raised, about 11,000 were German or Dutch mercenaries.[57] The percentage would steadily increase as the war progressed.

Fulfilling an important formality, Henry's Garter King of Arms, Christopher Barker, presented Francis I with a list of grievances on May 28, 1543, which expressed a "righteous indignation" over the French alliance with the Turks, the suspension of a pension agreed to in 1532, the unlawful imprisonment of English subjects, and the provocation of the emperor.[58] Francis was called on to make an alliance with Henry and Charles to drive the Infidel from Europe, for "the quiet of Christendom." In an attempt to strengthen his position, Henry published the propagandist *Statutes of War* in 1544, wherein he still claimed a legal right to the French throne, and that he went to war, "provoked by the manifold injuries committed by the French king, both in his confederation with the Turk, and by his private displeasures and wrongs done to his highness, against the commonweal of Christendom."

The English people did not seem entirely convinced that the common-

54. *LP,* 18(1), 804.
55. Millar, *Tudor Mercenaries,* 66–68; Elton, *Reform and Reformation,* 304–6; R. B. Wernham, *Before the Armada: The Growth of English Foreign Policy, 1485–1588* (New York: Norton, 1972), 154.
56. Having recently assumed the alias Theodore Basil to escape punishment for his advanced Protestantism, Becon may have written his *New Policy of War* as part of an attempt to get back into the government's good graces. Becon, *Early Works,* vii–ix, xvii; Bailey, *Thomas Becon,* 18–22.
57. Scarisbrick, *Henry VIII,* 434–35; Davies, "English People and War," 2–3.
58. *LP,* 18(1), 606, 622, 754.

weal was being threatened by external enemies. The subsidy bill for the Scottish campaign was debated in both houses of Parliament and the final version contained no usual preamble praising the king's excellent government, "instead resting the grant very coldly and precisely upon the needs of the Scottish war." While Parliament recognized the king's ancient right to the Scottish crown, enthusiasm for pressing it was noticeably absent. Attempts at installing a government sympathetic to the English there had already failed with Cardinal Beaton's (and the infant Queen Mary's) recent resumption of power.[59] As for the French campaign, no new levies were imposed the following year, since the previous subsidy was still being collected in installments. A 1542 loan, however, was remitted, justified in typical fashion — because of Francis's unholy alliance with the Turk, his "exciting Scotland to war," and a multitude of other injuries inflicted on England by him.[60]

It was an odd spectacle: a schismatic king allying with the emperor against the "Most Christian King and his ally, the infidel Turk."[61] After several delays, and an assurance that the Scots would pose no immediate trouble, Henry landed in Calais on July 14, 1544, and began the siege of Boulogne five days later. The chronicler Hall adopted what was perhaps the standard line of reasoning behind the Scottish incursions (which were used largely to screen the French campaign). He argued that the English had no choice but to invade Scotland:

> Being now enforced to the war, which we have always hitherto so much abhorred and fled, by our neighbor and nephew the king of Scots, one, who above all other, for our manifold benefits towards him, hath most just cause to love us, to honor us, and to rejoice in our quietness: We have thought good to notify unto the world his doings and behavior in the provocation of this war, and likewise the means and ways by us used to eschew and avoid it.[62]

59. A. J. Slavin, *Politics and Profit: A Study of Sir Ralph Sadler, 1507–1547* (Cambridge: The University Press, 1966), 125–31.

60. Stanford E. Lehmberg, *The Later Parliaments of Henry VIII, 1536–1547* (Cambridge: Cambridge University Press, 1977), 178–79, 189–90, 195–96.

61. *Statutes and Ordynances for the Warre* (London: Thomas Berthelet, 1544), sig. A1v; Scarisbrick, *Henry VIII*, 440; Millar, *Tudor Mercenaries*, 66–68, 97, 127.

62. Hall, *Hall's Chronicle*, 846 . For the council's even more direct linkage between the French and Scottish campaigns see Glyn Redworth, *In Defence of the Church Catholic: The Life of Stephen Gardiner* (Oxford: Basil Blackwell, 1990), 210.

If Hall could condone the Scottish war from a safe distance — by pointing out England's aversion to breaking the peace — those on the front lines in France had the right to be more ambivalent, especially since they were not fighting for ostensibly defensive reasons. The life of the English soldier on the Continent was no more endurable than it had been during the Hundred Years War. In fact, the 1544 statutes are distinguished by the degree to which they attempted to control the *jus in bello* (by invoking laws that would restrain soldiers from exercising their traditional license in war against property), but also by the national and official authorities through which they were promulgated. Nothing is to be taken or destroyed without proper authority, "upon pain to be imprisoned, and his life at the said lieutenant's will."[63] Captains were required to pay *full* wages to their soldiers as directed by the king, but the rank and file could not "play at dice, cardtables, closh, hand out, or any other game, whereby they shall waste their money, or cause debates to arise by the same, except such as shall be licensed by the king's majesty or his lieutenant, by bill assigned."[64] The penalty for those caught was one month's imprisonment and loss of one month's wages. Finally, no women could be brought into camp, and stiff punishment awaited those involved in brawls, quarrels, acts of plunder and pillage, or violence to civilians (servants, women, and children).[65] By way of contrast to the Tudor military ideal, Elis Gruffydd, the Welshman who found himself in his third French war since 1512, chronicled the actual day-to-day drudgery of war and just how closely the troops conformed to the high expectations of government directives. In his very personal and detailed account, Gruffydd lavished praise on only one soldier, Sir Thomas Poynings. The other officers were portrayed as being "more concerned with swindling the men out of their pay, and carousing on dead men's wages."[66] What follows is a virtual catalogue of military vices, including lazy seamen, immoral profit-making on victuals, gunners falling

63. *Statutes and Ordynances*, A2r. A few years earlier a similar but much briefer manual, *An Order Whych a Prince in Battayll Muste Observe, and Kepe, yf He Entende to Subdewe, or Passe thorough His Enemyes Landes* (London: Thomas Raynold and Wylliam Hall, [1540]), addressed the same issues by first cautioning the prince to make sure his cause for war is just, followed by simple directions for staging effective battles, including sieges.

64. *Statutes and Ordynances*, sigs. A3r–v, B1v.

65. Ibid., sigs. B2r–v, B3r–v, C1v–C2r.

66. Elis Gruffydd, "The 'Enterprise' of Paris and Boulogne," ed. M. Bryn Davies, in *Bulletin of the Faculty of Arts, Fouad I University*, vol. 11, pt. 1 (Cairo: Fouad I University Press, 1949), 45.

asleep, excessive drinking and cruelty, and the overall ineptitude of English soldiers, who were particularly gullible to French promises.[67]

To shore up the justification that had been offered for the war with France, and to set down additional guidelines on how to conduct it "humanely," Jacopo di Porcia's *Preceptes of Warre* were translated into English and published that same year.[68] The work begins with a traditional justification for the war, but emphasizes that peace must be the *only* legitimate objective:

> Before that thou begin to make battle, it is needful to take advisement once and again, whether the cause and beginning of thy warmaking be honest. But yet that is not a sufficient cause to give battle, except for thy purpose thou do it, to live afterward peaceable, and in quiet, not willing to sow and stir up battle after battle, the which thing is both foolish and cruel.

If the cause can be settled by any other means, the prince must forgo battle, "or else otherwise it were wicked, cruel, and rather beastly than manly, to make battle against him. . . . And so to destroy him by the sword, whom gentle words would have vanquished." In chapter 3, "Of sufferance in war," di Porcia argued that revenge, dissembling, and other "such injurious deeds" only stir up greater hatred and ill-will "that we be not able to bear their malice and force."[69] Building on this theme that war must be tactfully as well as tactically fought, in chapter 14, di Porcia declared that "a wise captain will not forsake any covenants and conditions of peace which may turn to his honor and profit, although the mastery be in his hands. Lest fortune which now appeareth gentle and favorable, hereafter show herself unkind and strange, and he that even now rejoiceth as victor, shortly after vanquished, may wail and sorrow."[70] Di Porcia incorporated into his just-war position the important humanist concepts of counsel, sufferance, and *fortuna*. A prince should always seek wise advice before entering into a war. He should be willing to suffer much before taking such a drastic step, since the harmful effects of war could easily

67. Ibid., 67–68, 70, 82, 87, 91.
68. Also known as the earl of Purlilias, this fifteenth-century Italian writer of treatises on education and war appears to have had little impact in his native land. The translator, Peter Betham, was a noted English humanist. Dibdin, *Typographical Antiquities*, 3:486.
69. Jacopo di Porcia, *The Preceptes of Warre*, trans. Peter Betham (London: Edwarde Wytchurche, 1544), sigs. B1r, B3v–B4r.
70. Ibid., sig. B7v.

outweigh the injuries that caused it. At the same time, the vicissitudes of fortune will double back on those who forsake peace by bringing eventual defeat on those who now appear to have won. Di Porcia's construction of the just war amid such considerations, and his particular emphasis on two particular aspects here, may reflect a growing appreciation for peaceful objectives among governments and their compatibility with current English attitudes. First, just or honest cause does not legitimize war if it is prosecuted with an attitude of vengeance or retribution. Since peace is to be maintained above all other conditions, a war can only be rightly fought with that end in mind. In addition, reversion to war must be a last resort, with diplomacy being the preferred method for settling disputes among nations. Treaties and covenants should be treated with utmost respect, not abrogated when one has the opportunity to gain by doing so. While this may seem an obvious position to hold, di Porcia integrated it into his overall discussion of a restrictive *jus in bello,* which encapsulates much of the intent of the entire work. Peace treaties are not just pauses in fighting so that each side can repair and regroup, but hard-fought compromises that are of lasting significance and working extensions of an emerging peace ethic that arose out of moral debates introduced by humanists into public discourse.

When Henry returned home on September 30 with the prize of Boulogne as the fruit of his efforts, he must have felt very satisfied by the results of the campaign. Yet on closer look, it had not been a brilliant success. When one calculated the amount of money and manpower expended for a victory that gave Boulogne to England for only eight years with a pension that would be hard to collect, there was really very little to celebrate.[71] In addition, there was a mounting shortage of men to serve in the garrisons at Boulogne and Calais precisely when more were required. The efficient, quick, and enthusiastic response by the people to the call to arms is one of many myths that have surrounded the Tudor army.[72] With the growing failure of Englishmen to fulfill their military obligations a new system was worked out in order to raise enough troops to serve in France. By the end of 1544, two thousand soldiers were transferred from Calais to become part of the five thousand eventually needed to garrison Boulogne that winter. Many of these men resented having to continue service after the campaigning season had ended. In a letter sent to William Paget in

71. Guy, *Tudor England,* 190–92; Barnett, *Britain and Her Army,* 15, Scarisbrick, *Henry VIII,* 448; Elton, *Reform and Reformation,* 394–95.
72. Goring, "Social Change and Military Decline," 187–88.

Calais dated October 27, the king's Privy Council spoke to this "understanding, by your letters of the 24th instructing that the 2,000 soldiers appointed to be sent to Boloyn were not very willing to go," by informing him that "the king has taken order that such things as did most annoy the soldiers at Boulogne shall be helped." Thereupon the council promised to provide more mattresses, canvasses, lathes, nails, and tilers, and so on.[73] It was at this juncture, also, that England began to experiment with a "national" system for raising additional troops more quickly (to serve in Boulogne) to exist alongside the older "quasi-feudal" method, which had provided the initial forces that went to France the previous year. As the hardships of war became more intense and insufferable in the sixteenth century (and to some less conscionable), newer means to create fresh supplies of men became necessary so that soldiers did not stay on campaigns long enough to lose all heart, sense of morality, and confidence.[74] It was no mere formality of a new regime, when in the second year of Edward's reign, a 1511 statute against unlicensed military leave and desertion was reenacted.[75]

On the Scottish front similar problems arose out of another spectacular victory. Hertford's complete rout of the Scots and the burning of Edinburgh in 1544, coming on the heels of the humiliation at Solway Moss two years earlier, left much of southern Scotland a wasteland. The campaign, however, was far from over, since the English still expected nothing less than complete surrender on the marriage issue. But, as with Boulogne, if they hoped to consolidate their gains in battle, a long-standing, expensive commitment of men and matériel would be required.[76] Those who sought to justify this enterprise went beyond the more negative, breaking-of-contracts rationale and argued also in a positive manner for the peace that would be a consequence of the marriage. In his account of Somerset's Scottish campaign William Patten witnessed

73. *LP,* 19(2), 489; Goring, "Military Obligations," 19, 264–73. In 1545 an oration supposedly given several times by Edward Walshe to his fellow soldiers in Boulogne was printed. The first part is a eulogy to fervent love for one's country as a way to thank God for the protection He provides. Walshe then proceeds to describe the overwhelming selfish preoccupations of man and the need to fight to protect righteous living. Edward Walshe, *The Office and Duety in Fightyng for Our Countrey* (London: Johannes Herford, 1545), sigs. A1r–C4v.

74. Goring, "Military Obligations," 178–287; Davies, "English People and War," 4–6.

75. Act of 3 Henry VIII, c. 5 reenacted as 2/3 Edward VI, c.2; Bush, *Government Policy,* 132.

76. Loades, *Mid-Tudor Crisis,* 94.

his Grace's godly disposition and behaviour, in the fiercest time of war, seeking nothing more than peace, neither cruel in victory, nor insolent upon good success, but with most moderate magnanimity, upon the respect of occasion, using, as the poet [Virgil] saith *Pacere subjectis et debellare superabos.*[77] In peace again, wholly bent to the advancement of GOD's glory and truth, the King's honour, and the common's quiet and wealth.[78]

So much for divine retribution and justice in a just war! The tract goes on to show how Hertford's policies were not harsh but temperate to the point of doing only what was necessary to subdue the rebellious Scots.[79] "And yet, notwithstanding all these our just causes and quarrels to kill them, we showed more grace, and took more to mercy, than the cause of our side . . . well deserve or require."[80]

Soon thereafter, just before the devastating English victory at Pinkie, Hertford, now the duke of Somerset and head of the government, wrote his own appeal to the Scots, pleading with them to make peace on English terms. It is a shrewd, cleverly argued tract that expounds exactly what Patten claimed had been Seymour's strategy in the war all along. The Protector argued from a position of strength, hoping that this would move the Scots to take advantage of England's magnanimity. Since it was obvious that English forces were superior and ultimately would be victorious, the Scots were entreated "to have us rather brothers, than enemies, rather Countrymen, than Conquerors," going "from servitude to foreign nations [i.e. France]: to liberty, to amity, to equality with us."[81] The similarities between the two nations are stressed, and that it is not England's intention to conquer, "but to have in amity, not to win by force, but to conciliate by love, not to spoil and kill, but to save and keep, not to dissever and divorce, but to join in marriage from high to low, both the realms, to make

77. "[To ordain the law of peace]: to be merciful to the conquered, and to keep the proud from waging war (or to subdue the proud)." Virgil, *Aeneid* 6.852–53.

78. William Patten, *The Expedition into Scotlande of . . . Edward, duke of Soomerset,* reprinted in *Tudor Tracts 1532–1588,* ed. A. F. Pollard (New York: Cooper Square Publishers, 1964), 57–62.

79. Ibid., 57–78, especially 79–106, 107–57.

80. Ibid., 127.

81. Edward Seymour, *An Epistle or Exhortacion, to Unitie & Peace, Sent from the Lorde Protector, & Others the Kynges Moste Honorable Counsaill of England To the Nobilitie, Gentlemen and Commons, and Al Others the Inhabitauntes of the Realme of Scotlande* (London: Richard Grafton, 1548), sigs. A2v–A3v.

one Isle one realm, in love, amity, concord, peace, and Charity."[82] Seymour blamed the Scots for the wars, which the English reduced simply to a matter of self-defense. (In a twisted sort of way he holds that since the contract made Princess Mary part of the English royal family, the English are actually protecting her!) But Somerset enjoined his northern neighbors to follow the more godly way of peace, and no matter what course is taken, since it "is to make an end of all wars, to conclude an eternal peace, we shall fight, and you to break, is it not easy to discern who hath the better part?" By the end of the treatise the duke was appealing to Scottish nationalism by promising not to "take from you your laws nor customs," but to make the queen's heirs "inheritors also to England."[83] Throughout the proclamation, he hoped that common sense would prevail, and that the Scots would weigh their position judiciously and realize that peace was the only worthwhile course of action available to them. In reading it, one gets the sense that Somerset truly wants peace on moral (as well as financial) grounds, and that he is catering to a similar sensibility among the Scots.[84] His brazen manipulation of the just-war argument testifies to its durability as a justification for military campaigns against foreign powers. But here credulity is stretched so much that even he appears to believe that only an appeal to a deep sentiment of Scottish self-preservation predicated on peace and cooperation has the slightest chance of ending this costly war.[85] It is another example of the mounting use of peace's practical advantages as an eloquent basis for ending wars and preventing future outbreaks.

In the end, however, Somerset made little impression as the Scots returned to the "auld alliance" against England in an attempt to salvage their self-respect and autonomy. The French army arrived in 1548 and spirited Mary away to marry the dauphin. As the new decade dawned, England's initial triumphs had turned into disasters. The peace with Scot-

82. Ibid., sigs. A4r–v, A5v–A7v, A8r.
83. Ibid., sigs. B2r–v, B3r.
84. Paul Crowson goes so far as to say that "Somerset had a genuine belief in Anglo-Scottish collaboration on the basis of the Treaty of Greenwich; he believed in equal partnership between the two countries and in the joint creation of a unified kingdom of Greater Britain." Paul S. Crowson, *Tudor Foreign Policy* (New York: St. Martin's Press, 1973), 169. The classical ideas of friendship and mutuality, drawn largely from Cicero and already found pertinent in earlier peace arguments, are once again used here.
85. See W. K. Jordan, *Edward VI: The Young King* (Cambridge: Harvard University Press, 1968), 252–63, for Somerset's objectives in this war and the Pinkie campaign, which followed the promulgation of this published proclamation. Cf. Bush, *Government Policy*, 12–18, for an argument that is largely accepted (though not without its faults), which finds the Protector's obsession with Scotland responsible for his foreign and domestic policy failures.

land included no marriage contract and Boulogne had already been returned to France.[86] The nature of sixteenth-century warfare, however, had tipped off many to this inevitable denouement. A much more realistic and less heroic approach to military science, along with a heightened sensitivity to the practical benefits of peace, caused some members of the government to question early on the wisdom of these wars.[87] The late Henrician wars were supervised within the Council by Stephen Gardiner, bishop of Winchester, and Sir William Paulet (later the marquis of Winchester), who helped plan logistics, especially the victualing arrangements.[88] Along with Sir William Paget, these men were probably the most informed Englishmen on all aspects of these wars. As they deliberated over policy and attempted to bring about a conclusion favorable to England, they knew that the best they could hope for were Pyrrhic victories and so wrestled with when and how England could end these wars with the least amount of loss in honor, resources, and money.

Considerations of Peace in the French and Scottish Wars (1545–1550)

There was an unusual amount of unity within the council at the start of the Scottish campaign, with Henry intentionally putting an end to the recent political manslaughter initiated by conservative forces and culminating in the failed Prebendaries Plot of 1543. The reduction of faction at court did not translate into uniform, unequivocal support for Henry's determination to invade France, and the king surely harbored no illusions that he could hope to gain enthusiastic backing. But he could control the activities to which his councillors directed their energies, and considering the renewed campaign's massive expense in soldiers and supplies, he demanded nothing less than full attention to the war effort. Council members formulated policy primarily by weighing available financial resources

86. Davies, "English People and War," 3–4; Guy, *Tudor England,* 201–3; Crowson, *Tudor Foreign Policy,* 39.

87. There is also evidence of significant popular dissatisfaction with both Edward's and Mary's wars against France, especially toward conscription. See Peter Clark, *English Provincial Society from the Reformation to the Revolution: Religion, Politics and Society in Kent, 1500–1640* (Hassocks, Eng.: Harvester Press, 1977), especially 72, 104; Elton, *Reform and Reformation,* 394–95.

88. C.S.L. Davies, "Supply Services of English Armed Forces, 1509–1550" (Ph.D. diss., Oxford University, 1963), 175, 244.

against the necessary cost of war. The equation never balanced, and the rising expenditures proved a constant source of anxiety. The privy councillors were concerned with long-term goals, and as they gave greater consideration to England's economic future and the need for better fiscal accountability, peace advocacy grew. Henry, however, squandered the wealth of the recent dissolutions for the quick money. His insistence that lead taken from the religious houses be sold in Antwerp immediately for whatever price it would fetch, despite a depressed market, was the most obvious indication that "the principle of action was always expediency."[89] The private correspondence of councillors in the 1540s reveals quite starkly that this side of Henry's management proved a constant irritant and source of frustration to those who wanted a quick end to the war. After peace was made with France in 1550, Henry's former councillors and courtiers reined in the excesses of the Privy Chamber and reorganized finances there according to the priorities of debt liquidation.[90] The road to financial reform was not so smooth. Military expenditures had necessitated the purchase of more foreign goods and additional loans, both of which affected the exchange rate adversely. As a result of these actions, and the currency debasements beginning in 1544, sterling lost much of its value during the war, even as the rates of interest on debts contracted abroad rose to "ruinously high" levels. Henry left his son an enormous financial burden that would only get worse.[91]

Different political objectives and the often related residual factional animosities carried over into how the council conducted the war. Gardiner handled the provisioning of the troops in Scotland, but Hertford and the bishop's other political enemies, Lisle and Paget, continued to vent their lingering resentment by exposing him to a barrage of constant criticism and grumbling about unmet supply needs.[92] Even this sniping came to a temporary halt when just before Henry's capture of Boulogne in September 1544, Emperor Charles began having serious reservations about the joint invasion and its prospects for lasting territorial remuneration. Right away and while still a favorite of the emperor, Winchester began his quest to maintain the Anglo-Imperial alliance. After Francis and Charles concluded

89. W. C. Richardson, "Some Financial Expedients of Henry VIII," *Economic History Review*, 2d ser., 7 (1954): 33–48.

90. Dale Hoak, "The Secret History of the Tudor Court: The King's Coffers and the King's Purse, 1542–1553," *Journal of British Studies* 26 (1987): 229.

91. Jones, *Tudor Commonwealth*, 135.

92. Redworth, *In Defence of the Church Catholic*, 210–12.

the peace of Crespy on September 18, this task became much more difficult, for by this time Henry was adamant about holding onto Boulogne while the emperor refused outright to support the claim.[93]

As peace became ever more a necessity, factions resurfaced at court and coalesced around two different peace/alliance orientations. Gardiner led the delegation that refused to give up hope for bringing the Habsburgs back into the English fold. Paget, according to his own political and religious proclivities, cast his lot with the reform element at the French court, especially Madame d'Etampes, and worked to find some compromise that would bring an honorable peace to England.[94] Winchester, along with Hertford, pressed their case before Charles in November, and after much procrastination on the emperor's part, returned home unsuccessful. French negotiator Cardinal du Bellay and Paget meanwhile had entered into negotiations at Calais, as Henry consciously kept open this other avenue of possible accommodation as long as it appeared the least bit promising. Amid the constantly shifting international scene, Paget had the formidable task of juggling the various peace options coming out of France, depending on the ascendant position at court at any particular moment. In the end, and after many months of sincere effort on both sides, he, like Gardiner before him, came back to England empty-handed on January 6, 1546.[95]

Despite the failure of this mission the possibility loomed in Charles's mind that England, France, and the German Protestants could eventually come to terms, leaving him potentially isolated and vulnerable. With the Schmalkaldic League particularly resurgent at the time, the emperor initiated once again negotiations for a renewal of the Anglo-Imperial alliance. Gardiner, its great champion, was dispatched quickly to Brussels, and there the treaty of Utrecht was concluded on January 16, 1546, reestablishing the alliance but this time without the intention of invading France.[96]

Throughout these intricate and sensitive negotiations, which impinged on princely honor and national prestige, the value of peace echoed clearly in the discourse of the protagonists. As potentialities for diplomacy grew

93. *Span. Cal.*, 7:364; *LP*, 19(1):249.

94. G. R. Elton, "Tudor Government: The Points of Contact, Part 3: The Court," *TRHS*, 5th ser., 26 (1976): 222–23, 226–27; Gunn, "The French Wars of Henry VIII," 44–47; Redworth, *In Defence of the Church Catholic*, 217–18.

95. Redworth, *In Defence of the Church Catholic*, 219–26; D. L. Potter, "Diplomacy in the Mid-Sixteenth Century: England and France, 1536–1550" (Ph.D. diss., Cambridge University, 1973), 50, 117–21.

96. *LP*, 21(1):71; D. L. Potter, "Foreign Policy in the Age of the Reformation: French Involvement in the Schmalkaldic War, 1544–1547," *Historical Journal* 20 (1977): 525–44.

concomitant with those for making war, the peace ideas were most often expressed in the developing language of political economy, which had in turn been affected by the Stoic-inspired humanists and the biblicism of the Christian reformers. Today scholars characterize Renaissance England more and more as a transitional period, noting in particular the writers of that time, who depicted the confusion, uncertainty, and liminal nature of their changing world.[97] Doubts concerning many traditional practices, institutions, and cultural norms extended beyond social displacements and problems of authority to include even conventional rationales for warfare.[98] One need only look to the correspondence of Gardiner and Paget during the height of their diplomatic machinations to find this situation illustrated. Both men seem convinced that society must move beyond wars and concentrate alternatively on the superior condition of peace. They were particularly distraught, especially Gardiner, over the petty and dubious justification for their own king's latest act of chivalric fancy and futility. By studying their personal letters we can perhaps get a more candid insight into their feelings toward the war, which they disguised somewhat in their official dispatches.

A meeting with the French on November 10, 1545, in Antwerp, during Winchester's final peacemaking mission, underscored the bishop's great exasperation over the war and his overwhelming desire for peace. With both nations in a financial bind, Gardiner pushed for peace at almost any price, even to the point of relinquishing Boulogne, which he considered a worldly prize, that if held onto would only encourage further greed and war.[99]

In a letter to Paget (who would join him at year's end) dated November 13, 1545, Gardiner lamented England's isolation in the French war and mused about whether a dishonorable peace would not be preferable to continuing along a course that must surely bring financial ruin: "Our war is noisome to all merchants that must traffic by us and pass the narrow seas as they cry out here wonderfully. Herewith we see at home a great

---

97. This approach to the period has been seized most readily by "new historicist" scholars who have rejected E.M.W. Tillyard's more unified and confident "Elizabethan world picture." See Jean Howard, "The New Historicism in Renaissance Studies," *English Literary Renaissance* 16 (1986): 3–33; also Stephen Greenblatt, *Renaissance Self-Fashioning: From More to Shakespeare* (Chicago: University of Chicago Press, 1980).

98. A. J. Slavin, "The Tudor State, Reformation, and Understanding Change: Through the Looking Glass," in *Political Thought and the Tudor Commonwealth*, 230–31.

99. J. A. Muller, *Stephen Gardiner and the Tudor Reaction* (New York: Macmillan, 1926; reprint, Octagon Books, 1970), 114–18.

appearance of lack of such things as the continuance of war necessarily requireth. And when, to put away this war, we show ourselves content to take a peace, we may have it."[100] Winchester's stress on profitable peace is indicative of the shift in peace discourse that many of his contemporaries had adopted, away from earlier platitudinous calls for restoration of good-will among peoples or the ease of conscience, to the practical advantages that would come with an end to war. Reiterating Lydgate's concern for protection of the commonweal, the bishop, however, infused his own with a more tangible quality. Gardiner worried that France would now demand too much: "Fie of such a peace as might be so displeasant. And yet in the war is misery." He concluded that the war never should have been started. For if one takes stock of the tragic situation at hand, the king was mired in a dilemma that held out two different options, neither of which was ultimately preferred.

Winchester's critique highlights a problem that was recognized in much of the mid-sixteenth-century discussion on war and peace. He posed a moral quandary that humanists and Protestants had only hesitatingly and half-heartedly resolved, that is, deciding the greater sin, continuing a cruel war or accepting the terms of a dishonorable peace. Gardiner, himself, was not at all sure about what should be done:

> Shall he [the king] take these base and unsure conditions of peace? I dare not but say, Nay; for I fear a miscontentment of the king's majesty to follow it. What mean I then? To continue in war still? . . . And yet, ye will say, either we must take such a peace as we can get or, of necessity, continue in war; for there is no third way.[101]

The amazing admission in this letter is that deep down, Gardiner acknowledged that the advantages of peace were of greater import than salvaging the king's honor (thereby tacitly rejecting the justification behind the war), even though unilateral withdrawal was not a recourse open to him. Because Henry's ego required so much stroking, the bishop actually feared for the king's mental health should a peace be concluded that did not include keeping Boulogne; but doubting that this could be accomplished, he writhed in indecision, declaring at one point: "I have written to you

100. Gardiner, *Letters*, 185–86.
101. Ibid., 186–89.

vehemently for peace, and I have noted the sentence of one that said the worst peace is better then the best war."[102] As noted earlier, Gardiner was repeating a Ciceronian dictum that had gained great currency among the peace advocates of the Renaissance, but here it acquired fresh utility from the one person most responsible for overseeing the French campaign!

There were at least thirty deeply personal and confessional letters written to Paget in November, but no evidence of reciprocity on the secretary's part. Considering the past resentment and animosity between these two councillors, Gardiner's motivation seems hard to explain — unless perhaps the two shared an affinity for peace that rested in common Christian, humanitarian, political, and even commercial interests that he felt he could count on. The bishop's most recent biographer finds in all of this a man torn among loyalties to a "warmongering monarch," the Habsburg alliance, and to "something of the humanist's ideal of peace between Christian princes."[103] These letters betray a deep desire for *concordia* among all European Christians and anticipate the reputation England might gain by leading the way; the sentiments in them are not unlike the ambitions harbored by humanists of 1518 who sought "universal peace."

Gardiner was not alone at court in holding to these opinions; almost every member of the Privy Council wanted a quick peace. The Lord Chancellor, Thomas Wriothesley, expressed a prevailing sentiment when he wrote in November: "I am at my wit's end how we shall possibly shift for three months following." The French, however, still refused all compromise, and so Gardiner drew back for the moment and left for home on November 25. With the completion of the treaty of Utrecht, the French found reason to reopen negotiations the following April, and this time finally came to terms with the bishop, much to his delight.[104]

As a postscript, it should be mentioned that Gardiner's distress over the deleterious effects of war on the realm continued into the next reign, when clearly out of favor, he expressed to Somerset the same concerns he had maintained under the old king, only this time addressing himself to the Scottish enterprise.[105]

102. Ibid., 189. Some movement by the French the next day raised Gardiner's hopes for peace once again. Sensing the dangerous sentiment inherent in the 13 November letter, in another one written to Paget the following day, he asked the recipient to burn it once it was read (p. 191).

103. Redworth, *In Defence of the Church Catholic,* 230.

104. Muller, *Stephen Gardiner,* 117–20; Crowson, *Tudor Foreign Policy,* 129.

105. In a strongly worded, antiwar, pro-peace letter to Somerset dated 28 February 1547, before his confinement, Winchester repeated Cicero's remark that any peace is preferable to

Gardiner's colleague, Paget, while perhaps not as passionate in his quest for peace, was just as critical of wars that provide no clear advantage to the nation. More of a *politique,* throughout much of his term in royal service he backed war and peace policies according to England's greatest advantage at the moment, hoping, however, to avoid war whenever possible. Of paramount importance to Paget during Henry's wars was the mounting burden of wartime subsidies on the English people. When a new parliament was scheduled to meet in January 1545 to consider new taxes (even though the last installment of the 1543 levy was not to be collected until the following year), Paget suggested that it would be better to postpone the convocation until sincere efforts had been made to raise a benevolence of £50,00–£60,000 and to secure peace through negotiation. In this way "no man shall pay, but such as may spare it, or will be contented to pay it; the common people shall not be grieved." When the new parliament, however, did meet in November of that year, supply was granted for two wars amid debasements, plague, and food shortages. With the rest of 1543's tax to be collected as well, the suffering was surely enormous.[106] In the 1545–46 negotiations Paget pursued a Protestant peace, while during Mary's reign he aligned himself with the Catholic cause. In neither case did he permit his personal religious proclivities to dictate policy decisions. His letters, in fact, demonstrate that an overriding concern for the nation's economic and political welfare had led him to believe that the prospect of peace itself had the most to offer in any case, and that this should be the active direction of government policy.[107]

As mentioned, Paget was incidentally responsible for the peace of 1546. As leader of the commission sent to negotiate in Calais he seemed as bothered by his own king's recalcitrance as by that of France. Writing to Petre, he encouraged his fellow councillor to use whatever influence he had to move Henry toward compromise, or else he might have to quit the conference in complete despair. The king at one point actually feared that Paget's insistence on an immediate peace would prevent him from seeking Henry's best advantage and so sent his minister a sharp rebuke to that effect. The royal secretary quickly replied that nothing could be further from the truth

---

the best war, and proclaimed the dire need for "quiet, tranquility, unity, and concord," especially during the new king's minority. Gardiner, *Letters,* 265–67.
    106. Lehmberg, *Later Parliaments of Henry VIII,* 200–220.
    107. Gunn, "The French Wars of Henry VIII," 44–47; Jordan, *The Young King,* 230–31; John Hayward, *The Life and Raigne of King Edward the Sixth,* ed. Barrett L. Beer (Kent, Ohio: Kent State University Press, 1993), 117–25.

but that the financial burden of the war was becoming unbearable. On May 23, once the king had sent his acceptance of the French terms, Paget "burst into a paean of joy." When it then appeared, however, that the French would balk due to a minor boundary dispute over the source of a stream, he once again wrote Petre a somber letter exclaiming that peace must be had, for "I see the honour of it and the commodities so great both they be wrought at home, at your friend's hands abroad, and at your enemies' hands also." The final treaty was signed on July 7. It is indicative that by the end of the reign, Henry had moved Paget, that "master of practices," into a position of chief adviser.[108] The councillor's political savvy extended to his use of a peace idea already an integral part of Tudor political discourse with its growing focus on strong, effective government, international status, and the economic welfare of the nation.

In the next reign the escalation of the Scottish war under Somerset found Paget once again advertising the benefits of a peace strategy. The high cost of this campaign caused the duke to summon Parliament at the end of 1548. When he had no bill prepared to submit, Paget wrote a confidential note on Christmas exhorting him to take control of a rapidly deteriorating situation. He reminded the Protector that when he came into power England was at peace with France, on friendly terms with the Holy Roman Empire, and indifferent to all other nations (except Scotland). Now there was open war with Scotland, a looming war with France, strained relations with the Holy Roman Empire, and "discord with all the rest of the World, besides dissension at home now at liberty to burst out." All of this has put the nation in dire straits: "You are in beggary, in debt, in scarcity of men to serve, in unwillingness of men to serve, in doubt to ask aid at home for your relief."[109] A subsidy was the only remedy for the moment, but Somerset cared about its effects on the commons. The bill that eventually appeared included a heavy tax on sheep, wool, and wool cloth (rather than a direct land tax). Paget feared that this attempt to relieve the people would backfire and have an adverse effect on English wool exports to the Netherlands. Any war with Charles V could lead to bankruptcy. Paget thus advised that Somerset at least keep the emperor neutral

---

108. *LP*, 21(1), 691, 763, 771, 831, 849, 855, 862, 891; S. R. Gammon, *Statesman and Schemer: William, First Lord Paget, Tudor Minister* (Hamden, Conn.: Archon Books, 1973), 103–7.

109. William Paget, "A Critique of the Protectorate: An Unpublished Letter of Sir William Paget to the Duke of Somerset," ed. Barrett L. Beer, *Huntington Library Quarterly* 34 (1971): 280–81.

and perhaps toward that end moderate his sweeping religious policy. In February 1549 the duke accepted his councillor's advice on the latter issue so as not to alienate Charles, even if there was probably no intention of returning to the Henrician church settlement.[110]

In spite of Paget's repeated warnings that the Scottish war, religious reform, and "sympathy for the poor" could lead to social unrest, Somerset lost control of the government when rising expectations spilled over into rebellion in the west country and Norfolk by the middle of the year.[111] In April 1549, Paget wrote the duke outlining "certain points to be resolved upon in Council." In this document he asserted that because of the broken marriage covenant "we have been in war with the Scots these eight years, and yet continue still [int]ending conquest of the realm upon pretence of forfeiture." Then, setting out the major question concerning the war he wondered "whether that this intent being not yet brought to pass it be most expedient to follow the same by war at this time till it be achieved or rather to devise and effectually prosecute by some honorable practice to shift of the war either utterly or at the least for a time."[112] Paget went on and made the same case for the renewed French war, whether England should continue to fight "or else devise by practice and treaty to set things between you and them in some more honorable and surer stage."[113] Yet this conflict dragged on ignominiously to the councillor's great chagrin.

With this predisposition toward peace, Paget played once again, in 1550, the role of peacemaker. After Charles V's candidate for pope was elected and Habsburg power again became ascendant, Henry II of France was prepared to come to terms with England. On January 8 he commissioned four ministers to treat with the English representatives (Paget, Petre, the earl of Bedford, and John Mason). Once more Paget took the lead in the discussions, which began on February 19. Three days later he wrote to Warwick in Boulogne, seeking advice and support for his "peace at any price" stand.[114] The basis for Paget's dissatisfaction with the war is most

110. William Paget, *The Letters of William, Lord Paget of Beaudesert, 1547–1563*, ed. Barrett L. Beer and Sybil M. Jack, C4S, vol. 13 (London: Royal Historical Society, 1974): 16/ To Somerset, February 2, 1548–59, pp. 22–25; Dale Hoak, *The King's Council in the Reign of Edward VI* (Cambridge: Cambridge University Press, 1976), 170–74.

111. Haigh, *English Reformations*, 175.

112. Paget, *Letters*: 22/Certain Points to be Resolved Upon in Council, April 17, 1549, pp. 30–31.

113. Ibid., 31.

114. Gammon, *Statesman and Schemer*, 169–72.

vividly expressed when he blamed the conflict for the economic and social evils plaguing England:

> The first, we must acknowledge (which we cannot deny) the evil condition of our estate at home; which recognizance is the first degree to amendment. The next is, to know the cause of the evil; and that is war, supposed to be, if not the only, at least one of the chiefest amongst many great. How many, how great occasions of mischief the war hath engendered to England?[115]

He went on to credit war with causing inflation (by supplying foreign armies with goods, which made them scarce at home),

> idleness among the people, . . . grudgings, devices to amend this and that, and an hundred mischiefs more; which make my heart sorry to think upon; and these be the fruits of war. Then if the disease will not be taken away, but the causes be taken away, also war (which is one chief cause) must be taken away.[116]

By arguing that the corrupting nature of war extends from personal vice to economic depression, Paget demonstrated the natural link that existed between spiritual, Christ-like peace and profitable peace which pervaded much thought on the subject by mid-century. In this case, as one disposed to realistic considerations of situations at hand, Paget believed that England should make peace and receive an indemnity, so that neither side would be dishonored. He proposed a way out of the impasse Gardiner had reached over Boulogne four years earlier. If his plan were not adopted, he feared the result would be "to lose Boulogne without any recompense, to live in war without sinews; and for lack of good opportunity, to be forced to let things at home unredressed." This is exactly what Henry did in 1523–24, when he squandered the fortune "left by the king his father marvellous wealthy, rich, and well obeyed of his subjects, in peace." By contrast, however, having been bequeathed a nation at peace with Spain, Flanders, Rome, and Germany, his son, "entered the wars to recover his right of France. But in conclusion what right get he?" He had to surrender Thérouanne and Tournai, getting nothing for the former and 600,000

---

115. To John Dudley, Earl of Warwick, February 22, 1549–50, in Strype, *Ecclesiastical Memorials,* 2(2): 439.
116. Ibid.

crowns for the latter.[117] "Thus being thus, as I take it to be (praying your Lordship to let it be looked up,) the exemple is much to move the place."[118] Drawing from rather recent historical illustration, therefore, Paget found Henry VII an exemplar of the practical value of peace and its corresponding relationship to strong government and a healthy economy and society. Finally, in another letter to Warwick, written on March 15, the royal secretary confessed that there was an honor greater than that acquired by the repute of military victory:

> For my part I doubt nothing utterly persuading to my self that peace is the first degree to it [the peace treaty]. And as for the other degrees if your lordship and the rest of my lords shall please to step, there is no doubt but you may shortly get up to the highest step, I mean the commonwealth and estate of the realm may be brought to a perfect and happy estate.[119]

The treaty was soon concluded and by March 29 he was back in London and the peace officially proclaimed.

In the end, Gardiner and Paget may have not have offered a comprehensive anatomy of what plagued the commonwealth, or fathomed the depths of ongoing economic transformation (as did their contemporary Thomas Smith), but they did possess an astute understanding of how peace could help repair the damage wrought by bad policy.[120] They employed a rhetoric that purposefully eschewed the legalisms that Henry had originally called up in his *Statutes of Warre* to justify his incursions into Scotland and France. They had little use for any scholastic arguments that neglected the overwhelming pragmatism of good government, economic solvency, and even Christian fellowship, and as such, continued to accommodate the

---

117. Ibid., 440–41.

118. Ibid. In other letters to Somerset and the Council, Paget makes similar comments on the disastrous nature of the present wars. See Paget, *Letters:* 16/To Somerset, February, 2, 1548–49; 41/To Somerset and Council, August, 28, 1549, also titled "A Discourse to the Duke of Somerset and Counsaill," pp. 24, 76–77.

119. Paget, *Letters:* 58/To Warwick, March 15, 1549–50, p. 98.

120. Even when Paget became a proponent of war, as he did in 1556–57, he seemed interested in the long-term benefits of maintaining the Spanish alliance above all else. Relatively unconcerned with nationalistic glories, he conceived of war in the further interest of lasting peace, as a means to intimidate France and Scotland, preventing future wars, and for protecting commerce with the Low Countries. Through Paget's unique insight, war could be envisioned as a means for ushering in a secure peace. See Gammon, *Statesman and Schemer,* 191–92; David M. Loades, *The Reign of Mary Tudor,* 2d ed. (London: Longman, 1991), 337–41.

idea of peace to those languages to which they now proved most conducive; and conversely, peace itself took on additional nuances of meaning
and application as conditional understandings *(paroles)* interacted with already existent and adaptive discourses *(langues)* that had been part of the
developing discussion on war and peace since the later Middle Ages.

Peace, Counsel, and Foreign Policy (1549–1559)

The struggle over the language of peace in early modern England beset
other mid-Tudor bureaucrats and politicians as well. The same thoughtful-
ness for the state of the commonwealth can be found in the advice literature written by influential advisers to both the Protector and the king. In
his *Defense,* dated September 1549, the M.P. from Lancashire, John Hales,
drew a strikingly more pointed correlation between problems of society
and of war.[121] He began by adopting the Protestant/Wycliffian argument
that the pope was responsible for the ruinous conditions that plagued the
realm, for continuing "to procure outward wars, to stir up rebellions, to
move amongst us seditions, till he hath recovered among us his primacy."
While concerned specifically with the Scottish conflict, Hales despaired
over the evils inherent in the institution of war itself, especially when contrasted with the fruits which always accompany peace: "God grant us his
grace and mollify our hearts that we may receive and follow his word.
Then no doubt he will withdraw from us these plagues and pour down on
us his benedictions and send us instead of wars and sedition, peace and
tranquility, instead of famine, and scarcity, abundance and plenty, and instead of sickness and sudden death, health and long life."[122] The four medieval understandings of peace can be detected in Hales's statement, but
profitable peace subsumes them all, for peace no matter how described is
presented as instrumental in the accomplishment of "abundance and
plenty," and "health and long life."

Another high-ranking government official of the time, William Thomas,
clerk of the Privy Council, played a role for Edward similar to that played

121. Hales's criticism of Tudor wars goes back at least to 1542, when he praised Henry's
"tender care of his subjects not wasting their lives in war but providing that they may live in
peace and quiet." *LP,* 17, App. 1:706.

122. John Hales, *Defence of John Hales* (1549), in *A Discourse of the Common Weal of
this Realm of England,* ed. Elizabeth Lamond (Cambridge: The University Press, 1929), lv,
lxvii.

by Paget for Henry. Both men were trusted implicitly by their sovereigns and seem to have developed close, personal friendships with them. As part of an embassy to demonstrate goodwill after the peace of 1550, Edward sent Thomas and the marquis of Northampton to France in May 1551 to invest Henry II with the Order of the Garter and to arrange a marriage between himself and the king's daughter Elizabeth. Impressed with his senior clerk's service and interest in long-term planning (which is evidenced through a long list of topics submitted for Edward's special attention), the king took Thomas up on his offer to expound more specifically on current pressing issues, especially in the area of foreign affairs.[123]

Two of the treatises that resulted give us insight into what he believed should be the government's policy in making peace the springboard for a more stable alliance system, which would then lessen the probability of future wars. His overall philosophy is spelled out in "What Princes Amity Is Best," which begins with a quotation from Cicero hailing friendship and charity as the most perfect gift to man from the gods, "for it maketh the prosperous things more resplendent, and adversities the more easy." However, man's nature "doth scarcely permit any perfect amity. Wherefore to treat of the politic amity that is to say the accustomable amity that may be had, it is first to be considered to what end the amity of foreign princes doth serve, and what need one prince hath of the other's amity."[124] Thomas's construction of peace policies as part of the game of politics is almost Machiavellian in its shrewd calculation and cost-benefit analysis. He has internalized the Stoic and Christian values for peace and universal concord, but, like many evangelicals of the time, found none capable of living up to the standard which Christ (or even Cicero) taught.

At the same time, however, the practical benefits of peace, which appeal to a person's (or country's) selfish nature, can provide a basis for bringing about a lasting peace. For Thomas the question was how a nation maximizes its own gain by avoiding war (now that the good of peace has already been established). His answer focused on alliances and deterrence. Achieving amity (an alliance) with a foreign power "consisteth in two points, one is giving aid to resist an enemy, and *ut sine iniuria in pace vivatur* [so as to live in peace and without injury], and the other in reliev-

---

123. E. R. Adair, "William Thomas: A Forgotten Clerk of the Privy Council," in *Tudor Studies,* ed. R. W. Seton-Watson (New York: Russell & Russell, 1924; reprint, 1970), 141–44.

124. William Thomas, *The Works of William Thomas, Clerk of the Privy Council in the Year 1549,* ed. Abraham D'Aubant (London: J. Almon, 1774), 147–48.

ing his friends' country with those commodities that it wanteth." Friendship with its nearest neighbors is especially important for England. Once alliances are struck, they must not be broken, because "being once violated, without time again cannot be recovered" and "the defiling of that amity must breed extreme displeasure in the Prince that receiveth the injury, whereof followeth the more hate of an ancient friend for the uncertain amity of a new reconciled foe."[125] The object of foreign policy, therefore, should be perpetual peace with other nations, and Thomas suggested various means for achieving alliances that would produce this state of affairs, and thereby rejected the medieval preference for tactical truces.

In specific reference to the state of peace just reached as a result of the treaty of Boulogne, Thomas applied his proposal for a stable alliance to England's own foreign policy, which he detailed in "My Private Opinion Touching Your Majesty's Outward Affairs at this Present." Referring back to the other treaties which were ultimately broken, he observed:

> And because there be infinite reasons that threaten us with war almost on every hand: therefore it is to be foreseen (as I have written in the Discourse of Princes Amity) that we fall not into such a war; as either we must be a prey to the enemy, or else throw ourselves into the lap of a dear purchased friend: the one and other being equally prejudicial unto us.[126]

Thomas then went on to offer suggestions about how to stay friendly with France, the emperor, and Scotland, while conceding that true peace is impossible when there are such divisive religious differences. But keeping the peace is not a vain hope: "Preparation doth not only discourage the enemy, but also encourage the subject; who sustaining a sudden war unlooked for, waxeth hardy."[127] By raising money to equip a possibly necessary army "your enemies shall either suffer your Majesty in peace, or at the worse have small advantage of you in war."[128]

In a work recently attributed to Thomas we can find other examples of his devotion to a rational peace policy. *An Argument, Wherin the Apparaile of Women is Both Reproved and Defended,* drawn from Livy's Fourth Decade of *Ab Urbe Condita Libri,* was composed by Thomas shortly after

125. Ibid., 148, 151–54.
126. Ibid., 180.
127. Ibid., 180–91.
128. Ibid., 193.

becoming Clerk of the Privy Council in April 1550 and published by the royal printer the following year. Although primarily concerned with the debate over the *lex oppia* enacted by the Roman Senate to restrict female extravagance after the defeat at Cannae (216 B.C.), Thomas used this episode to exposit further on the virtues of peace. Twenty years later (ca. 195 B.C.), the tribune Lucius Valerius debated the consul Cato in the Senate over whether to repeal the laws. For Valerius women should enjoy this present period of *pace et tranquillitas* as well as the men, which means the restrictions should be lifted. Women's glory is not "in magistrates, nor in priesthood, nor in triumphs, nor in arms, nor in gifts, nor in the spoils of war." If anything, Thomas was demonstrating the superior nature of women, who do not seek personal glory or stir up wars for personal gain. His association with peace and its economic benefits is clear in how he translated *nostras pacis et tranquillitatis publicae* to mean "public peace and prosperity." One recent scholar has suggested that Thomas had the 1551 English economy in mind in making this translation and was hoping, as with his position papers, to move the king toward peace and economic stability. The commonwealth idea is also present here, for Thomas pays special attention to Livy's pronouncement that private wealth is best maintained "for as long as we preserve the estate of our commonwealth."[129] One of the most celebrated of the *Inglesi italianati*, Thomas led an adventurous life that culminated in his execution during Mary's reign. More than his near contemporaries, such as Starkey, More, Morison, or Elyot, he believed that educated gentleman had a duty to be actively involved in government and in promoting higher national purposes. His practical approach to ensuring peace, which was predicated on the abandonment of shortsighted aggrandizements in the greater interest of the nation's long-term welfare set a benchmark in educated opinion on war and peace in early modern England.[130]

Thomas's conclusion that strong alliances and defenses do most in preserving peace is built on a steadfast belief in the ability of Tudor government to fashion a workable policy of peace that looked beyond immediate

---

129. "Res publica incolumis et privatas res facile salvas praestat; publica prodendo tua nequiquam serves." Livy, *Ab urbe condita* Fourth Decade 26.36.9.

130. Ibid., 34.7.2; Livy, *An Argument, Wherin the Apparaile of Women is Both Reproued and Defended,* [ed. and trans. William Thomas] (London: Thomas Berthelet, 1551), sigs. C7v, D2v; A. J. Carlson, "*Mundus Muliebris:* The World of Women Reviled and Defended ca. 195 B.C. and 1551 A.D. and Other Things. . . . ," *Sixteenth Century Journal* 24 (1993): 541–60.

slights to honor and expectations for heroism and glory. By the middle of
the sixteenth century war had become too expensive and wasteful for English governments to maintain for any extended amount of time. The
higher standards of conduct demanded of both crown and nobility, and
their own growing sense of the responsibilities needed to meet those standards, left many members to conclude that war was in essence an unproductive activity. The classical ideal of effective government office together with New Testament personal ethics enjoined princes to consider
higher moral imperatives (as the political nation was still viewed as essentially the personal domain of royal activity) when establishing all policies.
In the mid-Tudor wars of the 1540s, even more than the Hundred Years
War, the religious and intellectual currents were transforming and being
transformed by the economic and political realities that also took seriously
the ethic of peace. The discourse that became the vehicle for fashioning
this ethic demonstrates in this case both the autonomy of language and its
direct association with historical change.

This developing congruence in peace discourse between rhetoric and
policy can be seen clearly in the shifting language of war and peace found
in the proclamations of the mid-Tudor period. As we have already seen,
the announcements of treaties and peaces in the reign of Henry VII were
mostly legalistic and contractual in nature. Hostilities came to an end in
order to reestablish trade, or to return captured goods, and so on. Very
little was expressed about the nature of peace beyond those contexts which
conceived of it as a matter between two monarchs. By the time of his son,
such proclamations included brief paeans to the value of peace for the two
former adversaries, but there remained a certain tentativeness that suggests
these agreements were thought of as tactical maneuverings and temporary
truces rather than actual settlements meant to last.[131]

By the 1540s, however, a noticeable moralistic tone had appeared in
these proclamations, that expected, at least in theory, peace to be perpetual
and guarded as the most Christian and sensible way to live. The declaration of war against France in 1543 is predicated on Francis's alliance with

131. See *TRP*, vol. 1, especially, no. 79, "Peace Treaty with France," April 16, 1515; no.
105, "Peace with France," June 17, 1528; and no. 126 "Announcing Peace with the Emperor.
Only no. 105, "Announcing the Peace Treaty with France," September 6, 1525, includes a
more expanded introduction extolling the fruits of peace, perhaps because it was written by
Thomas More: "The King our sovereign lord, by the great and deliberate advice of his council, having always most tender remorse and regard unto the restfulness and tranquility of
Christendom, and namely to the weal, quiet, and increase of this his realm and his loving
subjects of the same," moved his ambassador to "pursue and labor for peace," so as to bring
about "a good . . . and amity."

the Turk, which caused "the peril and danger of the state of Christian religion and imminent destruction of the universal weal and quiet of Christendom." It went on to argue that Christian peace can be legitimately disrupted only when a Christian prince sides with heathens and threatens true religion. Francis is especially faulted for "refusing to receive their [English] heralds which were sent to him to offer honorable and reasonable conditions of peace."[132] This objective of restoring and keeping the peace is even more pronounced in the proclamations ending wars. The preface to the announcement of peace with France in 1546 (Treaty of Camp), testifies to the ostensible importance being attached to treaties:

> The King our sovereign lord, having always before his most gracious eyes the manifold benefits and commodities of peace, and considering how necessary it is at this time not only for his grace's own realms and dominions, but also for the whole state of Christendom, that Christian princes should agree and join in perfect love, concord and amity together, whereby they shall first please God, and be the more able to maintain their estates, and also procure great wealth and quietness to their subjects . . . hath . . . concluded, and agreed [to] a good, perfect, sincere, firm, assured and perpetual amity, peace, intelligence, confederation, union and amity, to remain and continue forever between his most excellent majesty and his heirs and successors on the one part, and the said right and mighty prince the French king on the other part . . . Peace it is provided and ordained, that from henceforth all hostility and war shall cease on either part.[133]

Upon consideration of this extended rationale for peace, the marriage between ethic and official policy seems almost complete, even natural. Of course, a new war did break out soon thereafter, but the language here indicates an appeal to maintaining peace as the primary good and duty of a prince. The moral arguments are lodged right alongside the practical ones that emphasize the "great wealth" to be had by heeding the treaty. An attempt is even made to make it binding upon each king's descendants,[134] demonstrating the good of peace itself, removed from strictly tactical con-

132. Ibid, no. 220, "Declaring War against France," August 2, 1543.
133. Ibid., no. 268, "Announcing the Peace Treaty with France," June 11, 1546.
134. M. L. Bush discusses a similar move attempted by Somerset and Paget when they tried to get Charles V to mirror English procedure, and make the peace with England binding on his descendants through the use of statute. Bush, *Government Policy*, 143.

siderations which in the past had associated peace with intervals in war
when nations could regroup, rearm, and overcome the complaints of war-
weary soldiers or people. The language of this proclamation is essentially
the same as that used in others issued during the following reign, including
another one announcing peace with France, only this time embracing Scotland and the Holy Roman Empire as well.[135]

The joy the Treaty of Boulogne (1550) brought to officialdom seems to
have extended to the rest of the nation. Once the proclamation was made
in London, "for a perpetual peace between the king's majesty and the
French king, their heirs and successors forever," celebrations broke out
everywhere. Wriothesley recounted that "this night were bonfires made
in every parish within the City of London, and drinkings by my Lord
Mayor's and the Council's commandment, for joy of the said peace." On
March 30 a Palm Sunday sermon "to give laud to God for the peace" was
followed by a great festival at court ending in a bonfire at Whitehall court
with "heralds or arms and trumpets."[136] The remainder of Edward's reign
remained relatively peaceful, and Northumberland turned his attention
largely to domestic affairs, most notably the currency problems and the
succession. In a speech given before the council on December 28, 1552, the
duke faulted his predecessor for England's being "plunged into wars" and
running up exorbitant debts that only further sales of crown lands could
alleviate.[137] By the time of Mary I's accession, there was little prospect of
war and even less desire to become engaged in one. But the situation,
despite major efforts to the contrary, could not be maintained. The war
that cost England its final foothold on the Continent also forced it to deal
with its inadequate military organization and left the Elizabethans more
equipped to employ deterrence as a major weapon against future wars and
for preserving the peace.

The Marian government was dragged reluctantly into the 1557–59 war
against France. The queen's marriage treaty with Philip included the
clause: "The Realm of England by occasion of this matrimony, shall not
directly or indirectly be entangled with the war that is" between Charles V

135. *TRP,* vol. 1, no. 354, "Announcing the Peace Treaty with France," March 28, 1550.
In no. 291, "Ordering Release of French Prisoners and Prizes," October 26, 1547, there is the
actual admission that neither nation has kept to the previous treaty by seizing prizes on the
sea "to the prejudice of peace and contrary to the form and tenor the treaty last made."

136. Charles Wriothesley, *A Chronicle of England During the Reigns of the Tudors,* ed.
William Douglas Hamilton, vol. 2, Camden Soc., n.s., no. 20 (London: J. B. Nichols & Sons,
1877), 35.

137. PRO, 10/15, no. 73; *SP Dom., Edw. VI:* 789.

and Henry II.[138] England had actually worked to keep peace between the two rulers, but failed. The two-year truce at Vaucelles was broken by Pope Paul IV in February 1556 soon after the emperor abdicated. The war essentially began over papal designs to expel Spain from Naples. Philip's invasion of the Papal States provoked the intervention of Henry, and before long the Habsburg-Valois rivalry had once again become violent. There was absolutely no reason for English involvement, but with the queen married to the Spanish king, pressure was immediately put on the Council in March 1557 to lend aid. Initially these requests were met with hostility, with members citing famine (inability to feed troops), lack of funds, threat of sedition, and the marriage treaty provision as reasons for remaining neutral. They slowly began to change their minds, especially after harvests improved and it became clear that Henry II was protecting and encouraging rebels, like Thomas Stafford, who wanted to overthrow the queen. War was finally declared on June 7, 1557.[139]

The conflict brought an initial flurry of excitement, as some among the nobility saw a chance to find favor with the still relatively new regime. Even Paget, a supporter of the imperial alliance, did not express the open hostility he had exhibited during the Edwardian wars. Yet the French invasion of Scotland, along with the all-too-easy loss of Calais, rekindled English dissatisfaction with the war and the miseries that followed in its wake. The commoners may have been against it from the start. New taxes demanded of Parliament in 1555 were hotly contested. The forced loan was reminiscent of the Amicable Grant debacle and was given nearly the same reception. The people might have also "voted against the war by staying away from the mass."[140] The continued impoverishment of the parish clergy during these years meant that there were probably rifts still within that estate over raising funds for the war.[141] The Council had no desire to launch a new expedition to recapture the coastal fortress, despite Philip's badgering and desperate efforts. A growing mistrust toward the Spaniard's overall designs in England was also coming to the fore. The 20,000 soldiers required would not be raised easily, and English troops

138. *Span. Cal.* 11:347; C.S.L. Davies, "England and the French War, 1557–9," in *The Mid-Tudor Polity, c. 1540–1560*, ed. Jennifer Loach and Robert Tittler (Totowa, N.J.: Rowman & Littlefield, 1980), 159–60.
139. Ibid., 159–61; Loades, *Mid-Tudor Crisis*, 66–67.
140. Haigh, *English Reformations*, 226; Elton, *Reform and Reformation*, 394–95.
141. Michael L. Zell, "Economic Problems of the Parochial Clergy in the Sixteenth Century," in *Princes and Paupers in the English Church, 1500–1800*, ed. Rosemary O'Day and Felicity Heal (Leicester, Eng.: Leicester University Press, 1981), 19–43.

had had their fill of French winters. Other excuses were also put forth by county authorities. Harvests had taken a turn for the worse, and a "sweating sickness" had broken out in 1558 as a result. Peace negotiations began in May as the war had reached a stalemate, and all parties were concerned about the costs involved in its continuation.[142]

The eventual outcome of this latest confrontation with France, and its socioeconomic injury to the commonwealth, had been foreseen several years earlier. In his final attempt to bring peace to Europe, Stephen Gardiner, or a member of his circle, completed a treatise of political theory, *Ragionanmento dell'advenimento delli inglesi et normanni in Britannia,* soon before his death in November 1555.[143] Employing a strategy for peace at variance with Thomas's advice for finding and maintaining strong allies, the author here warned the government about potential dangers in becoming entangled in a Habsburg alliance. In the form of a dialogue between Stephano and Alphonso (perhaps representing Gardiner and a Spaniard respectively) at the English court, the work discusses numerous affairs of state, mostly within the context of international war and peace. Unlike Paget, Gardiner, now chancellor, had opposed the Spanish marriage at first, seeing its capacity for dragging England into the Habsburg-Valois conflict. He led the opposition to England's entry in Mary's third parliament. He was also largely responsible for including the antiwar provision in the marriage contract itself, much to Philip's chagrin.[144]

Throughout the treatise, the writer made it clear that his hatred of war and its effect on the commonwealth had remained unaltered since the latter days of Henry VIII. He sarcastically acknowledged just wars, believing those fought "because of necessity" by a prince's command stood to bring "honor and profit" to him alone: "But the suffering which comes from a famine, plague or from a war in which people are driven from their land touches everyone, and thus you can see that wars made among princes do not come of necessity, but rather from the ambition of the prince who

142. Davies, "England and the French War," 161–81.
143. [Stephen Gardiner], *A Machiavellian Treatise,* ed. and intro. Peter Samuel Donaldson (Cambridge: Cambridge University Press, 1975), 2–4, 14, 26–29. There is some debate over whether Gardiner actually wrote the *Ragionamento.* Perhaps if Gardiner's hatred for wars were fully appreciated this work would not seem so unusual. It is doubtful a treatise attributed to Gardiner, but not authored by him, would have been presented to Philip when he simply could have checked its provenance. Basing authorship on speculations about Gardiner's competency in Italian is tricky, especially since he could have received help to compensate for any shortcomings. Redworth leans toward the work's translator, George Rainsford, a Gardiner intimate, as the writer. For the two sides of the issue see Redworth, *In Defence of the Church Catholic,* xi, 308, and Donaldson's introduction.
144. [Gardiner], *Machiavellian Treatise,* 2–4, 14, 26–29.

wishes to increase his empire or gain fame for himself like Alexander and Julius Caesar."[145] Stephano goes on at some length to decry all sorts of wars. The author must have been very familiar with Machiavelli's writings at the time, especially *The Prince*. He alluded to Machiavellian precepts throughout, but often gives them a new twist or meaning. For example, when Alphonso praises "those princes who value military matters," he and Stephano exhort them to "wage limited wars to secure lasting peace," rejecting military training for the commoners, and supporting instead the hiring of mercenaries. Wars corrupt humans, giving them violent natures that lead to thieving and other criminal behavior. And while it is sometimes necessary for the prince to appear cruel, in order to maintain order and peace, "mercy ought in any case to vanquish cruelty, otherwise the prince will not resemble God, of whom his is the living image." He "should prefer to reign rather in the hearts of men than in fortresses of stone."[146] In the final discussion of good government, Stephano calls upon Philip to usher in an age of peace throughout Europe,

> and the Christian people, after such long and cruel wars, would enjoy the precious and inestimable joy of peace so much desired and longed for by everyone. Peace, called the daughter of God, nurse of nature, conservatrix of the human race, sower of virtue, and mother of abundance. No voice is more pleasing to men's ears than the name of peace, nor is there anything which is desired more, or which is enjoyed with such delight, because there is no happiness or content in any heart where there is no peace. Therefore he who takes peace from men takes the sun from the world and life from the creature.

Philip, that "most merciful father" will "maintain his subjects in peace" because of his "love and great zeal for the common good and Christian benefit." Alphonso concurs, proclaiming that God has blessed the marriage and given Philip the "authority and power . . . for the peace and tranquility of Christendom."[147]

In this remarkable work, Gardiner, or one of his associates, has taken the severely practical manual of his Florentine predecessor and fashioned a whole new identity for a strong prince. As we have already seen with William Thomas, the *Inglesi italianati,* among whom we might possibly now

145. Ibid., 114–15, fols. 32r–33r.
146. Ibid., 118–19, 142–45; fols. 43r–47v, 115r–122r.
147. Ibid., 150–51; fols. 138v, 139r–140v.

include Gardiner, applied their humanist learning in various ways and for different purposes. Unlike Machiavelli, the writer did not envision a conquering military hero who would unify the nation and expel the foreigner, but rather a powerful king committed to world peace and the welfare of the commonwealth. Each man viewed his world in starkly realistic ways, and similar personal characteristics might be exhibited by both princes; but the ends which could justify various means were also in sharp contrast. The Englishman rejected war based on his commitment to the greater good of the commonweal, believing it to be the cause of Florence's many troubles, including those of the city's most famous political theorist.

The Peace of Câteau-Cambrésis (1559) made England's loss of all Continental territory official; yet as early as January 1558, Parliament began discussing the pressing need to modernize both army and defenses so that the nation could brace itself against future attacks.[148] The Militia Act (1558) resulted, and from that point on a national system of recruitment finally took precedence over the quasi-feudal pattern of old.[149] In large measure, the institutionalization of a new peace ethic had required a greater efficiency in war, again, the major reason being deterrence. By 1560 the limited *jus ad bellum* had made going to war less glorious and profitable; however, there remained an uneasiness over the times when war did break out and over the too few constraints that existed to prevent great cruelty and bloodshed. By improving the army and making it more efficient and disciplined, Tudor officials were attempting to address this problem, among many others. There was hope that wars could be ended and peace reestablished more quickly. The nation still felt uneasy with the idea of standing armies, and this issue would continue to plague the government for two more centuries.

Conclusion

The mid-Tudor period witnessed a significant outpouring of discourse that secured a lasting, if not unilateral, place for practical peace in overall considerations and arguments relating to war. This consolidation of a new

148. Davies, "England and the French War," 182–83.
149. Goring, "Social Change and Military Decline," 196–97; see also Goring, "Military Obligations," for a comprehensive study of the events and processes that led up to the reform of 1558.

peace position within the highest ranks of government grew out of complex social and economic changes that were overtaking England in the 1540s and 1550s. Some of these changes were the product of long-term shifts in cultural attitudes and roles, such as the expanded range of occupational alternatives for a more educated and recently endowed elite. The effects of both the Reformation, with the government appropriating and redistributing ecclesiastical properties, and the Renaissance, with its emphasis on practical and useful counsel to princes, reached their culmination during the later years of Henry VIII's monarchy and continued into the reigns of Edward VI, Mary I, and Elizabeth. The Reformation also provided a chance for many to rethink and determine afresh the morality of particular institutions and practices, including warfare. The more open discussion of a wide range of issues between 1547 and 1553 encouraged reconceptualization and innovative approaches to reform.

While there is danger in seeking coherence or consistency in social and political thought,[150] we can find certain trends that characterize attitudes toward peace during this period. Almost all writers, in a multitude of contexts, gave attention to the economic welfare of the English people as a basis for promoting peace at home and abroad. As we have seen, the commonwealth idiom had been uniquely powerful in England since at least the fifteenth century, perhaps even earlier.[151] By the middle of the following century, the potential for violent disruption based on religious and dynastic divisions had grown tremendously. The effects of war on England were far-reaching. The Valois-Habsburg feud constantly threatened the flow of trade and the security of the Antwerp staple. Since the later Middle Ages and the intracontinental expansion of commerce, wars had contributed to embargoes, piracy, domestic unrest, increased taxation, debasements of the coinage, contraction of trade, and shortages of goods. As technology developed and expenses multiplied, the depth of misery and national poverty grew concomitantly.[152] And while defense needs made armed conflict necessary at times, most English people seemed to hope that limited engage-

---

150. Skinner, "Meaning and Understanding," 3–53.

151. David Starkey, "Which Age of Reform?" in *Revolution Reassessed: Revisions in the History of Tudor Government and Administration*, ed. Christopher Coleman and David Starkey (Oxford: Clarendon Press, 1986), 13–27. For rebuttals, see also G. R. Elton, "A New Age of Reform?" *Historical Journal* 30 (1987): 709–16, and Ben Lowe, "War and the Commonwealth in Mid-Tudor England," *Sixteenth Century Journal* 21 (1990): 171–91.

152. John H. Munro, "Patterns of Trade, Money, and Credit," in *Handbook of European History, 1400–1600: Late Middle Ages, Renaissance, and Reformation*, ed. Thomas A. Brady, Jr., Heiko A. Oberman, and James D. Tracy (Leiden: E. J. Brill, 1994), 1:154–55.

ments would achieve the desired level of security. The inability to pacify
Scotland, for example, would leave England's northern border vulnerable
to foreign, especially French, invasion. At the same time Parliament was
finding it increasingly difficult to exact taxes from citizens who saw little if
any benefit from overseas wars, which, of course, raised the constant specter of rebellion at home. Members of the royal council and their agents
took note of the uprisings over the Amicable Grant of 1525 and considered it an omen for the future.[153] All of these situations threatened the
tranquillitas ordinis of the nation, but for the many who advocated justice
and prosperity for the commons, such concerns had to do not just with
the exercise of political control, but also with the ability of the people to
have enough to eat and drink and a viable livelihood to pursue. The commonwealth, as body politic by this time, linked fully the twin notions of
English nationalism under a strong monarchy with social obligations by
the state to its people and by the people toward one another.

Both the domestic and foreign policies of Thomas Cromwell in the
1530s signaled the conjunction of these two aspects of commonwealth.
Although initially the consequence of Henry's need for a divorce, the chief
minister's ability to infuse support for the royal supremacy with national
sentiment laid the basis for an attack on wars that might jeopardize England's independence.[154] Henry's return to warfare in the 1540s, when the
religious threats had subsided, provoked an outburst of negative opinion
against his obsolete claims. The Cromwellian approach had sprouted
roots. Not only were these wars vilified on just-war grounds, even by
someone as loyal as Stephen Gardiner, but they were detested even more
for the toll they took on the nation at home. By Edward's and Mary's
reigns, all practical benefits of the wars with France and Scotland had
proved elusive and been unconvincingly argued. Men who would not hesitate to support a war against a genuine threat to England's security, such
as William Paget, now interpreted national security not so much in resolv-
ing conflicting dynastic claims, as in protecting the livelihoods of the English people of all social classes. Some, such as John Hales and William
Thomas, went so far as to challenge the concept of war itself, seeing it as
naturally inimical to the health of the commonwealth.

153. Jennifer Loach, *Parliament under the Tudors* (Oxford: Oxford University Press,
1991), 12–13, 88–89.
154. G. R. Elton, *Policy and Police: The Enforcement of the Reformation in the Age of
Thomas Cromwell* (Cambridge: Cambridge University Press, 1972), 83–262.

Sixteenth-century writers on the effects of war, then, were much more interested than ever before in the preferable alternative of peace. As war came to be seen as the unavoidable result of sin, peace became a countervailing ethic that was pragmatized by Protestants who still took seriously Christ's command to be peacemakers. In the 1540s and 1550s, the humanist ethic, which was still intellectually vital, became coupled more with English Protestant (as loosely defined) "commonwealth" reform ideas, and in the end, generated a discourse that demanded peace be part of any plans to restore and revitalize society.[155] Or to put it another way, pragmatic and economic concerns came to dominate the decisions regarding war and peace, but the concepts inherent in the expanded language of peace provided the categories of analysis and argument. As this chapter has shown, men in important decision-making roles incorporated a commonwealth rationale into their determinations of whether or not a war was just. If dearth and depression were likely, the king's capacity for determining just wars might be seriously questioned. In addition, military campaigns — from the activities and provisioning of soldiers to the justice of cause and economic impacts — were scrutinized meticulously and assessed according to their potential for bringing a satisfactory peace in a way unknown during the Hundred Years War. The military elites that fought and stood to gain from war were greatly reduced in number, and their martial spirit did much to alienate them from the rest of society, causing a precipitous decline in respect for the military profession.[156]

The persistent cries for peace, even among those responsible for directing wars, may help explain England's reluctance to engage in the violent "religious" conflicts that plagued the Continent between 1540 and 1650. The general support of all estates for peace, from monarch and nobility to clergy and commons, contrasts with the violent regularities of semiautonomous noble faction and political instability that affected France, the Holy Roman Empire, Italy, the Low Countries, and even Spain during these years. Only when the body politic was being undermined toward the end of the period by perceived usurpations of rights that led to unnecessary wars and economic hardships, did English people take up arms, though reluctantly and with renewed hostility toward armies and their po-

155. Hattaway, "Blood Is Their Argument," 84; Marx, "Shakespeare's Pacifism," 49–55.
156. A number of recent studies support this conclusion, including Goring, "Social Change and Military Decline," 185–97; Hattaway, "Blood Is Their Argument," 84; Lowe, "Role of Peace," 3–14; Schwoerer, No Standing Armies, 8–18.

tential for harm.[157] In summary, England's need for peace had entered into its political culture by the 1550s and would never be completely expunged in the centuries that followed. Peace promised what was most desired by the people, and in continuing to put those benefits before their fellow citizens, producers of culture helped expand and enliven in a significant way, the national debate on war and peace. But as the Elizabethan era dawned, this respect for peace had become so great among both those who wanted to create a renewed respect for the military profession and those who believed a nation's greatness was founded on constructive, peaceful ventures rather than in commonwealth-destroying feats of arms that the arena of debate moved further toward circumscribing the *jus in bello*.

157. Underdown, *Revel, Riot and Rebellion*, 220–22; Schwoerer, *No Standing Armies*, 51–94.

Conclusion

The Elizabethan Age and Beyond

In this book I have attempted to trace clearly the emergence of an English peace discourse based on a Christian and humanistic ethic that supplemented and sometimes challenged traditional just-war theories by the middle of the sixteenth century. A deliberative and uneasy dichotomy that contrasted the benefits of peace on the one hand and the advantages of war on the other became an integral component of foreign policymaking by the 1540s; and while this in itself is remarkable enough, it indicates not only a significant shift in the conceptual framework of peace but also in its practicalities, especially as understood by members of the government. The emphasis on peace could also allow the subsidiary concerns for maintaining it to be sounded out and acted upon as well. Reforming the military, as has been shown, is but one way in which antipathy toward the incidents of war could be mollified in some part through more efficient organization. Perhaps of greater significance were the variety of means being employed to prevent wars by the last quarter of the sixteenth century. Along with renewed attention being given to diplomacy we find a solid body of teaching on peace and a growing number of government and military professionals arguing from a peace posture and offering hence the first comprehensive explications of the doctrine of deterrence.

Because the Elizabethan age embodied so fully the multifarious virtues connected with a peace stance, this postscript cannot offer the breadth and analysis that would most surely require a significant monograph. Yet we could not leave this subject without opening at least a small window onto the years that followed the mid-Tudor institutionalization of a peace ethic.

The Elizabethan Military Context

With a few exceptions there seems to be a general presentiment among historians of the Elizabethan military that the queen was at heart a woman of peace.[1] Her government, however, possessed a great variety of opinions and inclinations. While perhaps an overly simplistic view of the situation, it is still largely correct to identify prowar and antiwar factions at court. William Cecil (Lord Burghley), as leader of the latter, seems to have had the queen's ear most often on these matters, although at times she heeded the opposing counsel of Francis Walsingham and Robert Dudley, the earl of Leicester, who tended to believe that military vigilance was necessary to protect Protestantism. The Secretary, however, more *politique* than the rest, resisted alliances with great powers and realized the dangers of entrusting English aspirations against Spain, to any nation, including France.[2] He found dynastic wars barbaric and strikingly unproductive for the most part and verged on real skepticism for the institution of warfare as a whole. In a book of "precepts" written as counsel for his son Robert on various matters, Burghley offered this biting and sarcastic advice on the subject of educating children:

> Neither by mine advice shall you train them [sons] up to wars: for
> he that sets up his rest to live by that profession, in mine opinion,
> can hardly be an honest man, or a good Christian: for *every war of
> itself, the good cause make it lawful*: besides, it is a science no
> longer in request than use: for soldiers in peace, are like chimneys in
> summer, like dogs past hunting, or women when their beauty is

---

1. All of the following authors make some statement to this effect: Cruickshank, *Elizabeth's Army*, 16; Lindsay Boynton, *The Elizabethan Militia, 1558–1638* (London: Routledge & Kegan Paul, 1967), 4; R. B. Wernham, "Queen Elizabeth and the Portugal Expedition of 1589," *English Historical Review* 66 (1951): 218; Paul A. Jorgensen, "Theoretical Views of War in Elizabethan England," *Journal of the History of Ideas* 15 (1952): 470.
2. Jorgensen, "Theoretical Views of War," 470–71.

done. As a person of quality once noted to the like effect, in these verses following:

> Friends, Soldiers, Women in their prime,
> Are like to Dogs in hunting time:
> Occasion, Wars, and Beauty gone,
> Friends, Soldiers, Women here are none.[3]

In these few lines Cecil has identified those contemporary complaints which most damaged the age-old supports for military enterprises: the perceived anachronistic nature of warfare in a posthumanist world, the doubts regarding just wars, the incongruity between war and true Christianity, and the corruption of the military profession itself. Each of these concerns is dealt with in greater depth during this period by literate men from all walks of life, many professing a passion identified more with ethical concerns than with strictly pragmatic ones, much like peace activists today.

One of the ways that Elizabeth endeared herself to her people was in her great reluctance to go to war. In an unpublished chronicle of the Tudor years, probably written before the uprising of 1569, an anonymous author praised those monarchs who were most disposed toward peace. Elizabeth is singled out for special accolade, for after she became queen, there was a noticeable absence "of foreign wars of all sorts, invasion, repulsion of invasion open or declared, covert or underhand, by sea, by land, Scottish, French, Spanish."[4] The writer concluded that this policy had given England prominence in world affairs and allowed its people a high quality of life.[5] Unlike her father, half-brother, and half-sister, she was not criticized for demanding burdensome subsidies in order to prosecute foreign campaigns. During those few times when she did need to raise such revenues, one recent historian has concluded that "the government's main struggle, however, was not with the French, or the Spaniards, or the rebels who occupied Ireland. It was against its own citizens, whose enthusiasm for military service, never great, diminished in direct proportion to the demands made on them."[6]

Early modern society still endorsed Seneca's warning that indulgent

---

3. William Cecil, *Certaine Preceptes, or Directions for the Well Ordering and Carriage of a Mans Life* (Edinburgh: Andro Hart, 1618), 10–11.
4. Harley MS 532, fol. 46r–v.
5. Ibid., fol. 47r.
6. Cruickshank, *Elizabeth's Army*, 16. See also Boynton, *Elizabethan Militia*, 4, 88–89.

peaces might leave a nation militarily vulnerable to "the weakening effects of luxury and idleness." There also existed the common syllogism that depicted war and peace as turns in a perpetual and inescapable cycle to which all people need be resigned. But many Elizabethans challenged this hardened, deterministic outlook, and their humanist sensibilities denied such inevitability.[7] A healthy, productive, and active peace could be preserved, and there were many in the later sixteenth century who designed and advocated policies supporting this conviction.[8] But for others there was something wonderfully organic and healthy about the war/peace cycle. Historians and other scholars of Elizabethan political culture have sometimes bifurcated the range of opinion on war and peace among the intelligentsia by placing leading figures who commented on the subject into one of two diametrically opposed groups: those, on the one hand, who assert that "the theologians, the preachers, the authors of manuals of conduct and education, the merchants, the seamen, and so on" were tolerant or supportive of a long peace, while "most of the popular dramatists, the military-minded gentry and nobility, and a good part of the court" believed otherwise;[9] and those, on the other hand, who oppose this particular differentiation, preferring instead to accentuate the generational divide between the younger courtiers (coming of age after 1585), who were more interested in honor through martial exploits, and the older generation that had been responsible for creating the initial splendor of Elizabeth's reign by maintaining peace.[10] Both categorizations can be legitimately challenged, since other historians have been able to find in the proto-Puritan rhetoric among late Elizabethan and Jacobean divines a strong militancy that embraces the holy war, and one has deemed the earl of Essex's *Apolo-*

---

7. The strongest statement against the cyclical theory came from Thomas Fenne, who claimed it to be a sophistical argument because man is master of his own destiny: "War is not so incident to man, but that by wisdom it may easily be prevented." Drawing on Erasmus's "Dulce bellum inexpertis," Fenne is a notable example of the continuity of humanist idealism, though now in more mature form, prevalent in Elizabethan England. Thomas Fenne, *Fennes Frutes: Which Worke is Divided into Three Severall Parts . . . The Second, Intreateth of the Lamentable Ruines Which Attend on Warre: Also, What Politique Strategemes Have Been Used in Times Past: Necessarie for These Our Dangerous Daies* (London: Richard Oliffe, 1590), passim, especially, 53v–55v, 69r, 78r–v.

8. G. R. Waggoner, "An Elizabethan Attitude toward Peace and War," *Philological Quarterly* 33 (1954): 33; Jorgensen, "Theoretical Views of War," 476–78.

9. Waggoner, "Elizabethan Attitude toward Peace and War," 33.

10. Anthony Esler, *The Aspiring Mind of the Elizabethan Younger Generation* (Durham, N.C.: Duke University Press, 1966), 99–105; Wernham, "Queen Elizabeth and the Portugal Expedition," 218; McCoy, *Rites of Knighthood.*

gie (1603) the only "far-sighted" and truly "theoretical" argument in favor of a peace policy.[11]

The inconclusive nature of all of these statements should make it clear that it is almost impossible to identify one particular group with a consistent predilection for peace and another with an equally predictable bent toward war. As has been argued in the two preceding chapters, the debate that ensued on the problem of war moved beyond simple or clear-cut rationalizations. This complex issue did, however, create a tension wherein certain people at various times attempted either to justify or to decry the call to arms in both more theoretical and more practical ways. The automatic reflex that made appeals to proper authority, just cause, or right intention unequivocally unassailable had dissipated, largely as a result of the Reformation's stress on individual conscience. In applying this perceptual change to Elizabethan England, Paul Jorgensen is correct when he states that "even apart from the practical difficulties imposed by a cautious government, there were inhibitions of conscience limiting a philosophy of active militarism."[12] With the emerging peace ethic it had become much easier to argue that peace be the only objective in policy decisions, thus putting the military advocates on the defensive. The introduction of a thoroughly intellectually satisfying peace position did produce further reinterpretations of the just war. Many of those who took part, for example, in the explosive outpouring of martial literature in the late sixteenth century attempted to resurrect respect for the soldierly profession, often by downplaying the righting of wrongs and promoting alternatively the need for armies to ensure peace and prosperity. The legitimization of military careers thus — for these writers — became more a product of important social and economic transformations than of ideological or legal argument.

It is still not sufficient simply to dismiss the just war as if it did not exist during this time. It continued to thrive in some form (much as it does today) and remained the one touchstone of war/peace discourse that had deep roots. Its noticeable (if limited) appearance in late Tudor England can be found largely in the war of propaganda that accompanied the intensification of the rivalry between England and Spain. Each side, claiming to fight in defense of the true faith, exhibited a transparent didacticism built on specious reasoning, reminiscent of tactics employed earlier by men like

---

11. Jorgensen, "Theoretical Views of War," 470; Hale, "Incitement to Violence?" in *Renaissance War Studies,* 487–511.

12. Jorgensen, "Theoretical Views of War," 475.

Edward Seymour, and which were taken seriously only when invasion appeared imminent. In an intrigue that recalled Pole's mission in the 1530s, the exiled cardinal, William Allen, in *A True, Sincere, and Modest Defence of English Catholiques* (1583), defiantly proclaimed the right of popes to depose heretical monarchs even to the point of going to war to do so. As also with Pole, the maneuver served only to unite England against the threat of foreign and Catholic domination.[13] Such a charged atmosphere made it easy for the queen to move decisively against English recusancy, and most people probably felt that any royal endeavor to avert a Catholic resurgence would prevent wars, not encourage them. Burghley responded to Allen that same year with *The Execution of Justice in England for Maintenaunce of Publique and Christian Peace,* offering much the same argument as found in the earlier works of Starkey, Nicholas Wise, and Becon. The treatise targeted rebellious elements who would take sinister advantage of the pope's excommunication of Elizabeth and the missionary activities of Edmund Campion and Robert Parsons. He derided the propaganda accusing the queen of persecuting Catholics and detailed the greater atrocities of Mary's reign against those who had never even "denied their lawful Queen" or fomented rebellion at home with foreign assistance.[14] Obedience and loyalty to the government were becoming fundamental values that the occasional treatise sought to reaffirm.

The queen did not want to convey a bellicose image, and her noted reluctance to commit English forces to many religious hotspots can be attributed in part to a prevailing ideology that a long line of English humanists had helped craft for their nation—essentially that peace at home accomplished more for true religion (and national strength) than meddling erratically in what were ultimately internal problems of foreign nations and empires. Only when England became the target of a large Spanish invasion force did the just war find itself invoked with great passion. During the 1570s and 1580s the *jus in bello* considerations remained the most vital aspect of the just war. By emphasizing particular methods of fighting, many military authors looked for ways to minimize the cruelties of war, which were (embarrassingly) acknowledged, and upheld the preferable alternative of peace when at all possible. War was symptomatic of a breakdown in one person's ability to live sensibly and harmoniously with an-

13. William Allen, *A True, Sincere, and Modest Defence of English Catholiques That Suffer for Their Faith Both at Home and Abrode* (Rouen, France: Parsons' Press, 1584); Johnson, *Just War Tradition,* 54–55; Russell, *Peacemaking in the Renaissance,* 231.
14. William Cecil, *The Execution of Iustice in England for Maintenaunce of Publique and Christian Peace* (London, 1583), sigs. A2r, C2–C3r.

other. It was a condition that necessitated ready correction, and these treatises hoped to lend assistance in that direction.

The Elizabethans produced a self-conscious and determined expression
of this new outlook and its accompanying preoccupation with peace in a
breathtaking array of cultural manifestations that continued well into the
following reign. A preliminary review of the evidence suggests three distinct areas where this can be discovered. First, in the writings of those who
were most directly affected by the new ethic of peace—the career militar-
ists and their advocates. In trying to resuscitate the dying corpse of the *jus
gentium,* they were forced to smooth over its most brutal attributes so the
military profession could gain new prestige among citizens of a cynical
nation.[15] Second, in the examples of the peace theme in Elizabethan literature and iconography, where we can see that the *Pax Britannia* was a
deliberately orchestrated national image embodied by Astrea herself and
consciously patterned after the imperial and pastoral themes of antiquity.
And finally, in the Christian element found in the peace-laden sermons and
writings of Elizabethan clergy and through the official liturgies.[16]

The confluence of these three streams of peace justification, imagery,
and morality bestowed on late sixteenth-century England a remarkable
aura of attentiveness to peace that needs further investigation. There are a
tremendous number of examples where a strong peace message is conveyed, and while most of them are from the pre-Armada years (for obvious
reasons), it is remarkable how fully peace discourse recovered after 1588.
(In fact, it never really subsided, but was given to less conciliatory expressions for a time.) For the savvy queen herself, all of the above concentrations on peace meant one thing—the chance for her to make the nation
economically and politically strong, and thus establish an enduring legacy
for herself. Thus, a century later, Elizabeth fulfilled the dreams of the
critics of the Hundred Years War, who had dreamed in vain that through
peace kings like Richard II and Henry IV would bring prosperity to the
realm and lasting fame to their reigns.

Conclusion

We have seen in this study the interactive nature of early modern political
languages when through "multiple contexts" a new idiom (or sublan-

15. See Lowe, "Role of Peace," 3–14; Hattaway, "Blood Is Their Argument," 84–89.
16. Lowe, "Religious Wars and the 'Common Peace.'"

guage), such as that of peace, enters into the fray of current discourse. The Renaissance found writers resurrecting old rhetorics and fashioning new ones to give voice and definition to moral uncertainties, although events as unsettling as the Hundred Years War initiated profound questioning even in the later Middle Ages. New ways of thinking about war and peace (in the context of a growing belief in the necessity of peace) were all contingent on the replacement of older, worn-out ideas that were perceived to be largely irrelevant to rapidly changing, troubling conditions. Attempts at "purifying" language or refining meaning were one path taken, merely a small step removed from the more existential reformation that interested many contemporaries. The value of peace fits well into this purging mentality which characterized much of the sixteenth century. According to both humanists and Protestants (and these two groups were not mutually exclusive), humankind had seriously gone astray and left behind its true, divinely created self, with individuals becoming estranged from both God and one another. Restoration of a life-affirming natural order required peace. By contrast, the ravages of war could not be as easily tolerated in an age when the potential for destruction had increased exponentially. Princely power depended on financial health and economic wealth, and warfare drained away both, even as personal and social reform had taken on an added urgency also in the midst of a concurrent demographic crisis.

Careful attention to the "vocabulary, rules, preconditions and implications, tone and style" of peace discourse in mid-Tudor foreign policy yields a fascinating picture of how language is transformed permanently by those exigencies of long duration which encourage ideational entrenchment.[17] In England it was initially the circumstances surrounding the Hundred Years War that created fluid and mutable linguistic environments that expanded dramatically the connotations of peace between around 1370 and 1440. The incipient peace discourse that emerged highlighted new concerns and opened up additional doors to understanding current conditions. It was easy for contemporaries to detect in the wars of the 1540s features similar to late medieval conflicts, which, in turn, helped lead to a renewed attention to peace. This time the humanistic ethic and evangelical realism, both employing a hermeneutics derived at least in part from a persistent substratum of literary convention, gave the practical peace element a prominence in war policymaking that men high in government found compelling. Beginning with Thomas Becon's *New Policy of War* (1542), a

17. J.G.A. Pocock, "The Concept of a Language and the *Métier d'Historien:* Some Considerations on Practice," in *The Languages of Political Theory in Early Modern Europe,* ed. Anthony Pagden (Cambridge: Cambridge University Press, 1987), 21.

synthesis was achieved which argued that wars are basically evil enterprises, the products of grievous sin, while peace is the natural state of civil society and the end for which all Christians should strive unceasingly. This development presages attitudes found in Shakespeare, who was "conscious of war's cost," and whose plays "stressed not what is won in war but what is lost."[18]

The sixteenth century is thus a watershed of sorts in that peace — in the guise of benefit to the commonwealth — first assumes noticeable status in the making of foreign policy. Peace is valued for its own worth, released from the protocols of the *jus ad bellum* and *jus armorum*. It becomes an object of intense philosophical interest in and of itself. In determining the role of ideas in this process, J.G.A. Pocock points out the utility of historians seeking junctures where a "network or community of men of letters . . . employ the language of the professional corporations without necessarily belonging to them, and are capable, first, of adapting these idioms or rhetorics to the purposes of their own discourse; second, of generating and developing idioms and rhetorics of their own in the course of pursuing it." This type of study has the advantage of showing "how the performance of speech acts not merely modifies language, but leads to the creation and diffusion of new languages . . . by the activities, practices and contexts of society."[19] The development of the peace idea in its many manifestations within linguistic but also social, political, economic, religious, and cultural environments, gave birth to a new language. What ensued had much in common with those contemporary discourses from which the peace idioms arose in late medieval and early modern Europe, most notably their highly ethical natures and persuasive rhetorical styles. For discourse to become active and durable it must promote some moral value or values that give it purpose and substance. The early modern peace discourse that flourished in England was kept vital by its practitioners, who felt themselves ensnared in a crisis from which only true peace and concord offered real hope of escape. It was a discourse that engendered gradually a distinctive intellectual milieu built on new paradigms, but was also born out of a prolonged and painful labor.

A study of this kind is plagued with a number of drawbacks that frustrate the historian of ideas. Some of these disadvantages already have been highlighted in the introduction. But here it can also be said that for all of the context attempted so as to ground sufficiently the development of an idea,

18. Becon, *New Policy of War,* 240–48; Hattaway, "Blood Is Their Argument," 89.
19. Hattaway, "Blood Is Their Argument," 25, 29.

such as peace, it is still not enough. This study has attempted to compare and contrast England with other nations on this important conceptual development but more work needs to be done in examining the origins of the peace traditions of other countries in the age when the first modern states appeared. Further inquiry is needed also into the relationship between private and public acts of violence. My evidence seems to find few distinctions on this issue in the medieval and early modern periods, but today when we cherish our privacy and recoil at excessive outside intrusion, much greater differences are noticeable. And of course, peace ideas were *not* the dominant consideration in early modern English policy or social thought, and as for consistency and coherence, they often remained palliatives and sometimes even expedients for troubled times. But the period from 1337 to 1559 offered just such a crucible for a new discourse to arise, develop, and become a significant factor in English society. Some have referred to the period running from the beginning of the Hundred Years War to the Treaty of Câteau-Cambrésis (1559) as really the Two Hundred Years War.[20] The fits and starts of this long-standing conflict between England and its Continental and Scottish enemies contributed to great tensions and insecurities that were only exacerbated when conditions were shaped by other events and developments, such as the advent of humanism and Protestantism, contributing to expanding notions of reform. In fact, in the centuries that followed, the erosion of ethical valves to stem martial activities left only the practical rationales for peace, and these could be manipulated more easily by governments and other interested parties to support wars. The sixteenth century was a unique time, before English overseas empires and newfound commercial wealth became additional variables in the war-peace equation, and when public morality was still a social concern. Perhaps not until our own century did the respect and possibilities for peace again loom so large in England. But then it may be that Wilfred Owen and his contemporaries were not as revolutionary in their disgust for war as once thought.

Peace, a simple idea in 1337, had become much more complex and adaptable by the middle of the sixteenth century, and so its utility in formulating economic appraisals, in identifying moral and spiritual concerns, and even in setting priorities of statecraft blossomed. By noting the shifts in languages as the peace idea came to affect them, we can see how an easily neglected historical development could wield critical impact and yet

---

20. Collinson, *Birthpangs of Protestant England*, 6–7.

be practically unnoticed in traditional treatments of Tudor society and pol-itics. Here is the great value of discourse analysis for contemporary histo-riography. It permits those still, small voices to be heard in the midst of the thunderclaps and cannon blasts of professedly dominant ideologies and discourses that are assumed to be largely secure and hegemonic, and which seem to command, for that reason, undivided attention.

However, some have resisted the temptation to conceptualize war-torn England this way. Steven Marx, in his study of pacifism in Elizabethan drama, concludes that "the phenomenon of Renaissance pacifism is neither an anachronistic construct nor an ephemeral aberration," and that pacifist ideas "make their persistence known by the vituperation of attacks upon them in militaristic literature and religious propaganda" during the period of religious wars.[21] John Nef, who has studied thoroughly the relationship between early modern culture and economy, has pinpointed the late six-teenth century as a crucial period in laying the groundwork for those atti-tudes which would become the "foundation for the genesis of industrial civilization." For him, the English "during the last half of the sixteenth century . . . became increasingly pacific in their outlook and habits, until they had less relish for fighting than any of the continentals."[22] This indeed was an era when the peace idea had become so entrenched as a societal ethic that it burst forth in iconographical and literary allusion. Many clergy harmonized in exalting its teleological necessity while dazed martial-ists and soldier-writers scrambled to recover the military respect that had waned in consequence.[23] We cannot see the cultural institutionalization of the peace ethic as an autonomous entity, or even a secure one. The veri-similitude that gave peace, as the Tudors came to understand it, its sub-stance wafted over the waves of English policy for many years to come, unpredictable in all its magnitude, but nevertheless, enduring in some form. By attempting some greater understanding about the origins and effects of peace in early modern England, we can perhaps identify better the various strands of choice that bring a nation to the point of decision in such a critical arena as war and peace. It is a timeless exercise, much like the phenomenon we have herewith attempted to explain.

21. Marx, "Shakespeare's Pacifism," 55–56.
22. Nef, *War and Human Progress,* 21, 111. It is intriguing, although a bit presumptuous to see much of Britain's reluctance to engage in Continental conflicts in more modern times as a consequence of these late medieval and early modern developments.
23. The peace imagery characterizing James's entry into London in 1603 was unprecedented in scope. See Paul A. Jorgensen, *Shakespeare's Military World* (Berkeley and Los Angeles: University of California Press, 1956), 199–204, for a discussion of the new king's pacifism.

APPENDIX

STC 5611

A Pretty Complaint of Peace that was Banished
out of Diverse Countries and Brought by
Wealth into England, and then Fearing Both
to be Thence Exiled, Made Great Moan until
Prudence Retained Them Again.

The Prologue to the Reader

As one unworthy to write or dedicate,
For lack of cunning or pleasant eloquence,
This simple work, to any great estate,
Or unto them which have experience
Of goodly learning by grace and influence;
Yet my poor heart which misseth all things well,
Would Peace and Wealth in England still should dwell.

The poorest sort therefore I do now pray
This for to read, for they may daily see
That where a house is fallen in decay
It hath most need, new mended for to be;
So is this matter most meet for poverty
That need of Wealth, which doth complain and tell,
That Peace and he in England could not dwell.

Howbeit all men I heartily defy,
For to receive my true intention;
Which by this treatise shall plainly well appear,
That to my country I have so good affection;

To show the people, what hurt cometh of dissension,
Wherefore if ye will flourish and excel,
Let Peace and Wealth, in England ever dwell.

The end of the prologue.
[A3r]

The Complaint of Peace

Were it for their profit that on every side
Men me refused I could be content;
But seeing that in all the world so wide
Where I am not, they have cause to lament;
Why would I then their madness repent,
Which evermore are ready to rebel,
And me exile, which with them fain would dwell.

And yet of pity I greatly do bewail
Their unkindness and infelicity;
To see the sorrow, the labor, and travail
That followeth everywhere as they banish me;
Yet one by another cannot warned be,
Until they feel such woe and grievous pain,
That they are glad to wish for me again.

Who will mourn at their misery?
Or who may say one word in their defense?
For here I plead I never did offence,
But ever commanded, truth and obedience
Unto their prince, and one to love another,
As it beseemeth every Christian brother.

The brute beasts which lack reason and wit,
Unto your shame, show love and amity;
O foolish man why doest thou then forget
thy name, thy nature, and eke¹ thy dignity?
Remember like whom, that God hath formed thee,
And thee hath made a creature reasonable,
Were to receive his gifts incomparable.²
[A4v]

1. in addition.
2. This verse and the four that follow come almost directly from Erasmus's *Querela pacis,* 293–94 (CWE edition).

And if that beasts, truly did me despise,
I would impute thee contumely
thereof to nature, but ye that should be wise
And have of reason the very use only;
Which that they lack, yet show they forth daily,
More friendly concord according to their kind,
Than any men that I can see or find.

Behold the birds in companies that fly;
Note how the deer, and sheep in herds do feed,
The fish by schools that swim as ye may see,
The swarms of bees, and also ye may read
Of little ants the policy and guide,
And many beasts that seldom fight and rage,
But man with reason showeth him more savage.

Methinks that man of nature should desire
To live in peace, remembering in his mind
How poor and naked he first in entered here,
When nature only was to him such a friend
To give him suck, to swaddle, and to wind;
Which else forthwith than in his infancy
Must needs have died, there was no remedy.

And yet if nature with you can have no place,
In whom that reason ought to be resident;
Which in brute beasts availeth, in that case
I will you show a thing more excellent,
Which should persuade, your froward ill intent,
To love, which is of Christ the true doctrine,
And ought to be your only discipline.
                              [A5r]

That doctrine only ye say you have profit,
Where are the deeds that would it then declare?
Of concord, peace, quietness, and rest
When one with other, to fight still will not spare?
I am a bird that seen is very rare
In any land there to continue long;
Yet ever gladly I would them among.

But I am driven away on every side,
From land to land worse than a banished man;
In any country, small time I do abide,
I am full weary. What remedy now then?
Is there no counsel, that any give me can

Where that I may now have a resting place
Among some people, that have so good a grace?

In France I trusted among them for to dwell,
But there I found my purpose was in vain.
For they full fiercely away did me expel;
Then fled I thence to Flanders and to Spain,
But war mine enemy pursued fast again,
So that I was from thence full fain to flee,
In sundry countries, and so to Italy.

In Italy I was [in] a certain space
And saw the bishop [pope] with his cardinals
Dwelling in Rome, with whom I found small grace;
I may them like full well to painted walls
Record of Paul,[3] which one of them so calls,
Which did him strike, nothing unto his praise
Against my will, which that am called Peace.

                                          [A6v]

I did abhor their great abomination
To see how lordly they did both go and ride;
Nothing like to Christ's apostles' fashion
There was covetous[ness], lechery, and pride
With other knacks, that I could not abide;
For pretty poison, there wrought so privily
I had final comfort to dwell in Italy.

Then as I mused whether for to fare
When as an outlaw they did me reprehend,
A friend of mine bid me not to care
For into England he said he would me send,
Which country to me so highly did commend
And his report I took it also sure,
That there forever I thought still to endure.

Of Wealth I heard this goodly commendation,
Which to me truly was no small comfort,
To hear of England the goodly situation;
Wherefore in haste I got me to a port
And sailed thence until I did resort
Unto that land, where even as Wealth had said,
I found all things which made me well again.

3. Paul III, first of the great Counter-Reformation popes, reigned from 1534 to 1549.

For in that region I had full gentle cheer
With Wealth my friend that held me company,
Which in England had dwelled many year,
And me assured that even so should I,
Whereto I agreed, and so we both truly
Came to a city, where all thing was pleasant
Called London, sometimes Troy Nouvant.[4]

[A7r]

This city to me all other did excel,
Their goodly order was to me great pleasure;
There found I concord which liked me full well
With true dealing, just weight, and good measure,
Plenty of victual, gold, and great treasure;
And Justice ruled there most like a king,
Which was to me surely a full joyful thing.

The poor people I saw them fast apply
Their true labour, their households to maintain;
That glad I was to see how lovingly
One did for [an]other, refusing no great pain;
Love in their hearts appeared there so plain
That there was "neighbor, come dine and go with me"
And "I shall surely go twice as far with thee."

Those loving words greatly did me rejoice
So that I was in great felicity,
But suddenly I heard a wondrous noise
Of one, Dissension, come in the north country,[5]
Which was ever an enemy to me;
And men of him so greatly spoke and said,
That I was never before so much afraid.

4. The new Troy.
5. The poet was surely referring here to the Pilgrimage of Grace, a revolt that broke out
in Yorkshire in 1536. The rebels, led by a knight's son and servant of the earl of Northumberland, Robert Aske, found the recent religious changes unsettling and demanded the restoration of the monastaries, the eradication of heresy, and the replacement of Cromwell and his
Protestant supporters. On the economic side, they wanted an end to enclosure, landlords'
exactions, and rising prices. Coming as petitioners (pilgrims) to the king, under the banner of
the Five Wounds of Christ, the insurgents did not consider themselves resisters. Protracted
discussions between both sides and a royal pardon enabled the crown's forces to gather
strength and position while the rebel army began to disband. After a misguided attempt to
seize Hull and Scarborough in January 1537, the rebels were crushed, the pardon revoked,
and fierce retribution taken against the ringleaders.

Yet did I hide me there full privily
In hope that Wisdom, would put him to flight;
Howbeit I saw there was no remedy
But that to war all men were ready dight;⁶
Wanting⁷ nothing that would them help to fight,
Full woe was I to see poor wives moan
For their husbands which to the war were gone.

[A8v]

Methought London was changed suddenly,
For there was rumbling and searching on every side
For bows, bills,⁸ spears, and swords truly,
For guns, gunpowder, and horses for to ride;
Alas thought I what shall of me betide,
Such rattling of harness I did both hear and see,
That I am driven from hence away for [to] flee.

Then in a night I stole me thence away
And took my journey toward the west country;
The next morning soon after spring of day
I had espied a right great company
Of harnessed men, then in a bush crept I
Till they were past, I was full sore afraid,
They clattered Cornish I know not what they said.

But then I was brought into much despair,
For west nor east, I wist⁹ not where to go;
In all England I saw men did repair
To war, to war, my cruel mortal foe;
And as I was in this distress and woe
I saw one coming full sad with heavy cheer,
Not like to fight, to whom I drew me near.

He did salute me with all gentleness,
Me thought he was a man of honesty;
Howbeit his cheer such sorrow did express,
That I forgot plain what that he should be,
With his sad garments, which mourning were to see,
Until he spoke, and took me by the hand,
And said he was like to forsake this land.

[B1r]

6. equipped; arrayed.
7. lacking.
8. a type of broadsword.
9. knew.

Then by his voice I knew full well his name,
Which yet was changed through woe and pensiveness;
What, Wealth said I? Yea, Peace and he the same,
Where art thou bound in this great heaviness?
It doth appear thou art in woefulness,
And if in England there be no place for thee
Then know I well there is no grace for me.

Wealth

No no Peace, thou must from hence depart,
And so must I, which doth me much repent;
The people are so fond[10] and overthwart,[11]
That until we awhile have been absent
And war have made them bare and indigent,
They will not know the great diversity
Of Peace, and war, wealth, and adversity.[12]

O England, England it doth me greatly rue
Thee to forsake, which then must needs decay;
Howbeit thy people so frail are and untrue
That Peace and I with you abide not may,
Which will at length, surely cause you to say:
Alas that ever we were so mad and would
Them to exile which were our friends so good.[13]

Forsooth Peace, this dare I sure affirm,
Of England have I such experience:
That no country is able [to] do it harm,
And if they keep their true obedience,
This land sure is of such excellence,
They need not fear no Christian king nor Jew,
If in themselves they be both just and true.

                                    [B2v]

10. foolish; easily led.

11. contentious; quarrelsome; perverse.

12. This juxtaposition between the effects of war and peace can be found throughout the poem and are indicative of the dichotomy and tension that characterize much Protestant thought on the issue. See Chapter 6.

13. This lament is very similar to one written by Thomas Becon about four years later. Cf. Becon, *The New Policy of War* (PS edition), 243.

Peace

Wealth thou hast spoken not all that might be said
Of pleasant England, but now let it suffice;
For I ensure thee I am full sore afraid
To see the people on every side arise;
Wherefore I pray thee now give me thine advice,
This goodly country I would not yet forsake,
And if I wist [knew] the business would aslake.[14]

Wealth

To give thee counsel now being in distress
I am in doubt what I to thee may say;
Which am in danger as much as thou doubtless,
But if thou wilt needs tarry and assay,
if that the world will turn a better way,
Into some abbey among religious men,
There hide thyself, that is my counsel then.

Peace

Nay nay, by God I think not that way best,
I do mistrust their cloaked holiness;
There is no place for me to hide in rest,
For some men think that of this business,
If all were tried they would not be guiltless;
Wherefore those fellows I dare not come a nigh,
For fear something be found with them awry.[15]

What may I do now for a certain space
To see if that this matter will amend?
For in no town I dare once show my face.
Well into wilderness, I will now surely wend,
And there to tarry a time I do intend;
My friend Wealth, what shall become of thee?
Wilt thou not now awhile go dwell with me?

[B3r]

14. slacken; diminish; abate.
15. Considering the fact that the dissolutions had provided much of the impetus for the
Pilgrimage, it is natural that this Protestant poem would attempt to convince the reader that
the monasteries were better off liquidated, and that monks were in part responsible for wars
and rebellions of this type.

Wealth

Alas Peace to live in wild desert
I have not used,[16] wherefore it would me grieve;
How should I, Wealth, there have a merry heart
Where is no comfort, no succour nor relief?
But here of promise my troth[17] to thee I give,
And if thou wilt in wilderness go dwell
I will go see if thing[s] may be well.

For to the court I will straight take my way;
I am in favor with the king's council.
There shall I hear something what they do say
Of that false knave (Dissension) that rebel;
And if of truth that I may once hear tell
That he be gone; with speed I will me hie
To bring the word wherever that thou be.

Peace

I see well Wealth that thou canst not endure
In forests wild, among the bushes thick;
Thou hast been used so much unto pleasure
That cold and hunger perchance would make thee sick;
Wherefore farewell good dainty, gentle Greek,
For at the court ye will go fill your wallet,
And in the woods I must go pick a sallet.[18]

Wealth

My friend Peace, I pray thee be content,
My faithful mind thou needest not to mistrust;
But since thou has a coward's heart so faint,
That in the woods now needs hide thee must;
And if that wisdom may cause discord to flee,
That tidings in post I will sure bring to thee.
                                        [B4v]

And if I see no hope nor remedy
But that Dissension is like to prevail,
Yet unto thee again sure come will I

16. am not used to.
17. good faith.
18. a light medieval helmet, with a brim flaring in the back, sometimes fitted with a visor.

And out of England then will we both hence sail;
Which will at length cause them full sore to wail,
Wherefore farewell, since we must needs depart,
And after sorrow God send a merry heart.

A Woeful Complaint of Peace, When Wealth Had Forsaken Him

Now am I here poor Peace left all alone,
Which am constrained to live in wilderness;
For Wealth my friend unto the court is gone,
He must needs be where as all pleasure is;
Howbeit I have yet some comfort of this:
In court men say [it] is good to have a friend,
But out of sight perchance [I] will [be] out of mind.

For Wealth, in court where is so good welfare,
His old true friends doth many times forget,
And especially if they be poor and bare;
But if with Wealth no more that I may meet,
Yet such a letter to him then will I write;
That he shall know he is too much unkind,
That out of sight I should be out of mind.
                                                        [B5r]

But of one thing I am certain and sure,
Though Wealth in court live well and pleasantly;
That there be no great long time endure
Except I Peace, must thither come truly;
Wherefore some pain, awhile suffer will I,
And see which way that hurl will the wind,
Though out of sight I be, and out of mind.

O Wealth, Wealth, of thee may I complain,
That into England brought me first to dwell;
Which to forsake it were to me great pain,
This goodly country forsooth I like so well;
O mad people both foolish and cruel,
Small cause have ye to triumph or to joy,
Your pleasant land, unwisely to destroy.

Suppose ye by war to cause it to increase
In honour, substance, riches, and dignity;
Nay nay truly, for if that, I poor Peace,
Hence be exiled, then look for poverty;
War nothing bringeth but great calamity;

Ye foolish people, what thing do ye intend?
Your own destruction still followeth at the end.

For though I could now many things recite,
How evil ever that rebels have prevailed;
Which that I think not meet as now to write,
Yet men alive are, which that have bewailed;
Their noughty purpose which falsely hath them fatalke[19]
western men, which once were mad and wild;
How well they sped, for going to blackheath field led.[20]

[B6v]

I think small cause ye have for to complain
Except it be of pleasant wealthiness,
For no nation endureth lesser pain
Who hath it proved, the matter may express;
But sure in England there is much idleness
Which is the root of great debate and strife,
For every wretch will [would] lead an easy life.

Howbeit truly, there is a common saying:
That great rich men, and born to much land,
Are chief causers of good poor men's decaying;
With keeping of farms, and pastures in their hands
I know not I, how that the matter stands;
But I am sure that England may alone
Sustain his people, requiring help of none.

What should I meddle with rerages[21] and fines
Which with extremity, that some men do require;
Wherefore poor men, full often groan and whine,
their tenements set so high and dear;
They are ill-grieved and yet they know not where,
And of their pains would fain have remedy,
Howbeit their medicine like poison is contrary.

Ye seek for ease as men which lack all wit,
And worthy sure, of great reproof and blame;
God hath ordained a king royal and meet
For to command Justice in his name
all things to order, to settle and to frame,

19. falsely talk; fast-talk.
20. Perhaps a reference to the rebels' assembly at Pontefract in West Yorkshire, where they made their demands known to the government.
21. being in a state of arrears.

Whom that ye ought to honour and obey,
And not to seek by War a foolish way.[22]

[B7r]

War is the cause of great destruction,
It bringeth men to wretched poverty;
And they which are, in true possession,
Their very right causeth them to flee;
They are too blind, forsooth that will not see
The great ruin that followeth cruel war,
Where none is made, but every man doth mar.

For many a Duke, Earl, Lord, and knight
Which through Peace, do live full wealthly,
By force of war, are driven from their right,
And men of substance are brought to misery.
The poor plowman, also full woefully,
Which picketh out his living with great pain,
Soweth his corn, into the ground in vain.

For War destroyeth both city, town and land;
Who can express any wretchedness,
But that in war it ready may be found:
Extreme hunger, but sin with most excess,
Murder, burning, theft, and filthiness?
What Christian man can love that naughty life
Where they deflower both widow, maid and wife?[23]

Ye ought of truth greatly to be ashamed,
If that ye not, your froward ill intent,
That ye for Christians, would look once to be named,
Since Christ your master which was from heaven sent
Showed by his life, and his commandment
That he had Peace, in favor most of price,
But you love war, and count yourselves for wise.[24]

[B8v]

And yet as fools, ye will sure prove at length,
Ye make a rod to beat your tail withal;
God will be true, for all your power and strength;
Your foolish pride will have a shameful fall,
O froward man to thy remembrance call,

22. Erasmus, *Querela pacis*, 311–12.
23. Ibid., 316–17.
24. Ibid., 300–303.

That war's reward shall be to thee again,
For all thy labor but sorrow, woe, and pain.

Of Paul's epistles ye shall read few or none
But that with Peace he doth all men salute;
And how doth he extol my name alone
To the Corinthians, where he doth me repute[25]
Most worthy praise, which thing should you refute,
That favor war, the root of every vice,
Out of your folly for shame arise, arise.

What should I express that Isaiah doth me praise,
Which being inspired with the spirit divine,
Prophesied before that Christ should come in Peace,
Not like a warrior which causeth much ruin;[26]
Since that a heathen poet wrote so fine,
Counting Peace (to your great shame I was)
Chief of all things, whose name was Silius.[27]

Alas alas what may I farther say,
Since heathen poets your honour do deprive,
Which have nothing but reason for to lay,
And ye the testament of God's most holy life,
Ye may be counted unto your utter shame,
As usurping, of Christ a wrongful name.
                                        [C1r]

Of authors more, what need I to indict
Since God himself chief author of all things
Doth me commend, which ought you to excite
to love, Which doth so many pleasures bring?
And I doubt not, but that there is a king
In England, which so well doth favor me
That I again shall come to my degree.

But now of Wealth I long greatly to hear,
Which in the court hath such good banqueting;
He thinketh little upon my evil cheer
That in the woods, I have, where birds so sing
I would rejoice now much of his coming;

---

25. 1 Corinthians 7:15 and 14:33.

26. The prophet Isaiah makes numerous references to the fruits of peace, perhaps the most noted being in chapter 9, verse 6, where the expected Messiah is referred to as the Prince of Peace. See also Isaiah 14:7, 26:3, 32:17, 55:12 and 57:2.

27. Silius, *Punica* 11.591; cf. Pace, *Oration to Peace*, 235.

It is eight weeks since that on yonder plain
He went from me, God send him soon again.

I marvel much he is away so long,
Howbeit his tarrying I like it somewhat well;
For I suppose, and if all things were wrong,
He is too wise there to abide and dwell;
Some merry tidings I hope he will me tell.
Wherefore come Wealth my mind doth much desire,
To see thee once, now pleasantly appear.

Wealth saluteth Peace.

God bless thee Peace, and send thee well to fare,
Thou has methinks a changed pair of cheeks;
Is it with hunger, or else with woe and care?
What meat hast thou? onions, cheese, or leeks?
Thou are abated right evil in eight weeks;[28]
Pluck up thy heart, be merry, glad and fain,
Dissension is gone, with all his noughty train.
                                        [C2v]

Peace

Now welcome Wealth even with all my heart,
Thy merry tidings doth greatly me rejoice;
Methinks that gone is all my care and smart,
Thy joyful words do make so good a noise;
Now of my meat thou shalt sure have the choice,
And for thy drink, for lack of pleasant wine,
I will thee give sweet water, clear and fine.

Wealth

Gramercy Peace of thy great gentleness,
I marvel not that thou art maserate,[29]
To see thy fare so bare in wilderness;
For all things here thy courage doth abate,

28. The Pilgrimage of Grace lasted about eight weeks, from the time Aske began rallying supporters and organizing daily musters in Beverley (October 8), until his proclamation of peace to three thousand rebels in Pontrefact (December 7), after the duke of Norfolk's "pardon."
29. miserable.

Howbeit again, I trust to elevate
thee, For with wisdom I trust so sure to stand,
That false Dissension shall never hurt this land.

And who thinkest thou hath caused him to flee,
Which in this matter hath wrought most busily
but Prudence, that is a friend to thee and me;
And he hath handled the thing so wittily,
That we have cause to love him heartily,
For by his wisdom, his labor, and his pain,
All things are ended, and no man killed nor slain.

But Peace I pray thee now with all haste and speed,
Thee to prepare unto the court to wend,
And I shall hold thee company and guide;
The king's grace did me unto thee send,
To bring thee forth, which doth thee so commend,
That thou are bound for evermore to love
That godly prince, which war doth much reprove.
                                                       [C3r]

And noble men which are his councillors,
So doth thee favor, that thou canst never fall;
For some of them have pur[s]ued the chance of wars
Which know it is the spring of mischiefs all;
And I am sure that many one now shall
Which were great doers in this business,
While that they live, find pain of neediness.[30]

But woe, alas, this nation is so frail,
That oftentimes of folly mad and vain;
They would set forth the blind and foolish tail
To rule the head which hath both wit and brain;
I say no more, for many know the pain
That hath ensued of false discord and strife,
Though they have escaped the hazard of their life.

Peace

O lusty Wealth, now cheerful is my mood,
Though fools of folly the sorrow do sustain;
That I do find the king to me so good,
Within his land me still for to retain;

30. Wealth is here addressing another complaint of the Yorkshire rebels in his guarded
defense of the king's council.

And that his lords of me be also fain,
I do rejoice thereof so heartily,
That to the court I will go merrily.

Wealth

Now come on then, for thou art found absent,
In wilderness thou must not hide thy face;
Thou must obey the king's commandment,
With whom thou art in favor and in grace;
He will thee [de]fend abroad in every place,
To show his people his blessed godly will,
That thou and I, in England dwell shall still.

[C4v]

Peace

Now by my faith I will never deny
Him for to serve, which is so gracious;
Wherefore have with thee forth straight by and by,
My heart is pleased that was full tedious;
Since that the way is nothing dangerous,
Wherefore I trust to make a plenteous rame,[31]
Now war is gone, that cursed naughty came.

For I may triumph, which late in wilderness
Was in dispair lest Wealth had me deceived
When he departed from me; but now doubtless
Into the court I am so well received,
That many things which war would have decayed
I trust to see them flourish up and spring;
There is so noble and gracious a king;

Whom God I pray, his royal majesty
always preserve and make him fortunate;
Again all those whatever that they be,
That would unwisely or falsely violate
England his realm and maintain every estate;
With gentlemen and commons good and true,
And cause rebels their foolishness to rue.[32]

31. continuous shouting or crying out.
32. a final appeal to Peace as the lifeblood of the commonweal.

SELECTED
BIBLIOGRAPHY

Manuscripts

Bibliothèque Nationale

MS Paris BN 14524 x, 15: fols. 50va–vb; xv, 2, 3: fols. 63vb–64ra; xxvi, 10: fols. 92rb–va; xxx, 9: fol. 107ra
MS Paris BN 14556 fol. 220va
MS Paris BN 16385 fol. 69va–vb

British Library

Additional MS 21253, fol. 105
Arundel MS 73, fols. 96v–97
Cottonian MS, Titus C. VII, fol. 148r
Harley MS 45, fols. 150r–v
Harley MS 532, fols. 46–47
Harley MS 3760, fol. 193
Harley MS 4990, fol. 1
Landsdowne MS 393, fols. 26b, 48
Royal MS 18 B, xxiii, fols. 65, 123b–126, 139, 167

Bodleian Library

Bodley MS 240, fols. 548–50
University College MS 40, fols. 1–24

Cambridge University Library

St. John's College MS 57, fol. 204vb

Official Collections

Calendar of Letters, Dispatches and State Papers Relating to the Negotiations between England and Spain, Preserved in the Archives at Vienna, Simacas, and

Elsewhere. Edited by M.A.S. Hume, Royall Tyler et al. 13 vols. London: HMSO, 1862–1954.

Calendar of State Papers and Manuscripts Relating to English Affairs Existing in the Archives and Collections of Venice, and in Other Libraries of Northern Italy. Edited by Rawdon Brown. Vols. 2–8. London: Longman, 1862–81.

Calendar of the Patent Rolls Preserved in the Public Record Office, Edward VI, 1547–1553. Edited by R. H. Brodie. 5 vols. London: HMSO, 1936–39.

Calendar of State Papers Domestic Series of the Reign of Edward VI, 1547–1553. Preserved in the Public Record Office. Revised ed. Edited by C. S. Knighton. London: HMSO, 1992.

Certain Sermons or Homilies, Appointed to be Read in Churches, in the Time of Queen Elizabeth. 4th ed. London: M. Lewis, 1766.

English Historical Documents, 1042–1180. Edited by David C. Douglas and George W. Greenaway. Vol. 2. London: Eyre & Spottiswoode, 1953.

Gee, Henry, and William J. Hardy. *Documents Illustrative of English History*. London: Macmillan, 1896.

Leges Henrici Primi. Edited and translated by L. J. Downer. Oxford: Clarendon Press, 1972.

Letters and Papers, Foreign and Domestic, of the Reign of Henry VIII, 1509–47. Edited by J. S. Brewer, J. Gairdner, and R. H. Brodie. 21 vols. and addenda. London: HMSO, 1862–1932.

Letters and Papers Relating to the War with France, 1512–1513. Edited by A. Spout. London: HMSO, 1897.

Liturgical Services. Liturgies and Occasional Forms of Prayer Set Forth in the Reign of Queen Elizabeth. Edited by William Keatinge Clay. PS, vol. 30. Cambridge: The University Press, 1847.

The Register of Henry Chichele, Archbishop of Canterbury, 1414–1443. Edited by E. F. Jacob. 4 vols. Oxford: Clarendon Press, 1938–47.

Registrum Johannis Trefnant, episcopi Herefordensis, A.D. 1389–1404. Hereford, Eng.: Wilson & Phillips, 1914.

Statutes and Ordynances for the Warre. London: Thomas Berthelet, 1544.

Statutes of the Realm. Edited by A. Ludens et al. 11 vols. London: Record Commission, 1810–28.

Tanner, Norman P., ed. *Heresy Trials in the Diocese of Norwich, 1428–1431*. C4S, vol. 20. London: Royal Historical Society, 1977.

Tudor Royal Proclamations. Edited by Paul L. Hughes and James F. Larkin. 3 vols. New Haven, Conn.: Yale University Press, 1964–69.

The Two Books of Homilies Appointed to Be Read in Churches. Edited by John Griffiths. Oxford: Oxford University Press, 1859.

The Two Liturgies with Other Documents Set Forth by Authority in the Reign of King Edward the Sixth. Edited by Joseph Ketley. PS, vol. 29. Cambridge: The University Press, 1844.

Visitation Articles and Injunctions of the Period of the Reformation. Edited by W. H. Frere and W. M. Kennedy. Alcuin Club. London: Longmans, Green, 1910.

Wilkins, David, ed. *Concilia Magnae Britanniae et Hiberniae, a Syndodo Verolamiense, A.D. 446–1717*. 4 vols. London, 1737.

Chronicles

Bede. *Bede's Ecclesiastical History of the English People.* Edited by Bertram Colgrave and R.A.B. Mynors. Oxford: Clarendon Press, 1969.

Fabyan, Robert. *The New Chronicles of England and France in Two Parts.* Edited by Henry Ellis. London: F. C. and J. Rivington, et al., 1811.

Gesti Stephani. Edited and translated by K. R. Potter. London: Thomas Nelson & Sons, 1955.

Gruffydd, Elis. "Boulogne and Calais from 1545 to 1550." *Bulletin of the Faculty of Arts. Fouad I University* (Cairo) 12, no. 1 (1950): 1–90.

———. "The 'Enterprises' of Paris and Boulogne." In *Bulletin of the Faculty of Arts. Fouad I University* (Cairo) 11, no. 1 (1949): 37–95.

———. "Suffolk's Expedition to Montdidier 1523." *Bulletin of the Faculty of Arts. Fouad I University* (Cairo) 7 (1944): 33–43.

Hall, Edward. *Hall's Chronicle.* London: J. Johnson et al., 1809.

Holinshed, Raphael. *Chronicles of England, Scotland and Ireland.* 6 vols. London: J. Johnson, 1808.

Keynes, Simon, and Michael Lapidge, ed. and trans. *Asser's Life of King Alfred and Other Contemporary Sources.* Middlesex, Eng.: Penguin Books, 1983.

Knighton, Henry. *Chronicon Henrici Knighton.* Edited by Joseph R. Lumby. 2 vols. London: HMSO, 1889–95.

Polydore Vergil. *The Anglica Historia of Polydore Vergil, A.D. 1485–1537.* Edited and translated by Denys Hay. Camden Society, 3d ser., vol. 74. London: Royal Historical Society, 1950.

Venette, Jean de. *The Chronicle of Jean de Venette.* Translated by Jean Birdsall. Edited by Richard A. Newhall. New York: Columbia University Press, 1953.

cs*The Westminster Chronicle, 1381–1394.* Edited and translated by L. C. Hector and Barbara F. Harvey. Oxford: Clarendon Press, 1982.

William of Newburgh. *Historia Rerum Anglicarum.* In *Chronicles of the Reign of Stephen, Henry II, and Richard I,* edited by Richard Howlett, vol. 1. London: Longman, 1884.

Wriothesley, Charles. *A Chronicle of England During the Reigns of the Tudors.* Edited by William Douglas Hamilton. Vol. 2. Camden Society, n.s.., no. 20. London: J. B. Nichols & Sons, 1877.

Other Primary Sources

Albertano da Brescia. *Albertani Brixiensis liber consolationis et consilii: Ex quo hausta est fabula de Melibeo et Prudentia: Quam Anglice redditam et The Tale of Melibe inscriptam, Galfridus Chaucer inter Canterbury Tales recepit.* London: N. Trubner, 1873.

Allen, William. *A True, Sincere, and Modest Defence of English Catholiques That Suffer for Their Faith Both at Home and Abrode.* Rouen, France: [Parsons' Press], 1584.

The Alliterative Morte Arthure. Translated by Valerie Krishna. Washington, D.C.: University Press of America, 1983.

Allmand, C. T., ed. *Society at War.* Edinburgh: Oliver & Boyd, 1973.

Ambrose of Milan, *Of the Duties of the Clergy.* In *A Select Library of Nicene and Post-Nicene Fathers,* edited by Philip Schaff and Henry Wace, 2d ser., 10:1–89. New York: Christian Literature, 1896.

An Apology for Lollard Doctrines. Edited by James Henthorn Todd. Camden Society, vol. 20. London: J. B. Nichols & Son, 1842.

Aquinas, Thomas. *Summa Theologica.* New York: McGraw-Hill, 1972.

Ascham, Roger. *English Works.* Edited by William Aldis Wright. Cambridge: The University Press, 1904.

Ashby, George. *George Ashby's Poems.* Edited by Mary Bateson. EETS OS, no. 76. London: Kegan Paul, Trench, Trübner, 1899.

Augustine. *Opera omnia.* Vols. 7–8. Paris: Gaume Fratres, 1837–38.

Bacon, Roger. *Opus majus.* Edited and translated by Robert Belle Burke. 2 vols. Philadelphia: University of Pennsylvania Press, 1928.

Ballads from Manuscripts. Edited by F. J. Furnivall. 2 vols. Ballad Society. London: Taylor, 1868–73.

Becon, Thomas. *Early Works.* Edited by John Ayre. PS, vol. 2. Cambridge: The University Press, 1843.

Bonet, Honoré. *The Tree of Battles.* Translated by G. W. Coopland. Cambridge: Harvard University Press, 1949.

Brinton, Thomas. *The Sermons of Thomas Brinton, Bishop of Rochester, (1373–89).* Edited by M. A. Devlin. 2 vols. Camden 3d ser., vol. 75. London: Royal Historical Society, 1954.

Brixius, Germanus. "The *Antimorus* of Germanus Brixius, edited by Daniel Kinney. In *The Complete Works of St. Thomas More,* vol. 3, pt. 2, appendix B, pp. 469–547. New Haven, Conn.: Yale University Press, 1984.

Broadside Black-Letter Ballads. Edited by John Payne Collier. London: Thomas Richards, 1868.

Bromyard, John. *Summa prædicantium.* Venice: Dominicum Nicolinum, 1586.

Bueil, Jean de. *Le Jouvencel.* Edited by Léon Lecestre. 2 vols. Paris: Librairie Renouard, 1887.

Bullinger, Henry. *Decades.* Edited by Thomas Harding. PS, vols. 7–8. Cambridge: The University Press, 1849–50.

———. *An Holsome Antidotus or Counterpoysen, Ageynst the Pestylent Heresye and Secte of the Anabaptistes.* Translated by John Veron. London: Dumfrey Powell, 1548.

———. *A Treatise or Sermon of Henry Bullynger, Muche Fruitfull and Necessarye for This Tyme, Concernynge Magistrates and Obedience of Subiectes. Also Concernyng the Affayres of Warre, and What Scryptures Make Mention Thereof. Whether Christen Powers May War Against Their Enemies. And Whither It Be Laufull for a Christyan to Beare the Office of a Magistrate, and of the Duety of Souldiers with Many Other Holsom Instructions for Captaynes & Souldiers Both.* Translated by Walter Lynne. London: William Powell, 1549.

Bury, Richard de. *The Philobiblon.* Edited by Archer Taylor. Berkeley and Los Angeles: University of California Press, 1948.

Calvin, John. *Calvin's New Testament Commentaries*. Edited by David W. Torrance and Thomas F. Torrance. Grand Rapids, Mich.: William B. Eerdmans, 1972.

―――. *Institutes of the Christian Religion*. Translated by Ford Lewis Battles. 2 vols. Philadelphia: Westminster Press, 1960.

―――. *Minor Prophets*. Edited by John Owen. Vol. 3. Grand Rapids, Mich.: William B. Eerdmans, 1950.

―――. *The Sermons . . . Upon the Fifth Booke of Moses Called Deuteronomie*. Translated by Arthur Golding. London: Henry Middleton for George Bishop, 1583.

―――. *A Short Instruction for to Arme All Good Christian People Agaynst the Pestiferous Errours of the Common Secte of Anabaptistes*. London: John Daye, 1549.

Castiglione, Baldesar. *The Book of the Courtier*. Translated by Charles S. Singleton. Garden City, N.Y.: Anchor Books, 1959.

Cecil, William. *Certaine Preceptes, or Directions for the Well Ordering and Carriage of a Mans Life*. Edinburgh: Andro Hart, 1618.

―――. *The Execution of Iustice in England for Maintenaunce of Publique and Christian Peace*. London, 1583.

The Cely Letters, 1472–1488. Edited by Alison Hanham. EETS no. 273. London: Oxford University Press, 1975.

Chaucer, Geoffrey. *The Complete Works of Geoffrey Chaucer*. Edited by Walter W. Skeat. London: Oxford University Press, 1931.

Cheke, John. *The Gospel According to Saint Matthew and Part of the First Chapter of the Gospel According to Saint Mark, Translated into English . . . by Sir John Cheke*. Edited by James Goodwin. Cambridge: J. and J. J. Deighton, 1843.

―――. *The Hurt of Sedition Howe Greveous It Is to a Communewelth*. London: Iohn Day & Wylliam Seres, 1549.

Christine de Pisan. *The Book of Fayttes of Armes and of Chyvalrye*. Translated by William Caxton. Edited by A.T.P. Byles. London: Oxford University Press, 1932.

Clanvowe, John. *The Works of Sir John Clanvowe*. Edited by V. J. Scattergood. Cambridge: D. S. Brewer, 1975.

Colet, John. *Ioannis Coleti ennarratio in epistolam S. Pauli ad Romanos*. Translated by J. H. Lupton. London, 1873; reprint, Ridgewood, N.J.: Gregg Press, 1965.

Commynes, Philippe de. *Mémoires*. Edited by H. G. Bohn. 2 vols. London: H. G. Bohn, 1855.

Dives and Pauper. Edited by Priscilla Heath Barnum. 2 vols. EETS OS, nos. 275 and 280. Oxford: Oxford University Press, 1976, 1980.

Dobson, R. B., ed. *The Peasants' Revolt of 1381*. London: Macmillan, 1970.

Edgeworth, Roger. *Sermons Very Fruitfull, Godly and Learned, Preached and Sette Foorth by Maister Roger Edgeworth*. London: Roberti Caly, 1557.

Ellis, Henry, ed. *Original Letters Illustrative of English History*. Vol. 1. 3d series. London: Richard Bentley, 1846.

Elyot, Thomas. *The Book Named the Governour.* Edited by Arthur Turberville Eliot. Newcastle-upon-Tyne, Eng.: John Hernaman and Ridgeway & Sons, 1834.

———. *A Preservative Agaynste Deth.* London: Thomas Berthelet, 1545.

Erasmus, Desiderius. *The Adages of Erasmus.* Translated by Margaret Mann Phillips. Cambridge: The University Press, 1964.

———. *The Education of a Christian Prince.* Translated by Lester K. Born. New York: Columbia University Press, 1936.

———. *The First Tome or Volume of the Paraphrase of Erasmus Upon the Newe Testamente.* London: Edward Whitechurche, 1548.

———. *Lives of Johan Vitrier, Warden of the Franciscan Convent at St. Omer and Jean Colet, Dean of St. Paul's, London.* Edited and Translated by J. H. Lupton. London: George Bell & Sons, 1883.

———. *Querela pacis.* Translated by Betty Radice. In *Collected Works of Erasmus,* edited by A.H.T. Levi, 27:289–322. Toronto: University of Toronto Press, 1986.

———. *Panegyricus ad Philippum Austriae Ducem.* Translated by Betty Radice. In *Collected Works of Erasmus,* edited by A.H.T. Levi, 27:1–75. Toronto: University of Toronto Press, 1986.

———. *The Whole Familiar Colloquies.* Translated by Nathan Bailey. London: Hamilton, Adams, 1877.

Fenne, Thomas. *Fennes Frutes: Which Worke Is Divided into Three Severall Parts.* London: Richard Oliffe, 1590.

The First English Life of King Henry the Fifth. Written in 1513 by an Anonymous Author Known Commonly as the Translator of Livius. Edited by Charles L. Kingsford. Oxford: Clarendon Press, 1911.

Fortescue, John. *De laudibus legum Angliae.* Edited and translated by S. B. Chrimes. Cambridge: The University Press, 1949.

Four English Political Tracts of the Later Middle Ages. Edited by Jean-Philippe Genet. C4S, vol. 18. London: Royal Historical Society, 1977.

Four Supplications. Edited by F. J. Furnivall and J. M. Cowper. EETS ES, no. 13. London: N. Trübner, 1871.

Frontinus, Sextus Julius. *The Strategemes, Sleyghtes, and Policies of Warre Gathered Together, by S. Julius Frontinus, and Translated by Rycharde Morysine.* London: Thomas Berthelet, 1539.

Gardiner, Stephen. *The Letters of Stephen Gardiner.* Edited by James A. Muller. Cambridge: The University Press, 1933.

[Gardiner, Stephen]. *A Machiavellian Treatise.* Edited by Peter Samuel Donaldson. Cambridge: Cambridge University Press, 1975.

Gerson, Jean. *Ouevres complètes.* Edited by Palemon Glorieux. 7 vols. Paris: Desclée, 1960–66.

Gower, John. *Complete Works.* Edited by G. C. Macaulay. 4 vols. Oxford: Clarendon Press, 1899–1902.

———. *The Major Latin Works.* Edited and translated by E. W. Stockton. Seattle: University of Washington Press, 1962.

Gratian. *Hoc presens Graciani decretum una cum apparatu Bartho. Brixen in suis destinctionibus et causis bene visum et emendatum.* Basle: Michael Wenssler, 1481.

Grindal, Edmund. *Remains.* Edited by William Nicholson. PS, vol. 19. Cambridge: The University Press, 1842.

Hales, John. *Defence of John Hales.* In *A Discourse of the Common Weal of this Realm of England,* edited by Elizabeth Lamond, xlii–lxvii. Cambridge: The University Press, 1929.

Henry VII. *The Will of King Henry VII.* Edited by Thomas Astle. London: [Printed for the Editor], 1775.

Henry VIII. *The Letters of Henry VIII.* Edited by Muriel St. Clare Byrne. London: Cassell, 1936.

Hoccleve, Thomas. *Hoccleve's Works.* Edited by F. J. Furnivall. EETS ES, no. 72. London: Kegan Paul, Trench, Trübner, 1897; reprint, Millwood, N.Y.: Kraus, 1973.

Hooper, John. *Early Writings.* Edited by Samuel Carr. PS, vol. 20. Cambridge: The University Press, 1843.

———. *Later Writings.* Edited by Charles Nevinson. PS, vol. 21. Cambridge: The University Press, 1852.

Hudson, Anne, ed. *English Wycliffite Sermons.* Vol. 1. Oxford: Clarendon Press, 1983.

Hudson, Anne. "A Neglected Wycliffite Text." *Journal of Ecclesiastical History* 29 (1978): 257–79.

———, ed. *Selections from English Wycliffite Writings.* Cambridge: Cambridge University Press, 1978.

Humphrey, Laurence. *The Nobles, or Of Nobilitye.* London: Thomas Marshe, 1563.

The Institucion of a Gentleman. London: Thomas Marshe, 1555.

Jack Upland, Friar Daw's Reply and Upland's Rejoinder. Edited by P. L. Heyworth. Oxford: Oxford University Press, 1968.

John of Salisbury. *Policraticus, the Statesman's Book.* Edited by Murray F. Markland. New York: Frederick Ungar, 1979.

Knyghthode and Bataile. A 15th Century Verse Paraphrase of Falvius Vegitus Ranatus' Treatise "De Re Militari." Edited by R. Dyboski and Z. M. Arend. EETS OS, no. 201. London: Humphrey Milford, Oxford University Press, 1935.

Langland, William. *Piers Plowman: A New Translation of the B-Text.* Translated by A.V.C. Schmidt. Oxford: Oxford University Press, 1992.

———. *Piers Plowman, An Edition of the C-Text.* Edited by Derek Pearsall. London: Edward Arnold, 1978.

———. *Piers the Plowman, A Critical Edition of the A-Version.* Edited by Thomas Knott and David C. Fowler. Baltimore: Johns Hopkins University Press, 1952.

Latimer, Hugh. *Sermons.* Edited by George Elwes Corrie. PS, vol. 27. Cambridge: The University Press, 1844.

Lever, Thomas. *Sermons, 1550.* Edited by Edward Arber. Reprinted in *English Reprints.* Vol 6. London, 1871; reprint, New York: AMS Press, 1966.

The Libelle of Englyshe Polycye. Edited by Sir George Warner. Oxford: Clarendon Press, 1926.

Llull, Ramon. *The Book of the Ordre of Chyvalry.* Translated by William Caxton. Edited by A.T.P. Byles. EETS OS, no. 168. London: Oxford University Press, 1926.

Louen, Renaud de. *Le Livre de Mellibee et Prudence.* In *Sources and Analogues of Chaucer's Canterbury Tales,* edited by W. F. Bryan and Germaine Dempster, 568–614. New York: Humanities Press, 1958.

Luther, Martin. *Against the Robbing and Murdering Hordes of Peasants, 1525; On Whether Soldiers Can Be Saved, 1526; On Wars Against the Turk, 1529.* Edited by Robert C. Schultz. Translated by Charles M. Jacobs. In *Luther's Works,* Vol. 46: *The Christian in Society III,* edited by Helmut T. Lehmann, 161–65. Philadelphia: Fortress Press, 1967.

———. *Temporal Authority: To What Extent It Should Be Obeyed, 1523.* Edited by Walther I. Brandt. Translated by J. J. Shindel. In *Luther's Works,* Vol. 45: *The Christian in Society II,* edited by Helmut T. Lehmann, 123–29. Philadelphia: Muhlenberg Press, 1962.

Lydgate, John. *Lydgate's Siege of Thebes.* Edited by A. Erdmann and E. Ekwall. EETS ES, no. 125. London: K. Paul, Trench, Trübner, 1920.

———. *Lydgate's Troy Book.* Edited by Henry Bergen. EETS ES, no. 97. London: K. Paul, Trench, Trübner, 1906.

———. *The Minor Poems of John Lydgate. Part II: Secular Poems.* Edited by Henry N. MacCracken. EETS OS, no. 192. London: Humphrey Milford, Oxford University Press, 1934.

Marsh, Adam. *Epistolae.* In *Monumenta franciscana,* edited by J. S. Brewer. RS, no. 4. 2 vols. London: Longman, Brown, Green, Longman, and Roberts, 1858–82.

Marsilius of Padua. *The Defence of Peace.* Translated by Wyllyam Marshall. London: Robert Wyer, 1535.

Medwall, Henry. *The Plays of Henry Medwall.* Edited by Alan H. Nelson. Woodbridge, Eng.: D. S. Brewer, 1980.

Merriman, Roger B. *Life and Letters of Thomas Cromwell.* 2 vols. Oxford: Clarendon Press, 1902.

Mézières, Philippe de. *Le Songe du vieil pèlerin.* Edited by G. W. Coopland. 2 vols. Cambridge: Cambridge University Press, 1969.

———. *Letter to King Richard II: A Plea Made in 1395 for Peace between England and France.* Translated by G. W. Coopland. Liverpool: Liverpool University Press, 1975.

Michel, Dan. *Ayenbite of Inwyt, or Remorse of Conscience.* Edited by Richard Morris. EETS OS, no. 23. London: N. Trübner, 1866.

Middleton, Thomas. *The Peace-maker, or, Great Brittaines Blessing.* London: Thomas Purfoot, 1619.

Minot, Laurence. *The Poems of Laurence Minot, 1333–1352.* Edited by Thomas Beaumont James and John Simons. Exeter: University of Exeter, 1989.

More, Thomas. *Translations of Lucian.* Edited by Craig R. Thompson. In *The*

Complete Works of St. Thomas More, vol. 3, pt. 1. New Haven, Conn.: Yale University Press, 1974.

———. *Utopia.* Edited by Edward Surtz and J. H. Hexter. In *The Complete Works of St. Thomas More,* vol. 4. New Haven, Conn.: Yale University Press, 1965.

Morison, Richard. *A Remedy for Sedition.* In *Humanist Scholarship and Public Order: Two Tracts Against the Pilgrimmage of Grace,* edited by David Sandler Berkowitz. Washington, D.C.: Folger Shakespeare Library, 1984.

Mum and the Sothsegger. Edited by Mabel Day and Robert Steele. EETS OS, no. 199. London: Oxford University Press, 1936.

Origen, *Origen Against Celsus.* In *The Ante-Nicene Fathers,* edited by Alexander Roberts and James Donaldson, 4:395–669. Grand Rapids, Mich.: William B. Eerdmans, 1956.

Pace, Richard. *De fructu.* In *Early English Meals and Manners,* edited by F. J. Furnivall, xii–xiii. EETS OS, no. 32. London: Kegan Paul, Trench, Trübner, 1868.

———. *Oration on Peace.* London: Richard Pynson, 1518. Reprinted and translated in J. G. Russell, *Peacemaking in the Renaissance,* 234–41. Philadelphia: University of Pennsylvania Press, 1986.

Paget, William. "A Critique of the Protectorate: An Unpublished Letter of Sir William Paget to the Duke of Somerset." Edited by Barrett L. Beer. *Huntington Library Quarterly* 34 (1971): 277–83.

———. *The Letters of William, Lord Paget of Beaudesert, 1547–1563.* Edited by Barrett L. Beer and Sybil M. Jack. Camden Miscellany 25. C4S, vol. 13. London: Royal Historical Society, 1974.

Patten, William. *The Expedition into Scotlande of . . . Edward, Duke of Soomerset.* In *Tudor Tracts, 1532–88,* edited by A. F. Pollard, 53–78. New York: Cooper Square Publishers, 1964.

Pocock, Nicholas, ed. *Records of the Reformation.* 2 vols. Oxford: Clarendon Press, 1870.

Pole, Reginald. *The Seditious and Blasphemous Oration of Cardinal Pole Both Against God & His Country Which He Directed to Themperour in His Booke Intytuled the Defence of the Eclesiastical Unitye, Moving Themperour Therin to Seke the Destruction of England and All Those Whiche Had Professed the Gospel.* Translated by Fabyane Wythers. London: Owen Rogers, [1560].

Porcia, Jacopo di. *The Preceptes of Warre.* Translated by Peter Betham. London: Edwarde Wytchurche, 1544.

Powicke, F. M., and C. R. Cheney, ed. *Councils and Synods Relating to the English Church,* Vol. 2: 1265–1313. Oxford: Clarendon Press, 1964.

A Pretye Complaynt of Peace That Was Banyshed Out of Dyvers Countreys & Brought By Welth in to England, & Than Fearyng Both to Be Thins Exiled, Made Great Mone, Untyl Prudence Retayned Them Agayne. London: John Byddell, [1538].

Pseudo-Clement, *Recognitions of Clement.* In *The Ante-Nicene Fathers,* edited by

Alexander Roberts and James Donaldson, 8:75–211. Grand Rapids, Mich.: William B. Eerdmans, 1956.

Remigio de' Girolami. *De bono pacis (The Good of Peace)*. Edited by C. T. Davis. *Studi Danteschi* 36 (1959): 123–36.

Ross, Woodburn O., ed. *Middle English Sermons*. EETS OS, no. 209. London: Humphrey Milford, Oxford University Press, 1940.

Seymour, Edward. *An Epistle or Exhortacion, to Unitie & Peace, Sent From the Lorde Protector, & Others the Kynges Moste Honorable Counsaill of England To the Nobilitie, Gentlemen and Commons, and Al Others the Inhabitauntes of the Realme of Scotlande*. London: Richard Grafton, 1548.

Skelton, John. *The Complete English Poems*. Edited by John Scattergood. New Haven, Conn.: Yale University Press, 1983.

Smith, Thomas. *A Discourse of the Commonweal of This Realm of England*. Edited by Mary Dewar. Folger Shakespeare Library. Charlottesville: University Press of Virginia, 1969.

Starkey, Thomas. *An Exhortation to the People, Instructynge Theym to Unitie and Obedience*. London: Thomas Berthelet, [1536].

Taverner, Richard. *The Garden of Wysdom Wherin Ye Maye Gather Moste Pleasaunt Flowres, That Is to Say, Proper Wytty and Quycke Sayenges of Princes, Philosophers, and Dyvers Other Sortes of Men*. 2 vols. London: Richard Bankes, 1539.

———, ed. *Postilles or Homilies Upon the Epistles and Gospels from Ester Untyll Trinitie Sondaye*. London: Richard Bankes, 1540.

———. *Proverbes or Adagies with Newe Addicions Gathered Oute of the Chiliades of Erasmus*. London, 1539.

Tertullian, *On Idolatry* and *De corona*. In *The Ante-Nicene Fathers*, edited by Alexander Roberts and James Donaldson, 3:61–77, 93–104. Grand Rapids, Mich.: William B. Eerdmans, 1956.

Thomas of Chobham. *Summa confessorum*. Edited by F. Broomfield. Analecta Mediaevalia Namurcensia, 25, 1968.

Thomas, William. *The Works of William Thomas, Clerk of the Privy Council in the Year 1549*. Edited by Abraham D'Aubant. London: J. Almon, 1774.

Tunstall, Cuthbert. *A Sermon of Cvthbert Bysshop of Duresme, Made Upon Palme Sondaye Laste Past Before the Maiestie of Our Soverayne Lord Kyng Henry the VIII*. London: Thomas Berthelet, 1539.

Twenty-Six Political and Other Poems (Digby 102). Edited by J. Kail. EETS OS, no. 124. London: K. Paul, Trench, Trübner, 1904.

Tyndale, William. *Doctrinal Treatises*. Edited by Henry Walter. PS, vol. 42. Cambridge: The University Press, 1848.

———. *Expositions of Scripture and Practice of Prelates*. Edited by Henry Walter. PS, vol. 43. Cambridge: The University Press, 1849.

Upton, Nicholas. *The Essential Portions of Nicholas Upton's De Studio Militari, Before 1446*. Translated by John Blount. Edited by Francis P. Barnard. Oxford: Clarendon Press, 1931.

Victoria, Franciscus de. *De Indis et de jure belli relectiones*. Edited by Ernie Nys. Classics in International Law. Washington, D.C.: Carnegie Institute, 1917.

Vives, Juan Luis. *The Instruction of a Christen Woman*. Translated by Richard Hyrde. London: Thomas Berthelet, 1541.

———. *Saint Augustine, of the Citie of God: With the Learned Comments of Io. Lodovicus Vives*. Translated by J. Healey. London: G. Eld and M. Flesher, 1620.

The Vows of the Heron (Les Voeux du Héron): A Middle French Vowing Poem. Edited by John L. Grigsby and Norris J. Lacy. New York: Garland Publishing, 1992.

Walshe, Edward. *The Office and Duety in Fightyng for Our Countrey. Set Forth with Dyverse Stronge Argumentes Gathered Out of the Holy Scripture Provynge that the Affection to the Native Countrey Shulde Moche More Rule in Us Christians Then in the Turkes and Infidels, Who Were Therein So Fervent, as by the Hystoriis Doth Appere*. London: Johannes Herford, 1545.

William of Worcester. *The Boke of Noblesse: Addressed to King Edward IV on His Invasion of France in 1475*. Edited by John G. Nichols. London: J. B. Nichols & Son, 1860.

Wright, Thomas, ed. *Political Poems and Songs*. 2 vols. Roll Series 14. London: Longman, Green, Longman, and Roberts, 1859–61.

Wyclif, John. *The English Works*. Edited by F. D. Matthew. EETS OS, no. 74. London: K. Paul, Trench, Trübner, 1880.

———. *Select English Works of John Wyclif*. Edited by Thomas Arnold. Vol. 3. Oxford: Clarendon Press, 1871.

Wynnere and Wastoure. Edited by Israel Gallanz. Oxford: Oxford University Press, 1920; reprint, Cambridge: D. S. Brewer, 1974.

The Zurich Letters. Edited and translated by Hastings Robinson. 3 vols. PS, vol. 53, pts. 1 and 2. Cambridge: The University Press, 1842–46.

Zwingli, Ulrich. *Early Writings*. Edited by Samuel Macauley Jackson. Durham, N.C.: Labyrinth Press, 1987.

———. *Huldreich Zwinglis Sämtliche Werke*. Edited by E. Egli and G. Finsler. 13 vols. Berlin: C. A. Schwetschke und Sohn, 1904–68.

Secondary Sources

Adair, E. R. "William Thomas: A Forgotten Clerk of the Privy Council." In *Tudor Studies*, edited by R. W. Seton-Watson, 133–60. New York: Russell & Russell, 1924; reprint, 1970.

Adams, Robert P. *The Better Part of Valor: More, Erasmus, Colet, and Vives on Humanism, War, and Peace, 1496–1535*. Seattle: University of Washington Press, 1962.

———. "Bold Bawdry and Open Manslaughter." *Huntington Library Quarterly* 23 (1959–60): 33–48.

———. "Designs by More and Erasmus for a New Social Order." *Studies in Philology* 42 (1945): 131–45.

———. "The Literary Thought on War and Peace in English Literature of the

Renaissance." In *American Philosophical Society Year Book 1955*, 272–77. Philadelphia: American Philosophical Society, 1956.

———. "Pre-Renaissance Courtly Propaganda for Peace in English Literature." *Papers of the Michigan Academy* 32 ([1946]–48): 431–46.

Ainsworth, Peter F. *John Froissart and the Fabric of History: Truth, Myth, and Fiction in the Chronique*. Oxford: Clarendon Press, 1990.

Allen, J. W. *A History of Political Thought in the Sixteenth Century*. 3d ed. London: Methuen, 1951.

Allmand, Christopher T. *Henry V*. Berkeley and Los Angeles: University of California Press, 1992.

———. *The Hundred Years War: England and France at War, c. 1300–c. 1450*. Cambridge: Cambridge University Press, 1988.

———. "The War and the Non-Combatant." In *The Hundred Years War*, edited by Kenneth Fowler, 163–81. London: Macmillan, 1971.

———, ed. *War, Literature and Politics in the Late Middle Ages*. Liverpool: Liverpool University Press, 1976.

Ames, Russell. *Citizen Thomas More and His Utopia*. Princeton, N.J.: Princeton University Press, 1949.

Anglo, Sidney. "An Early Tudor Programme for Plays and Other Demonstrations against the Pope." *Journal of the Warburg and Courtauld Institutes* 20 (1957): 176–79.

———. *Spectacle, Pageantry and Early Tudor Policy*. Oxford: Clarendon Press, 1969.

Arnold, E. V. *Roman Stoicism*. Cambridge: The University Press, 1911.

Arthurson, Ian. "The King's Voyage into Scotland: The War that Never Was." In *England in the Fifteenth Century: Proceedings of the 1986 Harlaxton Symposium*, edited by Daniel Williams, 1–22. Suffolk, Eng.: Boydell Press, 1987.

Avineri, Shlomo. "War and Slavery in More's *Utopia*." *International Review of Social History* 7 (1962): 262–90.

Ayton, Andrew. "War and the English Gentry under Edward III." *History Today* 42 (1992): 34–40.

Bailey, Derrick S. *Thomas Becon and the Reformation of the Church in England*. Edinburgh: Oliver & Boyd, 1952.

Bainton, Roland H. *Christian Attitudes Toward War and Peace. A Historical Survey and Critical Re-Evaluation*. New York: Abingdon Press, 1960.

———. "The Querela Pacis of Erasmus, Classical and Christian Sources." *Archiv für Reformationsgeschichte* 42 (1951): 32–48.

Baker, J. H. "The English Legal Profession, 1450–1550." In *Lawyers in Early Modern Europe and America*, edited by Wilfrid Prest. New York: Holmes & Meier, 1981.

Baker-Smith, Dominic. "'Inglorious Glory': 1513 and the Humanist Attack on Chivalry." In *Chivalry in the Renaissance*, edited by Sidney Anglo, 129–44. Suffolk, Eng.: Boydell Press, 1990.

Baldwin, Anna P. *The Theme of Government in Piers Plowman*. Cambridge: D. S. Brewer, 1981.

Baldwin, John W. *Masters, Princes and Merchants: The Social Views of Peter the*

Chanter and His Circle. 2 vols. Princeton, N.J.: Princeton University Press, 1970.

Balke, Willem. *Calvin and the Anabaptist Radicals.* Translated by William Heynen. Grand Rapids, Mich.: William B. Eerdmans, 1981.

Barber, Richard. *The Knight and Chivalry.* New York: Charles Scribner's Sons, 1970.

Barnes, Jonathan. "The Just War." In *The Cambridge History of Later Medieval Philosophy,* edited by Norman Kretzmann, Anthony Kenny, and Jon Pinborg, 771–84. Cambridge: Cambridge University Press, 1982.

Barnett, Correlli. *Britain and Her Army, 1509–1970.* London: Allen Lane, The Penguin Press, 1970.

Barnie, John. *War in Medieval English Society: Social Values and the Hundred Years War, 1337–99.* London: Weidenfeld & Nicolson, 1974.

Beer, Barrett L. *Rebellion and Riot: Popular Disorder in England during the Reign of Edward VI.* Kent, Ohio: Kent State University Press, 1982.

Bense, W. F. "Paris Theologians on War and Peace, 1521–1529." *Church History* 41 (1972): 168–85.

Bergeron, David. *English Civic Pageantry 1558–1642.* London: Edward Arnold, 1971.

Bernard, G. W. *War, Taxation and Rebellion in Early Tudor England.* Brighton, Eng.: Harvester Press, 1986.

Bieler, André. *La Pensée économique et sociale de Calvin.* Geneva: Librairie de l'Université, 1959.

Blake, E. O. "The Formation of the 'Crusade Idea.'" *Journal of Ecclesiastical History* 21 (1970): 11–31.

Blench, J. W. *Preaching in England in the Late Fifteenth and Sixteenth Centuries.* New York: Barnes & Noble, 1964.

Bold, Alan, ed. *The Martial Muse: Centuries of War Poetry.* Exeter, Eng.: Wheaton, 1976.

Bond, Brian. "The 'Just War' in Historical Perspective." *History Today* 16 (1966): 111–19.

Bonnaud-Delamare, Roger. "Fondements des institutions de paix au XIe siècle." In *Mélanges d'histoire du moyen âge dédiés à la mémoire de Louis Halphen,* 21–26. Paris: Presses Universitaires de France, 1951.

Borstein, Diane. "Military Manuals in Fifteenth-Century England." *Medieval Studies* 37 (1975): 469–77.

Bouwsma, William J. *John Calvin: A Sixteenth Century Portrait.* Oxford: Oxford University Press, 1988.

Boynton, Lindsay. *The Elizabethan Militia, 1558–1638.* London: Routledge & Kegan Paul, 1967.

Brachin, Pierre. "*Vox clamantis in deserto:* Réflexions sur le pacifisme d'Erasme." In *Colloquia Erasmiana Turonensia,* edited by Jean-Claude Margolin, 1: 247–75. Toronto: University of Toronto Press, 1972.

Brewer, J. S. *The Reign of Henry VIII from His Accession to the Death of Wolsey.* Edited by James Gairdner. 2 vols. London: John Murray, 1884.

Bridoux, André. *Le Stoicisme et son influence.* Paris: Librairie Philosophique J. Vrin, 1966.

Brigden, Susan. "Thomas Cromwell and 'the Brethren.'" In *Law and Government under the Tudors,* edited by Claire Cross, David Loades, and J. J. Scarisbrick, 31–49. Cambridge: Cambridge University Press, 1988.

Brock, Peter. *Pacifism in Europe to 1914.* Princeton, N.J.: Princeton University Press, 1972.

Brundage, James A. *Medieval Canon Law and the Crusader.* Madison: University of Wisconsin Press, 1969.

Bush, M. L. *The Government Policy of Protector Somerset.* Montreal: McGill-Queen's University Press, 1975.

Cadoux, Cecil John. *The Early Christian Attitude to War.* London: Headley Bros., 1919; reprint, New York: Seabury Press, 1982.

Caillois, Roger. *Man and the Sacred.* Translated by Meyer Barash. Westport, Conn.: Greenwood Press, 1980.

Calvocoressi, Peter. *A Time for Peace: Pacifism, Internationalism and Protest Forces in the Reduction of War.* London: Hutchinson, 1987.

Cameron, Euan. *The European Reformation.* Oxford: Clarendon Press, 1991.

Carlson, A. J. "*Mundus Muliebris:* The World of Women Reviled and Defended ca. 195 B.C. and 1551 A.D. and Other Things. . . ." *Sixteenth Century Journal* 24 (1993): 541–60.

Caspari, Fritz. *Humanism and the Social Order in Tudor England.* Chicago: University of Chicago Press, 1954.

———. "Sir Thomas More and *Justum Bellum.*" *Ethics* 56 (1946): 303–8.

Charleton, Kenneth. *Education in Renaissance England.* London: Routledge & Kegan Paul, 1965.

Chester, Allan G. *Hugh Latimer: Apostle to the English.* Philadelphia: University of Pennsylvania Press, 1954.

Chew, Audrey. *Stoicism in Renaissance English Literature.* New York: Peter Lang, 1988.

Chrimes, S. B. *Henry VII.* Berkeley and Los Angeles: University of California Press, 1972.

Clair, Colin. *A History of Printing in Britain.* London: Cassell, 1965.

Clark, Peter. *English Provincial Society from the Reformation to the Revolution: Religion, Politics and Society in Kent, 1500–1640.* Hassocks, Eng.: Harvester Press, 1977.

Clough, Cecil H., ed. *Profession, Vocation, and Culture in Later Medieval England.* Liverpool: Liverpool University Press, 1982.

Coffman, George R. "John Gower in His Most Significant Role." In *Elizabethan Studies and Other Essays in Honour of George F. Reynolds,* 52–61. Boulder: University of Colorado Studies, 1945.

———. "John Gower, Mentor for Royalty: Richard II." *PMLA* 69 (1954): 953–64.

Coleman, Janet. "English Culture in the Fourteenth Century." In *Chaucer and the Italian Tricento,* edited by Piero Boitani, 33–63. Cambridge: Cambridge University Press, 1983.

———. *Medieval Readers and Writers, 1350–1400.* New York: Columbia University Press, 1981.

Collinson, Patrick. *The Birthpangs of Protestant England: Religious and Cultural*

Change in the Sixteenth and Seventeenth Centuries. New York: St. Martin's Press, 1988.

Condren, Conal. *The Status and Appraisal of Classical Texts: An Essay on Political Theory, Its Inheritance, and on the History of Ideas*. Princeton, N.J.: Princeton University Press, 1985.

Constant, Jean-Marie. *La Vie quotidienne de la noblesse française aux XVIe and XVIIe siècles*. Paris: Hachette Littérature, 1985.

Contamine, Philippe. "France at the End of the Middle Ages: Who Was Then the Gentleman?" In *Gentry and Lesser Nobility in Late Medieval Europe*, edited by Michael Jones, 210–16. New York: St. Martin's Press, 1986.

———. "La Théologie de la guerre à la fin du moyen âge: La Guerre de cent ans fut elle une guerre juste?" In *Jeanne d'Arc: Une époque, un rayonnement*, edited by J. Glenisson, 9–21. Paris: n.p., 1982.

———. *War in the Middle Ages*. Translated by Michael Jones. Oxford: Basil Blackwell, 1984.

Cooper, Helen. *Pastoral: Medieval Into Renaissance*. Ipswich, Eng.: D. S. Brewer, 1977.

Copeland, Rita. "Lydgate, Hawes, and the Science of Rhetoric in the Late Middle Ages." *Modern Language Quarterly* 53 (1992): 57–82.

Corvisier, André. *Armies and Societies in Europe, 1494–1789*. Translated by Abigail T. Siddall. Bloomington: Indiana University Press, 1979.

Cottle, Basil. *The Triumph of English, 1350–1400*. New York: Barnes & Noble, 1969.

Coulton, G. G. *Chaucer and His England*. London: Methuen, 1908.

Cowdrey, H.E.J. "The Peace and Truce of God in the Eleventh Century." *Past and Present* 46 (1970): 42–67.

Crane, Ronald. *The Vogue of Medieval Chivalric Romance During the English Renaissance*. Menasha, Wis.: George Banta, 1919.

Crowder, C.M.D. "Peace and Justice around 1400: A Sketch." In *Aspects of Late Medieval Government and Society. Essays Presented to J. R. Lander,* edited by J. G. Rowe, 53–81. Toronto: University of Toronto Press, 1986.

Crowson, Paul S. *Tudor Foreign Policy*. New York: St. Martin's Press, 1973.

Cruickshank, C. G. *Army Royal. Henry VIII's Invasion of France, 1513*. Oxford: Clarendon Press, 1969.

———. *Elizabeth's Army*. 2d ed. Oxford: Clarendon Press, 1966.

Curry, Anne. "The First English Standing Army? Military Organization in Lancastrian Normandy, 1420–1450." In *Patronage, Pedigree and Power in Later Medieval England,* edited by Charles Ross. Totowa, N.J.: Rowman & Littlefield, 1979.

Cuttino, G. P. *English Medieval Diplomacy*. Bloomington: Indiana University Press, 1985.

Cytowska, Maria. "Erasme et les Turcs." *Eos* 62 (1974): 311–21.

Daly, L. J. *The Political Theory of John Wyclif*. Chicago: Loyola University Press, 1962.

Davies, C.S.L. "England and the French War, 1557–9." In *The Mid-Tudor Polity,*

c. 1540–1560, edited by Jennifer Loach and Robert Tittler, 159–85. Totowa, N.J.: Rowman & Littlefield, 1980.

———. "The English People and War in the Early Sixteenth Century." In *Britain
and the Netherlands,* Vol. VI, *War and Society,* edited by A. C. Duke and
C. A. Tamse, 1–18. The Hague: Martinus Nijhoff, 1977.

———. "Provisions for Armies, 1509–1550: A Study in the Effectiveness of Early
Tudor Government." *Economic History Review* 17 (1964): 234–48.

———. "Supply Services of English Armed Forces, 1509–50." Ph.D. diss., Oxford
University, 1963.

Davies, R. G. "Lollardy and Locality." *TRHS,* 6th ser., 1 (1991): 191–212.

Davis, C. T. "Remigio de' Girolami and Dante. A Comparison of Their Conceptions of Peace." *Studi Danteschi* 36 (1959): 110–14.

Davis, J. F. "The Trials of Thomas Bilney and the English Reformation." *Historical
Journal* 24 (1981): 775–90.

Dean, James. "Gower, Chaucer, and the Rhyme Royal." *Studies in Philology* 88
(1991): 251–75.

Denholm-Young, N. "Richard de Bury (1287–1345)." *TRHS,* 4th ser., 20 (1937):
135–68.

Dibdin, Thomas F. *Typographical Antiquities of Great Britain.* Vol. 3. London:
John Murray, 1816.

Dickens, A. G. *The English Reformation.* 2d ed. University Park: Pennsylvania
State University Press, 1991.

Dickens, A. G., and Whitney R. D. Jones. *Erasmus the Reformer.* London: Methuen, 1994.

Donagan, Barbara. "Did Ministers Matter? War and Religion in England, 1642–
1649." *Journal of British Studies* 33 (1994): 119–56.

Dowling, Maria. *Humanism in the Age of Henry VIII.* London: Croom Helm,
1986.

Duby, Georges. *The Legend of Bouvines: War, Religion and Culture in the Middle
Ages.* Translated by Catherine Tihanyi. Berkeley and Los Angeles: University
of California Press, 1990.

Duff, E. Gordon. *The Printers, Stationers and Bookbinders of Westminster and
London from 1476 to 1535.* Cambridge: The University Press, 1906.

Duff, E. Gordon, H. R. Plomer, and R. Proctor. *Hand-Lists of English Printers
1501–1556.* Part 2. London: Blade, East & Blades, 1896.

Dunlop, David. "The Politics of Peace-Keeping: Anglo-Scottish Relations from
1503 to 1511." *Renaissance Studies* 8 (1994): 138–61.

Dust, Philip C. *Three Renaissance Pacifists. Essays in the Theories of Erasmus,
More, and Vives.* American University Studies, ser. 9, History, vol. 23. New
York: Peter Lang, 1987.

Eaves, Richard Glen. *Henry VIII's Scottish Diplomacy, 1513–1524: England's Relations with the Regency Government of James V.* New York: Exposition
Press, 1971.

Ebin, Linda A. *John Lydgate.* Boston: Twayne, 1985.

Eisenstein, Elizabeth. *The Printing Revolution in Early Modern Europe.* Cambridge: Cambridge University Press, 1983.

Eliav-Feldon, Miriam. "Grand Designs: The Peace Plans of the Late Renaissance." *Vivarium* 27 (1989): 51–76.

Elton, G. R. "English National Self-Consciousness and the Parliament in the Six-teenth Century." In *Studies in Tudor and Stuart Politics and Government,* vol. 4, *Papers and Reviews, 1983–1990,* 131–43. Cambridge: Cambridge University Press, 1992.

———. *Policy and Police: The Enforcement of the Reformation in the Age of Thomas Cromwell.* Cambridge: Cambridge University Press, 1972.

———. "Reform and the 'Commonwealth-Men' of Edward VI's Reign." In *The English Commonwealth, 1547–1640: Essays in Politics and Society,* edited by Peter Clark, Alan Smith, and Nicholas Tyacke, 23–38. New York: Barnes & Noble, 1979.

———. *Reform and Reformation: England, 1509–1558.* Cambridge: Harvard University Press, 1977.

———. "Taxation for War and Peace in Early Tudor England." In *War and Economic Development,* edited by J. M. Winter, 33–48. Cambridge: Cambridge University Press, 1975.

———. "Tudor Government: The Points of Contact, Part 3: The Court." *TRHS,* 5th ser., 26 (1976): 211–28.

Esler, Anthony. *The Aspiring Mind of the Elizabethan Younger Generation.* Durham, N.C.: Duke University Press, 1966.

Evans, G. R. *Problems of Authority in the Reformation Debates.* Cambridge: Cambridge University Press, 1992.

Ferguson, Arthur B. *The Articulate Citizen and the English Renaissance.* Durham, N.C.: Duke University Press, 1965.

———. *The Chivalric Tradition in Renaissance England.* Washington, D.C.: Folger Shakespeare Library, 1986.

———. *The Indian Summer of English Chivalry.* Durham, N.C.: Duke University Press, 1960.

———. "Renaissance Realism in the 'Commonwealth' Literature of Early Tudor England." *Journal of the History of Ideas* 16 (1955): 287–305.

———. "The Tudor Commonweal and the Sense of Change." *Journal of British Studies* 3 (1963): 11–35.

Fernandez, J. A. "Erasmus on the Just War." *History of the History of Ideas* 34 (1973): 209–26.

Fernandez-Santamaria, J. A. *The State, War and Peace: Spanish Political Thought in the Renaissance, 1516–1559.* Cambridge: Cambridge University Press, 1977.

Fideler, Paul A., and T. F. Mayer, ed. *Political Thought and the Tudor Commonwealth: Deep Structure, Discourse and Disguise.* London: Routledge, 1992.

Fisher, John H. *John Gower, Moral Philosopher and Friend of Chaucer.* New York: New York University Press, 1964.

Fowler, Kenneth, ed. *The Hundred Years War.* London: Macmillan, 1971.

Fox, Alistair. *Politics and Literature in the Reigns of Henry VII and Henry VIII.* Oxford: Basil Blackwell, 1989.

Fox, Alistair, and John Guy, eds. *Reassessing the Henrician Age: Humanism, Politics, and Reform, 1500–1550.* Oxford: Basil Blackwell, 1986.

Fryde, E. B. "Parliament and the French War." In *Essays in Medieval History Presented to Bertie Wilkinson,* edited by T. A. Sandquist and M. R. Powicke, 250–69. Toronto: University of Toronto Press, 1969.

Gammon, S. R. *Statesman and Schemer: William, First Lord Paget, Tudor Minister.* Hamden, Conn.: Archon Books, 1973.

Genet, Jean-Philippe. "Ecclesiastics and Political Theory in Late Medieval England: The End of a Monopoly." In *The Church, Politics and Patronage in the Fifteenth Century,* edited by Barrie Dobson, 23–43. New York: St. Martin's Press, 1984.

Gillingham, John. *The Wars of the Roses: Peace and Conflict in Fifteenth-Century England.* Baton Rouge: Louisiana State University Press, 1981.

Gillingham, John, and J. C. Holt, ed. *War and Government in the Middle Ages.* Woodbridge, Eng.: Boydell Press, 1984.

Gist, Margaret A. *Love and War in the Middle English Romances.* Philadelphia: University of Pennsylvania Press, 1947.

Gleason, John B. *John Colet.* Berkeley and Los Angeles: University of California Press, 1989.

Göller, Karl Hanz. "Reality versus Romance: A Reassessment of the *Alliterative Morte Arthure.*" In *The Alliterative Morte Arthure: A Reassessment of the Poem,* edited by Karl Hanz Göller, 15–29. Cambridge: D. S. Brewer, 1981.

———. "War and Peace in the Middle English Romances and Chaucer." In *War and Peace in the Middle Ages,* edited by Brian Patrick McGuire, 118–45. Copenhagen: C. A. Reitzels, 1987.

Goodman, Anthony. *The Wars of the Roses: Military Activity and English Society, 1452–97.* London: Routledge & Kegan Paul, 1981.

Goring, John Jeremy. "The Military Obligations of the English People, 1511–1558." Ph.D. diss., University of London, 1955.

Grady, Frank. "The Lancastrian Gower and the Limits of Exemplarity." *Speculum* 70 (1995): 552–75.

———. "Social Change and Military Decline in Mid-Tudor England." *History* 60 (1975): 185–97.

Greenblatt, Stephen. *Renaissance Self-Fashioning: From More to Shakespeare.* Chicago: University of Chicago Press, 1980.

Greenslade, Stanley L. *The English Reformers and the Fathers of the Church.* Oxford: Clarendon Press, 1960.

Gunn, Steven. "The French Wars of Henry VIII." In *The Origins of War in Early Modern Europe,* edited by Jeremy Black, 28–51. Edinburgh: John Donald Publishers, 1987.

Gunn, S. J., and P. G. Lindley, ed. *Cardinal Wolsey: Church, State and Art.* Cambridge: Cambridge University Press, 1991.

Guy, J. A. *The Public Career of Sir Thomas More.* Brighton, Eng.: Harvester Press, 1980.

———. *Tudor England.* Oxford: Oxford University Press, 1988.

———. "Wolsey and the Parliament of 1523." In *Law and Government Under the Tudors,* edited by Claire Cross, David Loades, and J. J. Scarisbrick, 1–18. Cambridge: Cambridge University Press, 1988.

Gwynn, Aubrey. "Richard FitzRalph. Part III." *Studies* 23 (1934): 395–411.

———. "The Sermon-Diary of Richard FitzRalph, Archbishop of Armagh." *Proceedings of the Royal Irish Academy* 44, sec. C (1937–38): 1–57.

Haigh, Christopher. *English Reformations: Religion, Politics, and Society under the Tudors.* Oxford: Clarendon Press, 1993.

Haines, Keith. "Attitudes and Impediments to Pacifism in Medieval Europe." *Journal of Medieval History* 7 (1981): 369–89.

Haines, Roy M. "An English Archbishop and the Cerberus of War." In *The Church and War,* edited by W. J. Sheils, 153–70. SCH, vol. 20. Oxford: Basil Blackwell, 1983.

Hale, John R. *Renaissance War Studies.* London: Hambledon Press, 1983.

———. "Sixteenth-Century Explanations of War and Violence." *Past and Present* 51 (1971): 3–26.

———. *War and Society in Renaissance Europe, 1450–1620.* Leicester: Leicester University Press, 1985.

Harlan, David. "Intellectual History and the Return of Literature." *American Historical Review* 94 (1989): 581–609.

Hartigan, Richard S. "Saint Augustine on War and Killing." *Journal of the History of Ideas* 27 (1966): 195–204.

Hattaway, Michael. "Blood Is Their Argument: Men of War and Soldiers in Shakespeare and Others." In *Religion, Culture and Society in Early Modern Britain: Essays in Honour of Patrick Collinson,* edited by Anthony Fletcher and Peter Roberts, 84–101. Cambridge: Cambridge University Press, 1994.

Hayward, John. *The Life and Raigne of King Edward the Sixth.* Edited by Barrett L. Beer. Kent, Ohio: Kent University Press, 1993.

Heath, Michael J. "Erasmus and War against the Turks." In *Acta Conventus Neo-Latini Turonensis,* edited by Jean-Claude Margolin, 991–99. Paris: Vrin, 1980.

Hewitt, Herbert J. *The Organization of War under Edward III: 1338–62.* New York: Barnes & Noble, 1966.

Hexter, J. H. "The Education of the Aristocracy in the Renaissance." *Journal of Modern History* 22 (1950): 1–20.

———. *More's Utopia, the Biography of an Idea.* Princeton, N.J.: Princeton University Press, 1952.

Hillerbrand, Hans J. "Martin Luther and the Bull *Exsurge Domine.*" *Theological Studies* 30 (1969): 108–12.

Hoak, Dale. *The King's Council in the Reign of Edward VI.* Cambridge: Cambridge University Press, 1976.

———. "The Secret History of the Tudor Court: The King's Coffers and the King's Purse, 1542–1553." *Journal of British Studies* 26 (1987): 208–31.

Holdsworth, C. J. "Ideas and Reality: Some Attempts to Control and Defuse War in the Twelfth Century." In *The Church and War,* edited by W. J. Sheils, 59–78. SCH, vol. 20. London: Basil Blackwell, 1983.

Hooker, James R. "Notes on the Organization and Supply of the Tudor Military under Henry VII." *Huntington Library Quarterly* 23 (1959–60): 19–31.

Howard, Jean H. "The New Historicism in Renaissance Studies." *English Literary Renaissance* 16 (1986): 3–33.

Howard, Michael. "Constraints on Warfare." In *The Laws of War: Constraints on Warfare in the Western World,* edited by Michael Howard, George J. Andreopoulos, and Mark R. Shulman, 1–11. New Haven, Conn.: Yale University Press, 1994.

———. *War and the Liberal Conscience.* New Brunswick, N.J.: Rutgers University Press, 1978.

Hudson, Anne. *The Premature Reformation.* Oxford: Clarendon Press, 1988.

———. "Wycliffism in Oxford, 1381–1411." In *Wyclif in His Times,* edited by Anthony Kenny, 67–84. Oxford: Clarendon Press, 1986.

Huizinga, Johan. *Men and Ideas.* Translated by James S. Holmes and Hans van Merle. London: Eyre & Spottiswoode, 1960.

Huppé, B. F. "The A-Text of *Piers Plowman* and the Norman Wars." *PMLA* 54 (1939): 37–64.

Hutton, James. "Erasmus and France: the Propaganda for Peace." *Studies in the Renaissance* 8 (1961): 103–27.

———. *Themes of Peace in Renaissance Poetry.* Ithaca, N.Y.: Cornell University Press, 1984.

Jacob, E. F. *The Fifteenth Century, 1399–1485.* Oxford: Clarendon Press, 1961.

James, Mervyn. *English Politics and the Concept of Honour, 1485–1642. Past and Present,* Supplement, no. 3 (1969).

Jesperson, Knud J. V. "Social Change and Military Revolution in Early Modern Europe." *Historical Journal* 26 (1983): 1–14.

Johnson, James Turner. *Ideology, Reason, and the Limitation of War: Religious and Secular Concepts, 1200–1740.* Princeton, N.J.: Princeton University Press, 1975.

———. *Just War Tradition and the Restraint of War.* Princeton, N.J.: Princeton University Press, 1981.

———. *The Quest for Peace: Three Moral Traditions in Western Cultural History.* Princeton, N.J.: Princeton University Press, 1987.

———. "Two Kinds of Pacifism: Opposition to the Political Use of Force in the Renaissance-Reformation Period." *Journal of Religious Ethics* 12 (1984): 39–60.

Johnson, Lynn Staley. "Inverse Counsel: Contexts for the *Melibee.*" *Studies in Philology* 87 (1992): 137–45.

Jones, Terry. *Chaucer's Knight: The Portrait of a Medieval Mercenary.* Baton Rouge: Louisiana State University Press, 1980.

Jones, W. R. "The English Church and Royal Propaganda During the Hundred Years War." *Journal of British Studies* 19 (1979): 18–30.

Jones, Whitney R. D. *The Tudor Commonwealth, 1529–1559.* London: Athlone Press, 1970.

Jordan, W. K. *Edward VI: The Threshold of Power.* Cambridge: Harvard University Press, 1970.

———. *Edward VI: The Young King.* Cambridge: Harvard University Press, 1968.

Jorgensen, Paul A. "Theoretical Views of War in Elizabethan England." *Journal of the History of Ideas* 15 (1952): 469–79.

Kaeuper, Richard W. *War, Justice, and Public Order. England and France in the Later Middle Ages.* Oxford: Oxford University Press, 1988.

Keen, Maurice. "Chaucer's Knight, the English Aristocracy and the Crusade." In *English Court Culture in the Later Middle Ages,* edited by V. J. Scattergood and J. W. Sherborne, 45–61. New York: St. Martin's Press, 1983.

———. "The Influence of Wyclif." In *Wyclif in His Times,* edited by Anthony Kenny, 127–45. Oxford: Clarendon Press, 1986.

———. *The Laws of War in the Late Middle Ages.* London: Routledge & Kegan Paul, 1965.

———. "War, Peace and Chivalry." In *War and Peace in the Middle Ages,* edited by Brian Patrick McGuire, 94–117. Copenhagen: C. A. Reitzels, 1987.

Keeney, Barnaby C. "Military Service and the Development of Nationalism in England, 1272–1327." *Speculum* 22 (1947): 534–49.

Kekewich, Margaret. "George Ashby's 'The Active Policy of a Prince': An Additional Source." *Review of English Studies* 41 (1990): 533–35.

Kelley, Donald R. "Ideas of Resistance before Elizabeth." In *The Historical Renaissance: New Essays on Tudor and Stuart Literature and Culture,* edited by Heather Dubrow and Richard Strier, 48–76. Chicago: University of Chicago Press, 1988.

Kelso, Ruth. *The Doctrine of the English Gentleman in the Sixteenth Century.* Urbana: University of Illinois Press, 1929; reprint, Gloucester, Mass.: Peter Smith, 1964.

Kilgour, Raymond Lincoln. *The Decline of Chivalry as Shown in the French Literature of the Late Middle Ages.* Cambridge: Harvard University Press, 1937; reprint, Gloucester, Mass.: Peter Smith, 1966.

King, John N. "Crowley's Editions of *Piers Plowman*: A Tudor Apocalypse." *Modern Philology* 73 (1973): 346–48.

Klein, Arthur J. *Intolerance in the Reign of Elizabeth, Queen of England.* Boston: Houghton Mifflin, 1917; reprint, Port Washington, N.Y.: Kennikat Press, 1968.

Knappen, M. M. *Tudor Puritanism.* Chicago: University of Chicago Press, 1939.

Kristeller, Paul Oskar. "The Moral Thought of Renaissance Humanism." In *Renaissance Thought and the Arts: Collected Essays,* 20–68. Princeton, N.J.: Princeton University Press, 1990.

Kunz, Josef L. "*Bellum Justum* and *Bellum Legale.*" *American Journal of International Law* 45 (1951): 528–34.

LaCapra, Dominick. "Rethinking Intellectual History and Reading Texts." In *Modern European Intellectual History: Reappraisals and New Perspectives,* edited by Dominick LaCapra and Steven L. Kaplan, 47–85. Ithaca, N.Y.: Cornell University Press, 1982.

Lange, Christian L. *Histoire de la doctrine pacifique et de son influence sur le développement du droit international.* Academy of International Law. Recueil des cours, no. 3, 13:171–426. The Hague: Academy of International Law, 1926; reprint, New York: Garland, 1973.

Lanham, Richard A. *The Motives of Eloquence: Literary Rhetoric in the Renaissance.* New Haven, Conn.: Yale University Press, 1976.

Lake, Peter, and Maria Dowling, ed. *Protestantism and the National Church in Sixteenth-Century England.* London: Croom Helm, 1987.

Lander, J. R. "The Hundred Years War and Edward IV's 1475 Campaign in France." In *Tudor Men and Institutions: Studies in English Law and Government,* edited by Arthur J. Slavin, 70–100. Baton Rouge: Louisiana State University Press, 1972.

———. *The Limitations of English Monarchy in the Later Middle Ages.* Toronto: University of Toronto Press, 1989.

———. *The Wars of the Roses.* London: White Lion Publishers, 1965.

Langsam, G. Geoffrey. *Martial Books and Tudor Verse.* New York: King's Crown Press, 1951.

Lawrence, William W. "The Tale of Melibeus." In *Essays and Studies in Honor of Carleton Brown,* 100–110. New York: New York University Press, 1940.

Leeds, Josiah. *Wiclif's Anti-War Views,* 2d ed. London: Friends Tract Association, 1902.

Lehmberg, Stanford E. *The Later Parliaments of Henry VIII, 1536–1547.* Cambridge: Cambridge University Press, 1977.

———. *Sir Thomas Elyot, Tudor Humanist.* Austin: University of Texas Press, 1960.

Levy, F. J. *Tudor Historical Thought.* San Marino, Calif.: Huntington Library, 1967.

Lewis, P. S. "War, Propaganda and Historiography in Fifteenth-Century France and England." *TRHS,* 5th ser., 15 (1965): 1–21.

Lloyd, Simon D. *English Society and the Crusade, 1216–1307.* Oxford: Oxford University Press, 1988.

Loach, Jennifer. *Parliament under the Tudors.* Oxford: Oxford University Press, 1991.

Loades, David. *The Mid-Tudor Crisis, 1545–1565.* New York: St. Martin's Press, 1992.

———. "The Origins of English Protestant Nationalism." In *Religion and National Identity,* edited by Stuart Mews, 297–307. SCH, vol. 18. Oxford: Basil Blackwell, 1983.

———. "Martin Luther and the Early Stages of the English Reformation." In *Politics, Censorship and the English Reformation.* London: Pinter, 1991.

———. *The Reign of Mary Tudor.* 2d ed. London: Longman, 1991.

Logan, George M. *The Meaning of More's Utopia.* Princeton, N.J.: Princeton University Press, 1983.

Lowe, Ben. "The Emergence of a Peace Ethic in England, 1337–1600." Ph.D. diss., Georgetown University, 1990.

———. "Peace Discourse and Mid-Tudor Foreign Policy." In *Political Thought and the Tudor Commonwealth: Deep Structure, Discourse, and Disguise,* edited by Paul A. Fideler and T. F. Mayer, 108–39. London: Routledge, 1992.

———. "Religious Wars and the 'Common Peace': Anglican Anti-War Sentiment in Elizabethan England." *Albion* 28 (1996): 415–35.

———. "The Role of Peace in Elizabethan Military Strategy, 1572–1593: A Look at the Manuals." *Fides et Historia* 24 (1992): 3–14.

———. "War and the Commonwealth in Mid-Tudor England." *Sixteenth Century Journal* 21 (1990): 171–91.

Lupton, J. H. *A Life of John Colet.* London: G. Bell & Sons, 1909.

MacCracken, Henry N. "Vegetius in English." In *Anniversary Papers by Colleagues and Pupils of George Lyman Kittredge,* edited by E. S. Sheldon, W. A. Neilson, and F. N. Robinson, 389–403. Boston: Ginn, 1913.

MacCulloch, Diarmaid. "England." In *The Early Reformation in Europe,* edited by Andrew Pettigree, 66–87. Cambridge: Cambridge University Press, 1992.

———. "Two Dons in Politics: Thomas Cranmer and Stephen Gardiner, 1503–1533." *Historical Journal* 37 (1994): 1–22.

Maclure, Millar. *The Paul's Cross Sermons, 1534–1642.* Toronto: University of Toronto Press, 1958.

Maddicott, J. R. "Poems of Social Protest in Early Fourteenth-Century England." In *England in the Fourteenth Century: Proceedings of the 1985 Harlaxton Symposium,* edited by W. M. Ormrod, 130–44. Woodbridge, Eng.: Boydell Press, 1986.

Manning, Roger B. "Poaching as a Symbolic Substitute for War in Tudor and Early Stuart England." *Journal of Medieval and Renaissance Studies* 22 (1992): 185–210.

Margolin, Jean-Claude. "Erasme et la guerre contre les turcs." *Il pensiero politico* 13 (1980): 3–38.

———. *Guerre et paix dans la pensée d'Erasme.* Paris: Aubier Montaigne, 1973.

Markus, R. A. "Saint Augustine's Views on the 'Just War.'" In *The Church and War,* edited by W. J. Sheils, 1–13. SCH, vol. 20. Oxford: Basil Blackwell, 1983.

Marrin, Albert, ed. *War and the Christian Conscience: From Augustine to Martin Luther King, Jr.* Chicago: Henry Regnery, 1971.

Marx, Steven. "Shakespeare's Pacifism." *Renaissance Quarterly* 45 (1992): 49–96.

Mayer, Thomas F. *Thomas Starkey and the Commonweal: Humanist Politics and Religion in the Reign of Henry VIII.* Cambridge: Cambridge University Press, 1989.

McConica, James K. *English Humanists and Reformation Politics under Henry VIII and Edward VI.* Oxford: Clarendon Press, 1965.

McCoy, Richard C. *The Rites of Knighthood: The Literature and Politics of Elizabethan Chivalry.* Berkeley and Los Angeles: University of California Press, 1989.

McFarlane, K. B. *John Wycliffe and the Beginnings of English Nonconformity.* London: English Universities Press, 1952.

———. *Lancastrian Kings and Lollard Knights.* Oxford: Clarendon Press, 1972.

———. "William Worcester: A Preliminary Survey." In *Studies Presented to Sir Hilary Jenkinson,* edited by J. Conway Davies, 198–214. London: Oxford University Press, 1937.

McGrath, Alister. *The Intellectual Origins of the European Reformation.* Oxford: Blackwell, 1987.

McGuire, Brian Patrick. "The Church and the Control of Violence in the Early Middle Ages: Friendship and Peace in the Letters of Gerbert, 982–97." In

War and Peace in the Middle Ages, edited by Brian Patrick McGuire, 30–55. Copenhagen: C. A. Reitzels, 1987.

McHardy, A. K. "The English Clergy and the Hundred Years War." In *The Church and War,* edited by W. J. Sheils, 171–78. SCH, vol. 20. Oxford: Basil Blackwell, 1983.

————. "Liturgy and Propaganda in the Diocese of Lincoln during the Hundred Years War." In *Religion and National Identity,* edited by Stuart Mews, 215–27. SCH, vol. 18. Oxford: Basil Blackwell, 1983.

McKenna, J. W. "Henry VI of England and the Dual Monarchy: Aspects of Royal Political Propaganda, 1422–32." *Journal of the Warburg and Courtauld Institutes* 28 (1965): 145–62.

McKisack, May. *The Fourteenth Century, 1307–1399.* The Oxford History of England. Oxford: Clarendon Press, 1959.

McQuail, Denis. *Mass Communication Theory.* 2d ed. London: Sage, 1987.

McShane, Edith. *Tudor Opinions of the Chivalric Romance.* Microcards. Washington, D.C.: Catholic University of America Press, 1950.

Meron, Theodor. *Henry's Wars and Shakespeare's Laws: Perspective on the Law of War in the Later Middle Ages.* Oxford: Clarendon Press, 1993.

Millar, Gilbert J. *Tudor Mercenaries and Auxiliaries.* Charlottesville: University Press of Virginia, 1980.

Miller, Helen. *Henry VIII and the English Nobility.* Oxford: Basil Blackwell, 1986.

Mitchell, Jerome. *Thomas Hoccleve: A Study in Early Fifteenth-Century English Poetics.* Urbana: University of Illinois Press, 1969.

Monsarrat, Gilles D. *Light from the Porch: Stoicism and English Renaissance Literature.* Collection Etudes Anglaises no. 86. Paris: Didier-Erudition, 1984.

Moran, Jo Ann H. *The Growth of English Schooling, 1340–1548: Learning, Literacy, and Laicization in Pre-Reformation York Diocese.* Princeton, N.J.: Princeton University Press, 1985.

Moreau, Jean-Pierre. *Rome ou l'Angleterre? Les réactions politiques des catholiques anglais au moment du schisme (1529–1553).* Paris: Presses Universitaires de France, 1984.

Muller, J. A. *Stephen Gardiner and the Tudor Reaction.* New York: Macmillan, 1926; reprint, New York: Octagon Books, 1970.

Munro, John H. "Patterns of Trade, Money, and Credit." In *Handbook of European History, 1400–1600: Late Middle Ages, Renaissance, and Reformation,* edited by Thomas A. Brady Jr., Heiko A. Oberman, and James D. Tracy; vol. 1, *Structures and Assertions,* edited by Thomas A. Brady Jr., 147–95. Leiden: E. J. Brill, 1994.

Musto, Ronald G. *The Catholic Peace Tradition.* Maryknoll, N.Y.: Orbis Books, 1986.

————. "Just Wars and Evil Empires: Erasmus and the Turks." In *Renaissance Society and Culture: Essays in Honor of Eugene F. Rice, Jr.,* edited by John Monfasani and Ronald G. Musto, 197–216. New York: Italica Press, 1991.

Nef, John U. "War and Economic Progress, 1540–1640." *Economic History Review* 12 (1942): 13–38.

————. *War and Human Progress: An Essay on the Rise of Industrial Civilization.* Cambridge: Harvard University Press, 1950.

Neillands, Robin. *The Hundred Years War.* London: Routledge, 1990.

Norris, Christopher. *Deconstruction and the Interests of Theory.* London: Pinter, 1989.

Nussbaum, Arthur. "Just War—A Legal Concept?" *Michigan Law Review* 42 (1943): 453–79.

Nuttall, Geoffrey F. *Christian Pacifism in History.* Oxford: Basil Blackwell, 1958.

Olin, John C. "The Pacifism of Erasmus." In *Six Essays on Erasmus,* 17–31. New York: Fordham University Press, 1979.

Oman, C.W.C. *The Art of War in the Middle Ages.* Revised and edited by John H. Beeler. Ithaca, N.Y.: Cornell University Press, 1953.

Ong, Walter J., S.J. *The Presence of the Word: Some Prolegomena for Cultural and Religious History.* New Haven, Conn.: Yale University Press, 1967.

Orme, Nicholas. "The Education of the Courtier." In *English Court Culture in the Later Middle Ages,* edited by V. J. Scattergood and J. W. Sherborne, 63–85. New York: St. Martin's Press, 1983.

Ormrod, W. M. *The Reign of Edward III: Crown and Political Society in England, 1327–1377.* New Haven, Conn.: Yale University Press, 1990.

Owst, G. R. *Literature and the Pulpit in Medieval England.* 2d ed. Oxford: Basil Blackwell, 1961.

————. *Preaching in Medieval England.* Cambridge: The University Press, 1926.

Painter, Sidney. *French Chivalry: Chivalric Ideas and Practices in Medieval France.* Baltimore: Johns Hopkins University Press, 1940; reprint, Ithaca, N.Y.: Cornell University Press, 1957.

————. *William Marshal.* Baltimore: Johns Hopkins University Press, 1933.

Palmer, J.J.N. *England, France and Christendom, 1377–99.* Chapel Hill: University of North Carolina Press, 1972.

————. "The War Aims of the Protagonists and the Negotiations for Peace." In *The Hundred Years War,* edited by Kenneth Fowler, 51–74. London: Macmillan, 1971.

Parker, Geoffrey. "Early Modern Europe." In *The Laws of War: Constraints on Warfare in the Western World,* edited by Michael Howard, George J. Andreopoulos, and Mark R. Shulman, 40–58. New Haven, Conn.: Yale University Press, 1994.

Parrow, Kathleen Ann. "The Use of Defense and Just War Concepts during the French Wars of Religions: A Preliminary Study in the Justification of Violence." Ph.D. diss., University of Rochester, 1986.

Patterson, Annabel. *Reading Holinshed's Chronicles.* Chicago: University of Chicago Press, 1994.

Pearsall, Derek. *John Lydgate.* London: Routledge & Kegan Paul, 1970.

————. "Lydgate as Innovator." *Modern Language Quarterly* 53 (1992): 5–22.

Peck, Russell A. *Kingship and Common Profit in Gower's "Confessio Amantis."* Carbondale: Southern Illinois University Press, 1978.

Pettegree, Andrew. *Foreign Protestant Communities in Sixteenth-Century London.* Oxford: Clarendon Press, 1986.

Plomer, H. R. *Hand-Lists of English Printers, 1501–1556.* Pt. 2. London: Blades, East & Blades, 1896.

Pocock, J.G.A. "The Concept of a Language and the *Métier d'Historien:* Some Considerations on Practice." In *The Languages of Political Theory in Early Modern Europe,* edited by Anthony Pagden, 19–38. Cambridge: Cambridge University Press, 1987.

Pollard, A. F. *The Reign of Henry VII from Contemporary Sources.* Vol. 1, *Narrative and Extracts.* London: Longmans, Green, 1913.

Porter, Elizabeth. "Chaucer's Knight, the *Alliterative Morte Arthure,* and Medieval Laws of War: A Reconsideration." *Nottingham Medieval Studies* 27 (1983): 56–78.

Postan, M. M. "Some Social Consequences of the Hundred Years' War." *Economic History Review* 12 (1942): 1–8.

Potter, D. L. "Diplomacy in the Mid-Sixteenth Century: England and France, 1536–1550." Ph.D. diss., Cambridge University, 1973.

———. "Foreign Policy in the Age of the Reformation: French Involvement in the Schmalkaldic War, 1544–1547." *Historical Journal* 20 (1977): 525–44.

Powicke, F. M. *Stephen Langton.* London: Merlin Press, 1965.

Powicke, Michael Rhys. "Lancastrian Captains." In *Essays in Medieval History Presented to Bertie Wilkinson,* edited by T. A. Sandquist and M. R. Powicke, 371–82. Toronto: University of Toronto Press, 1969.

———. *Military Obligation in Medieval England: A Study in Liberty and Duty.* Oxford: Clarendon Press, 1962.

Prest, Wilfred, ed. *The Professions in Early Modern England.* New York: Croom Helm, 1987.

Prestwich, Michael. *War, Politics and Finance under Edward I.* Totowa, N.J.: Rowman & Littlefield, 1972.

Purcell, Maureen. "Changing Views of Crusade in the Thirteenth Century." *Journal of Religious History* 7 (1972): 3–19.

Ramsey, Lee C. *Chivalric Romances: Popular Literature in Medieval England.* Bloomington: Indiana University Press, 1983.

Redworth, Glyn. *In Defence of the Church Catholic: The Life of Stephen Gardiner.* Oxford: Basil Blackwell, 1990.

Reeves, Marjorie. *The Influence of Prophecy in the Later Middle Ages: A Study of Joachimism.* Oxford: Clarendon Press, 1969.

Reiss, Timothy J. *The Discourse of Modernism.* Ithaca, N.Y.: Cornell University Press, 1982.

Renna, Thomas. "The Idea of Peace in the West, 500–1150." *Journal of Medieval History* 6 (1980): 143–67.

Rex, Richard A. W. "The English Campaign Against Luther in the 1520s." *TRHS,* 5th ser., 39 (1989): 85–106.

———. *Henry VIII and the English Reformation.* New York: St. Martin's Press, 1993.

Richardson, W. C. "Some Financial Expedients of Henry VIII." *Economic History Review,* 2d ser., 7 (1954): 33–48.

Ricoeur, Paul. *Hermeneutics and the Human Sciences.* Cambridge: Cambridge University Press, 1981.

Riley-Smith, Jonathan. "Crusading as an Act of Love." *History* 65 (1980): 177–92.

Rist, John M, ed. *The Stoics.* Berkeley and Los Angeles: University of California Press, 1978.

——. *Stoic Philosophy.* Cambridge: Cambridge University Press, 1969.

Robinson, I. S. "Gregory VII and the Soldiers of Christ." *History* 58 (1973): 169–92.

Rogge, Joachim. *Zwingli und Erasmus: Die Friedensgedanken des jungen Zwingli.* Stuttgart: Calwer Verlag, 1962.

Rosenwein, B. H. "Feudal War and Monastic Peace: Clunaic Liturgy as Ritual Aggression." *Viator* 2 (1971): 129–57.

Ross, Charles. "Rumour, Propaganda and Popular Opinion during the Wars of the Roses." In *Patronage, the Crown and the Provinces,* edited by Ralph A. Griffiths, 15–32. Gloucester, Eng.: Alan Sutton, 1981.

Roy, Ian. "The Profession of Arms." In *The Professions in Early Modern England,* edited by Wilfrid R. Prest, 181–219. London: Croom Helm, 1987.

Russell, Frederick H. *The Just War in the Middle Ages.* Cambridge: Cambridge University Press, 1975.

Russell, J. G. *Peacemaking in the Renaissance.* Philadelphia: University of Pennsylvania Press, 1986.

Scarisbrick, J. J. *Henry VIII.* Berkeley and Los Angeles: University of California Press, 1968.

Scase, Wendy. *"Piers Plowman" and the New Anti-clericalism.* Cambridge: Cambridge University Press, 1989.

Scattergood, V. J. "Chaucer and the French War: *Sir Thopas* and *Melibee.*" In *Court and Poet: Selected Proceedings of the Third Congress of the International Courtly Literature Society (Liverpool 1980),* edited by Glyn S. Burgess, 287–96. Liverpool: Francis Cairns, 1981.

——. "Literary Culture at the Court of Richard II." In *English Court Culture in the Later Middle Ages,* edited by V. J. Scattergood and J. W. Sherborne, 29–43. New York: St. Martin's Press, 1983.

——. *Politics and Poetry in the Fifteenth Century.* London: Blandford Press, 1971.

Schmandt, Raymond H. "The Fourth Crusade and the Just-War Theory." *Catholic Historical Review* 61 (1975): 191–221.

Schwoerer, Lois G. *No Standing Armies: The Antimilitary Ideology in Seventeenth-Century England.* Baltimore: Johns Hopkins University Press, 1974.

Scribner, R. W. "Oral Culture and the Transmission of Ideas in the Lutheran Reformation." In *The Transmission of Ideas in the Lutheran Reformation,* edited by Helga Robinson-Hammerstein, 83–104. Dublin: Irish Academic Press, 1989.

Sherborne, James. "John of Gaunt, Edward III's Retinue and the French Campaign of 1369." In *Kings and Nobles in the Later Middle Ages: A Tribute to*

Charles Ross, edited by Ralph A. Griffiths and James Sherborne, 41–61. New York: St. Martin's Press, 1986.

———. *War, Politics and Culture in Fourteenth-Century England.* Edited by Anthony Tuck. London: Hambledon Press, 1994.

Siegel, Paul N. "English Humanism and the New Tudor Aristocracy." *Journal of the History of Ideas* 13 (1952): 450–68.

Severs, J. B. "The Source of Chaucer's Melibeus." *PMLA* 50 (1935): 92–99.

Skinner, Quentin. *The Foundations of Modern Political Thought.* 2 vols. Cambridge: Cambridge University Press, 1978.

———. "Meaning and Understanding in the History of Ideas." In *Meaning and Context: Quentin Skinner and His Critics,* edited by James Tully, 29–67. Princeton, N.J.: Princeton University Press, 1988.

Slavin, A. J. *Politics and Profit: A Study of Sir Ralph Sadler, 1507–1547.* Cambridge: The University Press, 1966.

———. "'Tis Far Off, and Rather Like a Dream': Common Weal, Common Woe, and Commonwealth." *Explorations in Renaissance Culture* 14 (1988): 1–28.

———. "The Tudor State, Reformation and Understanding Change: Through the Looking Glass." In *Political Thought and the Tudor Commonwealth: Deep Structure, Discourse and Disguise,* edited by Paul A. Fideler and T. F. Mayer, 223–53. London: Routledge, 1992.

Smeeton, Donald Dean. *Lollard Themes in the Reformation Theology of William Tyndale.* Kirksville, Mo.: Sixteenth Century Journal Publishers, 1986.

Stacey, Robert C. "The Age of Chivalry." In *The Laws of War: Constraints on Warfare in the Western World,* edited by Michael Howard, George J. Andreopoulos, and Mark R. Shulman, 27–39. New Haven, Conn.: Yale University Press, 1994.

Stayer, James M. *Anabaptists and the Sword.* Lawrence, Kans.: Coronado Press, 1972.

Steel, Anthony. *Richard II.* Cambridge: The University Press, 1962.

Stephens, W. P. *Zwingli: An Introduction to His Thought.* Oxford: Clarendon Press, 1992.

Stillwell, Gardiner. "John Gower and the Last Years of Edward III." *Studies in Philology* 45 (1948): 454–71.

———. "The Political Meaning of Chaucer's *Tale of Melibee.*" *Speculum* 19 (1944): 433–44.

———. "*Wynnere and Wastoure* and the Hundred Years War." *English Literary History* 8 (1941): 241–47.

Strype, John. *Annals of the Reformation . . . In the Church of England.* 6 vols. Oxford: Clarendon Press, 1824.

———. *Ecclesiastical Memorials.* 6 vols. Oxford: Clarendon Press, 1822.

Surtz, Edward. *The Praise of Wisdom.* Chicago: Loyola University Press, 1957.

Swift, Louis J. "St. Ambrose on Violence and War." *Transactions and Proceedings of the American Philological Association* 101 (1970): 533–43.

Tallett, Frank. *War and Society in Early Modern Europe, 1495–1715.* London: Routledge, 1992.

Teichman, Jenny. *Pacifism and the Just War: A Study in Applied Philosophy.* Oxford: Basil Blackwell, 1986.

Thorne, J. R., and Marie-Claire Uhart. "Robert Crowley's *Piers Plowman.*" *Medium Aevum* 55 (1986): 243–53.

Throop, Palmer A. *Criticism of the Crusade: A Study of Public Opinion and Crusade Propaganda.* Amsterdam: N. V. Swets and Zeitlinger, 1940; reprint, Philadelphia: Porcupine Press, 1975.

Tooke, Joan D. *The Just War in Aquinas and Grotius.* London: S.P.C.K., 1965.

Tracy, James D. *The Politics of Erasmus: A Pacifist Intellectual and His Political Milieu.* Toronto: University of Toronto Press, 1978.

Trueman, Carl R. *Luther's Legacy: Salvation and English Reformers, 1525–1556.* Oxford: Clarendon Press, 1994.

Tuck, J. Anthony. "Carthusian Monks and the Lollard Knights: Religious Attitude at the Court of Richard II." In *Studies in the Age of Chaucer. Proceedings, No. 1, 1984: Reconstructing Chaucer,* edited by Paul Strohm and Thomas J. Heffernan, 149–61. Knoxville, Tenn.: New Chaucer Society, 1985.

———. *Richard II and the Nobility.* London: Edward Arnold, 1973.

———. "Why Men Fought in the Hundred Years War." *History Today* 33 (April 1983): 35–40.

Tully, James, ed. *Meaning and Context: Quentin Skinner and His Critics.* Princeton, N.J.: Princeton University Press, 1988.

Underdown, David. *Revel, Riot and Rebellion: Popular Politics and Culture in England, 1603–1660.* Oxford: Oxford University Press, 1985.

Vale, M.G.A. "New Techniques and Old Ideals: The Impact of Artillery on War and Chivalry at the End of the Hundred Years War." In *War, Literature and Politics in the Late Middle Ages,* edited by C. T. Allmand. Liverpool: Liverpool University Press, 1976.

———. *War and Chivalry. Warfare and Aristocratic Culture in England, France, and Burgundy at the End of the Middle Ages.* Athens: University of Georgia Press, 1981.

Van Der Wee, Herman. *The Growth of the Antwerp Market and the European Economy (Fourteenth–Sixteenth Centuries).* Vol. 2, *Interpretation.* The Hague: Martinus Nijhoff, 1963.

Waggoner, G. R. "An Elizabethan Attitude toward Peace and War." *Philological Quarterly* 33 (1954): 20–33.

Walker, Greg. *John Skelton and the Politics of the 1520s.* Cambridge: Cambridge University Press, 1988.

Wallace-Hadrill, J. M. "War and Peace in the Earlier Middle Ages." *TRHS,* 5th ser., 25 (1975): 157–74.

Walsh, Katherine. *A Fourteenth Century Scholar and Primate: Richard Fitzralph in Oxford, Avignon and Armagh.* Oxford: Clarendon Press, 1981.

Walters, LeRoy. "Five Classic Just War Theories: A Study in the Thought of Thomas Aquinas, Vitoria, Suarez, Gentili and Grotius." Ph.D. diss., Yale University, 1971.

———. "The Just War and the Crusade: Antithesis or Analogies?" *The Monist* 57 (1973): 584–94.

Walzer, Michael. "Exodus 32 and the Theory of the Holy War: The History of a Citation." *Harvard Theological Review* 61 (1968): 1–14.

———. *The Revolution of the Saints: A Study in the Origins of Radical Politics.* Cambridge: Harvard University Press, 1965.

Waugh, Scott L. *England in the Reign of Edward III.* Cambridge: Cambridge University Press, 1991.

Wegg, Jervis. *Richard Pace: A Tudor Diplomatist.* New York: Barnes & Noble, 1971.

Wernham, R. B. "Elizabethan War Aims and Strategy." In *Elizabethan Government and Society: Essays Presented to Sir John Neale,* edited by S. T. Bindoff, Joel Hurstfield, and C. H. Williams, 340–68. London: Athlone Press, 1961.

———. *The Making of Elizabethan Foreign Policy, 1558–1603.* Berkeley and Los Angeles: University of California Press, 1980.

———. "Queen Elizabeth and the Portugal Expedition of 1589." *English Historical Review* 66 (1951): 1–26, 194–218.

White, Hayden. *The Content of the Form.* Baltimore: Johns Hopkins University Press, 1987.

Williams, Penry. "Rebellion and Revolution in Early Modern England." In *War and Society: Historical Essays in Honour and Memory of J. R. Western, 1928–1971,* edited by M.R.D. Foot, 225–240. London: Paul Elek, 1973.

Windass, Stanley. *Christianity versus Violence: A Social and Historical Study of War and Christianity.* London: Sheed & Ward, 1964.

Wingfield-Stratford, Esme. *The History of English Patriotism.* Vol. 1. London: John Lane, the Bodley Head, 1913.

Wood, Mary Morton. *The Spirit of Protest in Old French Literature.* New York: Columbia University Press, 1917; reprint, New York: AMS Press, 1966.

Wright, N.A.R. "The *Tree of Battles* of Honoré Bouvet and the Laws of War." In *War, Literature and Politics in the Late Middle Ages,* edited by C. T. Allmand, 12–31. Liverpool: Liverpool University Press, 1976.

Yates, F. A. *Astrea: The Imperial Theme in the Sixteenth Century.* London: Routledge & Kegan Paul, 1975.

Yeager, R. E. "*Pax Poetica:* On the Pacifism of Chaucer and Gower." *Studies in the Age of Chaucer* 9 (1987): 97–121.

Zeeveld, W. Gordon. *Foundations of Tudor Policy.* Cambridge: Harvard University Press, 1948; reprint, Westport, Conn.: Greenwood Press, 1981.

Zell, Michael L. "Economic Problems of the Parochial Clergy in the Sixteenth Century." In *Princes and Paupers in the English Church, 1500–1800,* edited by Rosemary O'Day and Felicity Heal, 19–43. Leicester: Leicester University Press, 1981.

INDEX